ORSON SCOTT CARD

EMILY JANICE CARD

WITH ZINA CARD

Laddertop

ILLUSTRATED BY **HONOEL A. IBARDOLAZA** VOLUME 1

Laddertop
VOLUME 1

story by Orson Scott Card & Emily Janice Card
with Zina Margaret Card

art by Honoel A. Ibardolaza

STAFF CREDITS

lettering & interiors	**Nicky Lim**
toning	**Ludwig Sacramento**
cover design	**Seth Lerner**
story consultant	**Jason DeAngelis**
production editor	**Adam Arnold**

This is a work of fiction. All of the characters, organizations, and events portrayed in this novel are either products of the authors' imaginations or are used fictitiously.

LADDERTOP: VOLUME 1

Copyright © 2011 by Orson Scott Card and Emily Janice Card

All rights reserved.

A Tor/Seven Seas Paperback
Published by Tom Doherty Associates, LLC
175 Fifth Avenue
New York, NY 10010

Visit us online at **www.gomanga.com** and **www.tor-forge.com**.

Seven Seas and the Seven Seas logo are trademarks of Seven Seas Entertainment, LLC. Tor® and the Tor logo are registered trademarks of Tom Doherty Associates, LLC.

ISBN 978-0-7653-2460-3

First Edition: October 2011

Printed in the United States of America

0 9 8 7 6 5 4 3 2 1

TOR ® Seven Seas

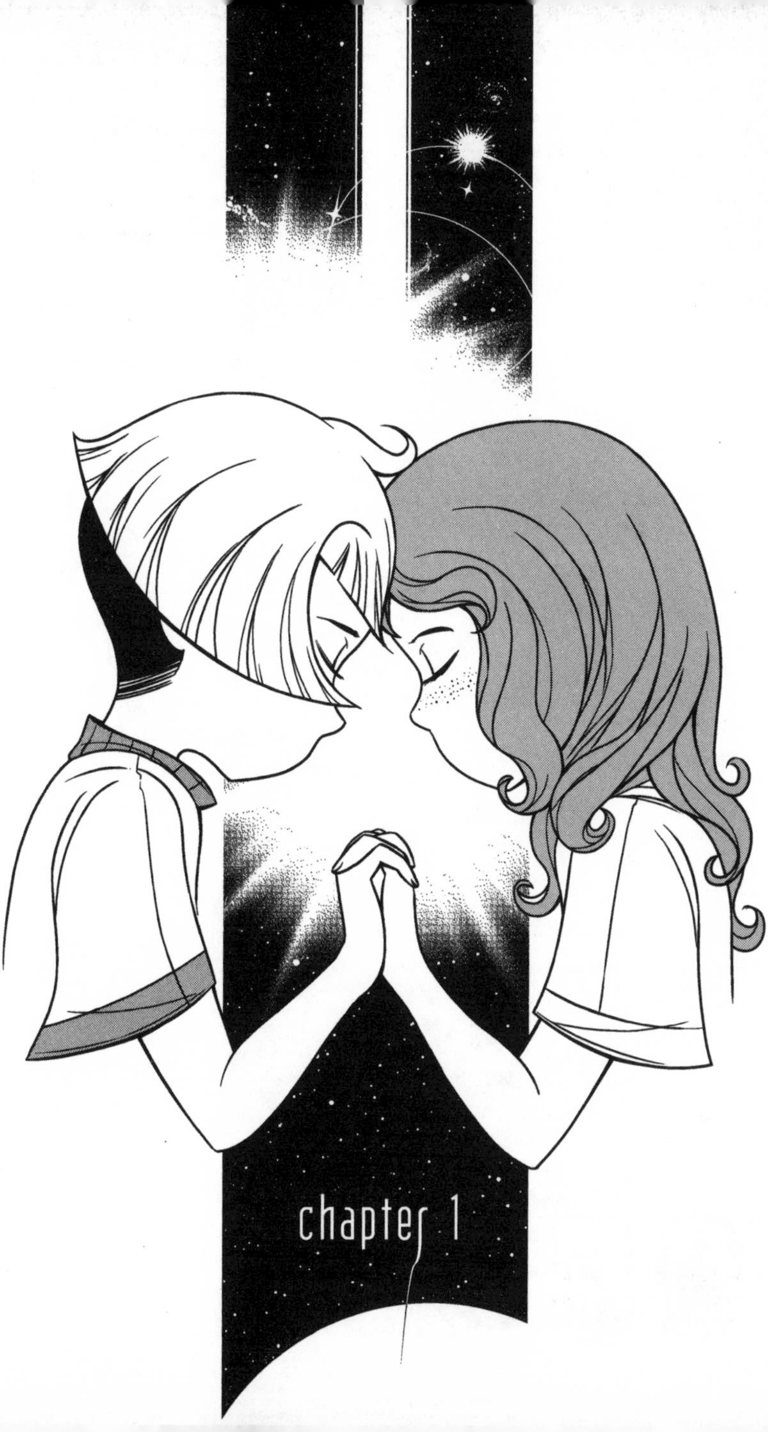
chapter 1

Laddertop

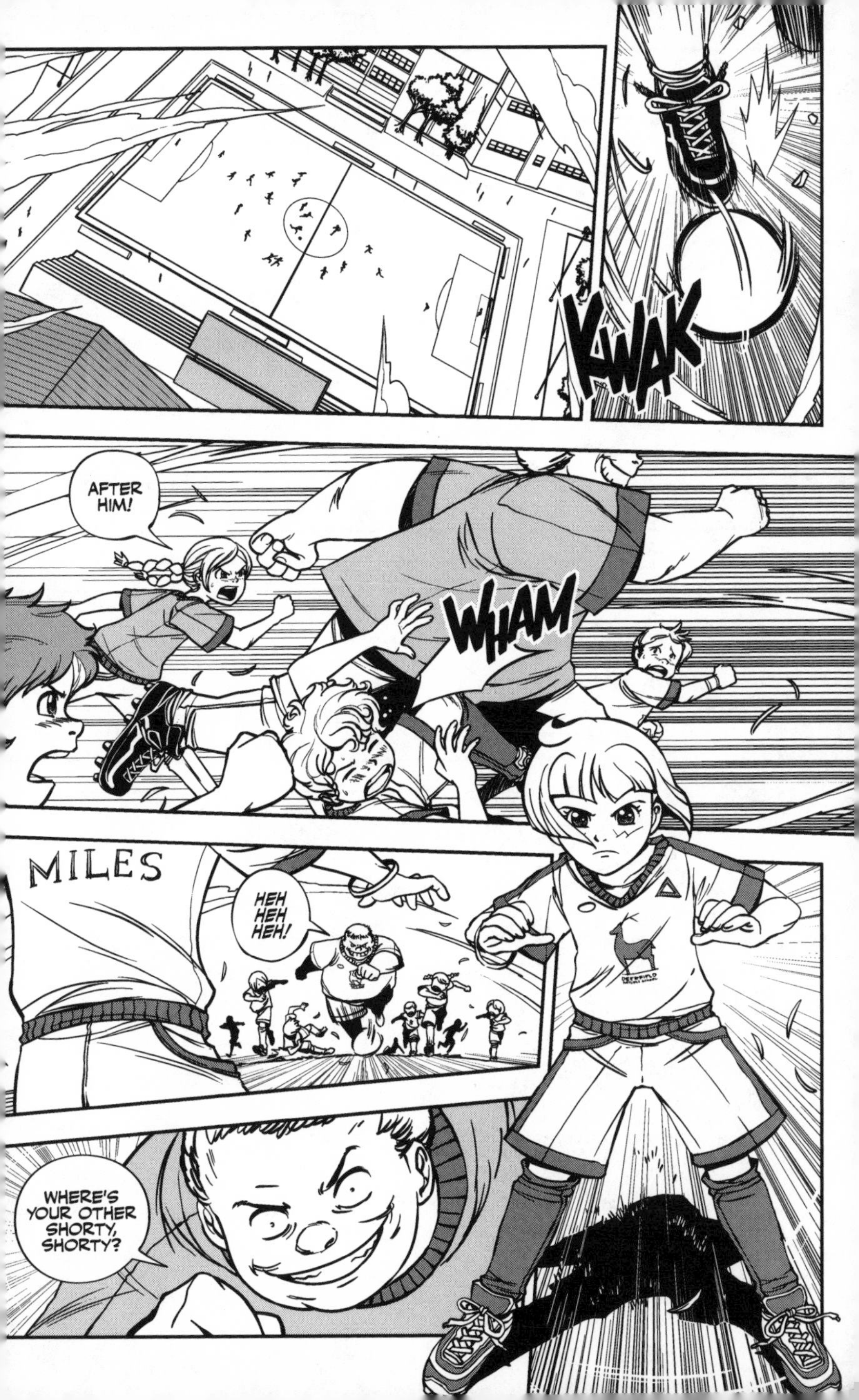
KWAK
AFTER HIM!
WHAM
MILES
HEH HEH HEH!
WHERE'S YOUR OTHER SHORTY, SHORTY?

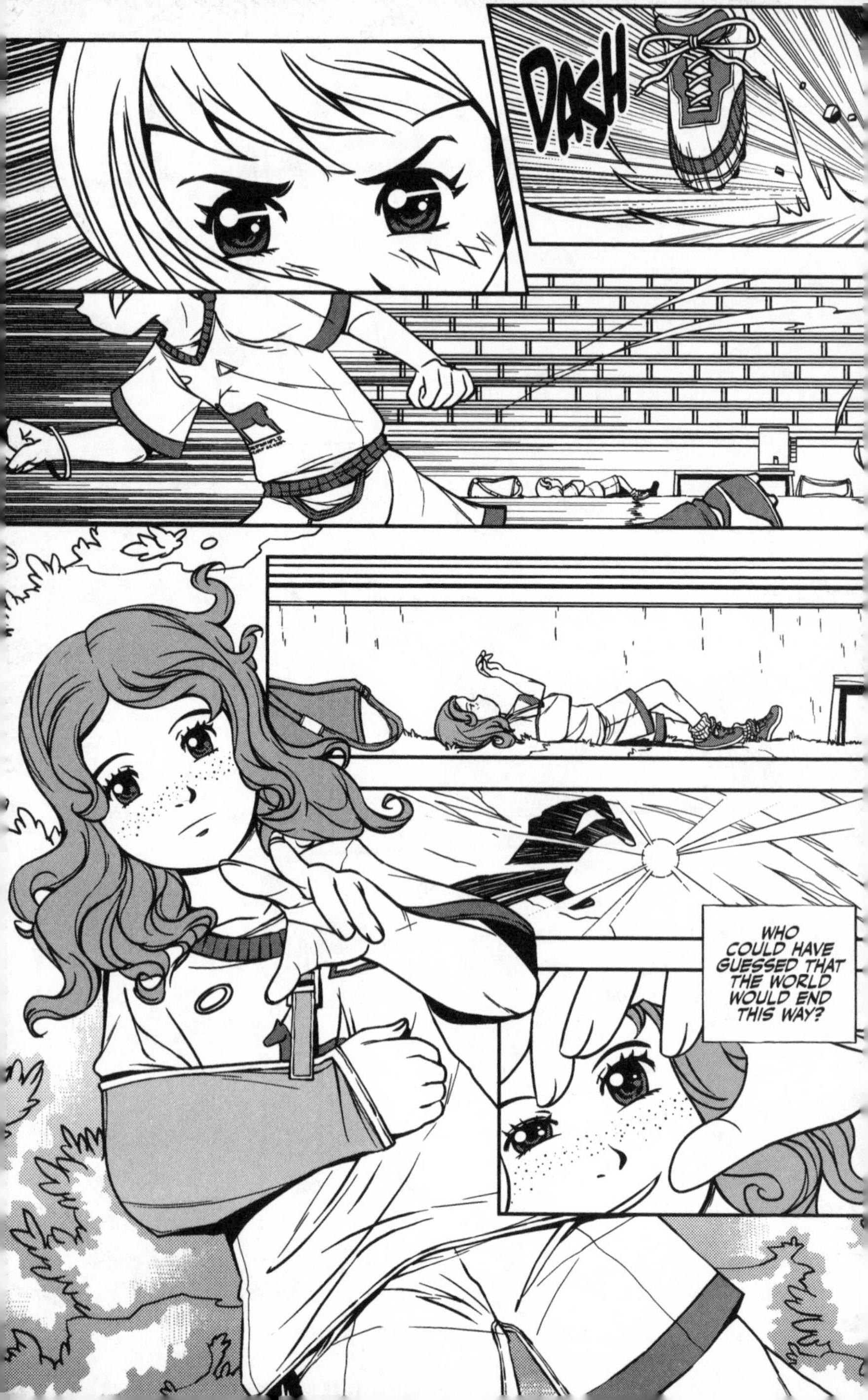
DASH
WHO COULD HAVE GUESSED THAT THE WORLD WOULD END THIS WAY?

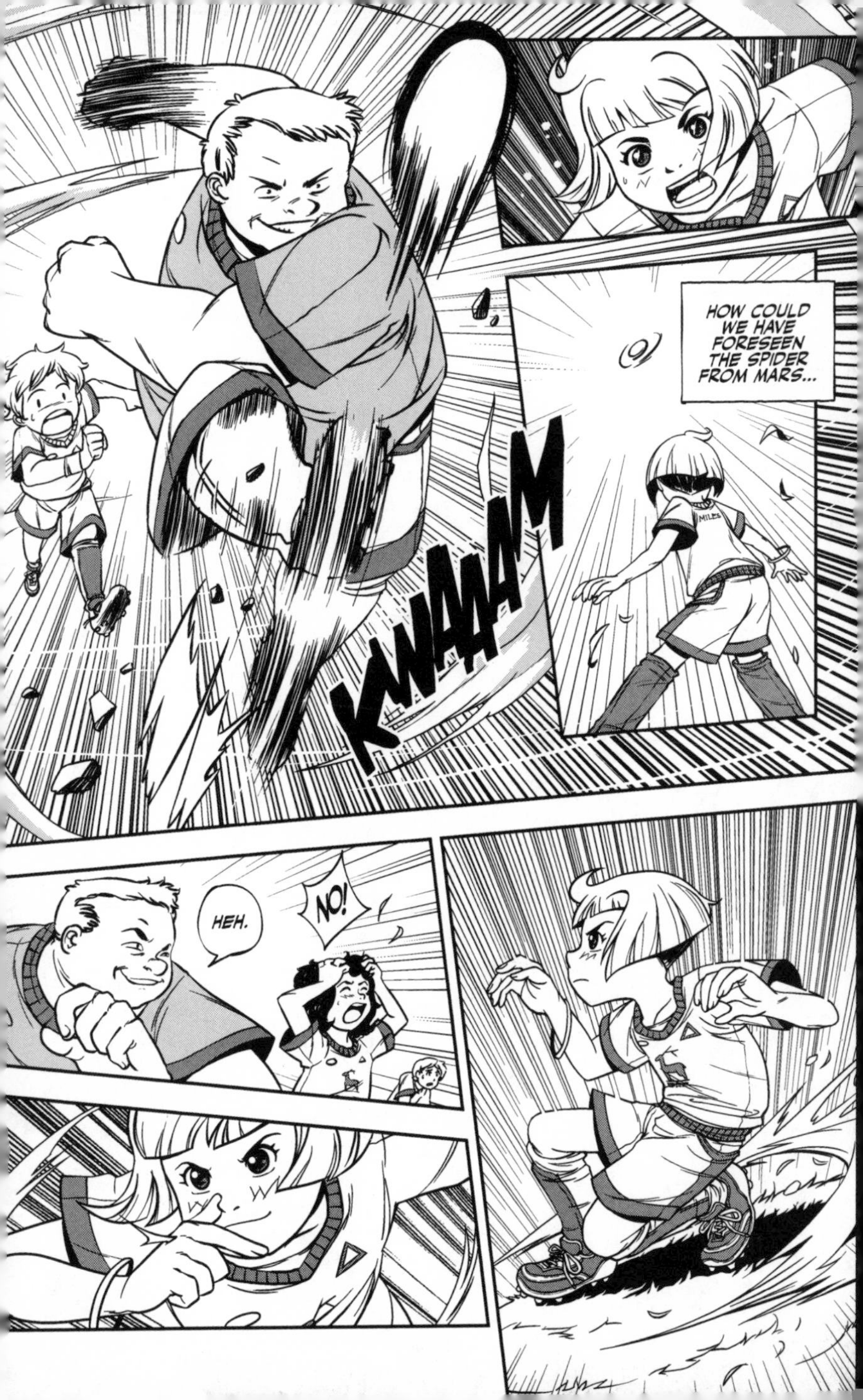
HOW COULD WE HAVE FORESEEN THE SPIDER FROM MARS...
KWAAAM
MILES
HEH.
NO!

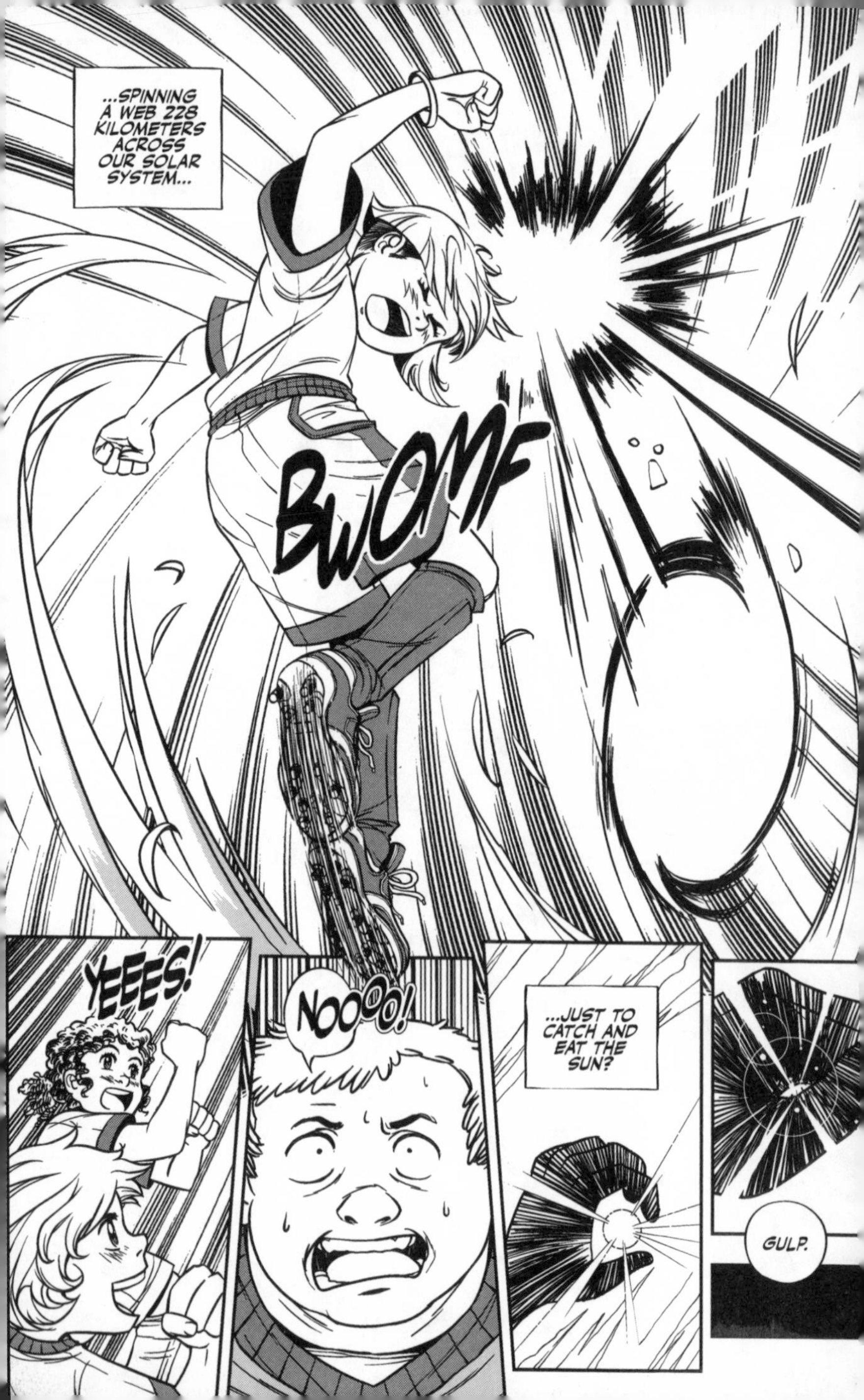
...SPINNING A WEB 228 KILOMETERS ACROSS OUR SOLAR SYSTEM...
BWOMF
YEEES!
NOOOO!
...JUST TO CATCH AND EAT THE SUN?
GULP.

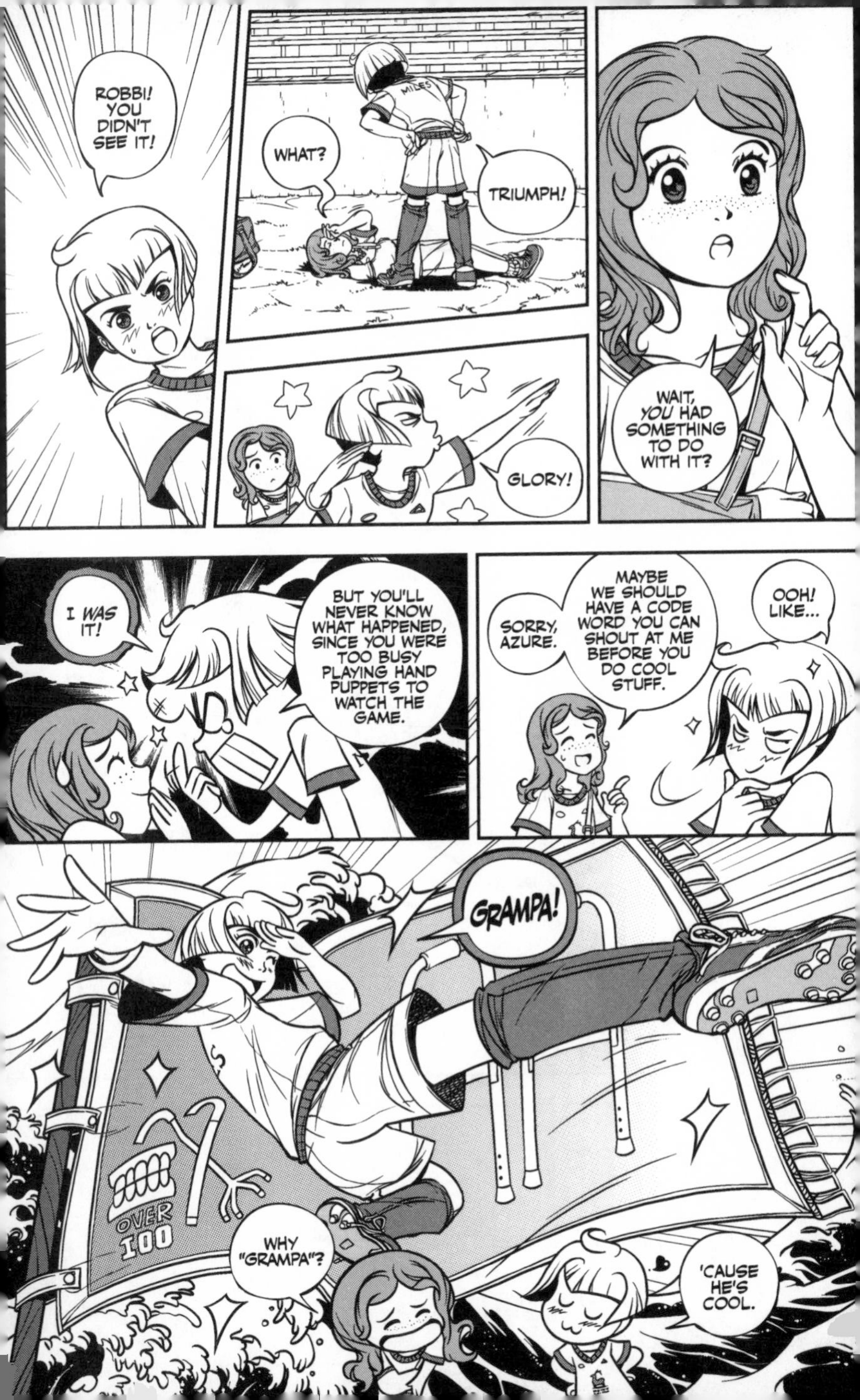
ROBBI! YOU DIDN'T SEE IT!
MILES
WHAT?
TRIUMPH!
GLORY!
WAIT, *YOU* HAD SOMETHING TO DO WITH IT?
I *WAS* IT!
BUT YOU'LL NEVER KNOW WHAT HAPPENED, SINCE YOU WERE TOO BUSY PLAYING HAND PUPPETS TO WATCH THE GAME.
SORRY, AZURE.
MAYBE WE SHOULD HAVE A CODE WORD YOU CAN SHOUT AT ME BEFORE YOU DO COOL STUFF.
OOH! LIKE...
GRAMPA!
OVER 100
WHY "GRAMPA"?
'CAUSE HE'S COOL.

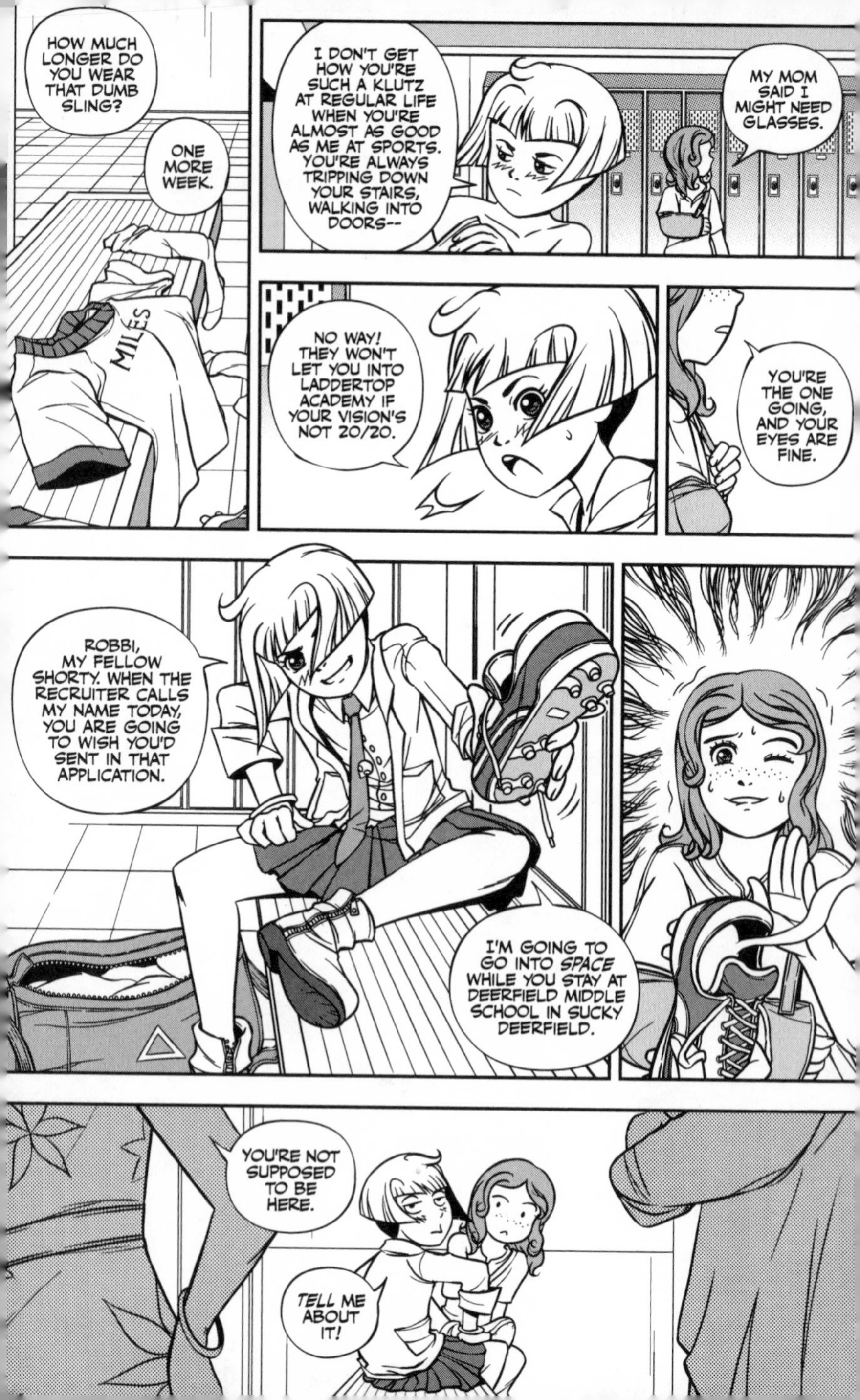
HOW MUCH LONGER DO YOU WEAR THAT DUMB SLING?
ONE MORE WEEK.
MILES
I DON'T GET HOW YOU'RE SUCH A KLUTZ AT REGULAR LIFE WHEN YOU'RE ALMOST AS GOOD AS ME AT SPORTS. YOU'RE ALWAYS TRIPPING DOWN YOUR STAIRS, WALKING INTO DOORS--
MY MOM SAID I MIGHT NEED GLASSES.
NO WAY! THEY WON'T LET YOU INTO LADDERTOP ACADEMY IF YOUR VISION'S NOT 20/20.
YOU'RE THE ONE GOING, AND YOUR EYES ARE FINE.
ROBBI, MY FELLOW SHORTY. WHEN THE RECRUITER CALLS MY NAME TODAY, YOU ARE GOING TO WISH YOU'D SENT IN THAT APPLICATION.
I'M GOING TO GO INTO *SPACE* WHILE YOU STAY AT DEERFIELD MIDDLE SCHOOL IN SUCKY DEERFIELD.
YOU'RE NOT SUPPOSED TO BE HERE.
TELL ME ABOUT IT!

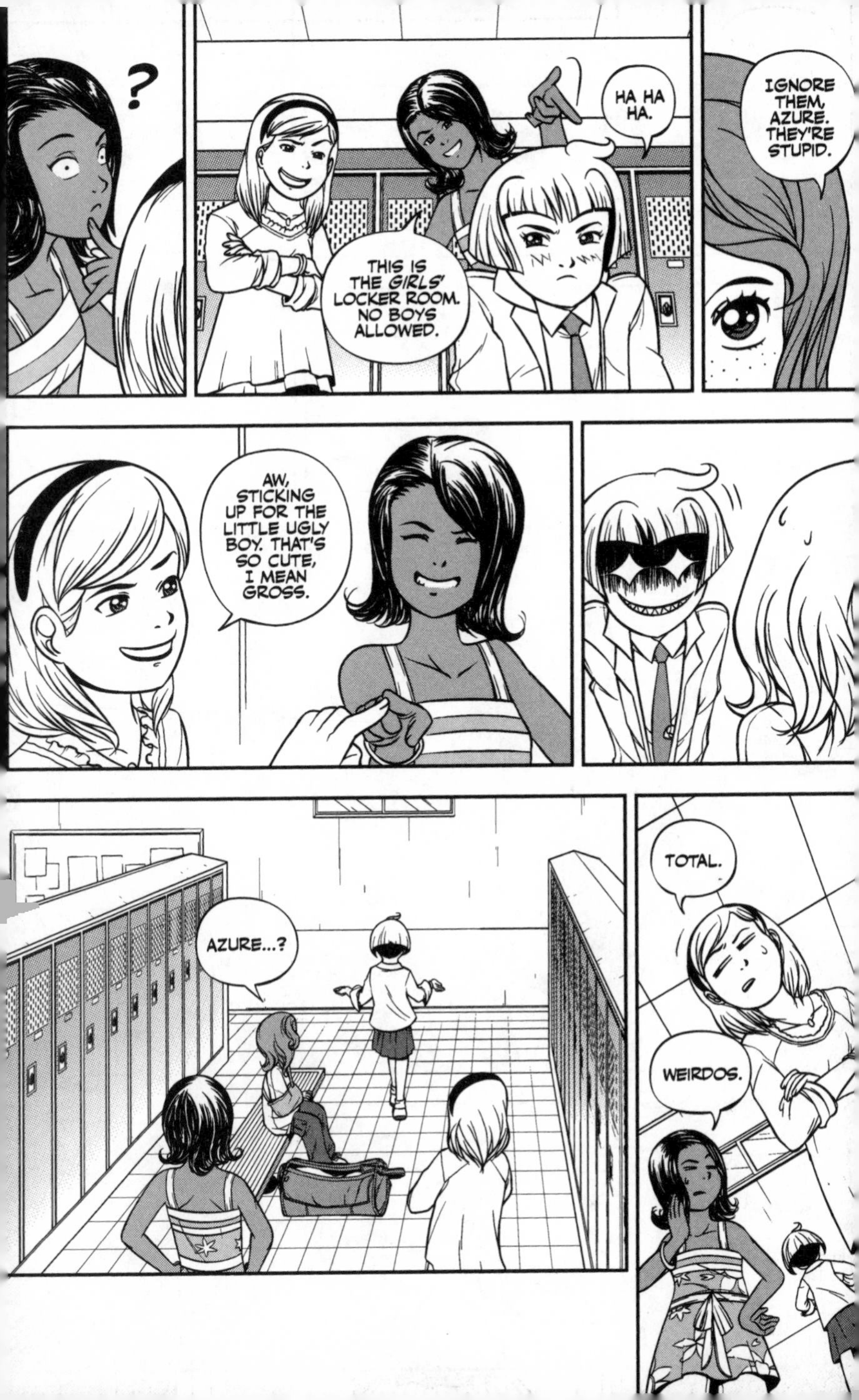
?
THIS IS THE GIRLS' LOCKER ROOM. NO BOYS ALLOWED.
HA HA HA.
IGNORE THEM, AZURE. THEY'RE STUPID.
AW, STICKING UP FOR THE LITTLE UGLY BOY. THAT'S SO CUTE, I MEAN GROSS.
AZURE...?
TOTAL.
WEIRDOS.

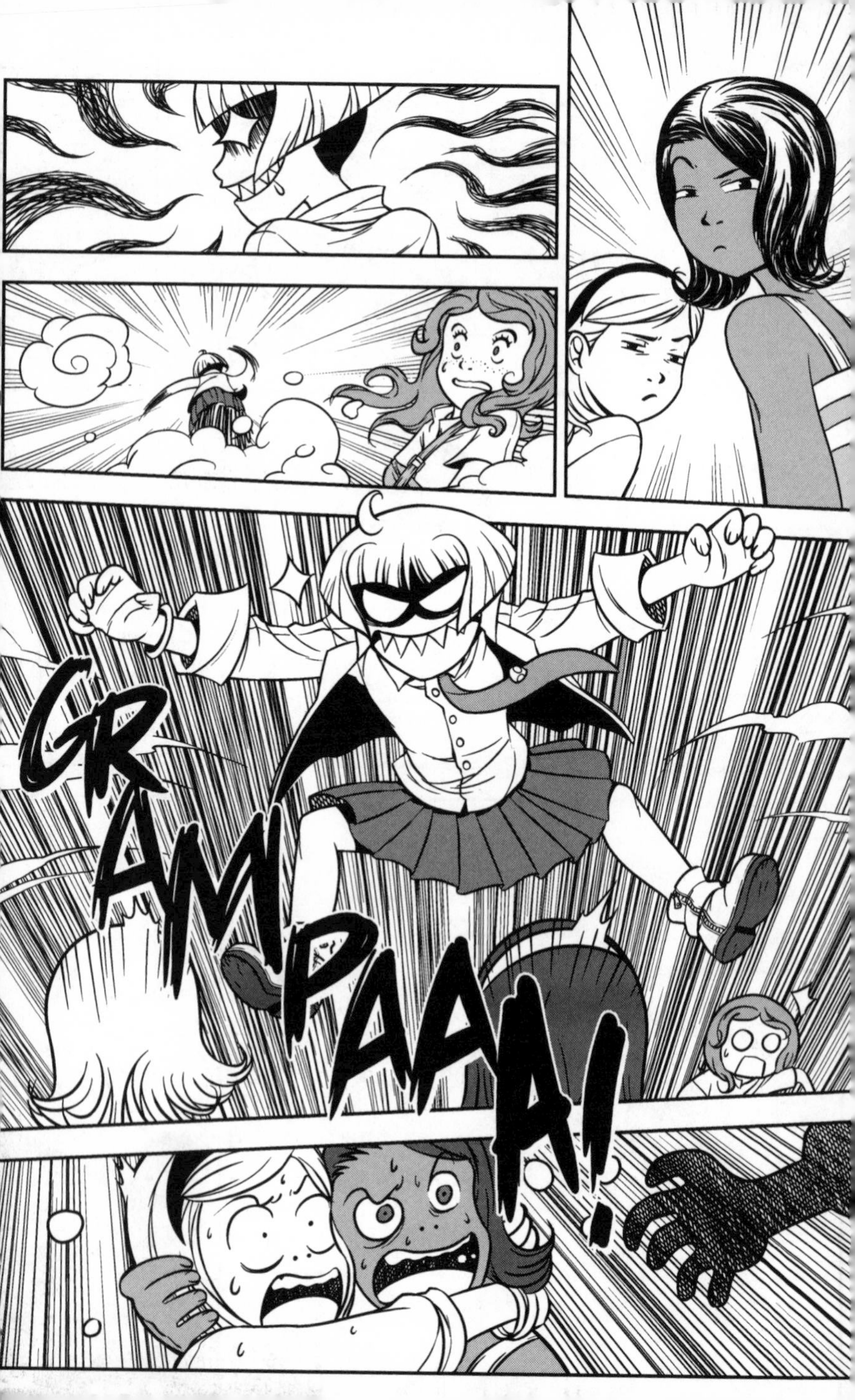
GRAMPAAA!

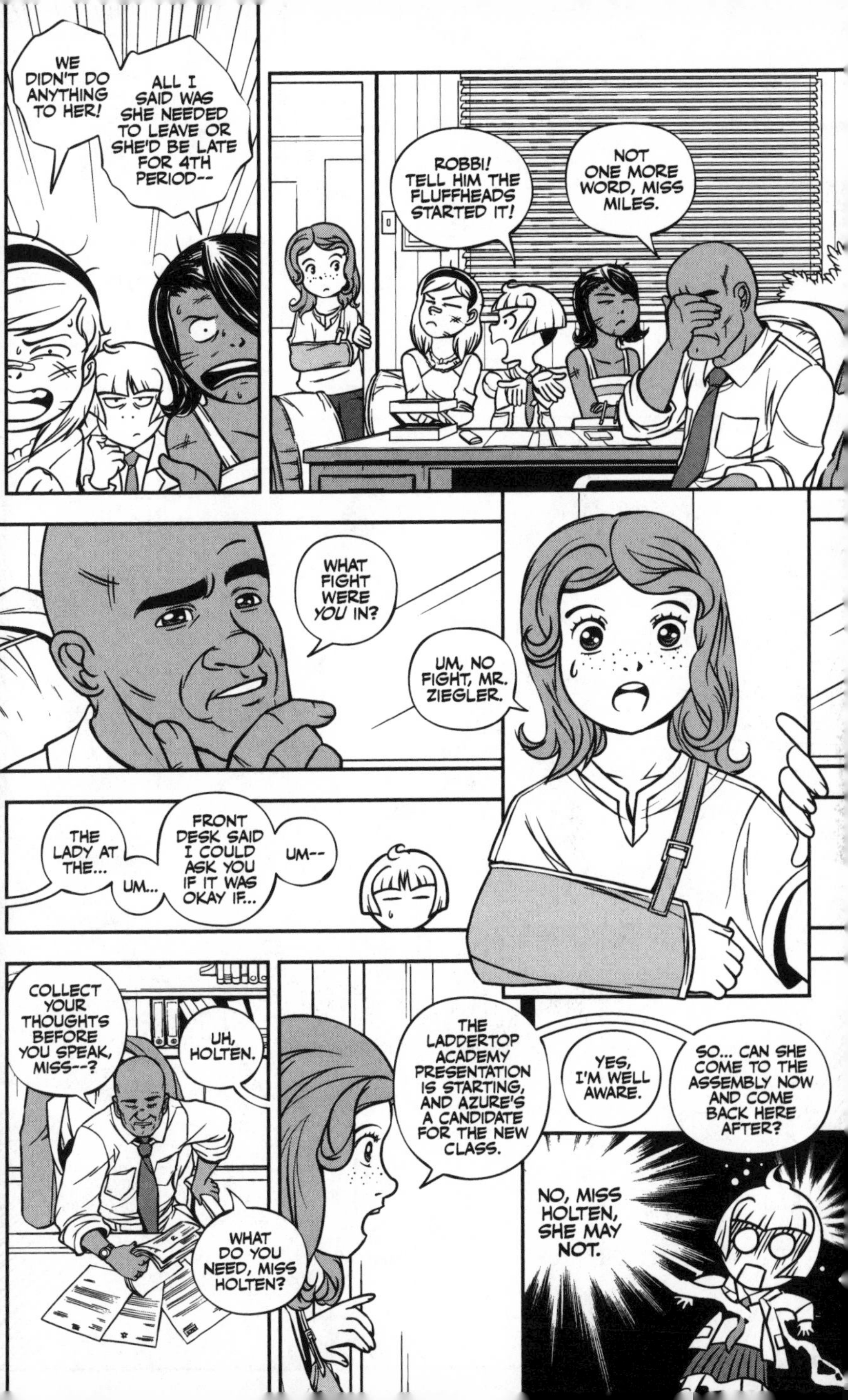
WE DIDN'T DO ANYTHING TO HER!
ALL I SAID WAS SHE NEEDED TO LEAVE OR SHE'D BE LATE FOR 4TH PERIOD--
ROBBI! TELL HIM THE FLUFFHEADS STARTED IT!
NOT ONE MORE WORD, MISS MILES.
WHAT FIGHT WERE *YOU* IN?
UM, NO FIGHT, MR. ZIEGLER.
THE LADY AT THE...
UM...
FRONT DESK SAID I COULD ASK YOU IF IT WAS OKAY IF...
UM--
COLLECT YOUR THOUGHTS BEFORE YOU SPEAK, MISS--?
UH, HOLTEN.
WHAT DO YOU NEED, MISS HOLTEN?
THE LADDERTOP ACADEMY PRESENTATION IS STARTING, AND AZURE'S A CANDIDATE FOR THE NEW CLASS.
YES, I'M WELL AWARE.
SO... CAN SHE COME TO THE ASSEMBLY NOW AND COME BACK HERE AFTER?
NO, MISS HOLTEN, SHE MAY NOT.

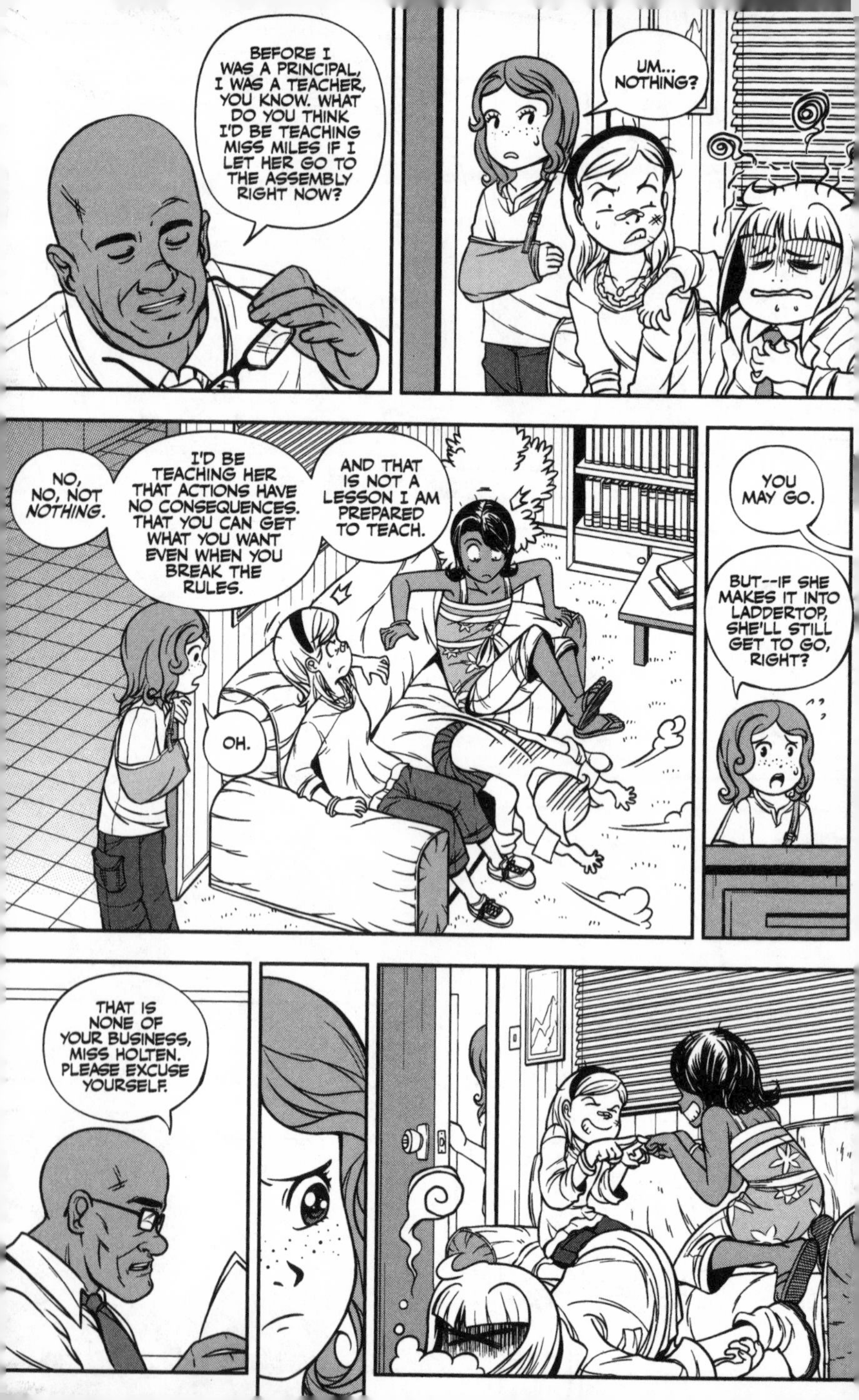
BEFORE I WAS A PRINCIPAL, I WAS A TEACHER, YOU KNOW. WHAT DO YOU THINK I'D BE TEACHING MISS MILES IF I LET HER GO TO THE ASSEMBLY RIGHT NOW?
UM... NOTHING?
NO, NO, NOT *NOTHING*.
I'D BE TEACHING HER THAT ACTIONS HAVE NO CONSEQUENCES. THAT YOU CAN GET WHAT YOU WANT EVEN WHEN YOU BREAK THE RULES.
AND THAT IS NOT A LESSON I AM PREPARED TO TEACH.
OH.
YOU MAY GO.
BUT--IF SHE MAKES IT INTO LADDERTOP, SHE'LL STILL GET TO GO, RIGHT?
THAT IS NONE OF YOUR BUSINESS, MISS HOLTEN. PLEASE EXCUSE YOURSELF.

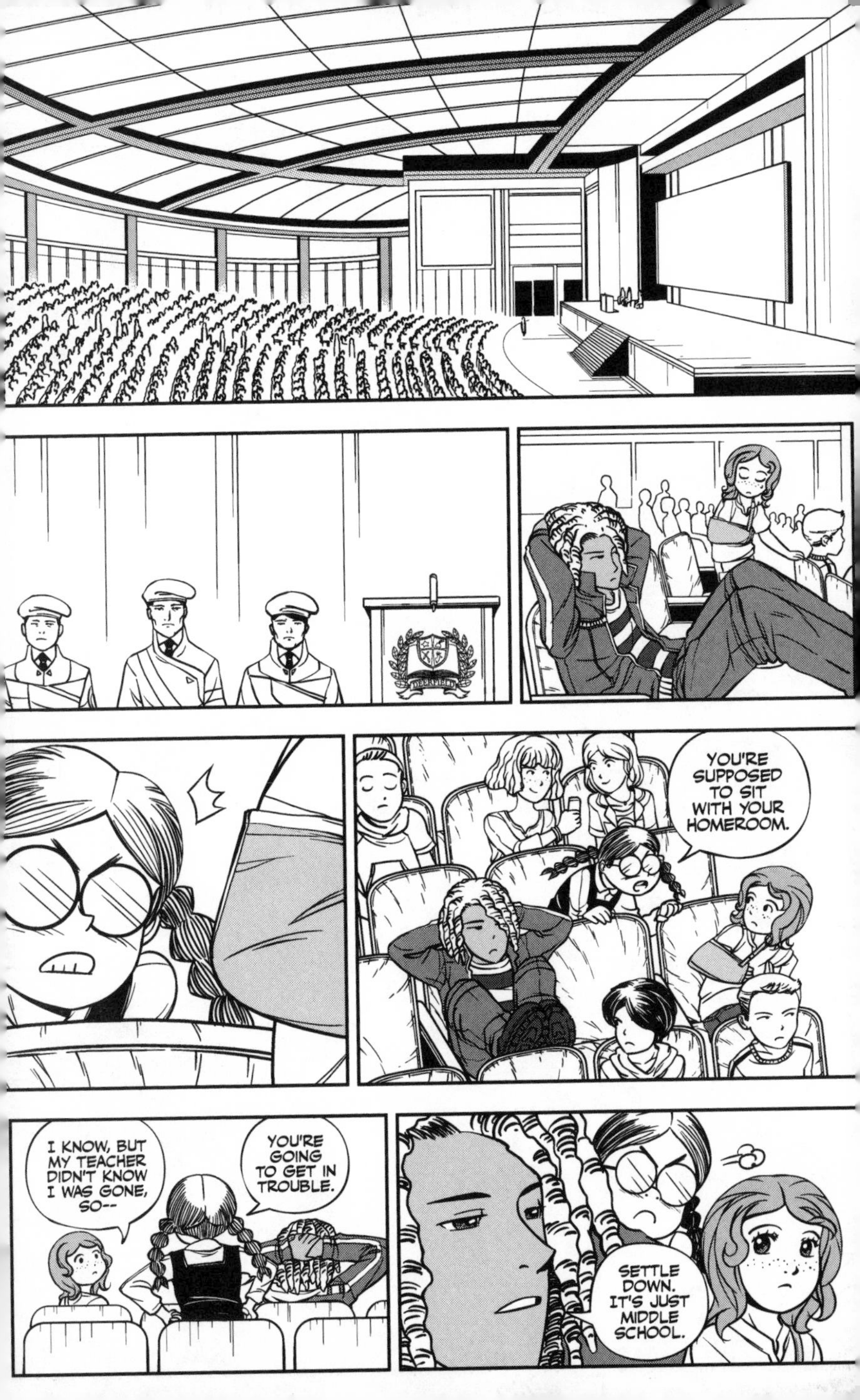
DEERFIELD
YOU'RE SUPPOSED TO SIT WITH YOUR HOMEROOM.
I KNOW, BUT MY TEACHER DIDN'T KNOW I WAS GONE, SO--
YOU'RE GOING TO GET IN TROUBLE.
SETTLE DOWN. IT'S JUST MIDDLE SCHOOL.

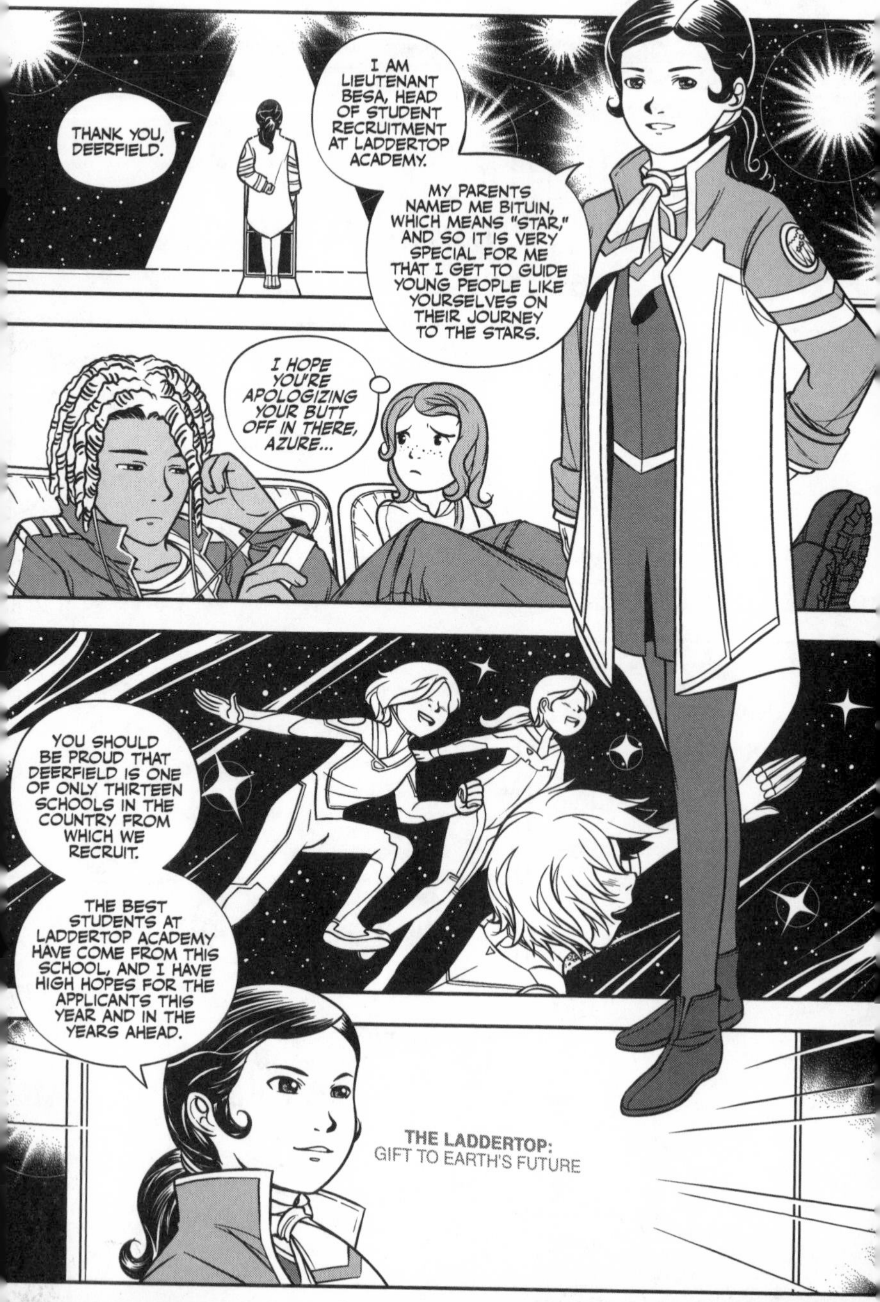
THANK YOU, DEERFIELD.
I AM LIEUTENANT BESA, HEAD OF STUDENT RECRUITMENT AT LADDERTOP ACADEMY.
MY PARENTS NAMED ME BITUIN, WHICH MEANS "STAR," AND SO IT IS VERY SPECIAL FOR ME THAT I GET TO GUIDE YOUNG PEOPLE LIKE YOURSELVES ON THEIR JOURNEY TO THE STARS.
I HOPE YOU'RE APOLOGIZING YOUR BUTT OFF IN THERE, AZURE...
YOU SHOULD BE PROUD THAT DEERFIELD IS ONE OF ONLY THIRTEEN SCHOOLS IN THE COUNTRY FROM WHICH WE RECRUIT.
THE BEST STUDENTS AT LADDERTOP ACADEMY HAVE COME FROM THIS SCHOOL, AND I HAVE HIGH HOPES FOR THE APPLICANTS THIS YEAR AND IN THE YEARS AHEAD.
THE LADDERTOP:
GIFT TO EARTH'S FUTURE

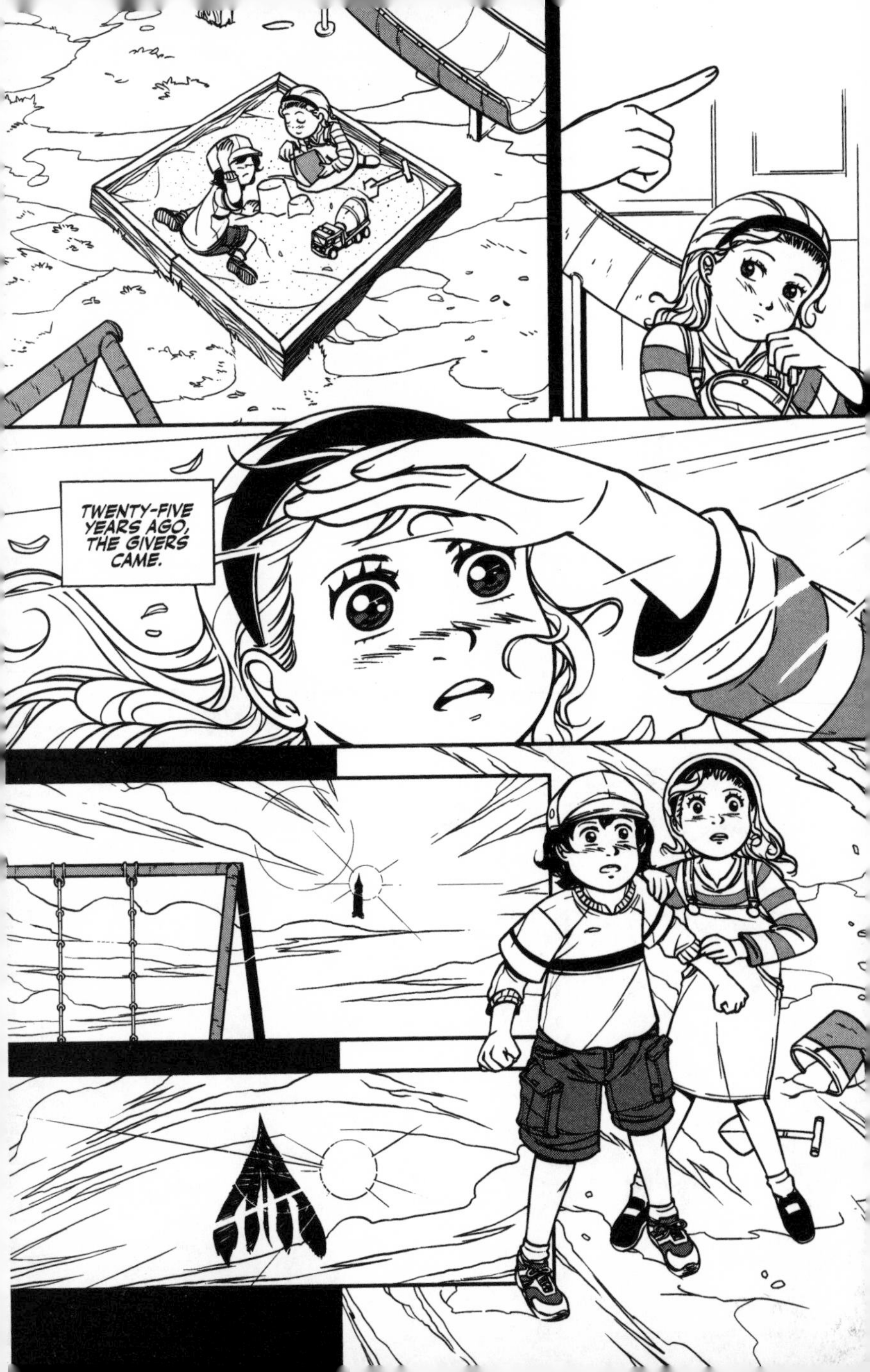
TWENTY-FIVE YEARS AGO, THE GIVERS CAME.

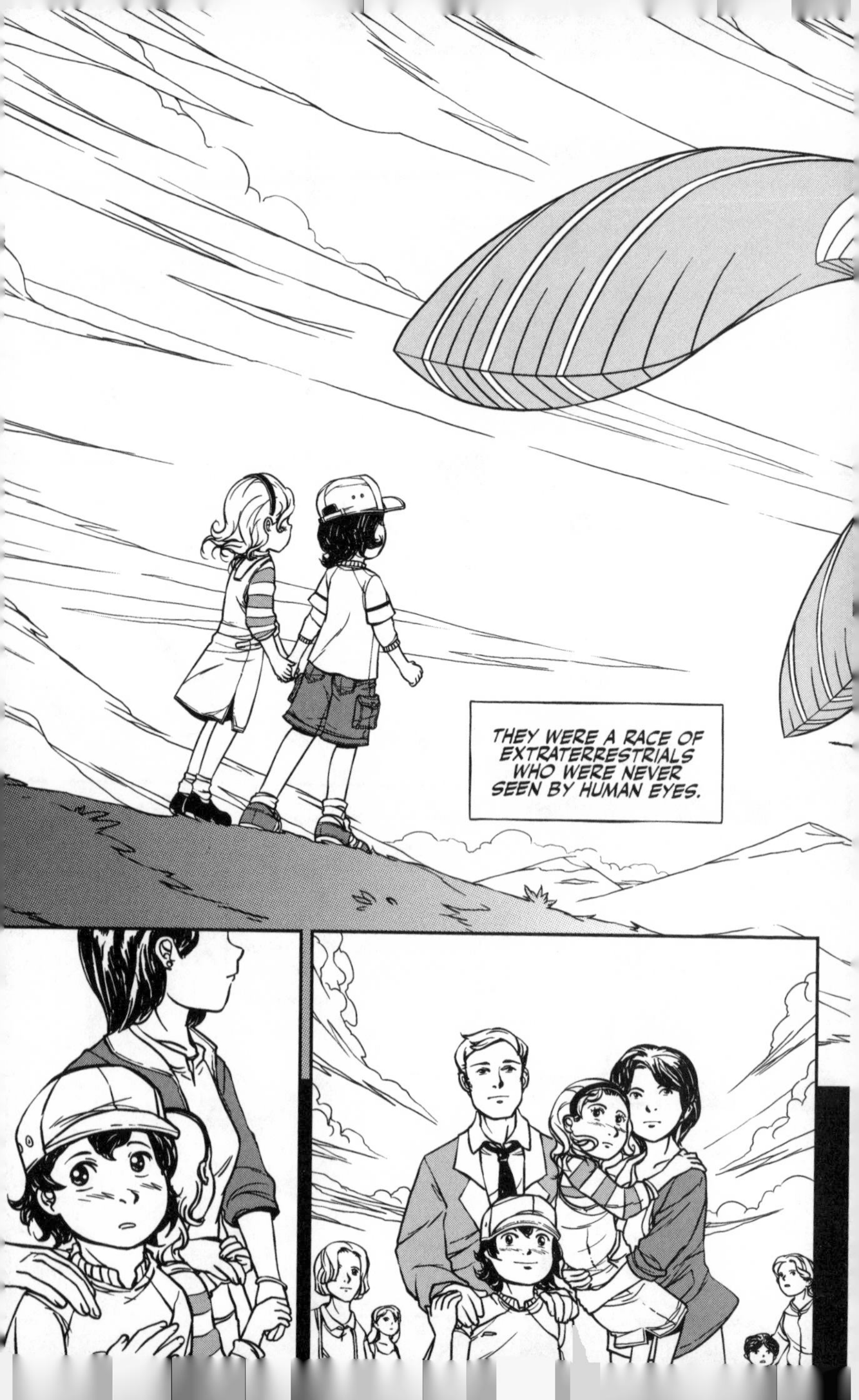
THEY WERE A RACE OF EXTRATERRESTRIALS WHO WERE NEVER SEEN BY HUMAN EYES.

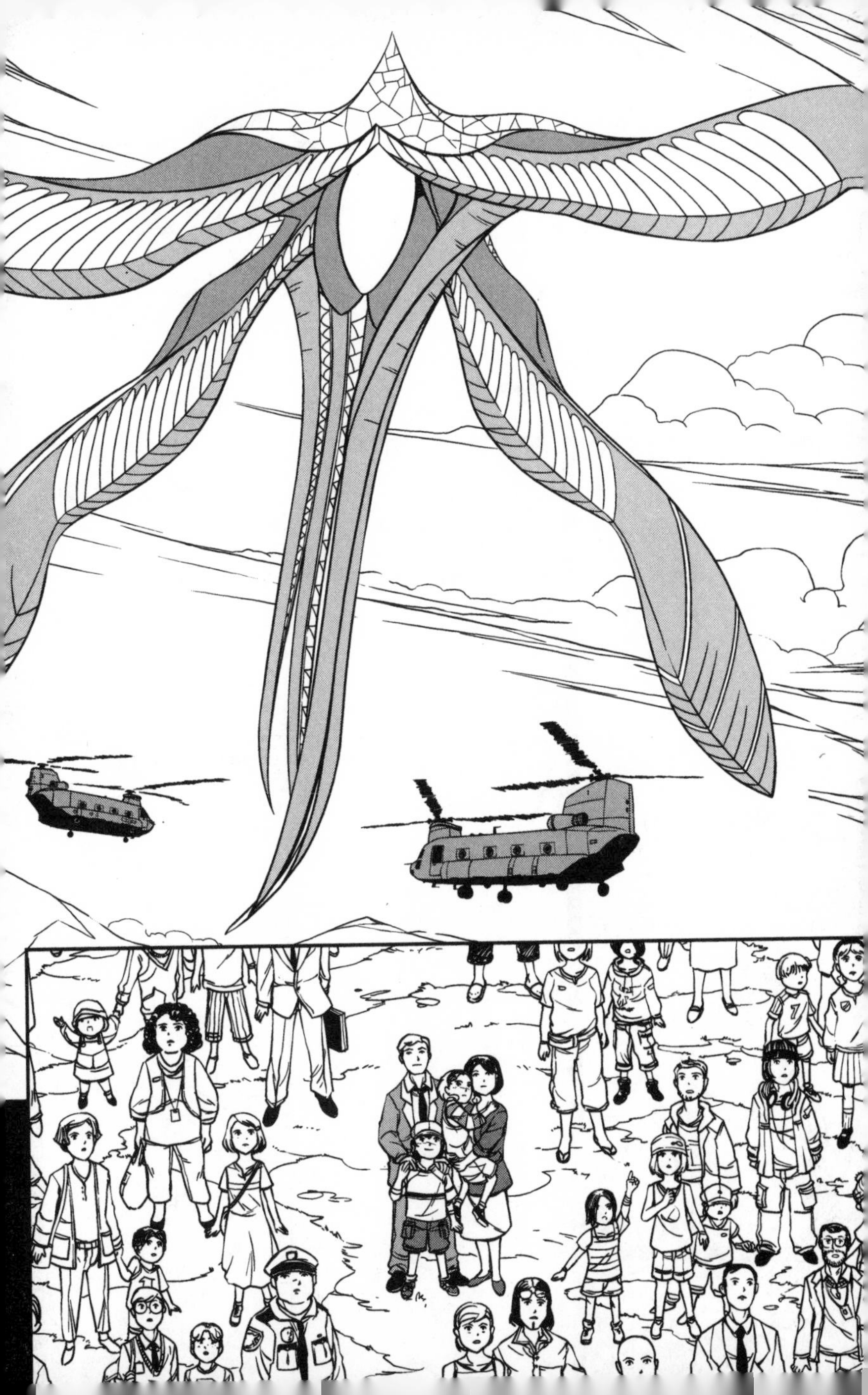

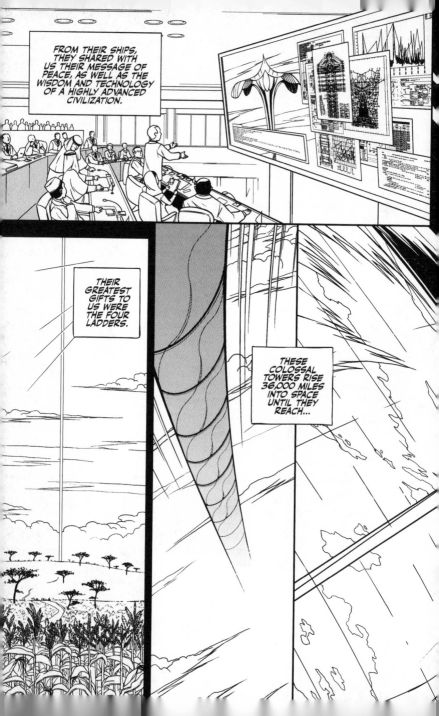

FROM THEIR SHIPS, THEY SHARED WITH US THEIR MESSAGE OF PEACE, AS WELL AS THE WISDOM AND TECHNOLOGY OF A HIGHLY ADVANCED CIVILIZATION.

THEIR GREATEST GIFTS TO US WERE THE FOUR LADDERS.

THESE COLOSSAL TOWERS RISE 36,000 MILES INTO SPACE UNTIL THEY REACH...

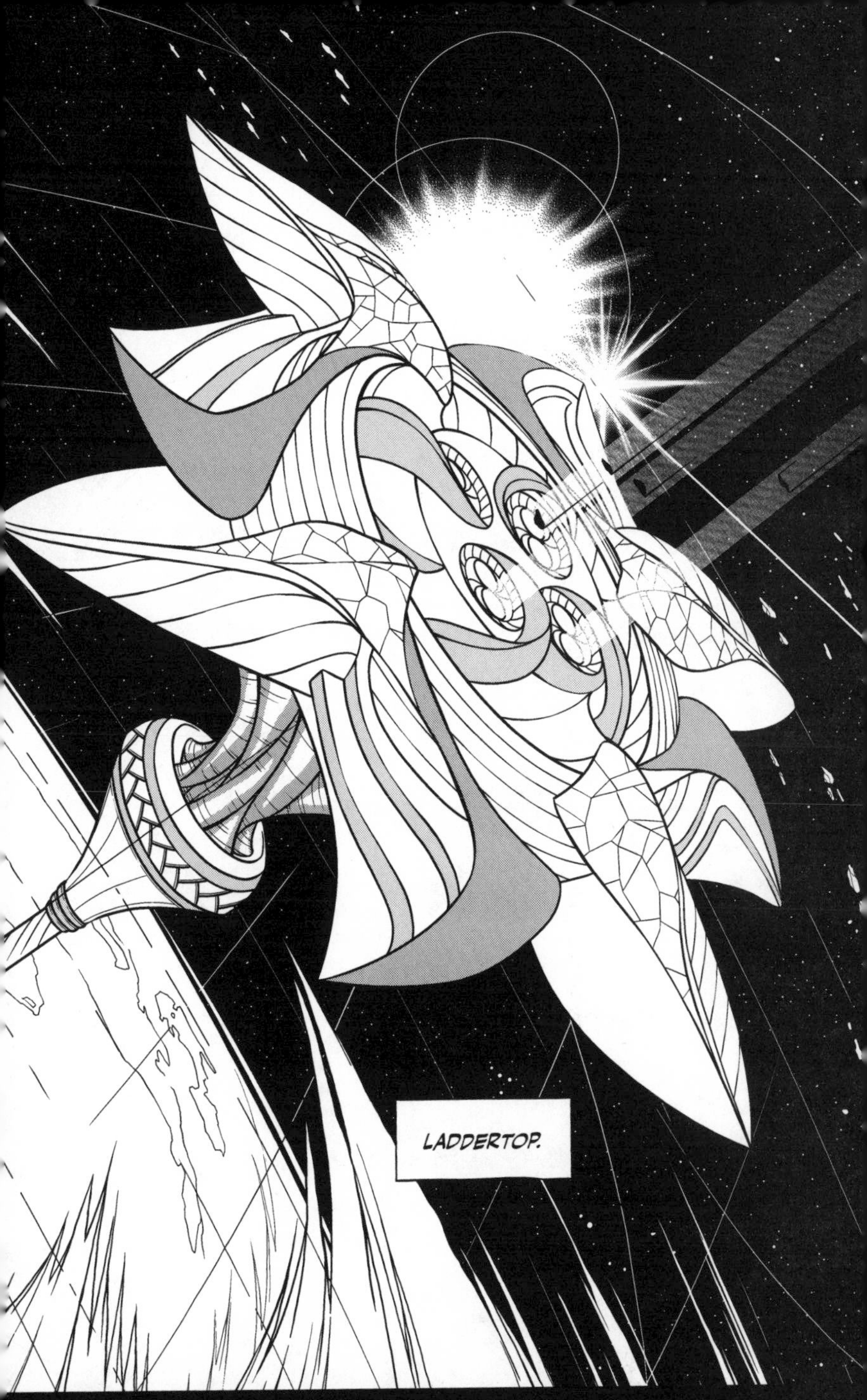
LADDERTOP.

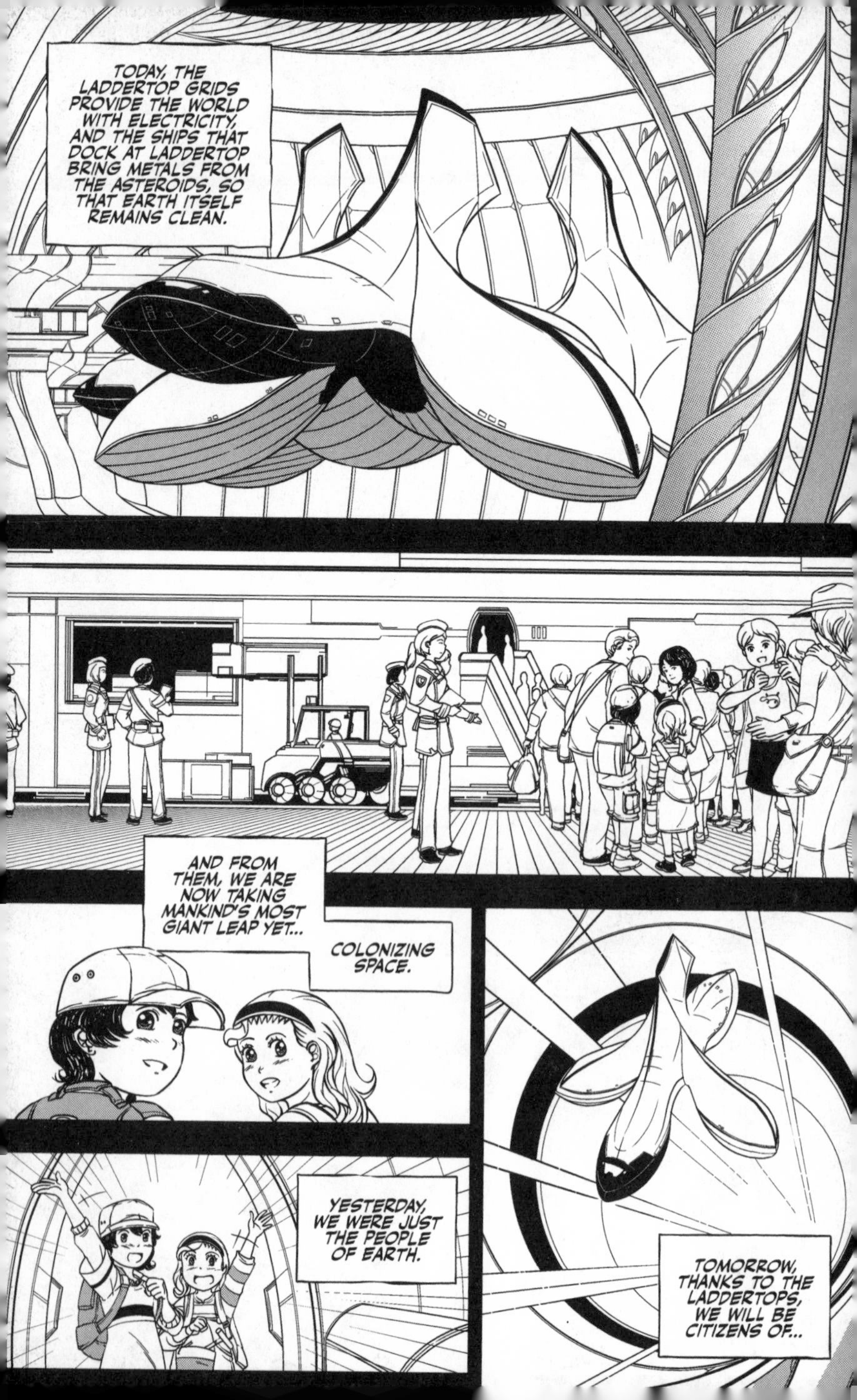
TODAY, THE LADDERTOP GRIDS PROVIDE THE WORLD WITH ELECTRICITY, AND THE SHIPS THAT DOCK AT LADDERTOP BRING METALS FROM THE ASTEROIDS, SO THAT EARTH ITSELF REMAINS CLEAN.
AND FROM THEM, WE ARE NOW TAKING MANKIND'S MOST GIANT LEAP YET...
COLONIZING SPACE.
YESTERDAY, WE WERE JUST THE PEOPLE OF EARTH.
TOMORROW, THANKS TO THE LADDERTOPS, WE WILL BE CITIZENS OF...

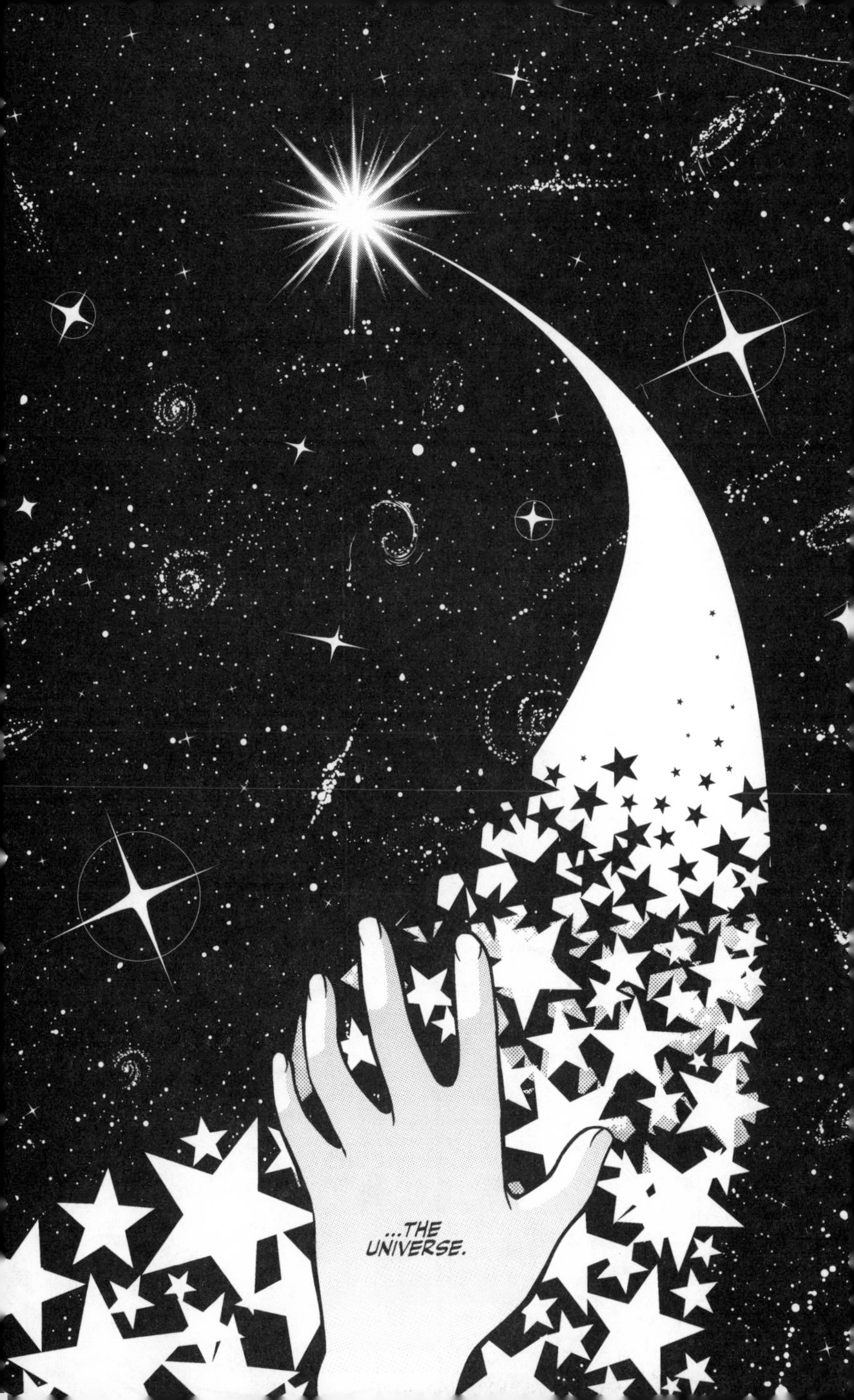
...THE UNIVERSE.

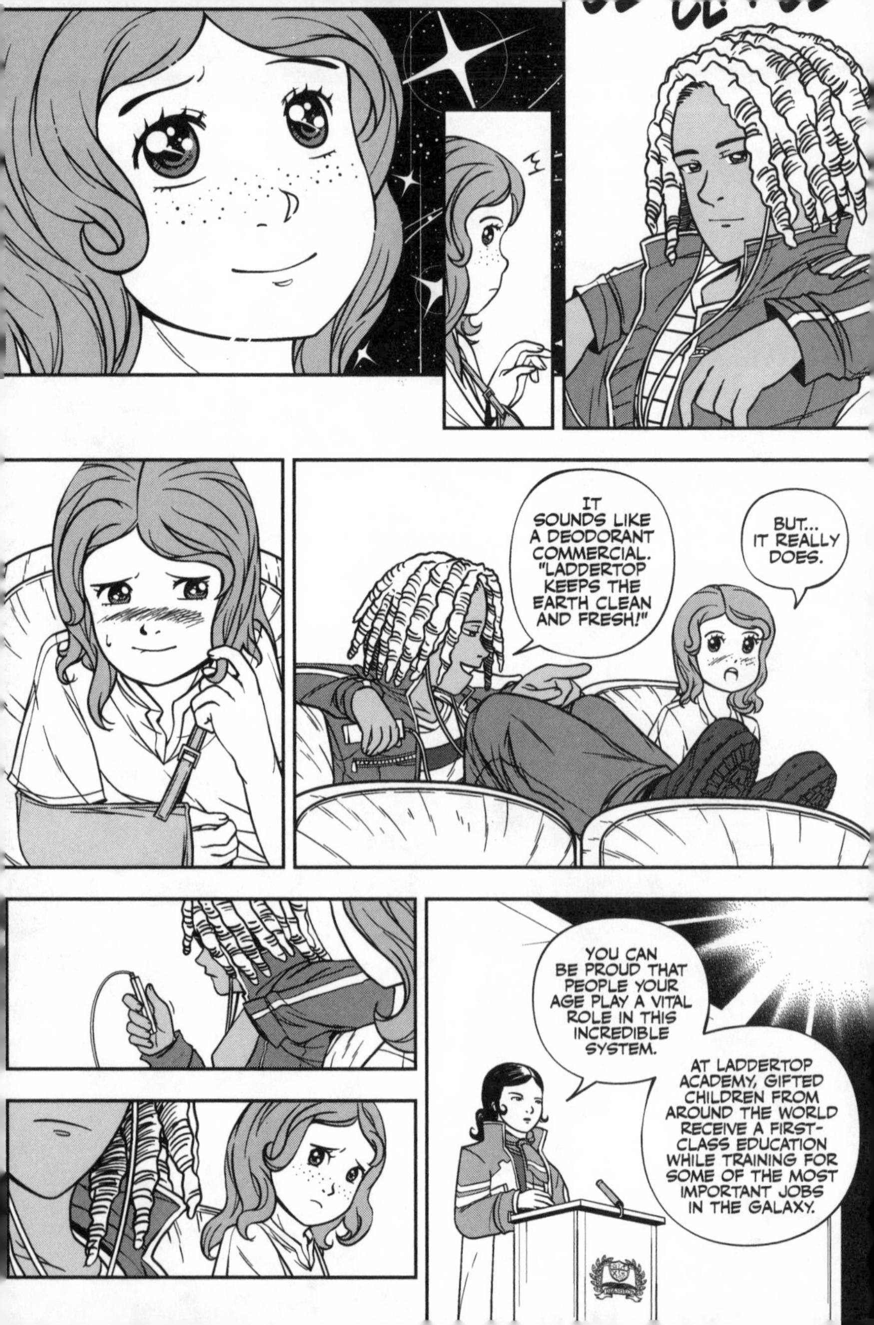
IT SOUNDS LIKE A DEODORANT COMMERCIAL. "LADDERTOP KEEPS THE EARTH CLEAN AND FRESH!"
BUT... IT REALLY DOES.
YOU CAN BE PROUD THAT PEOPLE YOUR AGE PLAY A VITAL ROLE IN THIS INCREDIBLE SYSTEM.
AT LADDERTOP ACADEMY, GIFTED CHILDREN FROM AROUND THE WORLD RECEIVE A FIRST-CLASS EDUCATION WHILE TRAINING FOR SOME OF THE MOST IMPORTANT JOBS IN THE GALAXY.

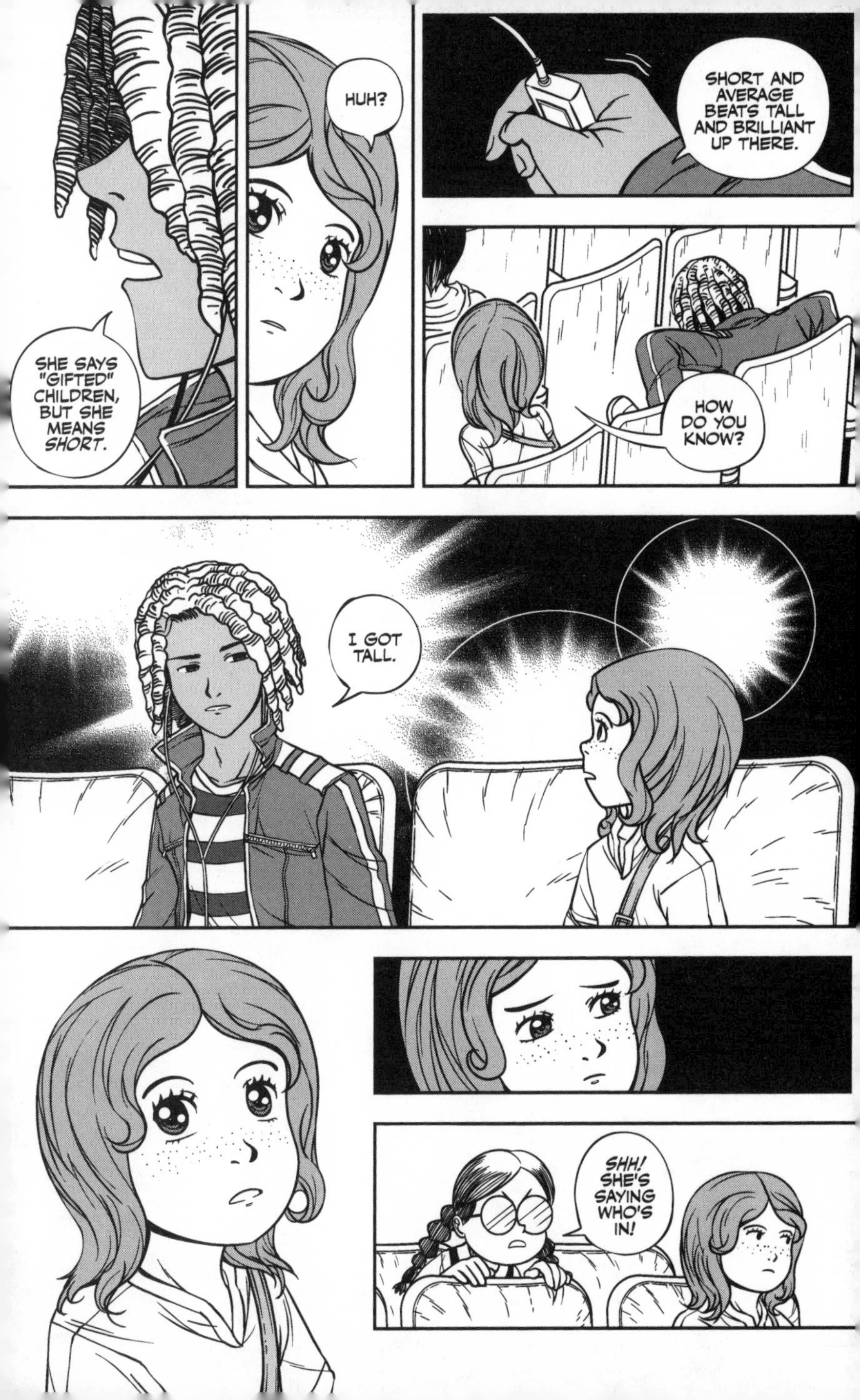
SHE SAYS "GIFTED" CHILDREN, BUT SHE MEANS *SHORT*.
HUH?
SHORT AND AVERAGE BEATS TALL AND BRILLIANT UP THERE.
HOW DO YOU KNOW?
I GOT TALL.
SHH! SHE'S SAYING WHO'S IN!

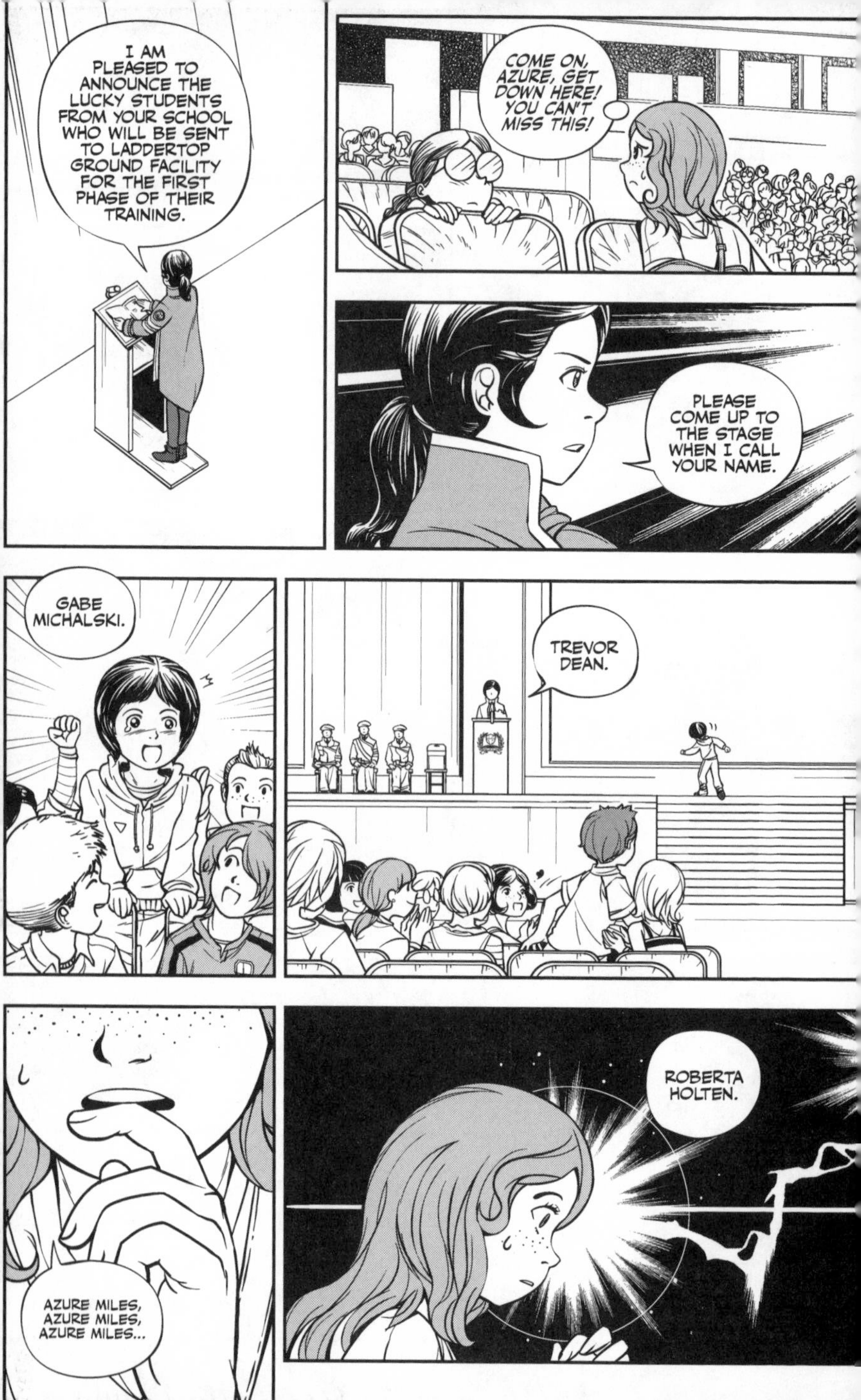
I AM PLEASED TO ANNOUNCE THE LUCKY STUDENTS FROM YOUR SCHOOL WHO WILL BE SENT TO LADDERTOP GROUND FACILITY FOR THE FIRST PHASE OF THEIR TRAINING.
COME ON, AZURE, GET DOWN HERE! YOU CAN'T MISS THIS!
PLEASE COME UP TO THE STAGE WHEN I CALL YOUR NAME.
GABE MICHALSKI.
TREVOR DEAN.
AZURE MILES, AZURE MILES, AZURE MILES...
ROBERTA HOLTEN.

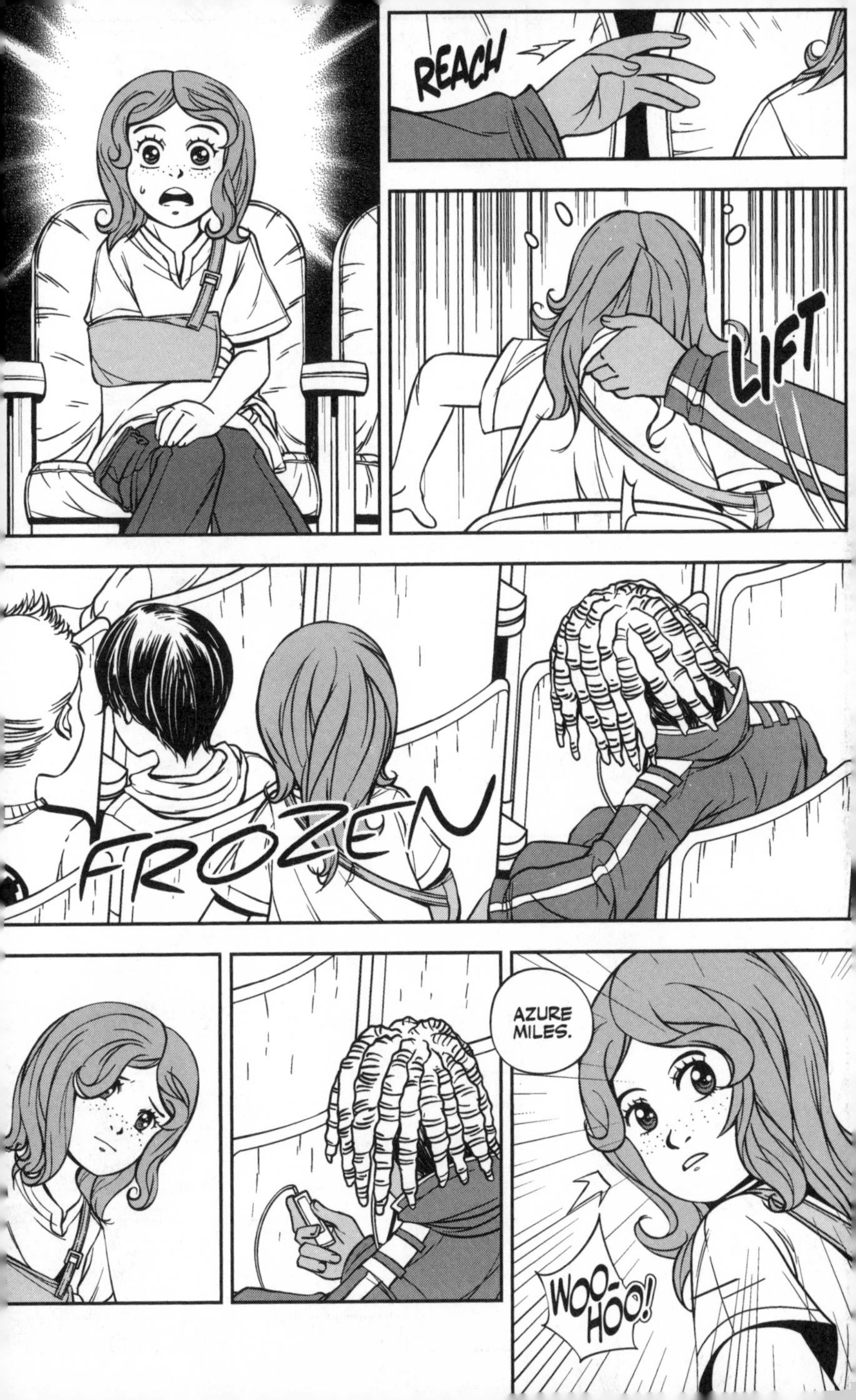
REACH
LIFT
FROZEN
AZURE MILES.
WOO-HOO!

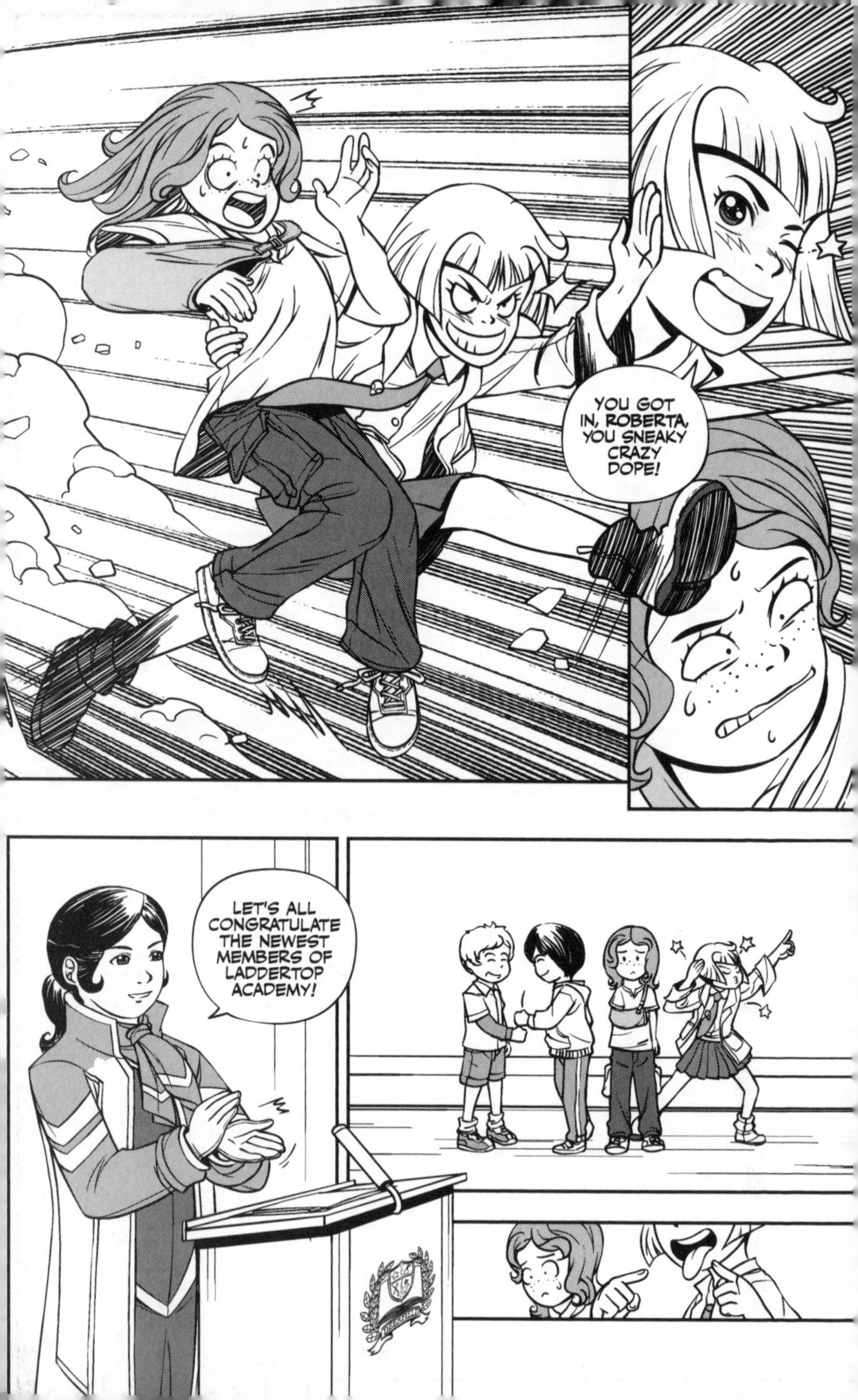
YOU GOT IN, ROBERTA, YOU SNEAKY CRAZY DOPE!
LET'S ALL CONGRATULATE THE NEWEST MEMBERS OF LADDERTOP ACADEMY!

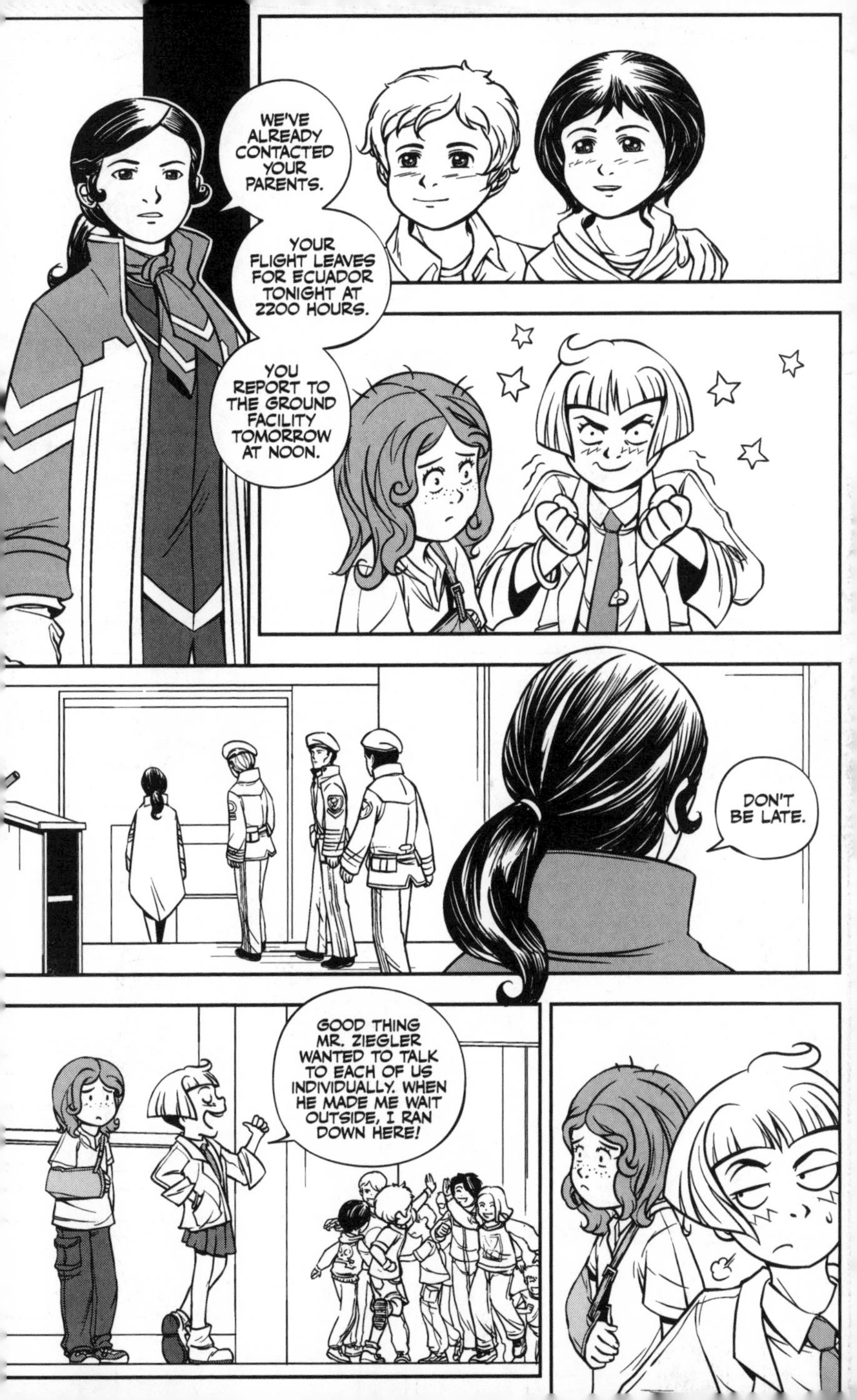
WE'VE ALREADY CONTACTED YOUR PARENTS.
YOUR FLIGHT LEAVES FOR ECUADOR TONIGHT AT 2200 HOURS.
YOU REPORT TO THE GROUND FACILITY TOMORROW AT NOON.
DON'T BE LATE.
GOOD THING MR. ZIEGLER WANTED TO TALK TO EACH OF US INDIVIDUALLY. WHEN HE MADE ME WAIT OUTSIDE, I RAN DOWN HERE!

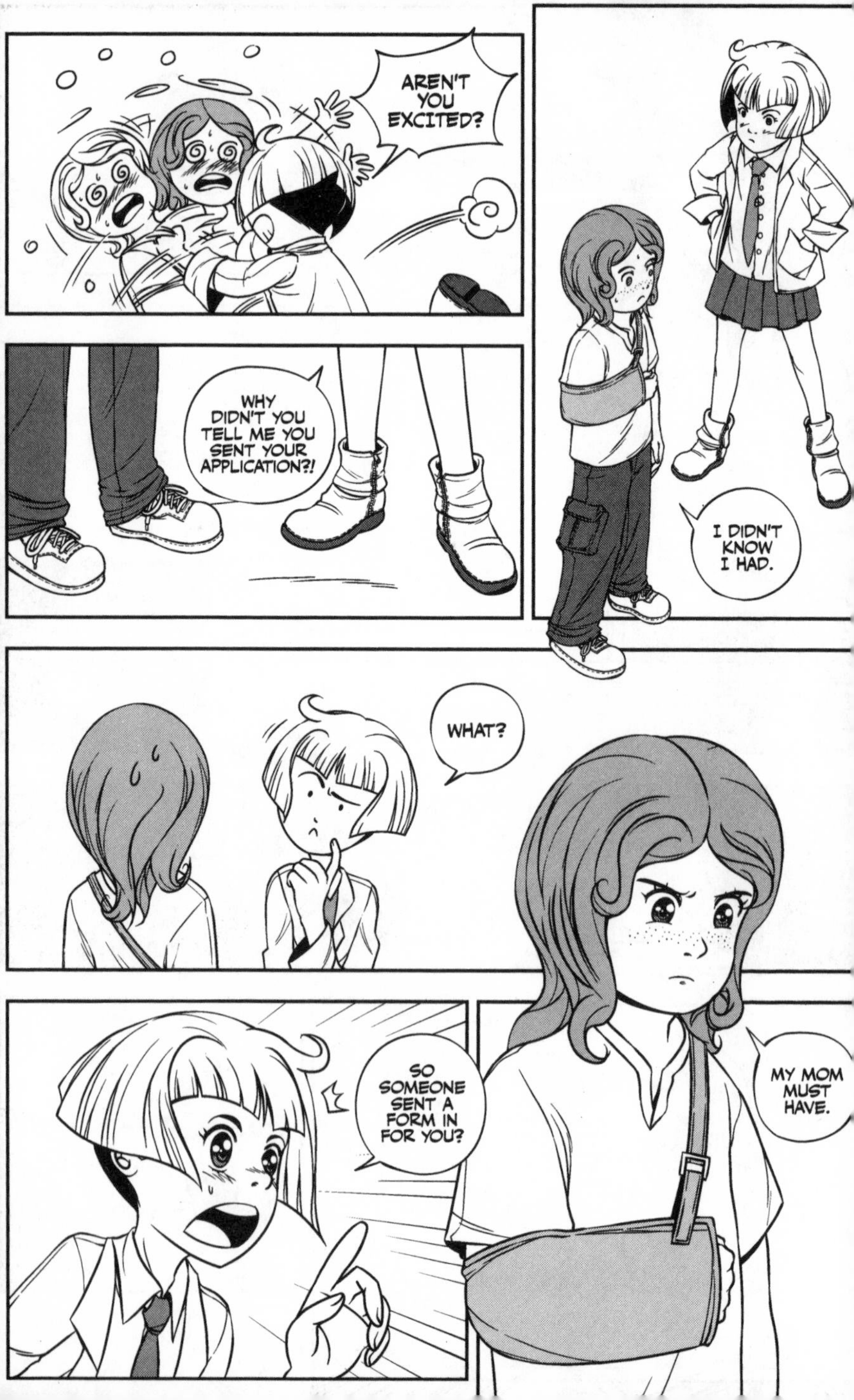
AREN'T YOU EXCITED?
WHY DIDN'T YOU TELL ME YOU SENT YOUR APPLICATION?!
I DIDN'T KNOW I HAD.
WHAT?
SO SOMEONE SENT A FORM IN FOR YOU?
MY MOM MUST HAVE.

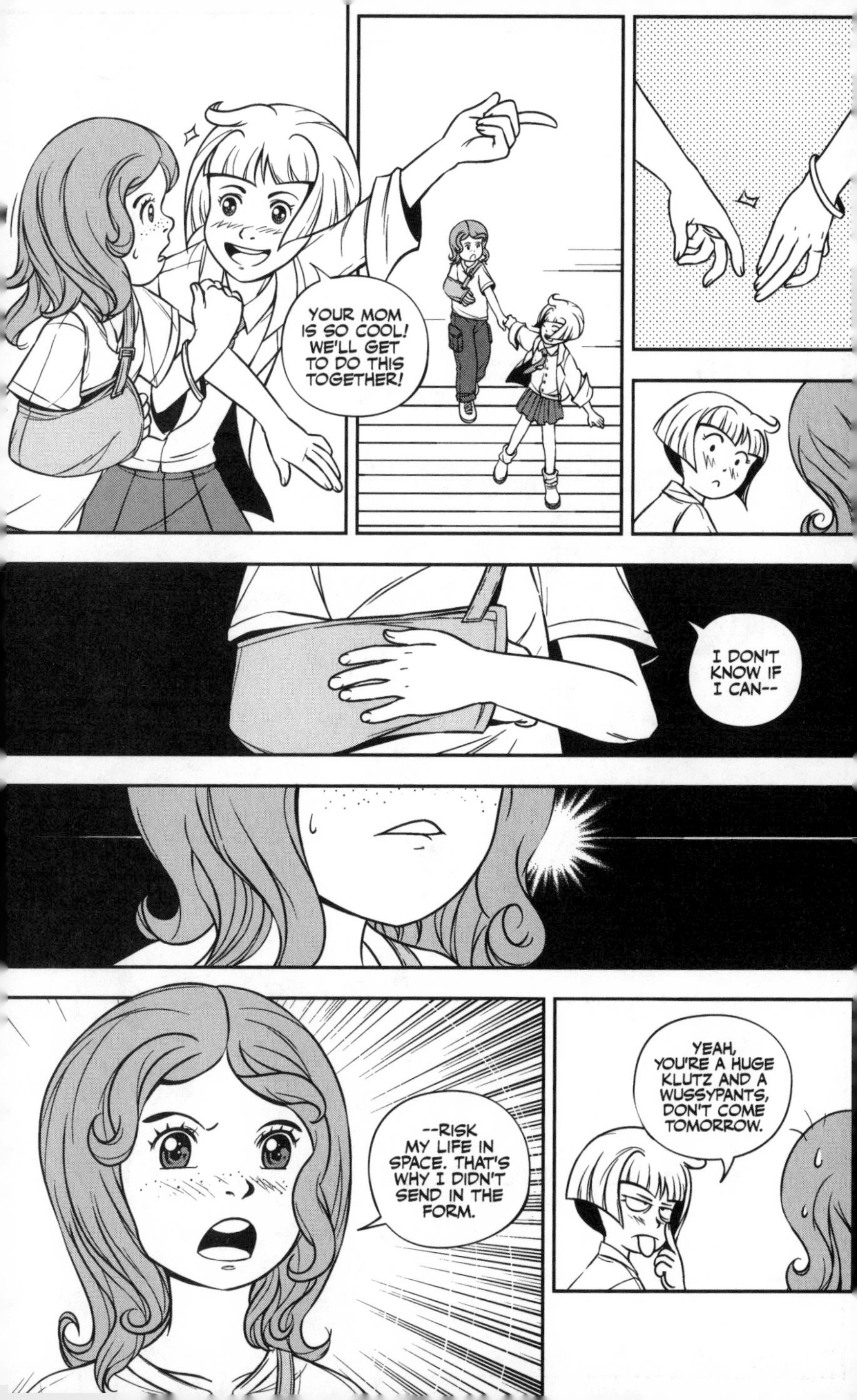
YOUR MOM IS SO COOL! WE'LL GET TO DO THIS TOGETHER!
I DON'T KNOW IF I CAN--
--RISK MY LIFE IN SPACE. THAT'S WHY I DIDN'T SEND IN THE FORM.
YEAH, YOU'RE A HUGE KLUTZ AND A WUSSYPANTS, DON'T COME TOMORROW.

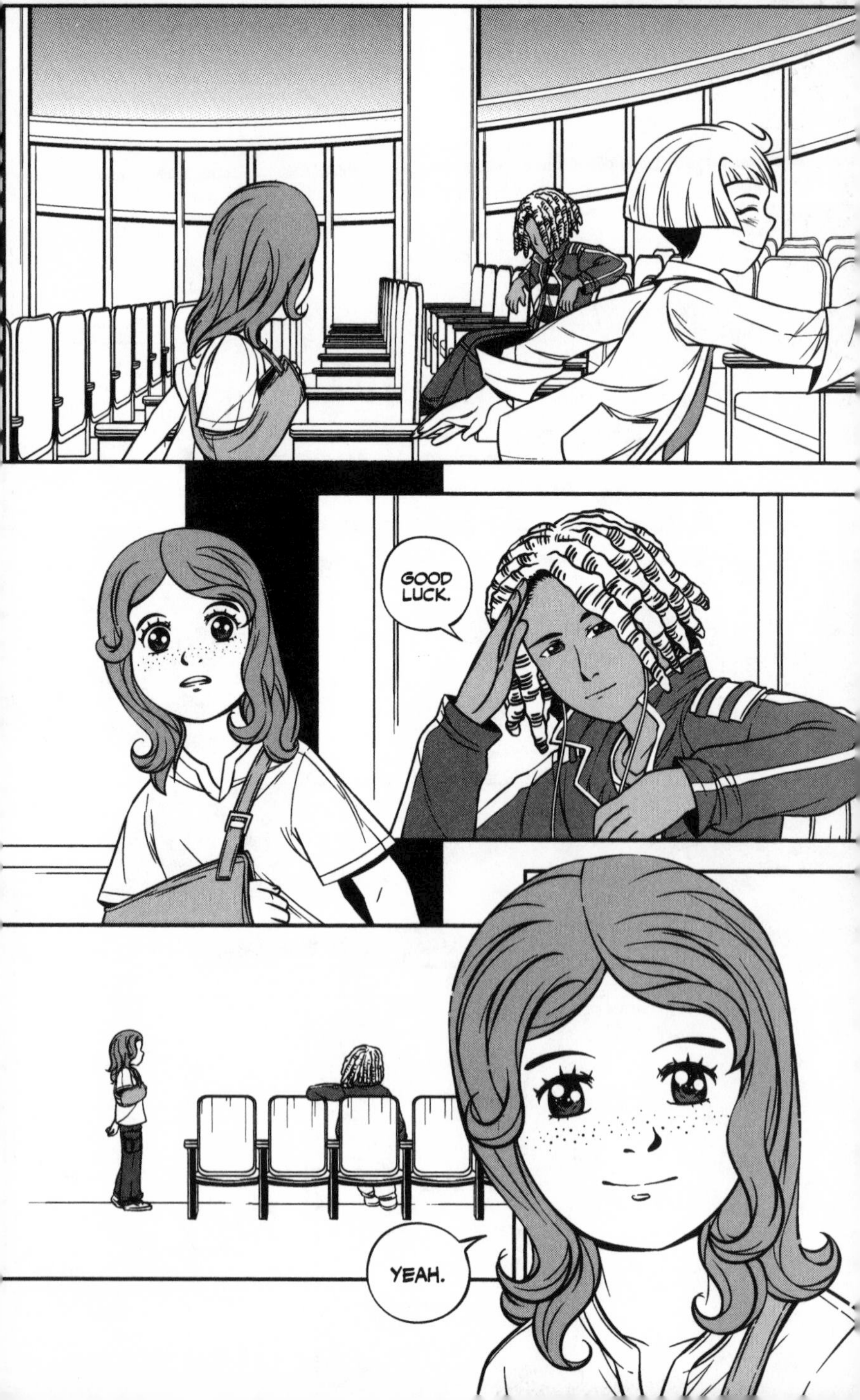
GOOD LUCK.
YEAH.

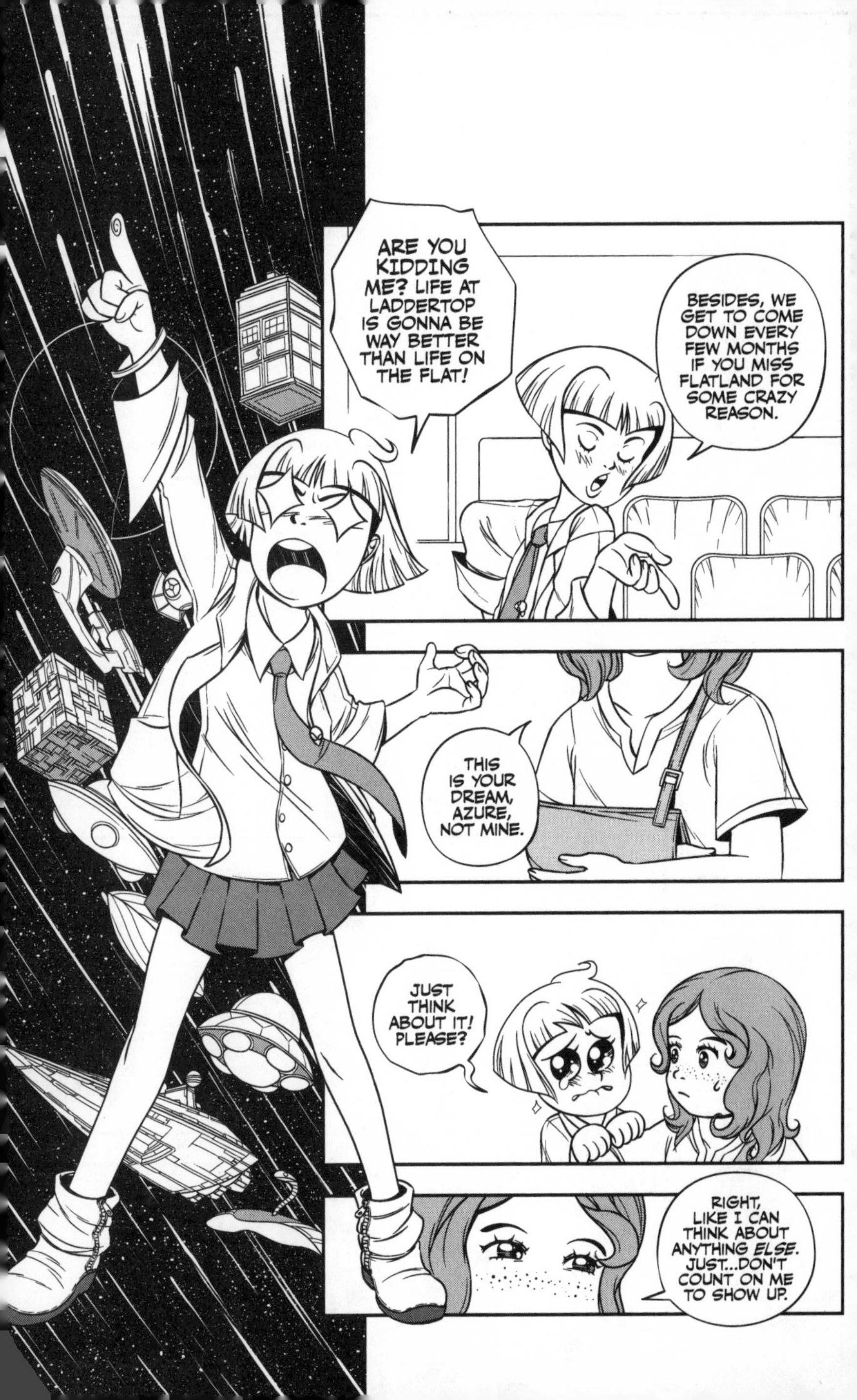
ARE YOU KIDDING ME? LIFE AT LADDERTOP IS GONNA BE WAY BETTER THAN LIFE ON THE FLAT!
BESIDES, WE GET TO COME DOWN EVERY FEW MONTHS IF YOU MISS FLATLAND FOR SOME CRAZY REASON.
THIS IS YOUR DREAM, AZURE, NOT MINE.
JUST THINK ABOUT IT! PLEASE?
RIGHT, LIKE I CAN THINK ABOUT ANYTHING *ELSE*. JUST...DON'T COUNT ON ME TO SHOW UP.

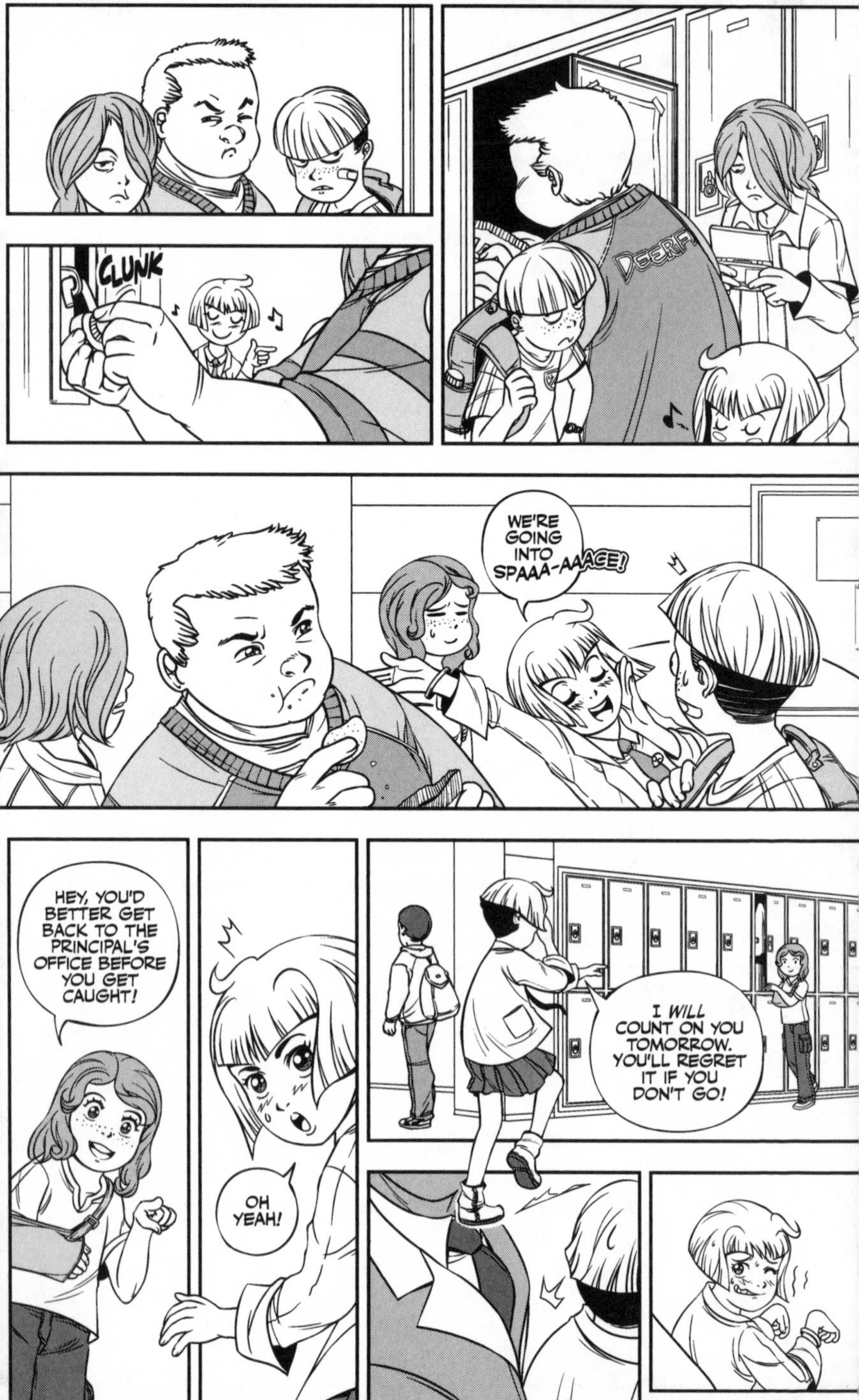
CLUNK
DEERF
WE'RE GOING INTO SPAAA-AAACE!
HEY, YOU'D BETTER GET BACK TO THE PRINCIPAL'S OFFICE BEFORE YOU GET CAUGHT!
OH YEAH!
I *WILL* COUNT ON YOU TOMORROW. YOU'LL REGRET IT IF YOU DON'T GO!

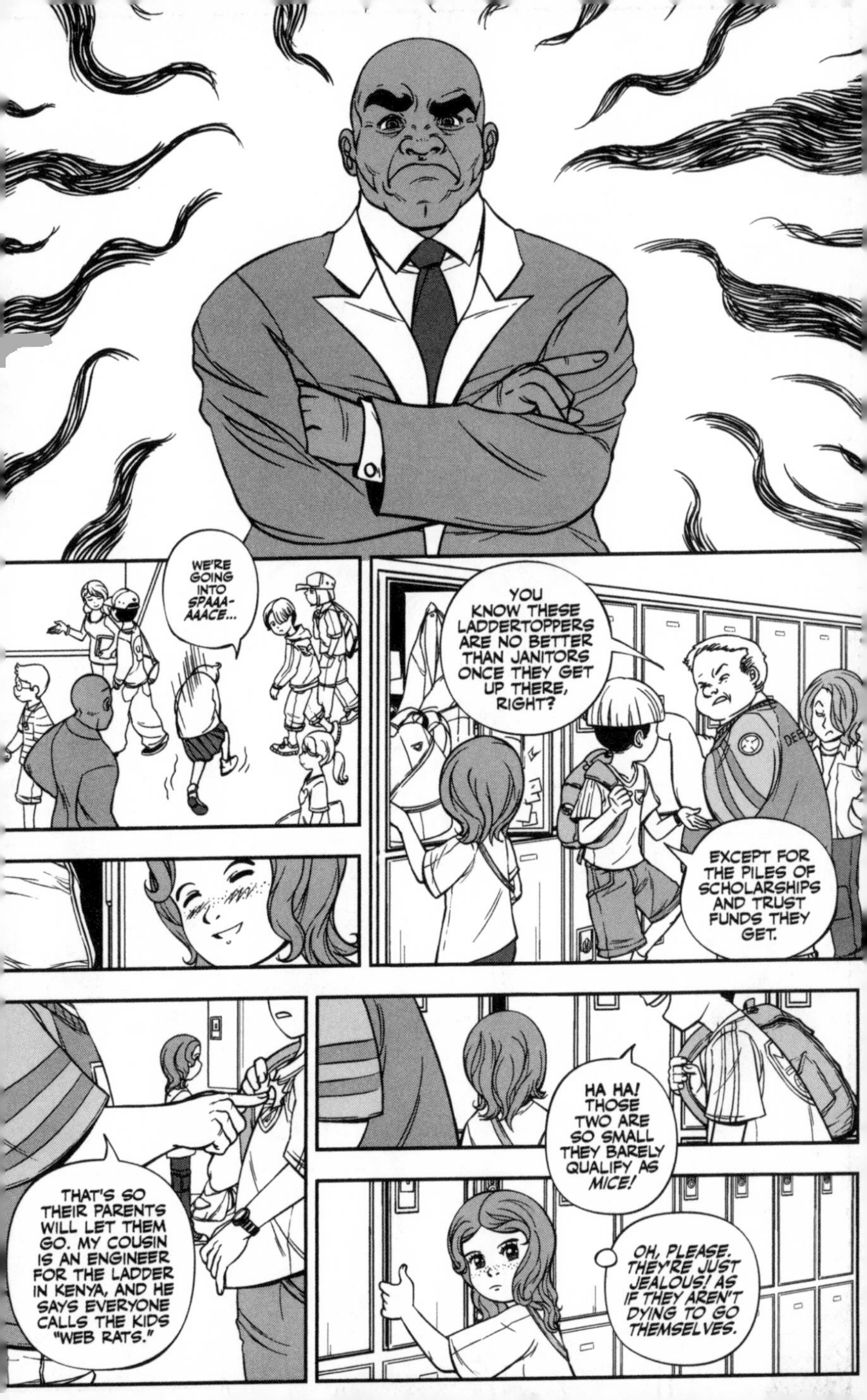
WE'RE GOING INTO SPAAA-AAACE...
YOU KNOW THESE LADDERTOPPERS ARE NO BETTER THAN JANITORS ONCE THEY GET UP THERE, RIGHT?
EXCEPT FOR THE PILES OF SCHOLARSHIPS AND TRUST FUNDS THEY GET.
THAT'S SO THEIR PARENTS WILL LET THEM GO. MY COUSIN IS AN ENGINEER FOR THE LADDER IN KENYA, AND HE SAYS EVERYONE CALLS THE KIDS "WEB RATS."
HA HA! THOSE TWO ARE SO SMALL THEY BARELY QUALIFY AS MICE!
OH, PLEASE. THEY'RE JUST JEALOUS! AS IF THEY AREN'T DYING TO GO THEMSELVES.

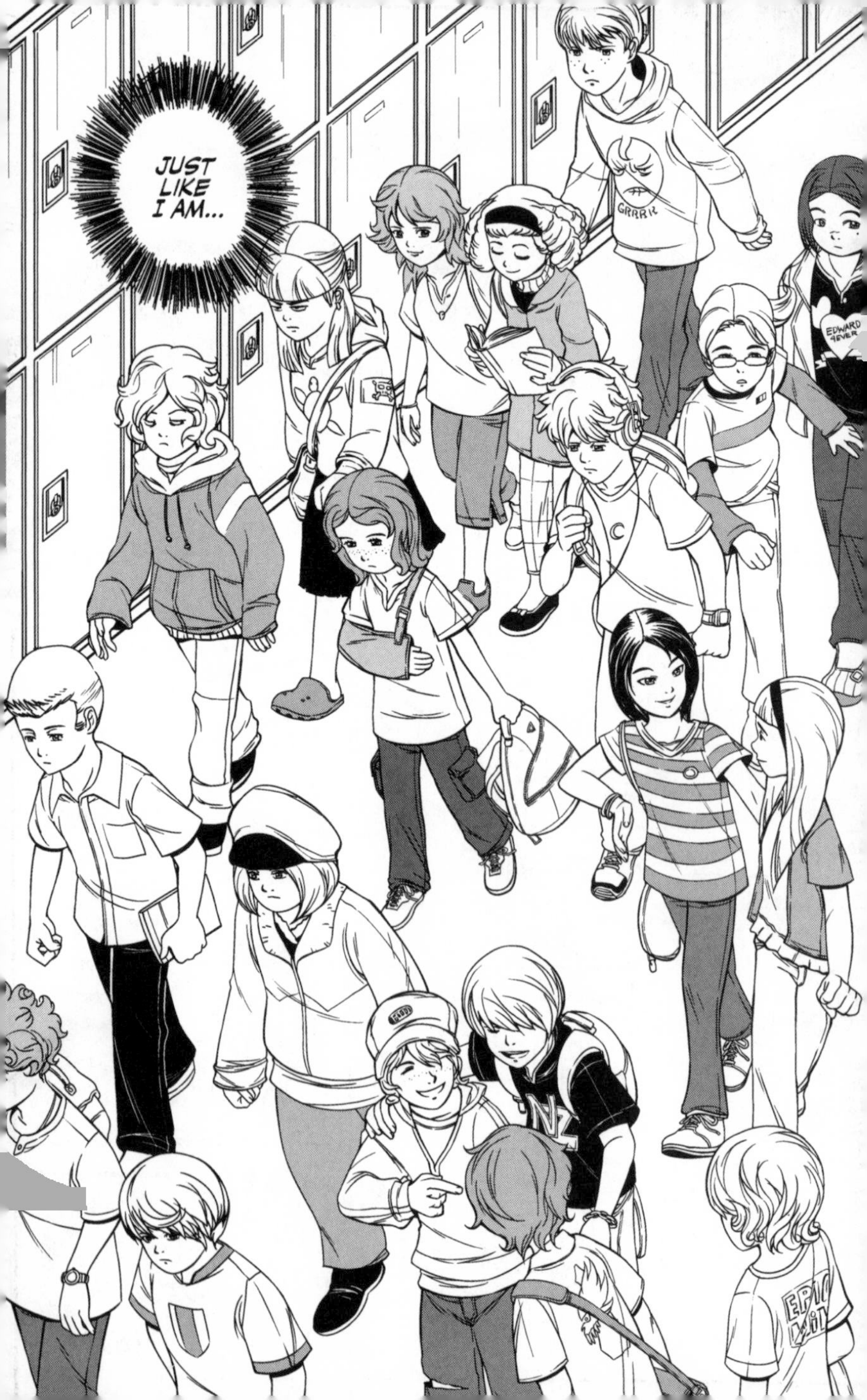
JUST LIKE I AM...
EDWARD 4EVER

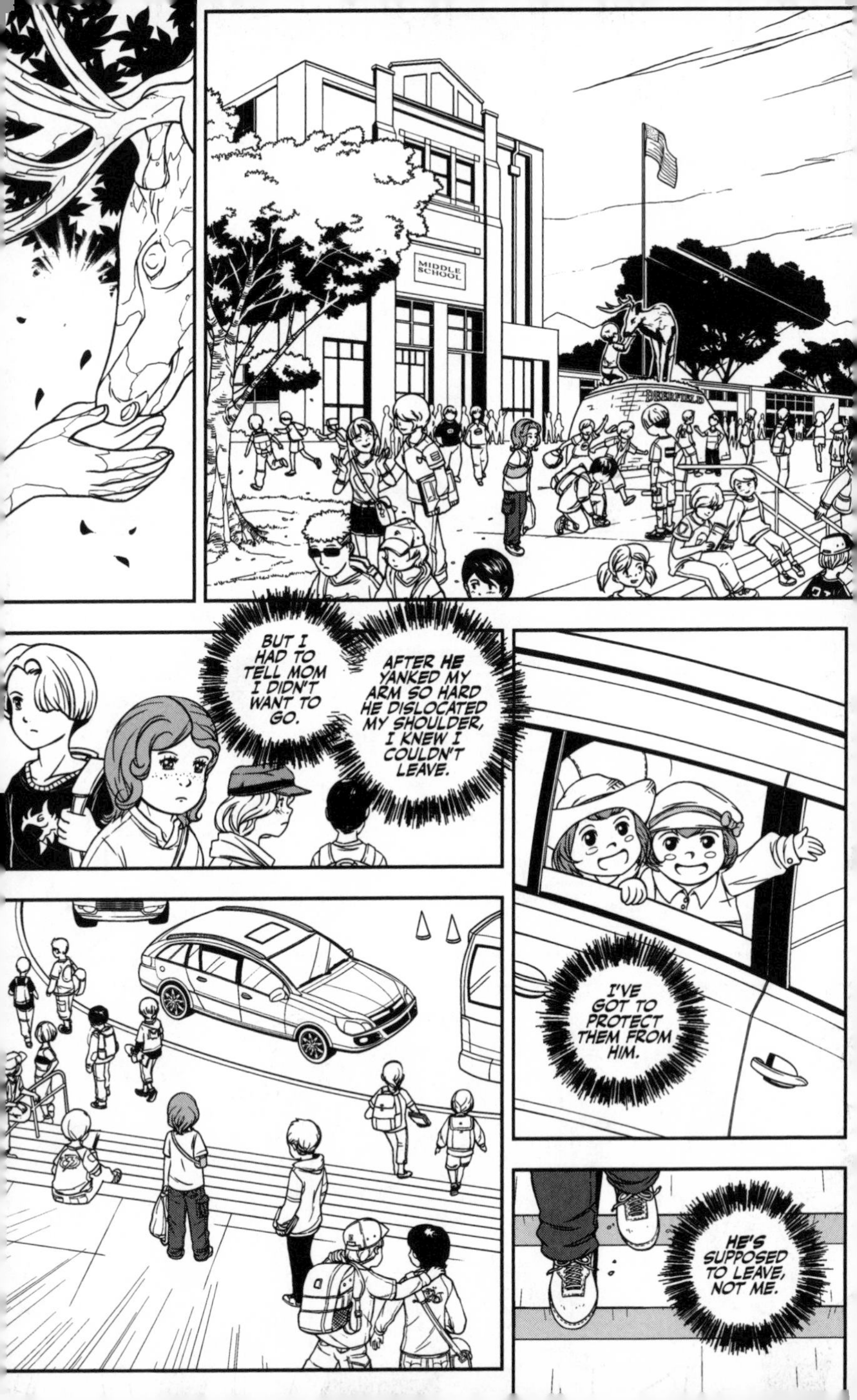
MIDDLE SCHOOL
DEERFIELD
BUT I HAD TO TELL MOM I DIDN'T WANT TO GO.
AFTER HE YANKED MY ARM SO HARD HE DISLOCATED MY SHOULDER, I KNEW I COULDN'T LEAVE.
I'VE GOT TO PROTECT THEM FROM HIM.
HE'S SUPPOSED TO LEAVE, NOT ME.

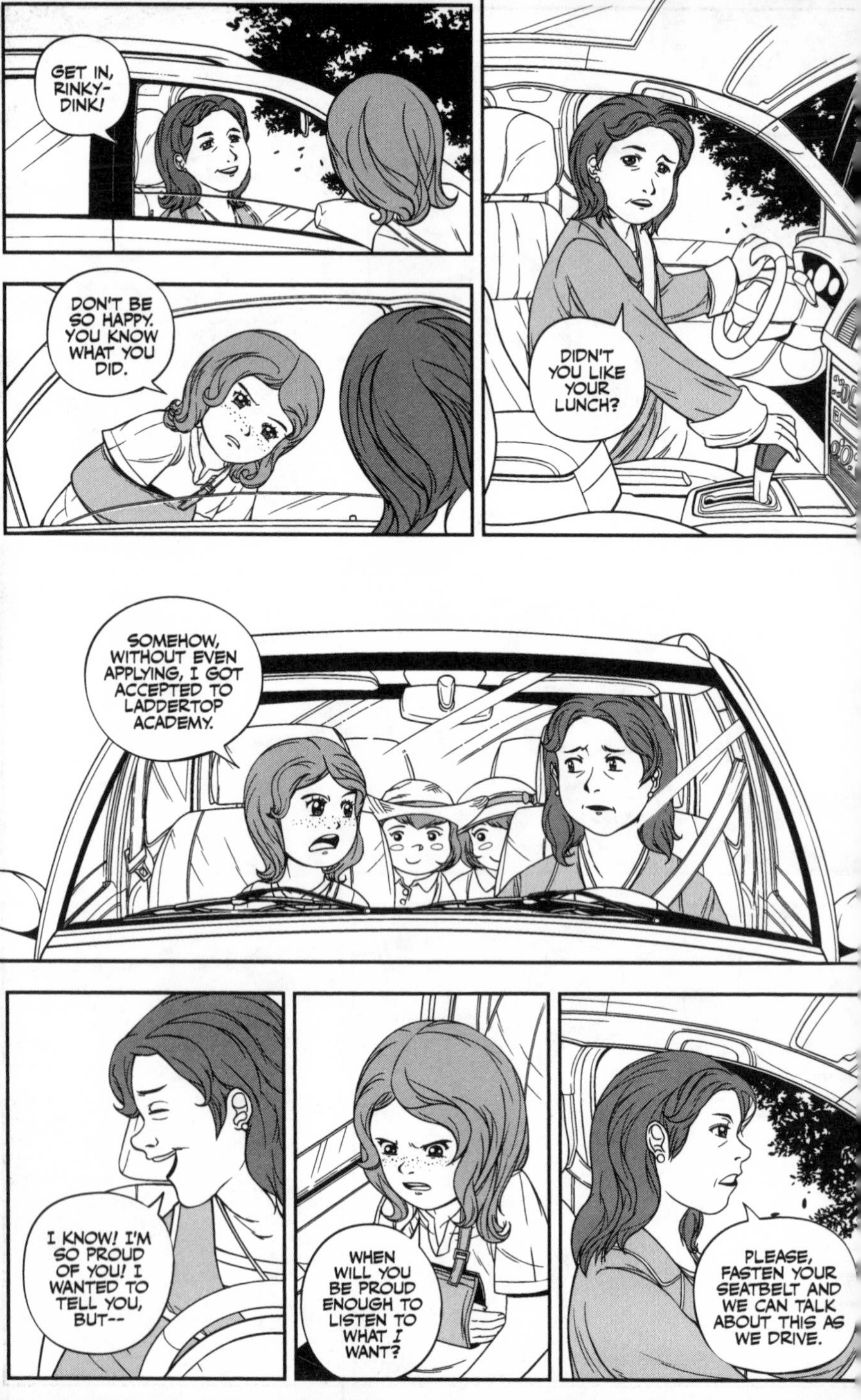
GET IN, RINKY-DINK!
DON'T BE SO HAPPY. YOU KNOW WHAT YOU DID.
DIDN'T YOU LIKE YOUR LUNCH?
SOMEHOW, WITHOUT EVEN APPLYING, I GOT ACCEPTED TO LADDERTOP ACADEMY.
I KNOW! I'M SO PROUD OF YOU! I WANTED TO TELL YOU, BUT--
WHEN WILL YOU BE PROUD ENOUGH TO LISTEN TO WHAT *I* WANT?
PLEASE, FASTEN YOUR SEATBELT AND WE CAN TALK ABOUT THIS AS WE DRIVE.

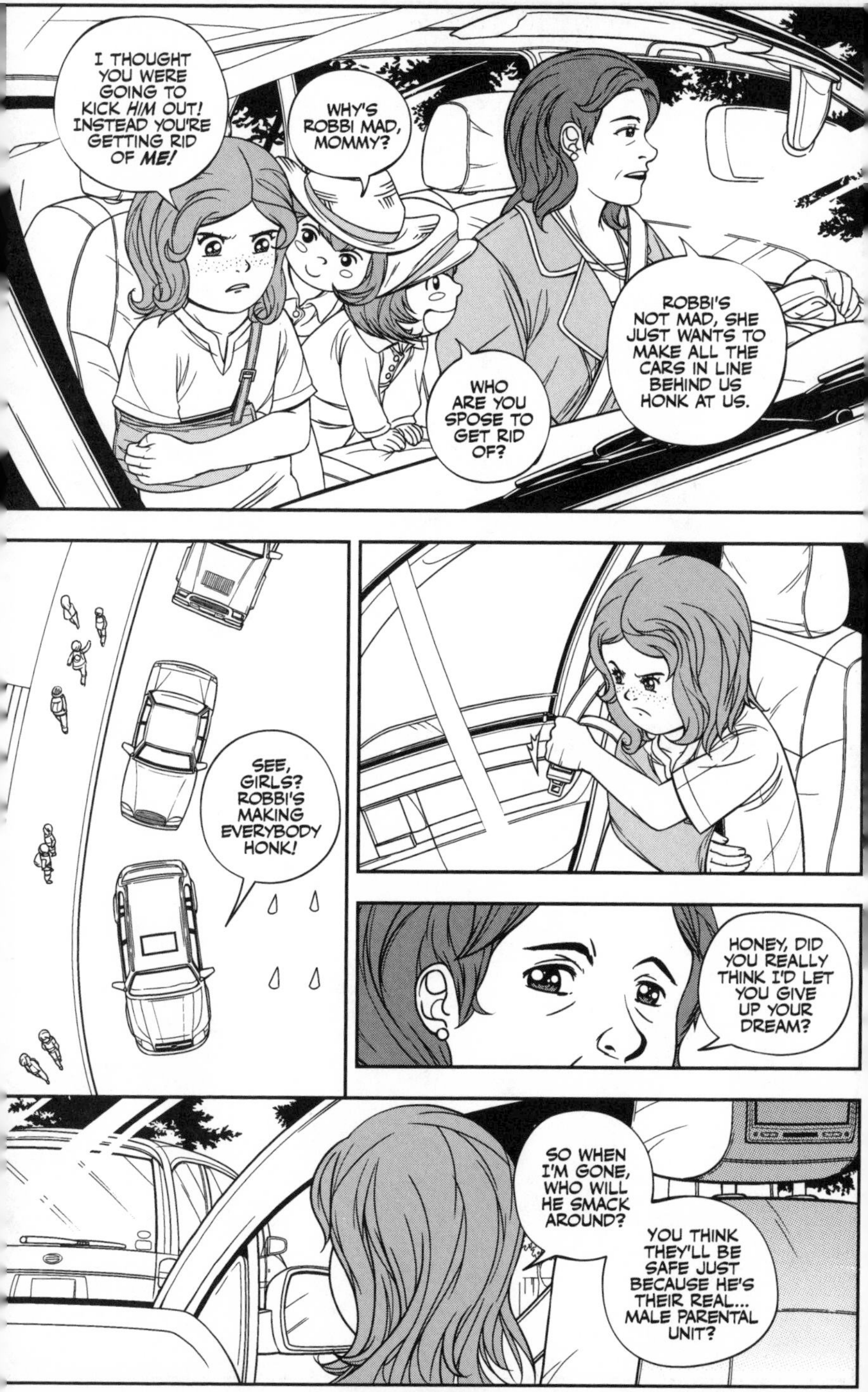
I THOUGHT YOU WERE GOING TO KICK *HIM* OUT! INSTEAD YOU'RE GETTING RID OF *ME!*
WHY'S ROBBI MAD, MOMMY?
ROBBI'S NOT MAD, SHE JUST WANTS TO MAKE ALL THE CARS IN LINE BEHIND US HONK AT US.
WHO ARE YOU SPOSE TO GET RID OF?
SEE, GIRLS? ROBBI'S MAKING EVERYBODY HONK!
HONEY, DID YOU REALLY THINK I'D LET YOU GIVE UP YOUR DREAM?
SO WHEN I'M GONE, WHO WILL HE SMACK AROUND?
YOU THINK THEY'LL BE SAFE JUST BECAUSE HE'S THEIR REAL... MALE PARENTAL UNIT?

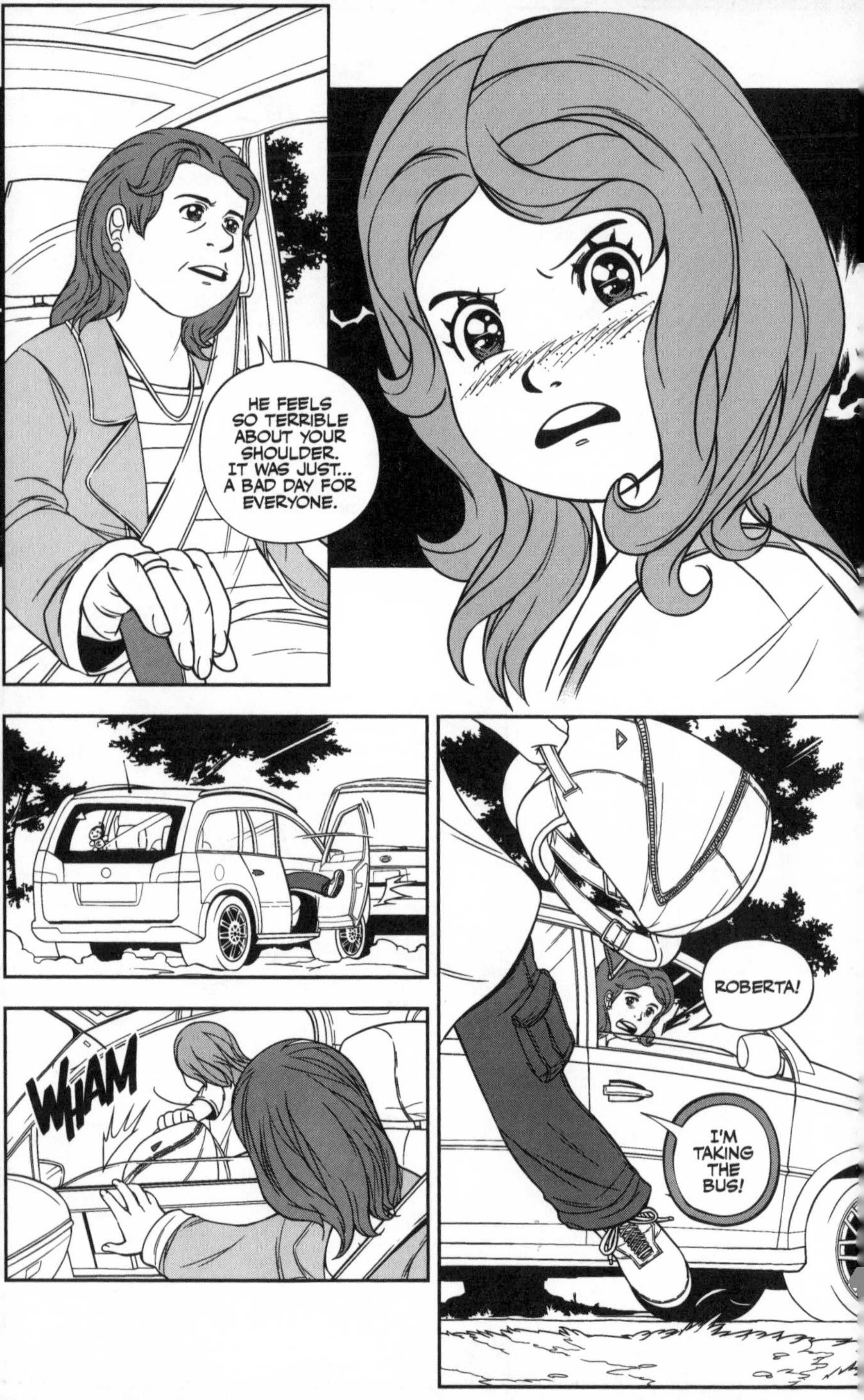
HE FEELS SO TERRIBLE ABOUT YOUR SHOULDER. IT WAS JUST... A BAD DAY FOR EVERYONE.
WHAM
ROBERTA!
I'M TAKING THE BUS!

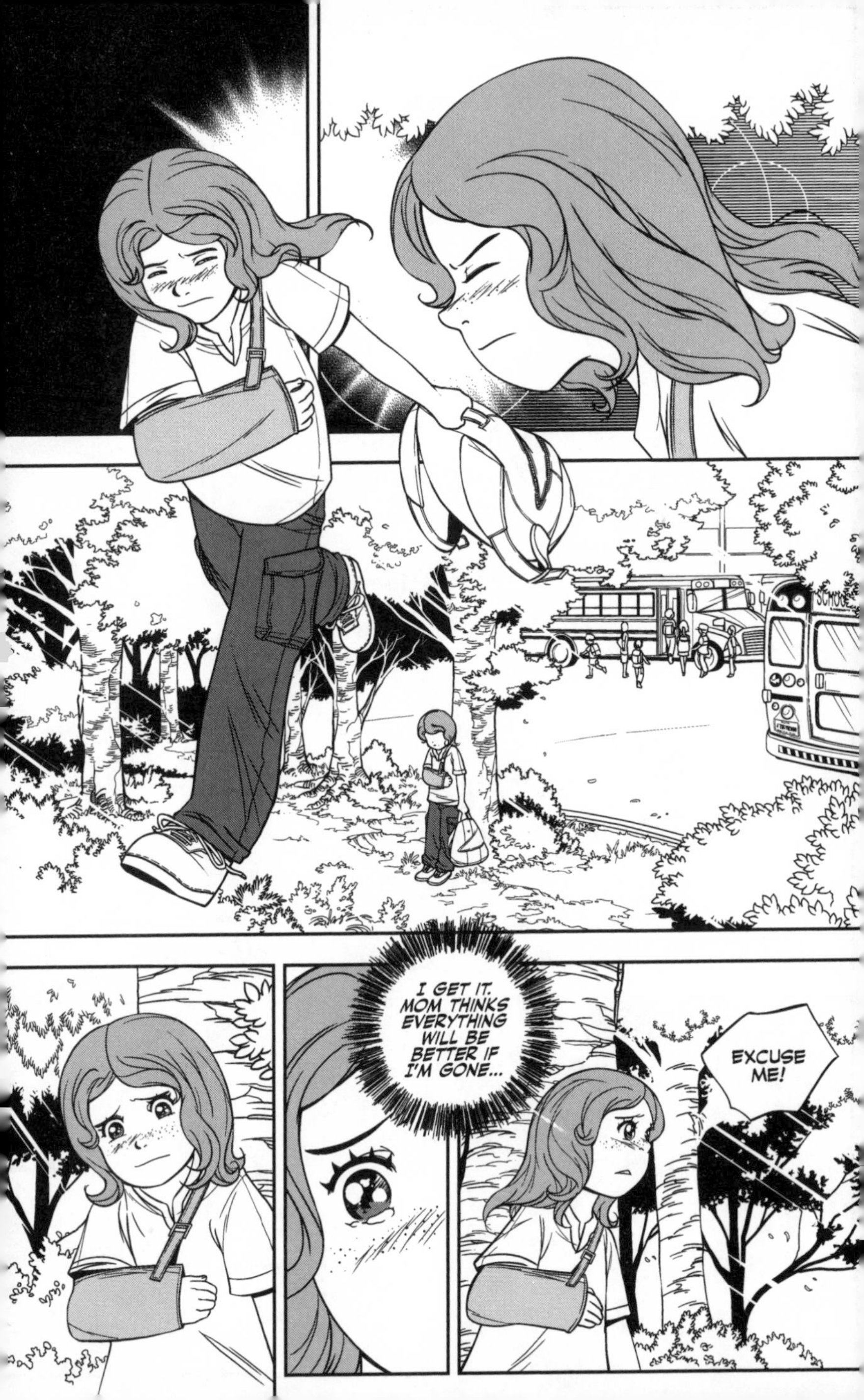
I GET IT. MOM THINKS EVERYTHING WILL BE BETTER IF I'M GONE...
EXCUSE ME!

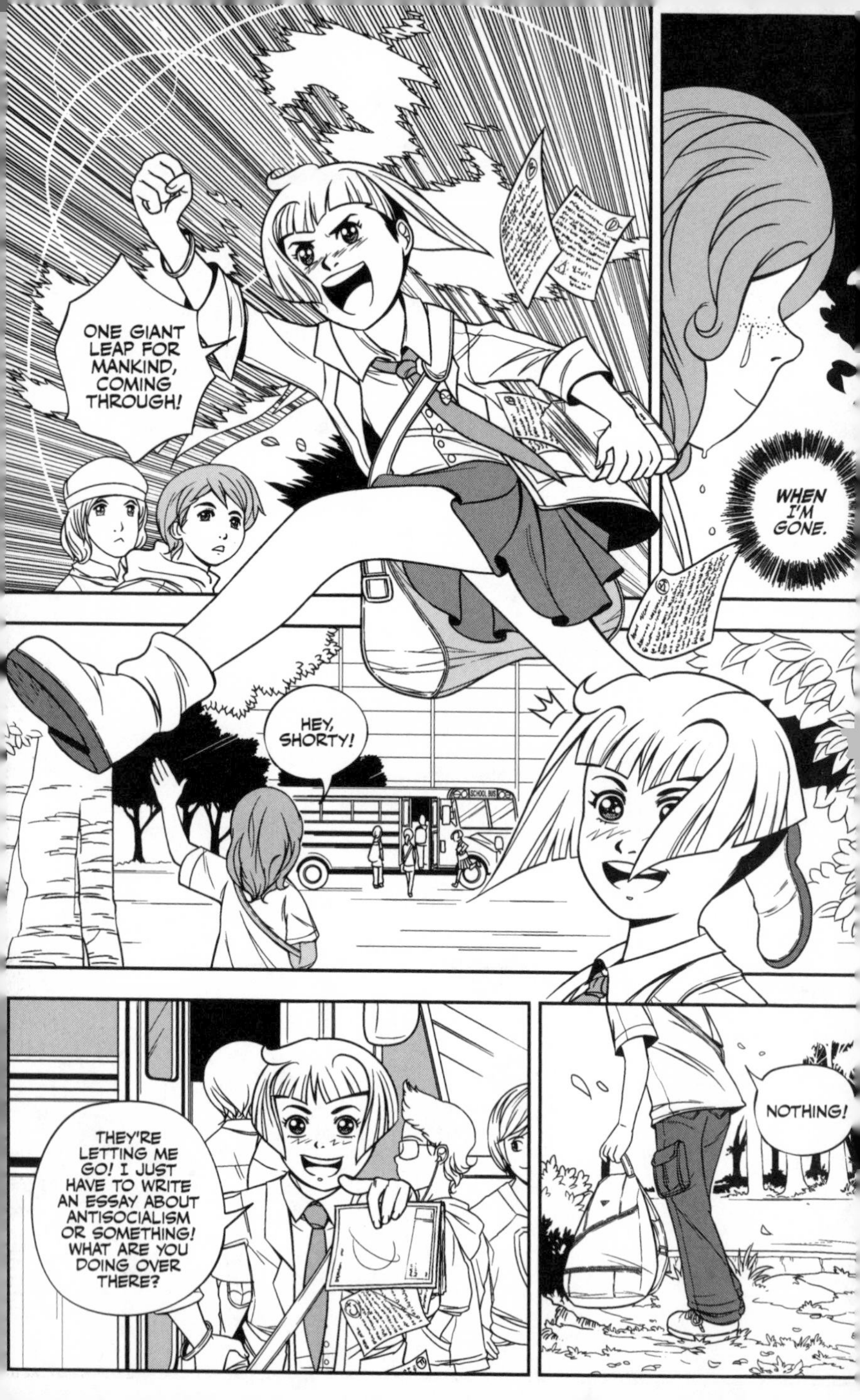
ONE GIANT LEAP FOR MANKIND, COMING THROUGH!
WHEN I'M GONE.
HEY, SHORTY!
THEY'RE LETTING ME GO! I JUST HAVE TO WRITE AN ESSAY ABOUT ANTISOCIALISM OR SOMETHING! WHAT ARE YOU DOING OVER THERE?
NOTHING!

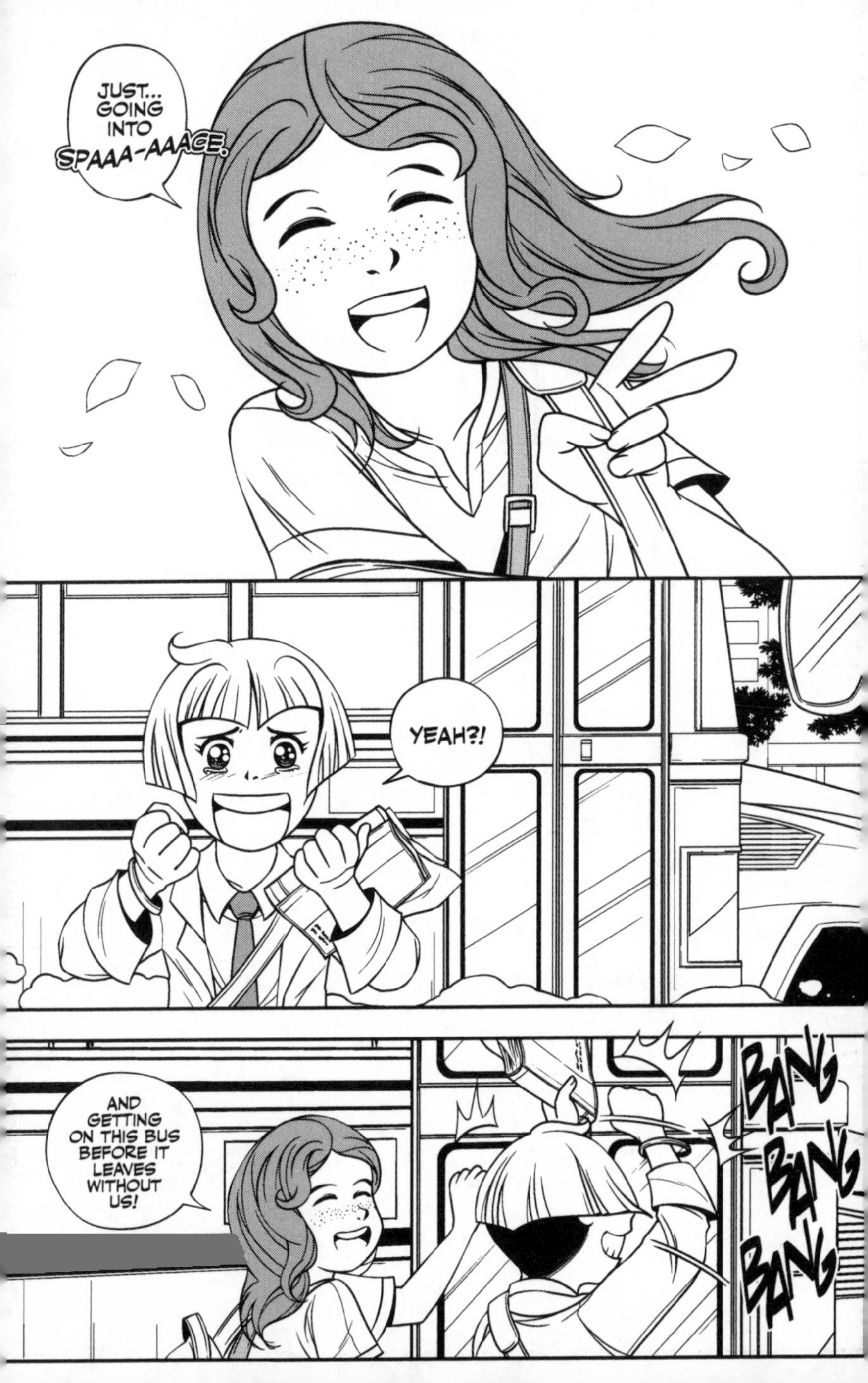
JUST... GOING INTO SPAAA-AAAGE.
YEAH?!
AND GETTING ON THIS BUS BEFORE IT LEAVES WITHOUT US!
BANG BANG BANG

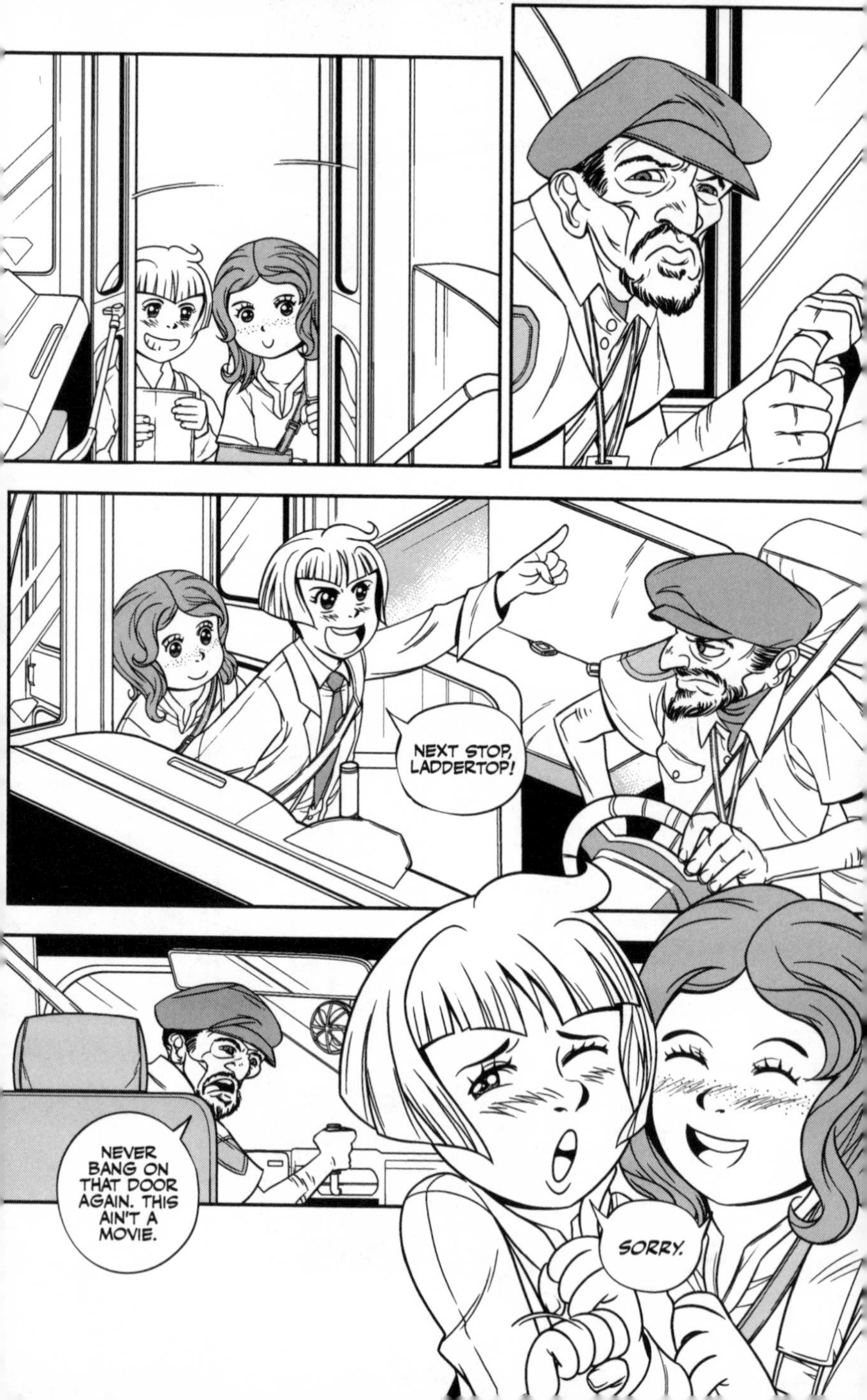
NEXT STOP, LADDERTOP!
NEVER BANG ON THAT DOOR AGAIN. THIS AIN'T A MOVIE.
SORRY.

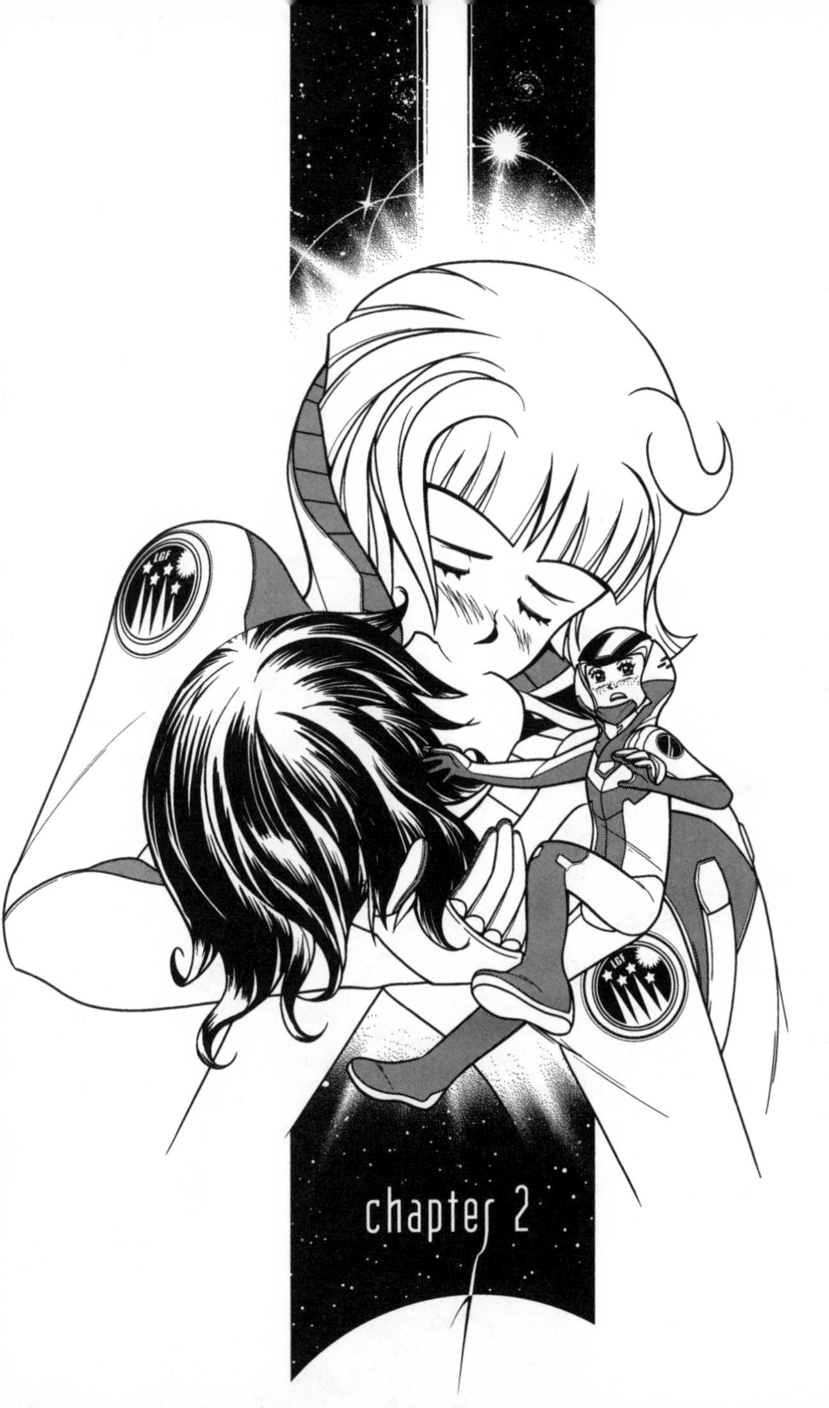
LGF
LGF
chapter 2

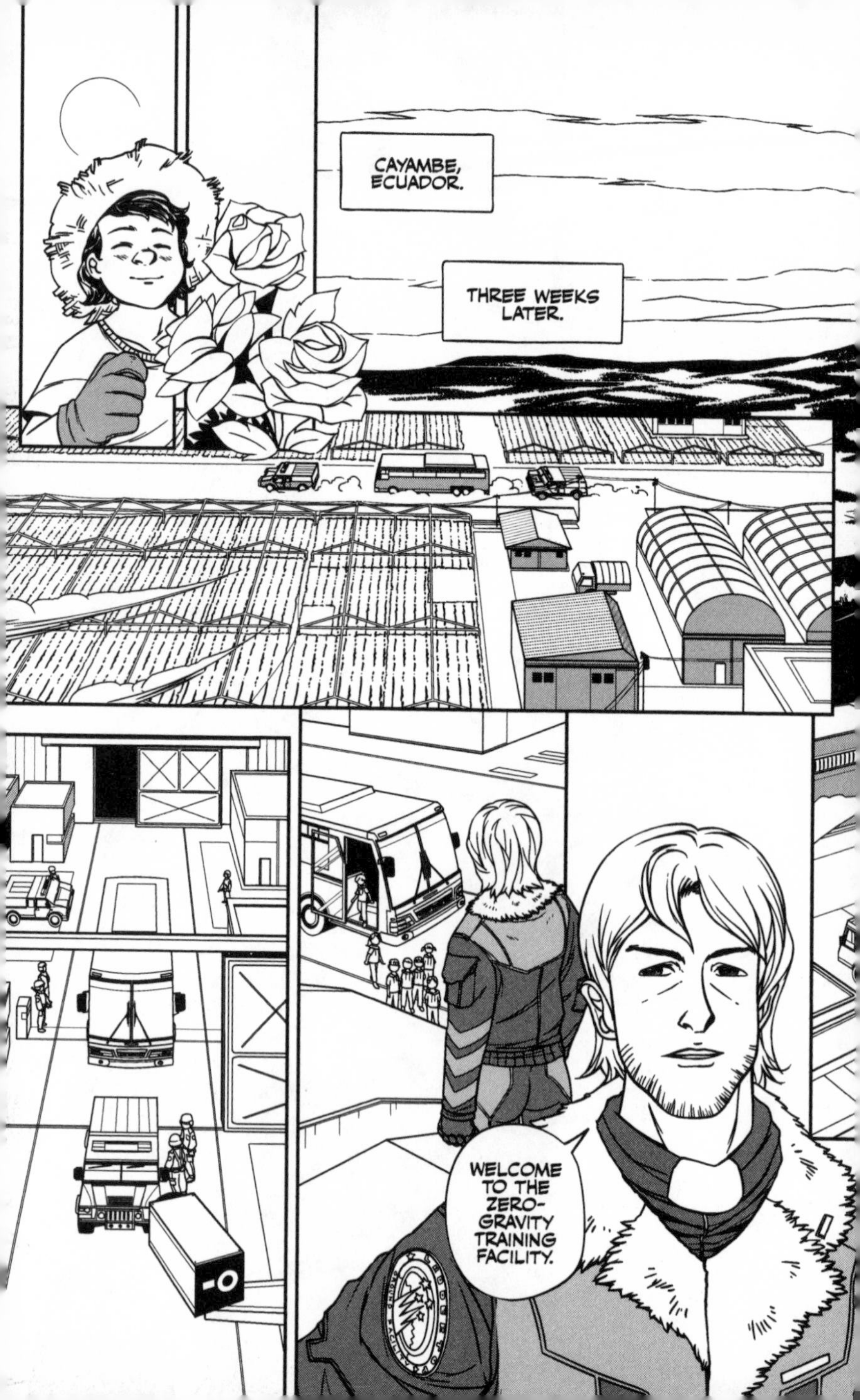
CAYAMBE, ECUADOR.
THREE WEEKS LATER.
WELCOME TO THE ZERO-GRAVITY TRAINING FACILITY.

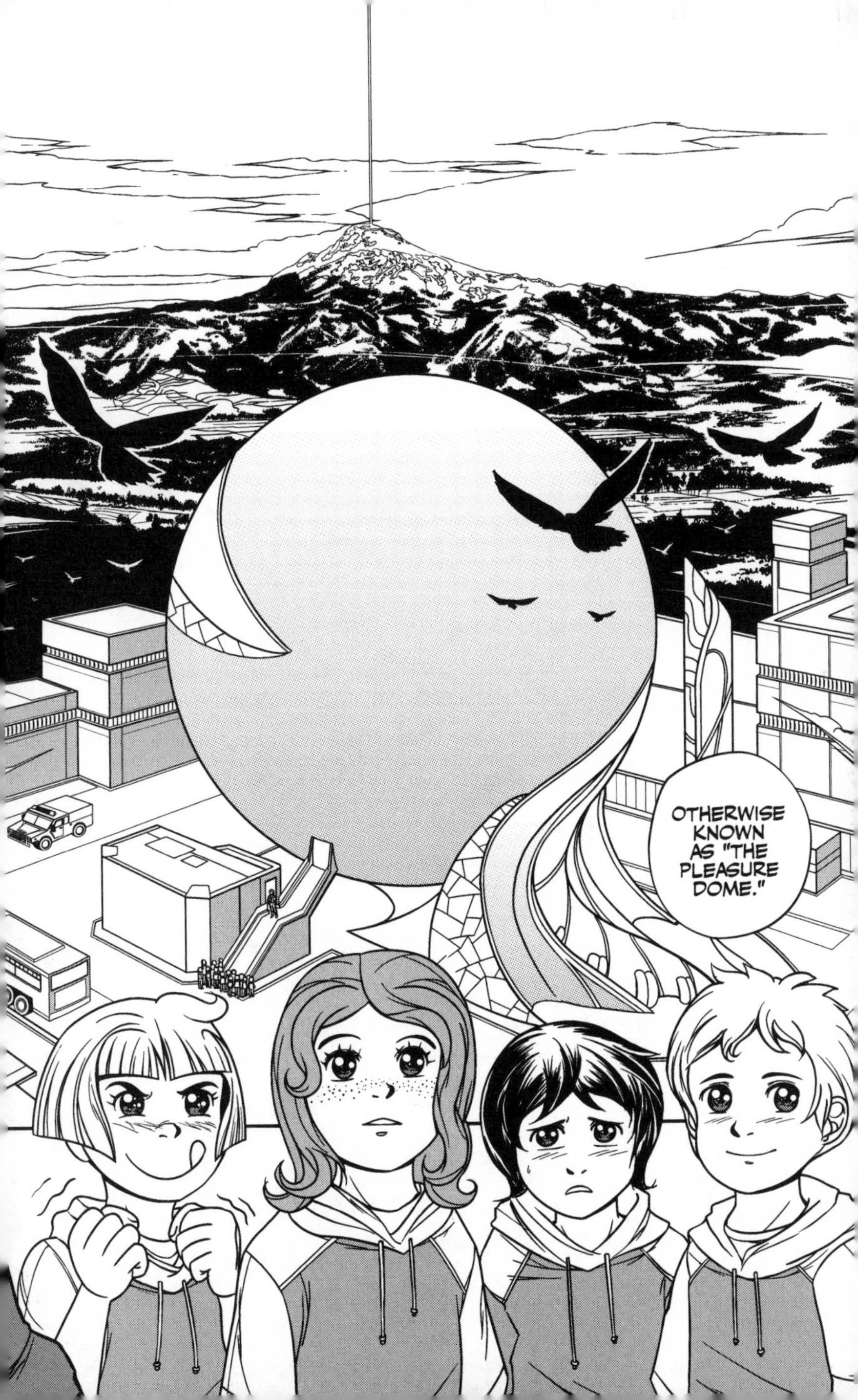
OTHERWISE KNOWN AS "THE PLEASURE DOME."

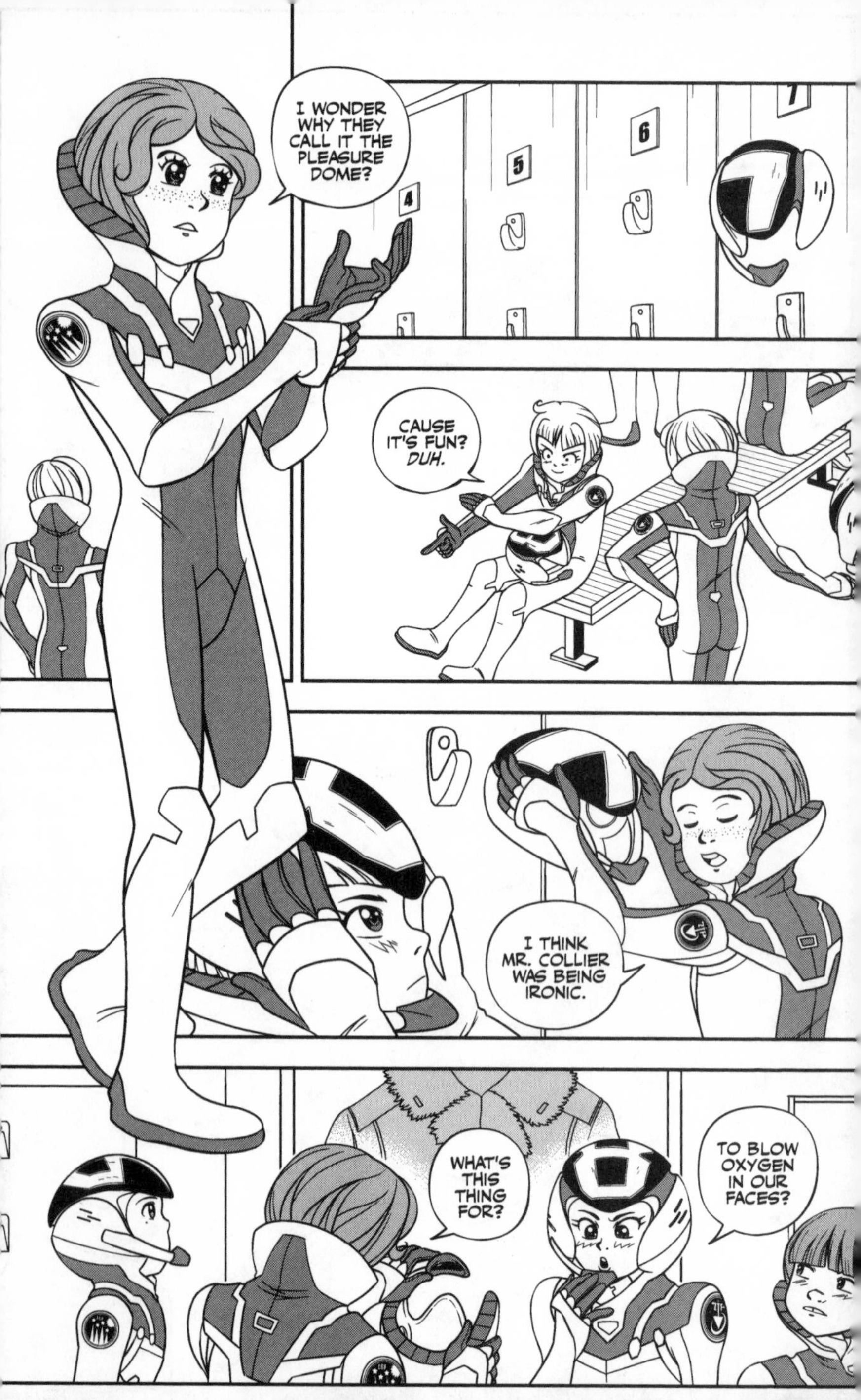
I WONDER WHY THEY CALL IT THE PLEASURE DOME?
4
5
6
7
CAUSE IT'S FUN? *DUH.*
I THINK MR. COLLIER WAS BEING IRONIC.
WHAT'S THIS THING FOR?
TO BLOW OXYGEN IN OUR FACES?

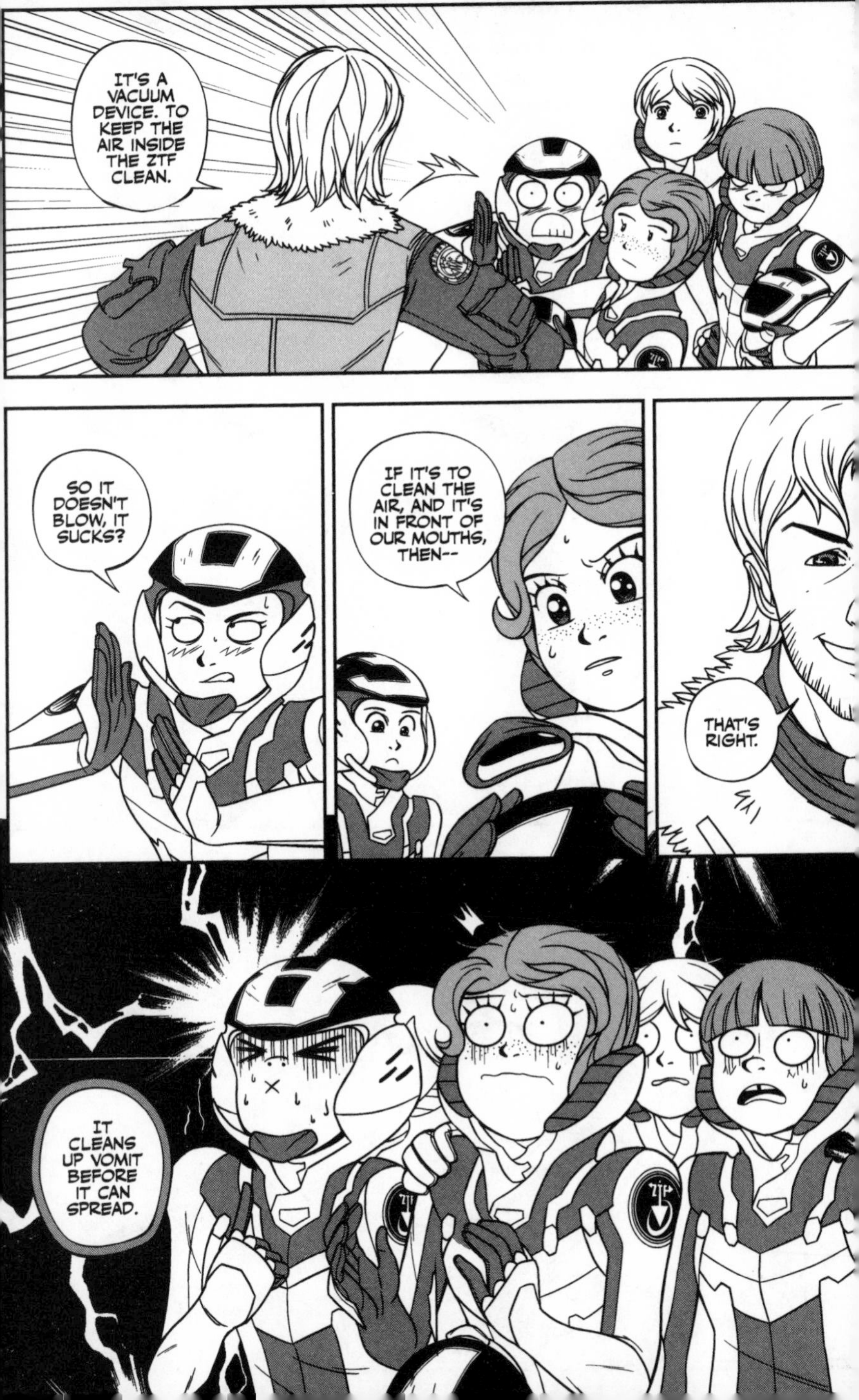
IT'S A VACUUM DEVICE. TO KEEP THE AIR INSIDE THE ZTF CLEAN.
SO IT DOESN'T BLOW, IT SUCKS?
IF IT'S TO CLEAN THE AIR, AND IT'S IN FRONT OF OUR MOUTHS, THEN--
THAT'S RIGHT.
IT CLEANS UP VOMIT BEFORE IT CAN SPREAD.

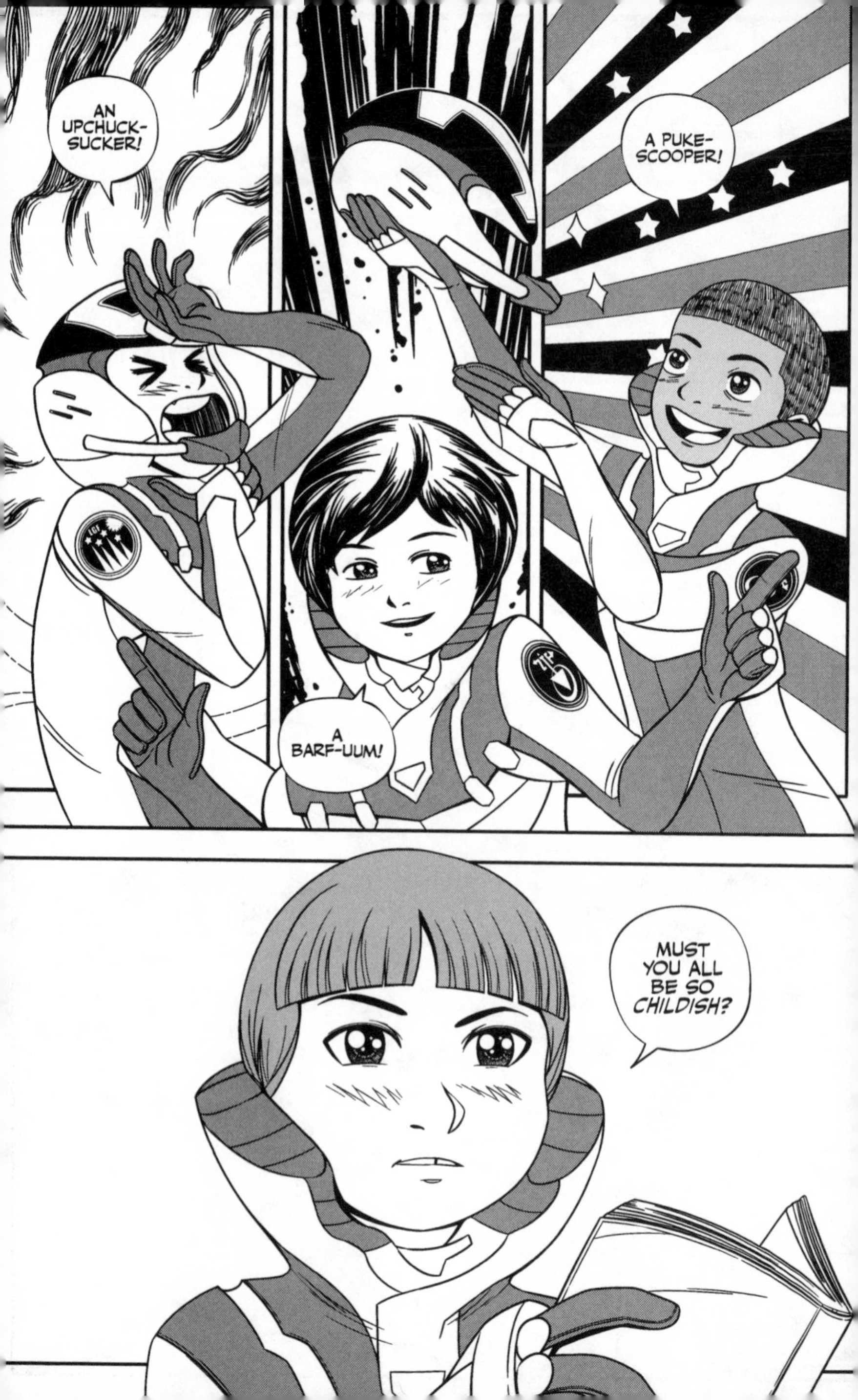
AN UPCHUCK-SUCKER!
A BARF-UUM!
A PUKE-SCOOPER!
MUST YOU ALL BE SO *CHILDISH?*

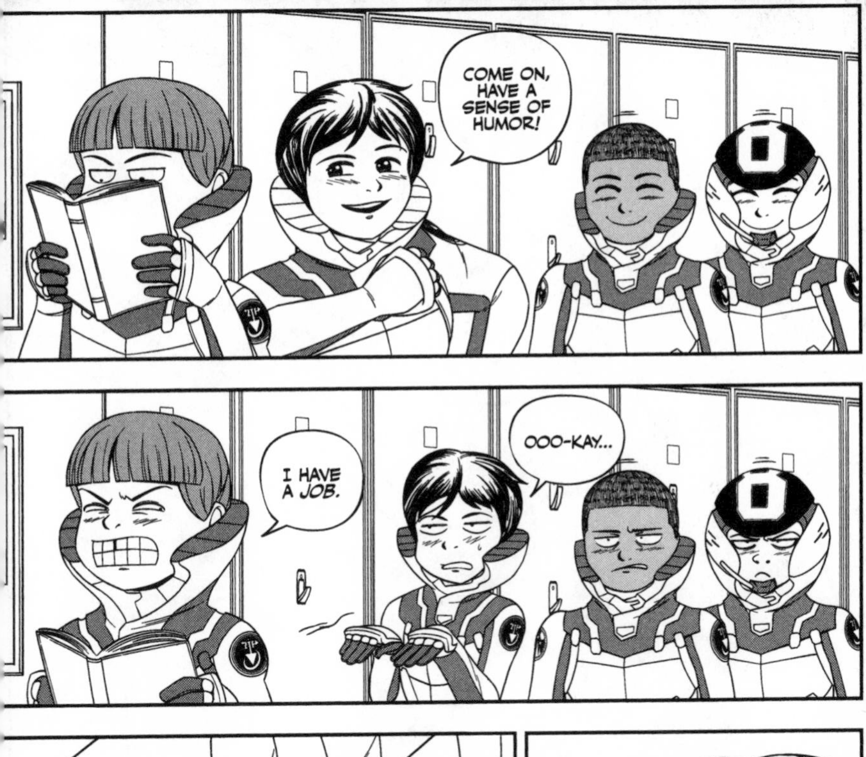
COME ON, HAVE A SENSE OF HUMOR!
I HAVE A *JOB.*
OOO-KAY...
MR. COLLIER, I'M NOT GOING TO NEED THIS SUCK-THING. I *NEVER* THROW UP.
EVERYBODY THROWS UP THEIR FIRST FEW TIMES IN ZERO-G.

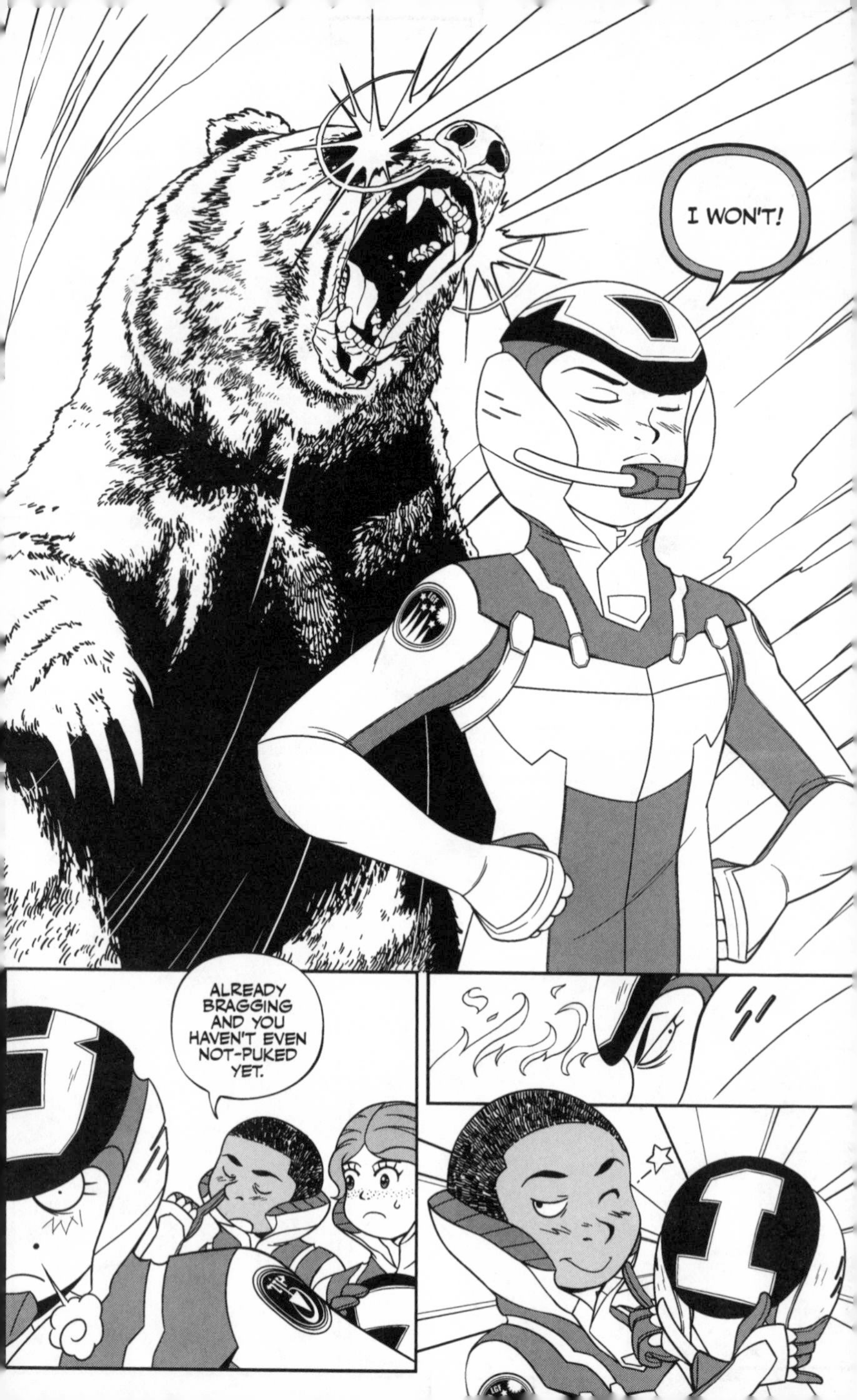
I WON'T!
ALREADY BRAGGING AND YOU HAVEN'T EVEN NOT-PUKED YET.

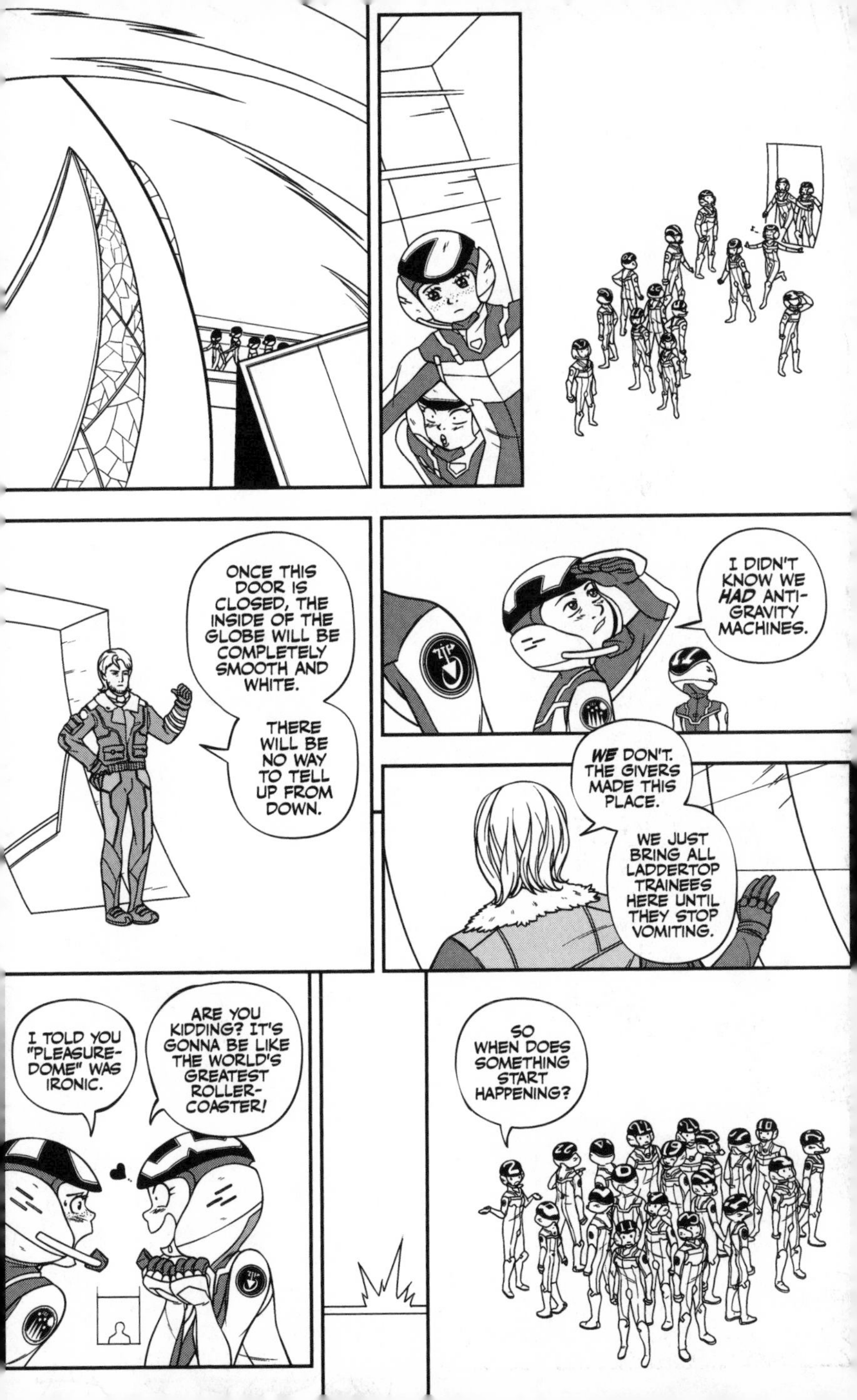
ONCE THIS DOOR IS CLOSED, THE INSIDE OF THE GLOBE WILL BE COMPLETELY SMOOTH AND WHITE.
THERE WILL BE NO WAY TO TELL UP FROM DOWN.
I DIDN'T KNOW WE *HAD* ANTI-GRAVITY MACHINES.
WE DON'T. THE GIVERS MADE THIS PLACE.
WE JUST BRING ALL LADDERTOP TRAINEES HERE UNTIL THEY STOP VOMITING.
I TOLD YOU "PLEASURE-DOME" WAS IRONIC.
ARE YOU KIDDING? IT'S GONNA BE LIKE THE WORLD'S GREATEST ROLLER-COASTER!
SO WHEN DOES SOMETHING START HAPPENING?

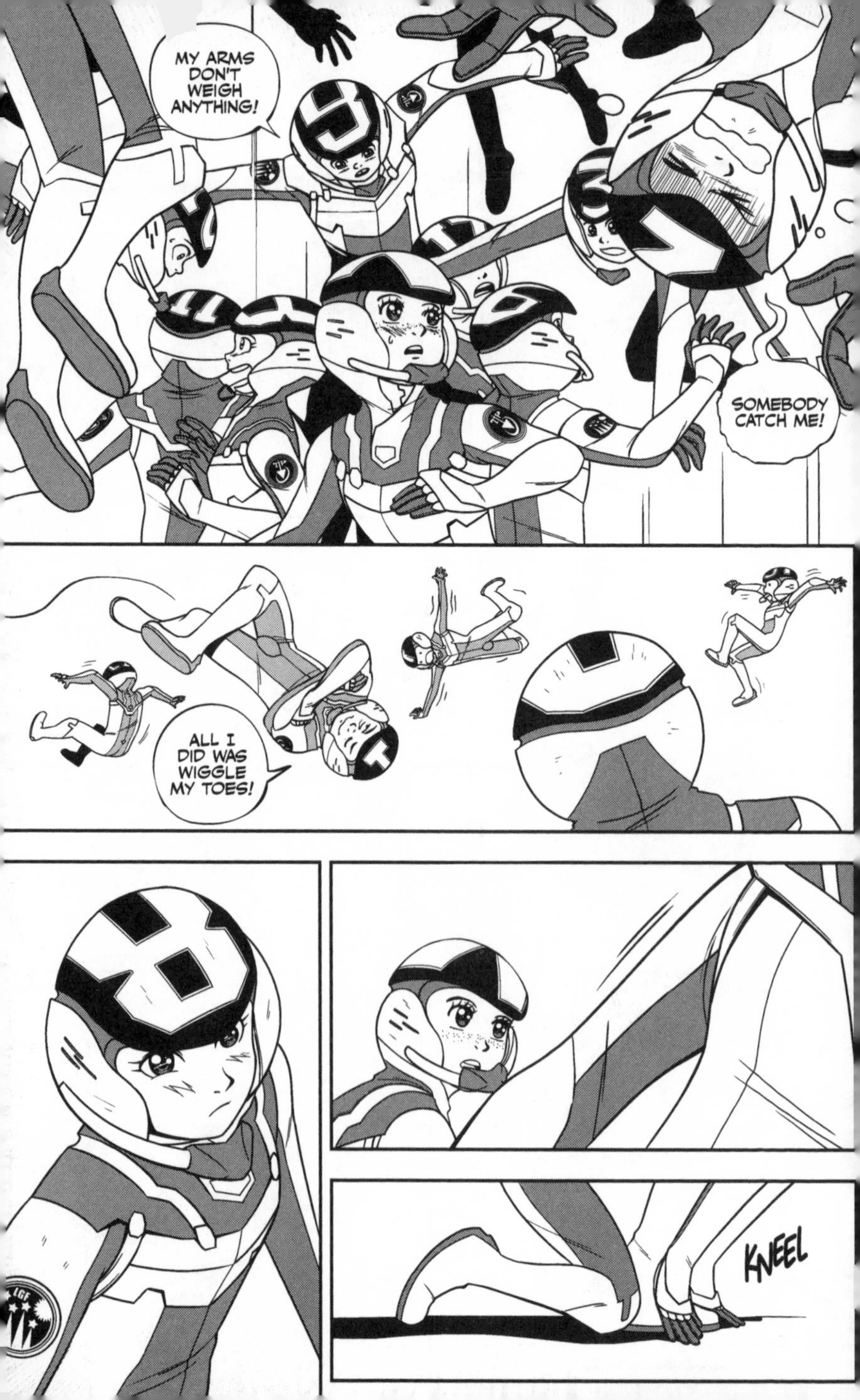
MY ARMS DON'T WEIGH ANYTHING!
SOMEBODY CATCH ME!
ALL I DID WAS WIGGLE MY TOES!
KNEEL

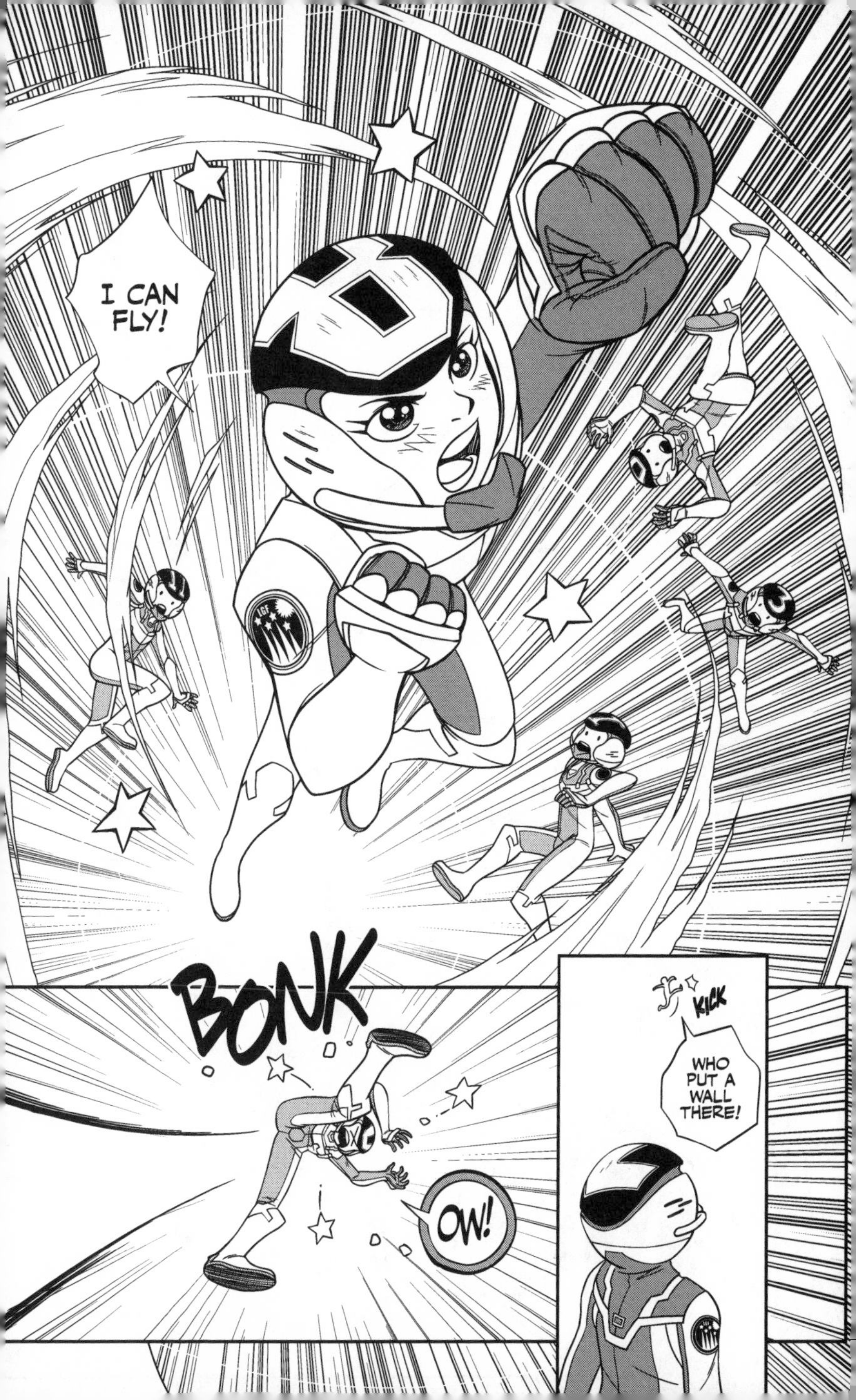
I CAN FLY!
LGF
BONK
OW!
KICK
WHO PUT A WALL THERE!

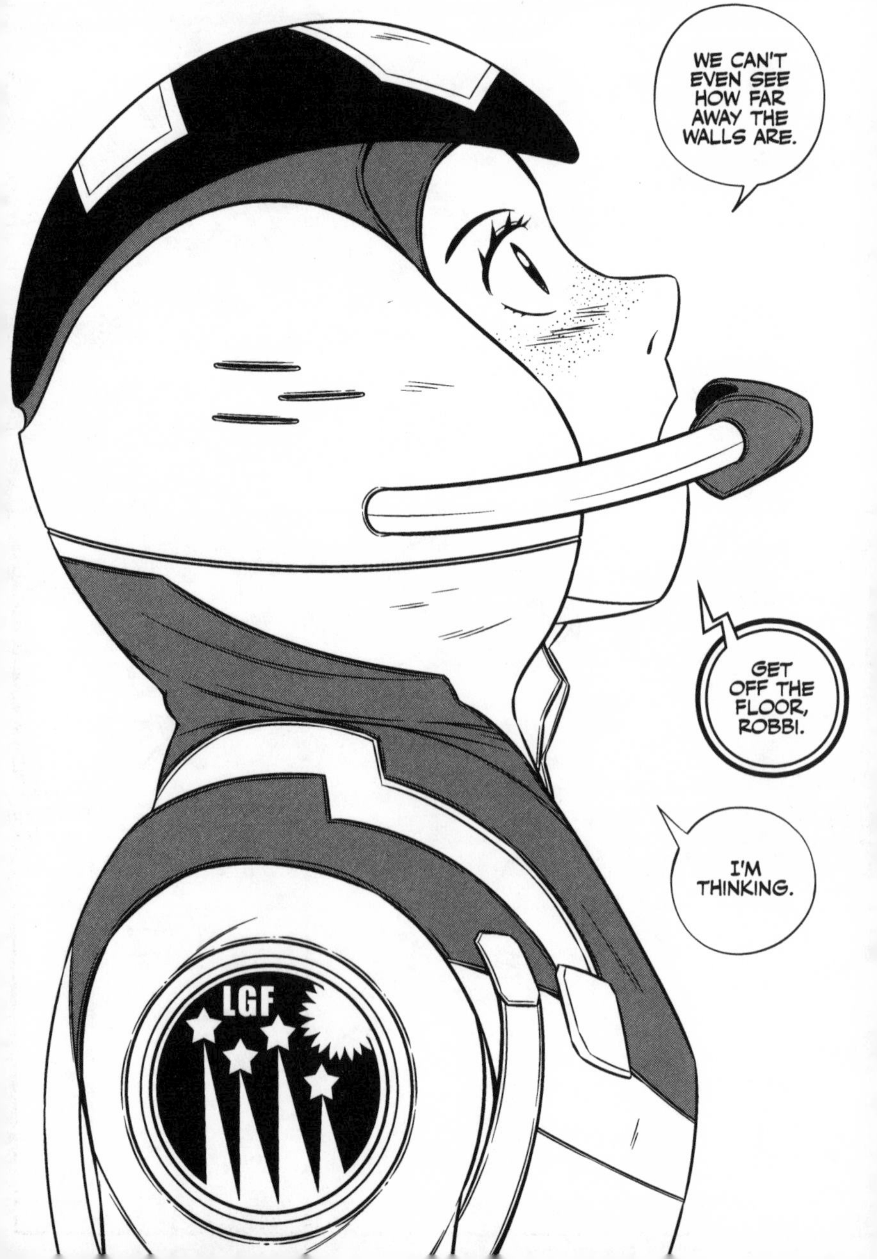
WE CAN'T EVEN SEE HOW FAR AWAY THE WALLS ARE.
GET OFF THE FLOOR, ROBBI.
I'M THINKING.
LGF

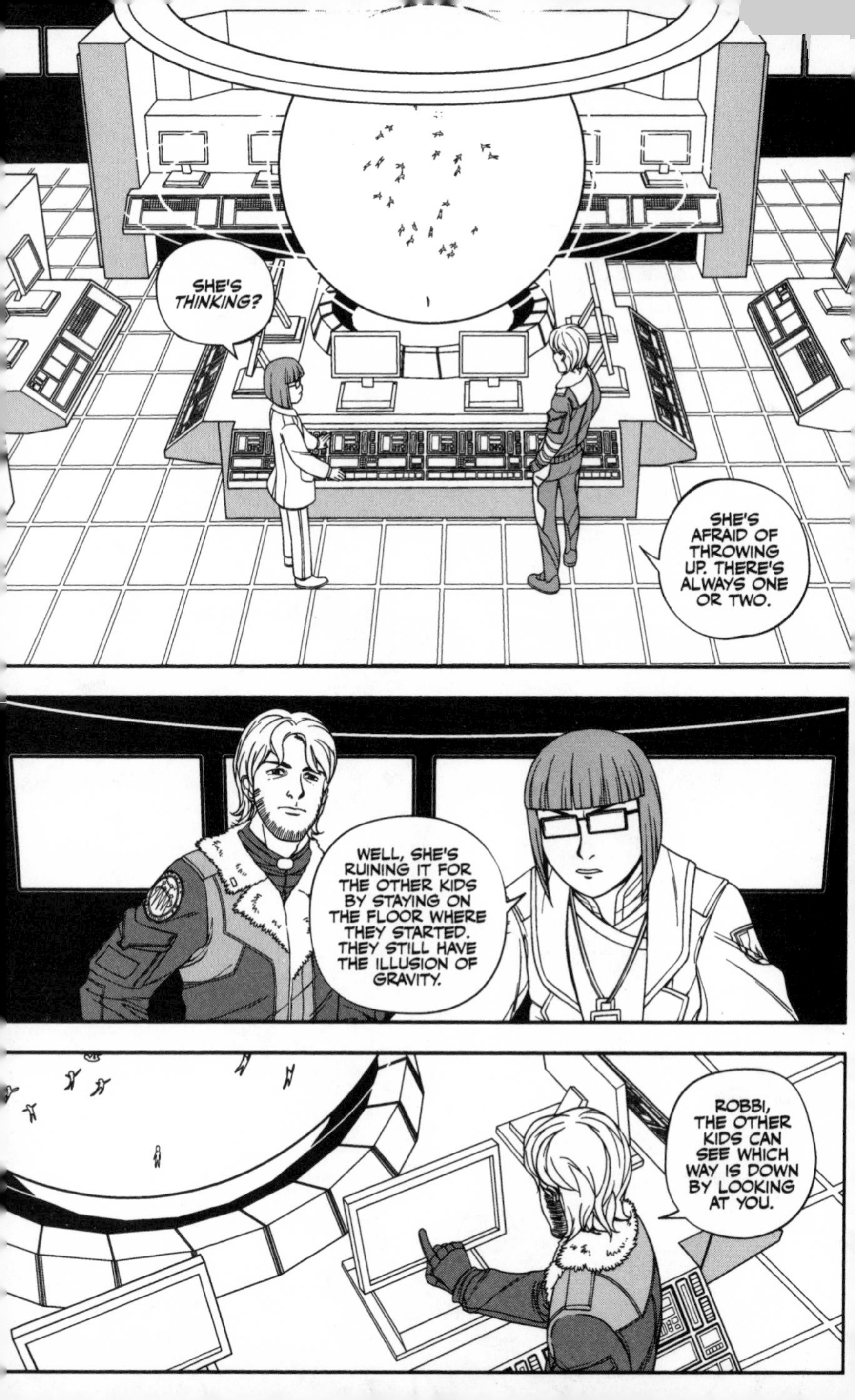
SHE'S THINKING?
SHE'S AFRAID OF THROWING UP. THERE'S ALWAYS ONE OR TWO.
WELL, SHE'S RUINING IT FOR THE OTHER KIDS BY STAYING ON THE FLOOR WHERE THEY STARTED. THEY STILL HAVE THE ILLUSION OF GRAVITY.
ROBBI, THE OTHER KIDS CAN SEE WHICH WAY IS DOWN BY LOOKING AT YOU.

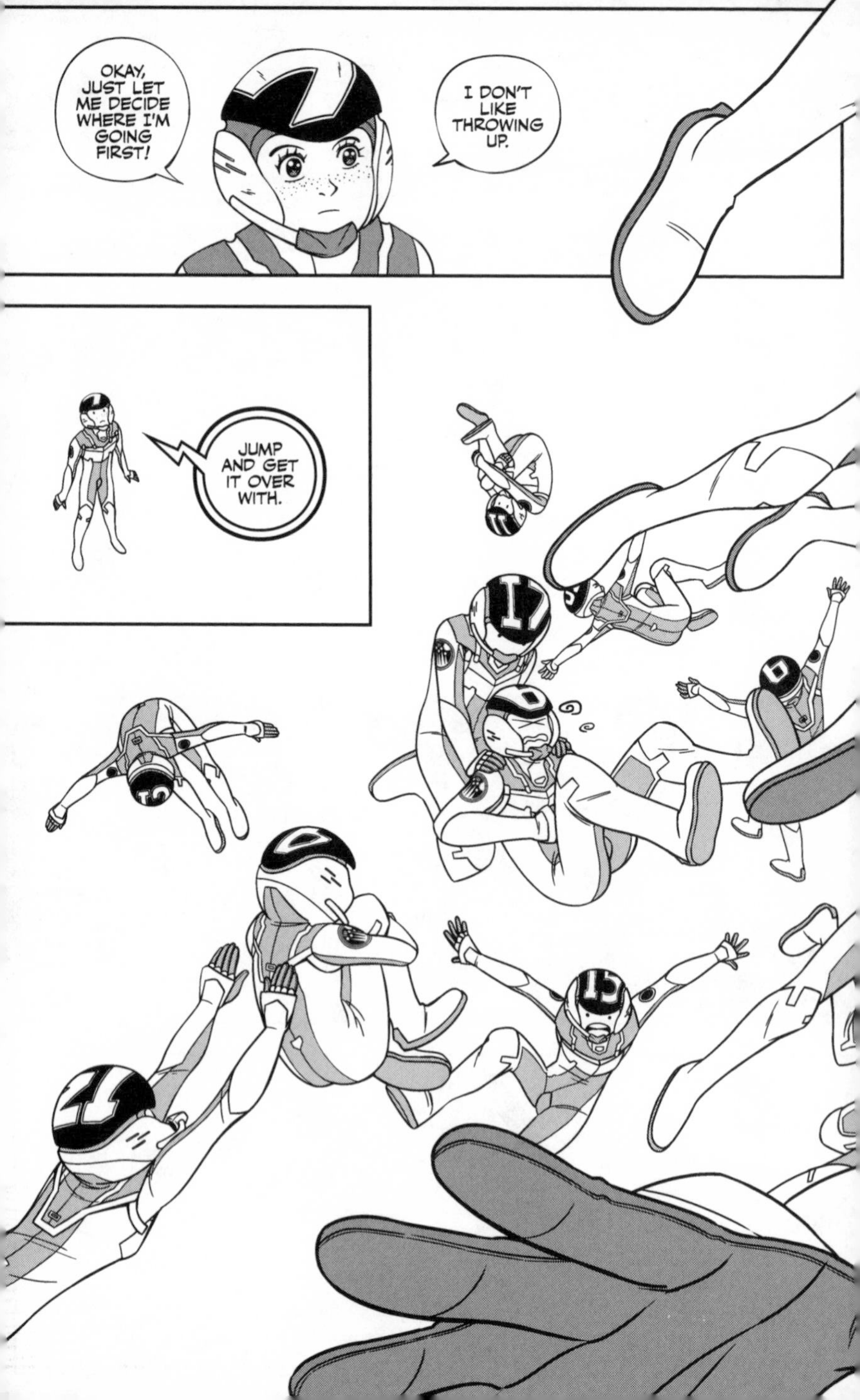
OKAY, JUST LET ME DECIDE WHERE I'M GOING FIRST!
I DON'T LIKE THROWING UP.
JUMP AND GET IT OVER WITH.

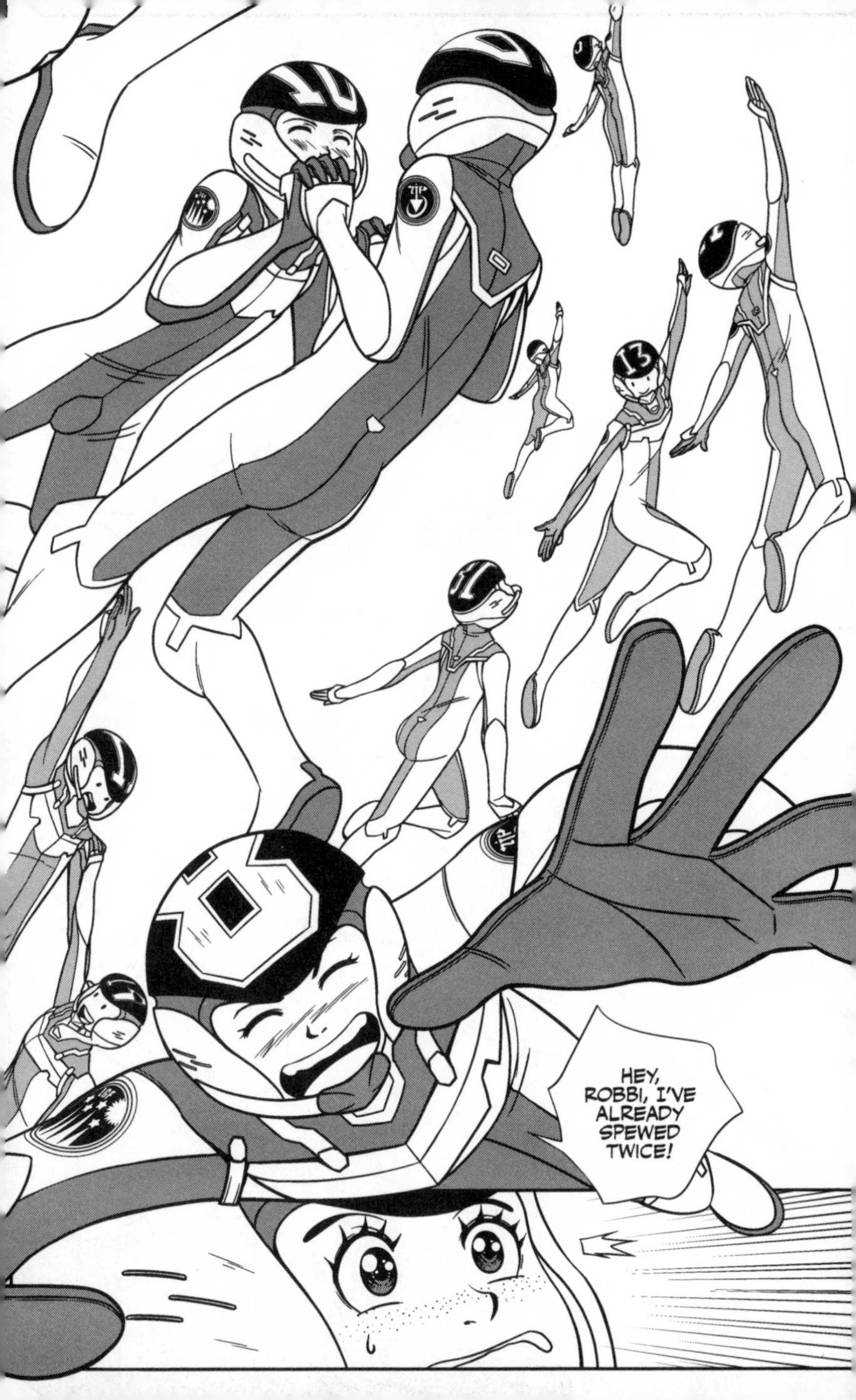
HEY, ROBBI, I'VE ALREADY SPEWED TWICE!

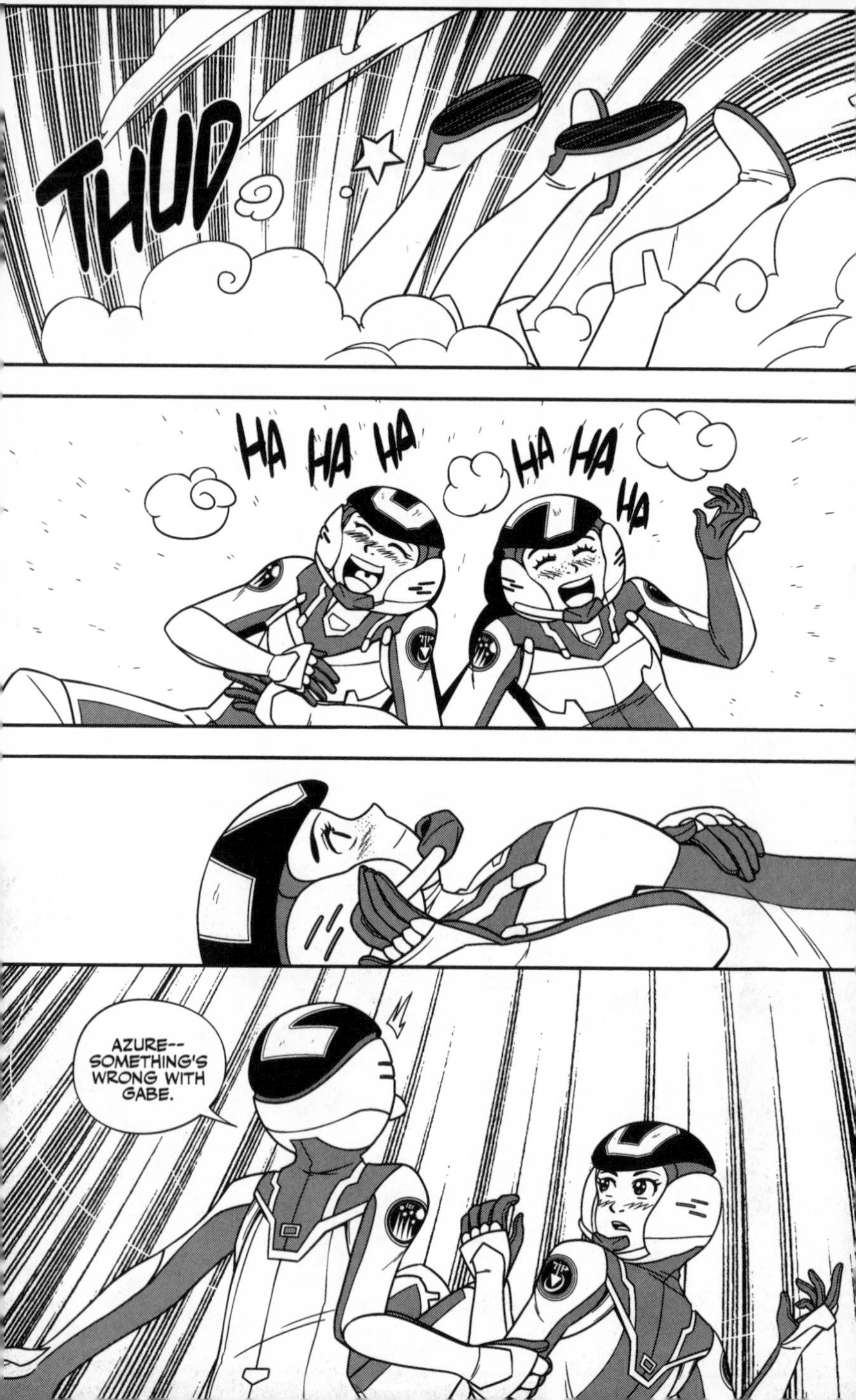
THUD
HA HA HA
HA HA HA
AZURE-- SOMETHING'S WRONG WITH GABE.

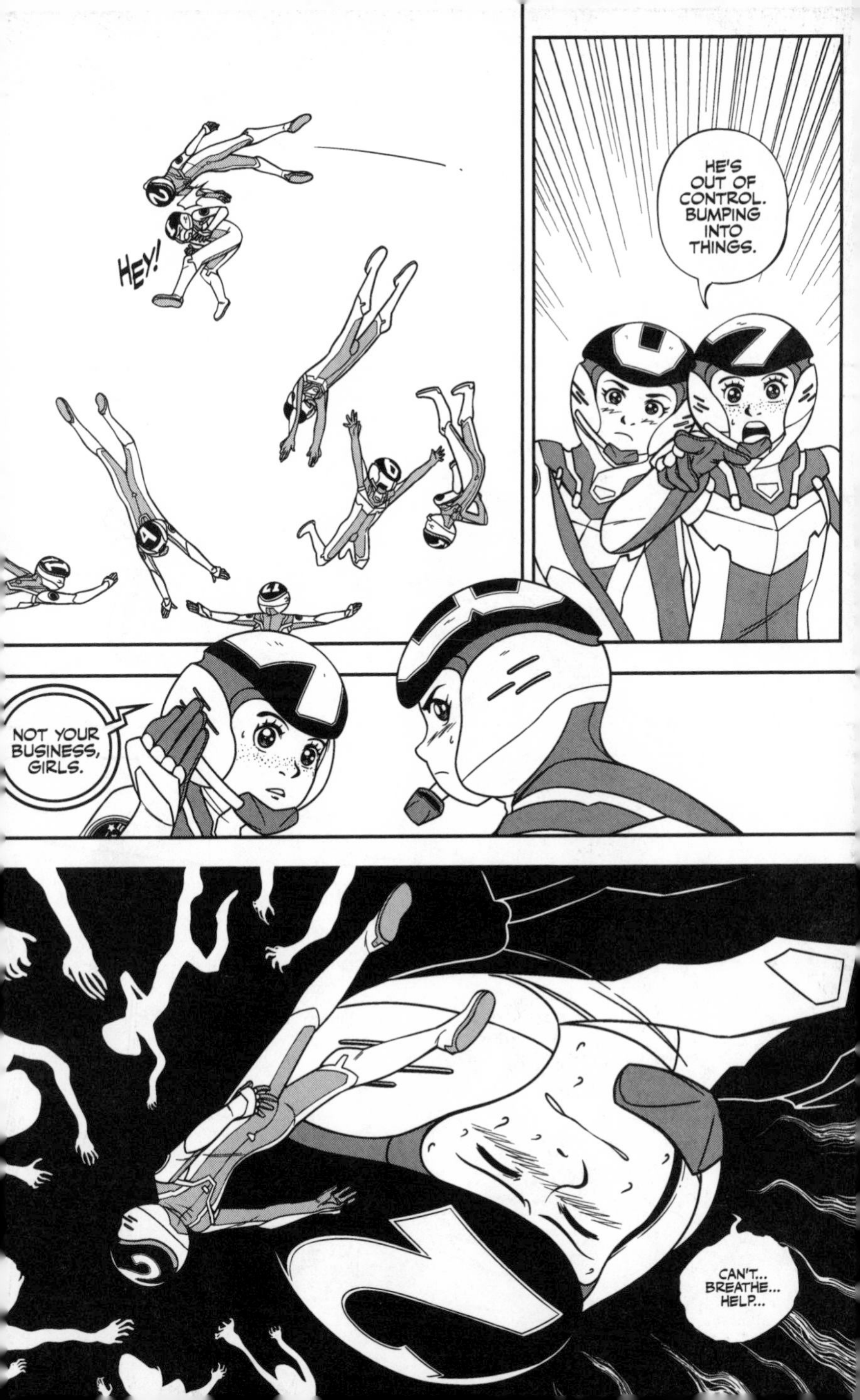
HEY!
HE'S OUT OF CONTROL. BUMPING INTO THINGS.
NOT YOUR BUSINESS, GIRLS.
CAN'T... BREATHE... HELP...

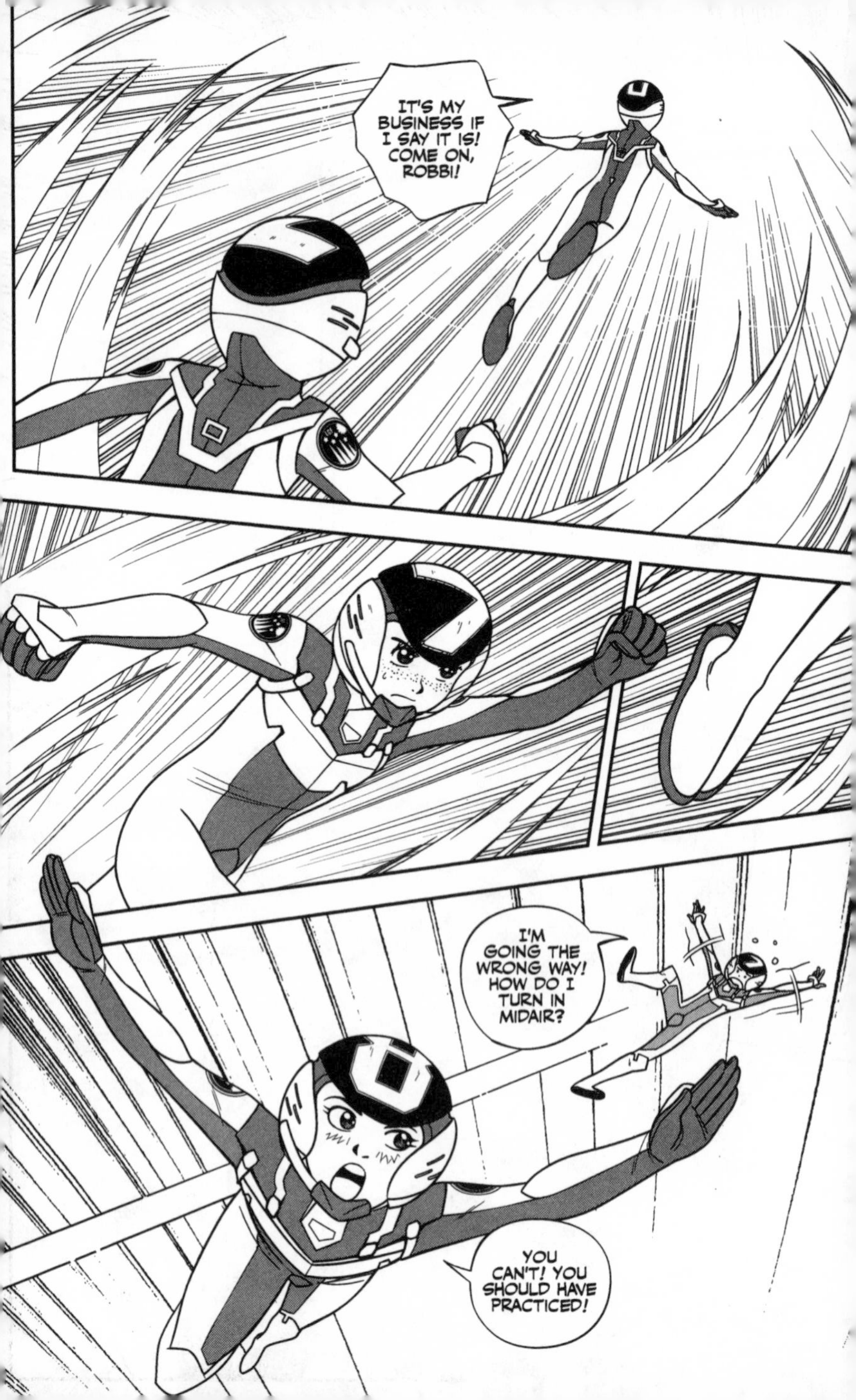
IT'S MY BUSINESS IF I SAY IT IS! COME ON, ROBBI!
I'M GOING THE WRONG WAY! HOW DO I TURN IN MIDAIR?
YOU CAN'T! YOU SHOULD HAVE PRACTICED!

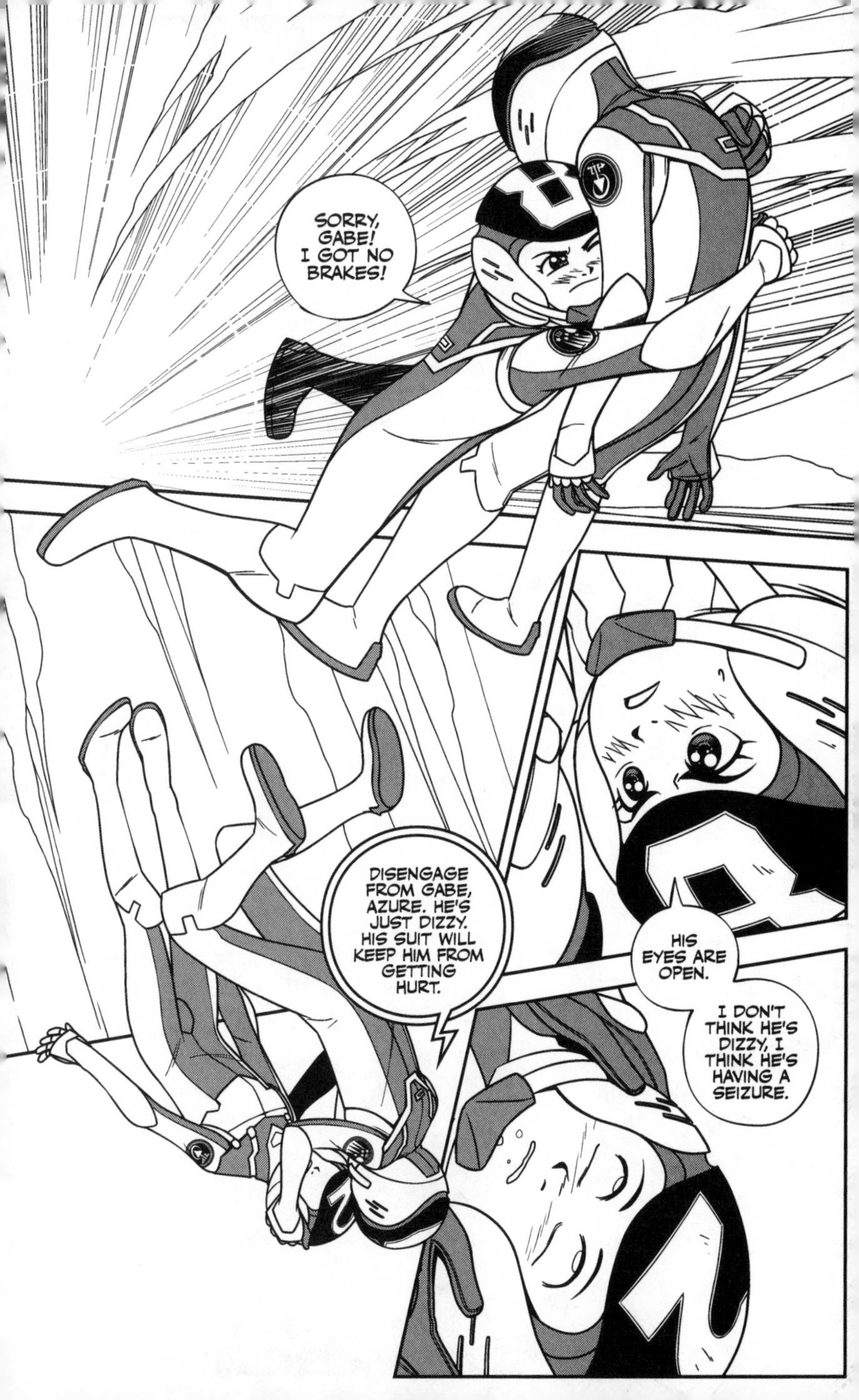
SORRY, GABE! I GOT NO BRAKES!
DISENGAGE FROM GABE, AZURE. HE'S JUST DIZZY. HIS SUIT WILL KEEP HIM FROM GETTING HURT.
HIS EYES ARE OPEN.
I DON'T THINK HE'S DIZZY, I THINK HE'S HAVING A SEIZURE.

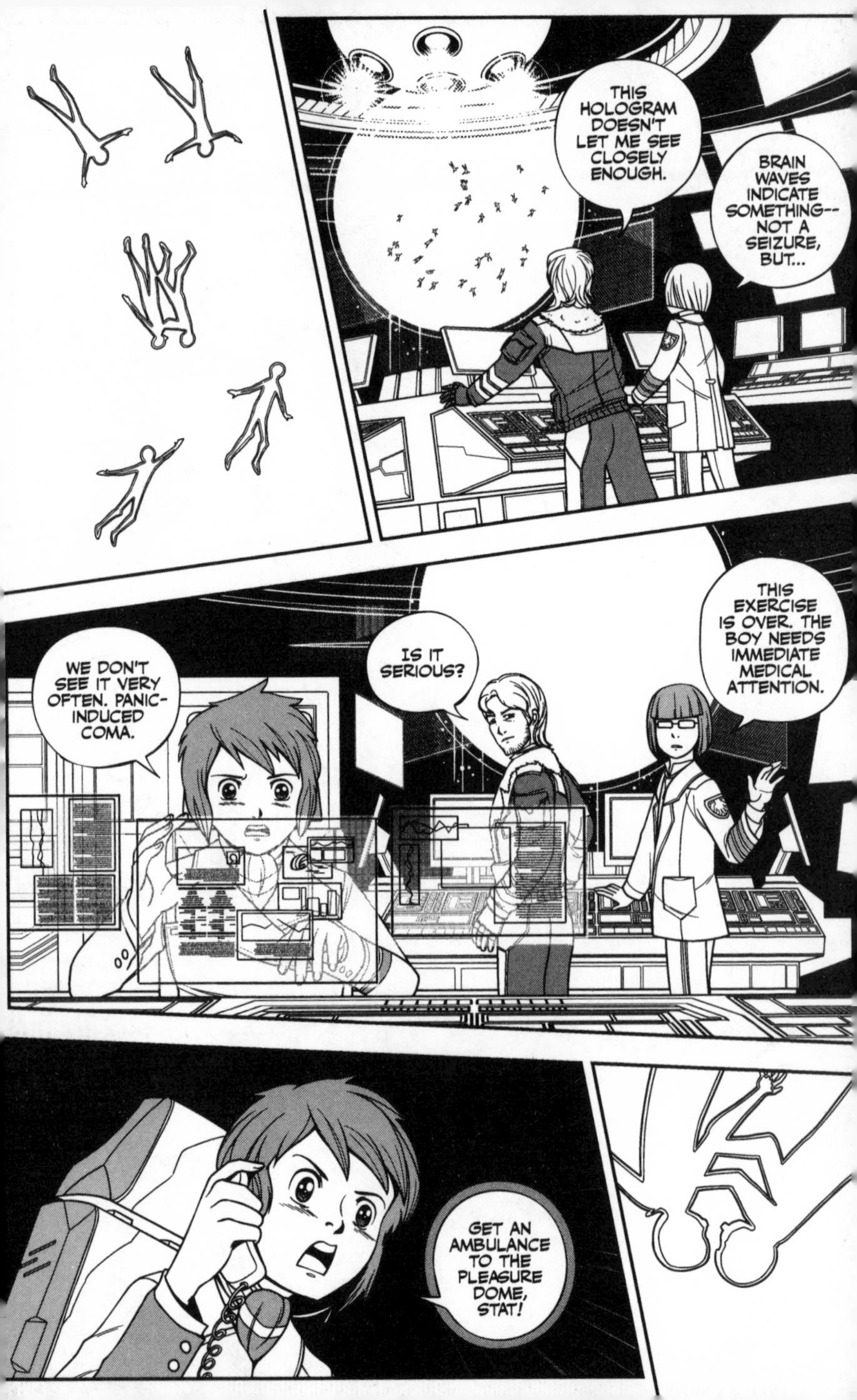
THIS HOLOGRAM DOESN'T LET ME SEE CLOSELY ENOUGH.
BRAIN WAVES INDICATE SOMETHING-- NOT A SEIZURE, BUT...
WE DON'T SEE IT VERY OFTEN. PANIC-INDUCED COMA.
IS IT SERIOUS?
THIS EXERCISE IS OVER. THE BOY NEEDS IMMEDIATE MEDICAL ATTENTION.
GET AN AMBULANCE TO THE PLEASURE DOME, STAT!

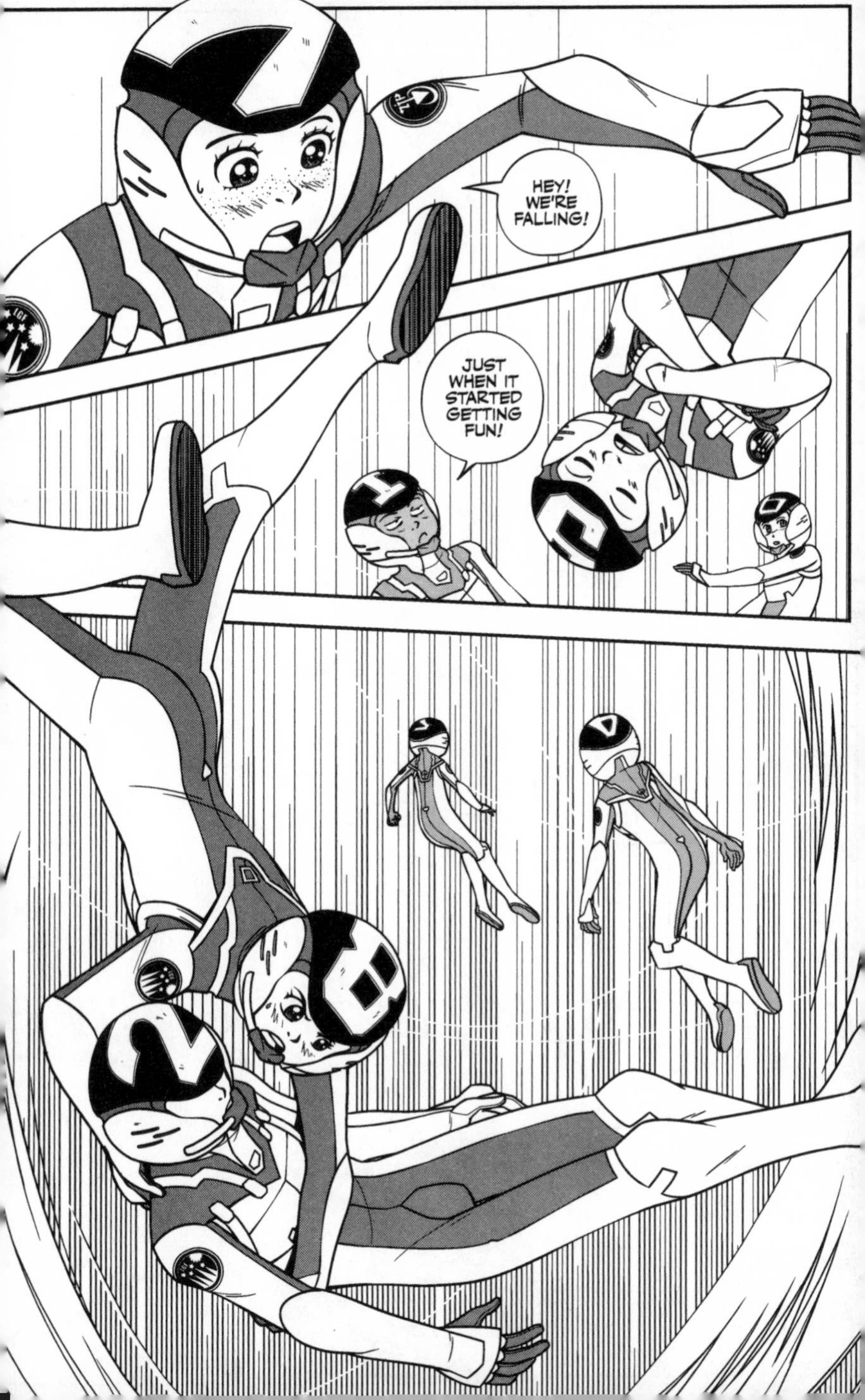
HEY! WE'RE FALLING!
JUST WHEN IT STARTED GETTING FUN!

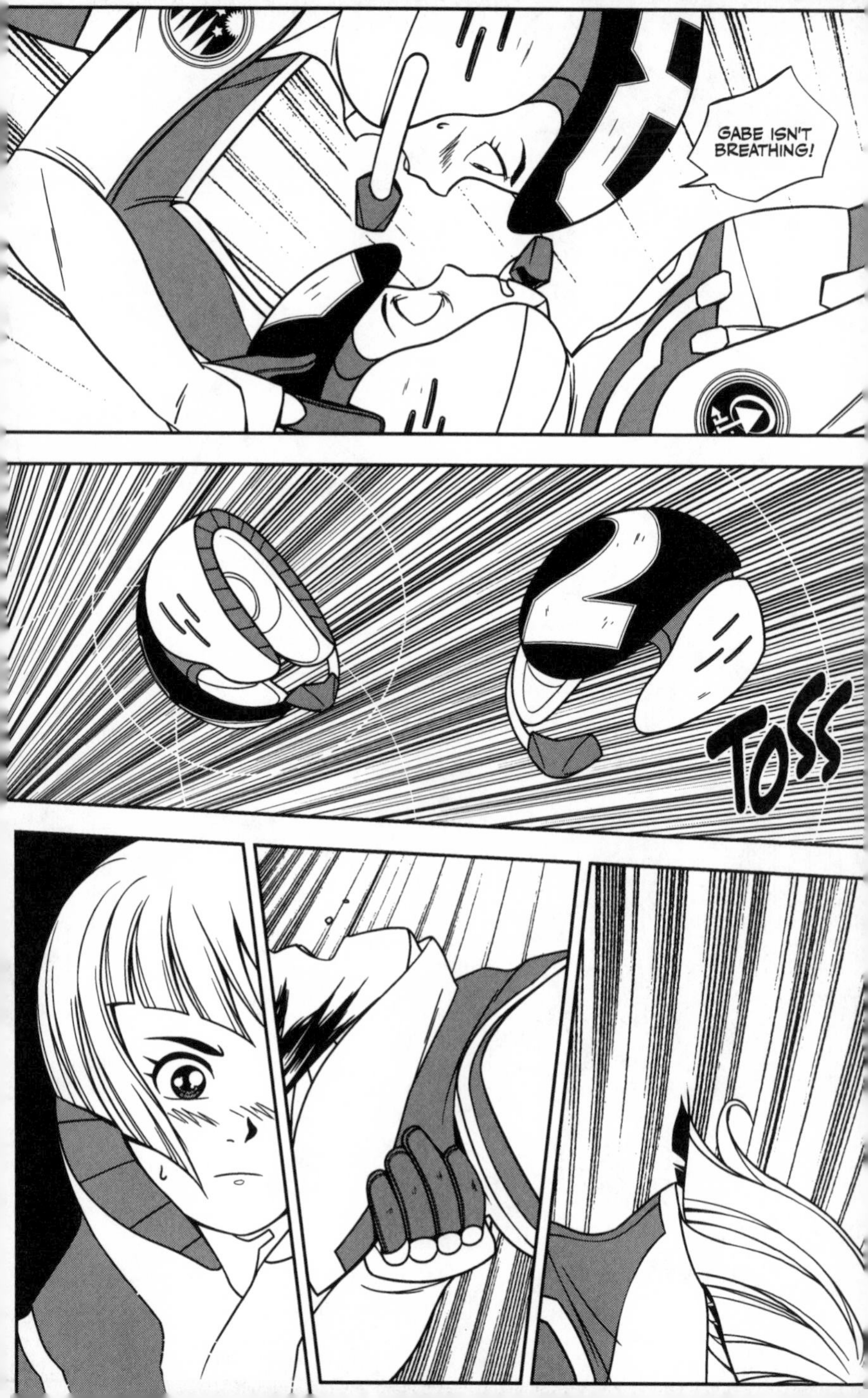
GABE ISN'T BREATHING!
TOSS

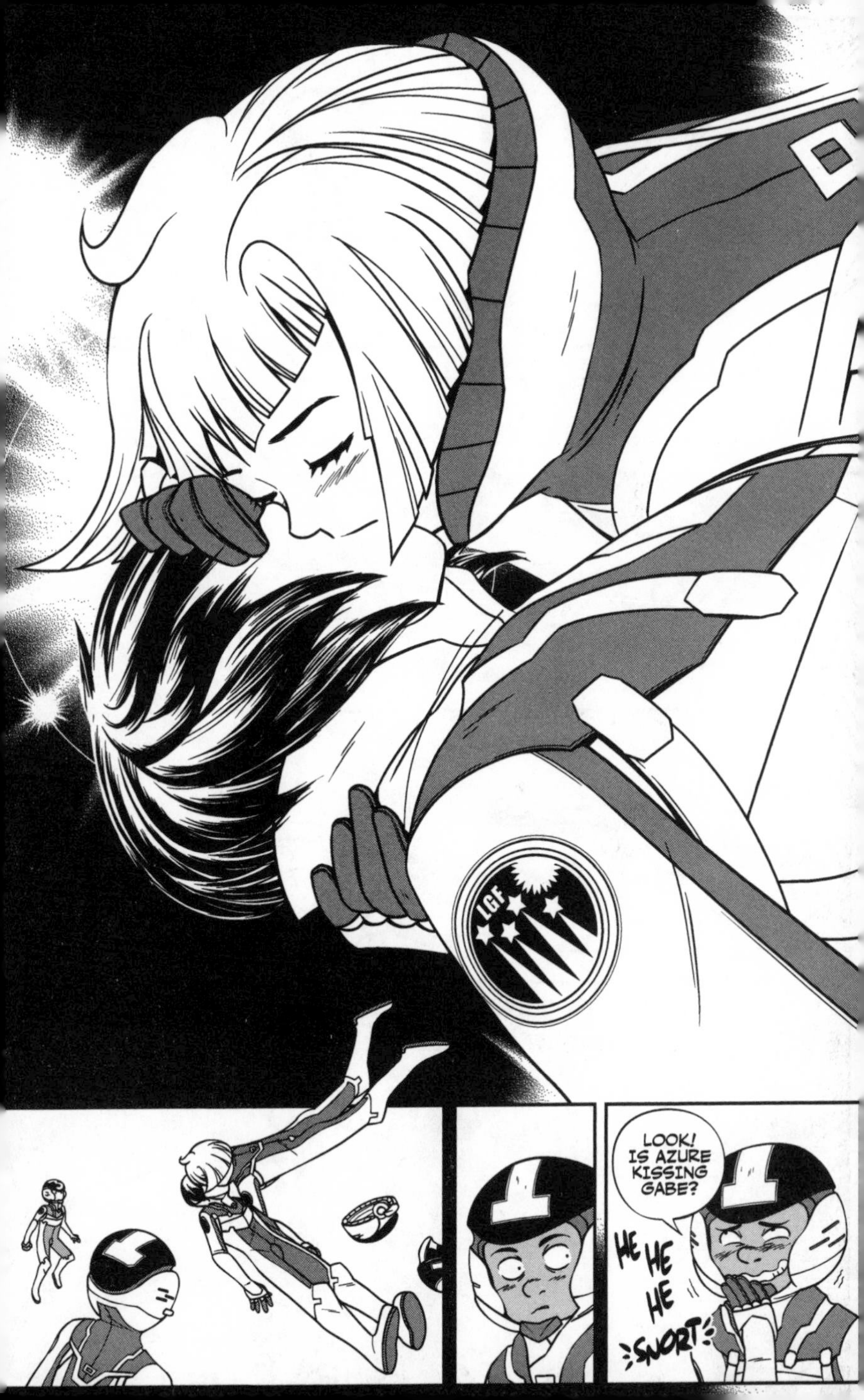
LGF
LOOK! IS AZURE KISSING GABE?
HE HE HE
SNORT

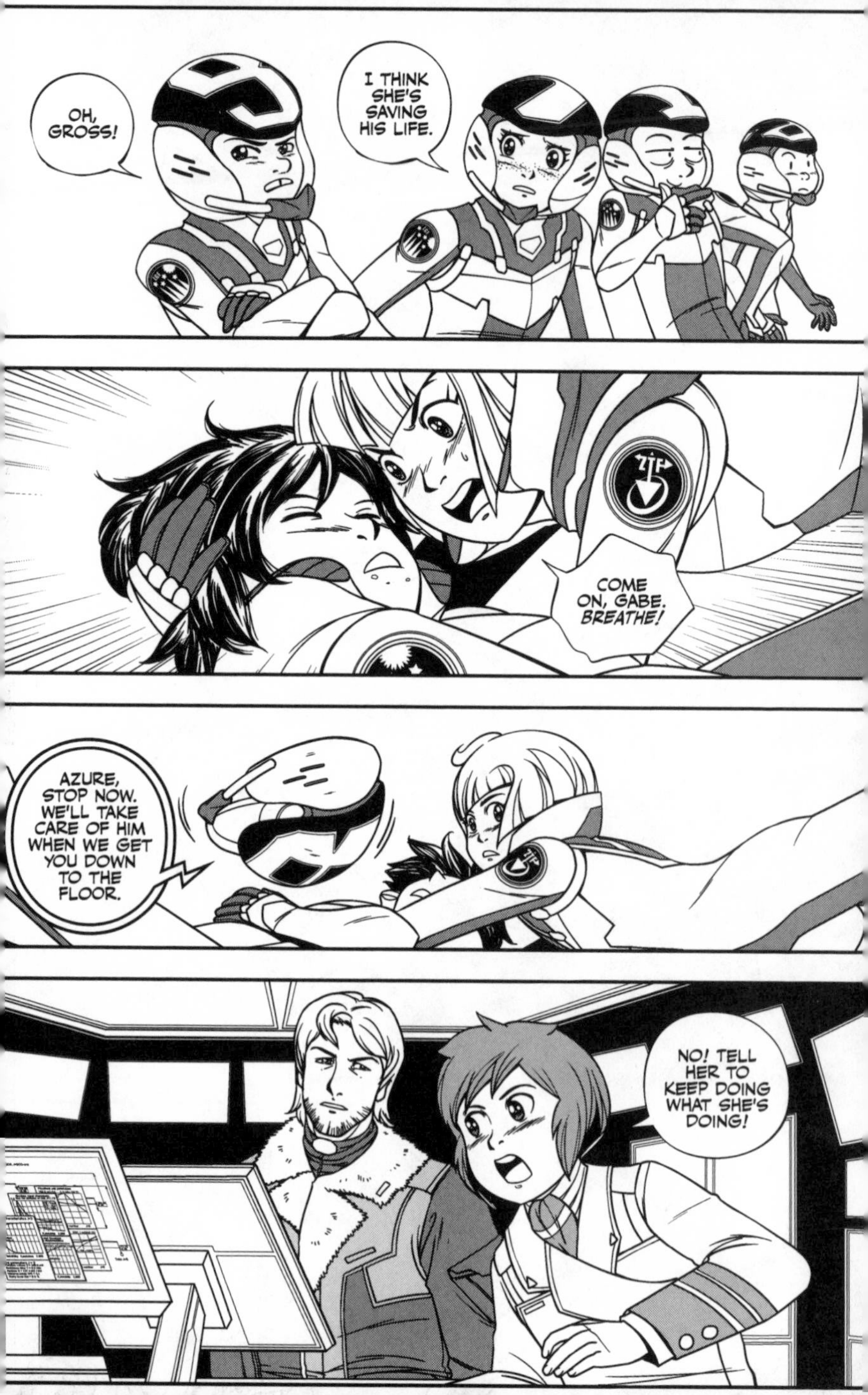
OH, GROSS!
I THINK SHE'S SAVING HIS LIFE.
COME ON, GABE. BREATHE!
AZURE, STOP NOW. WE'LL TAKE CARE OF HIM WHEN WE GET YOU DOWN TO THE FLOOR.
NO! TELL HER TO KEEP DOING WHAT SHE'S DOING!

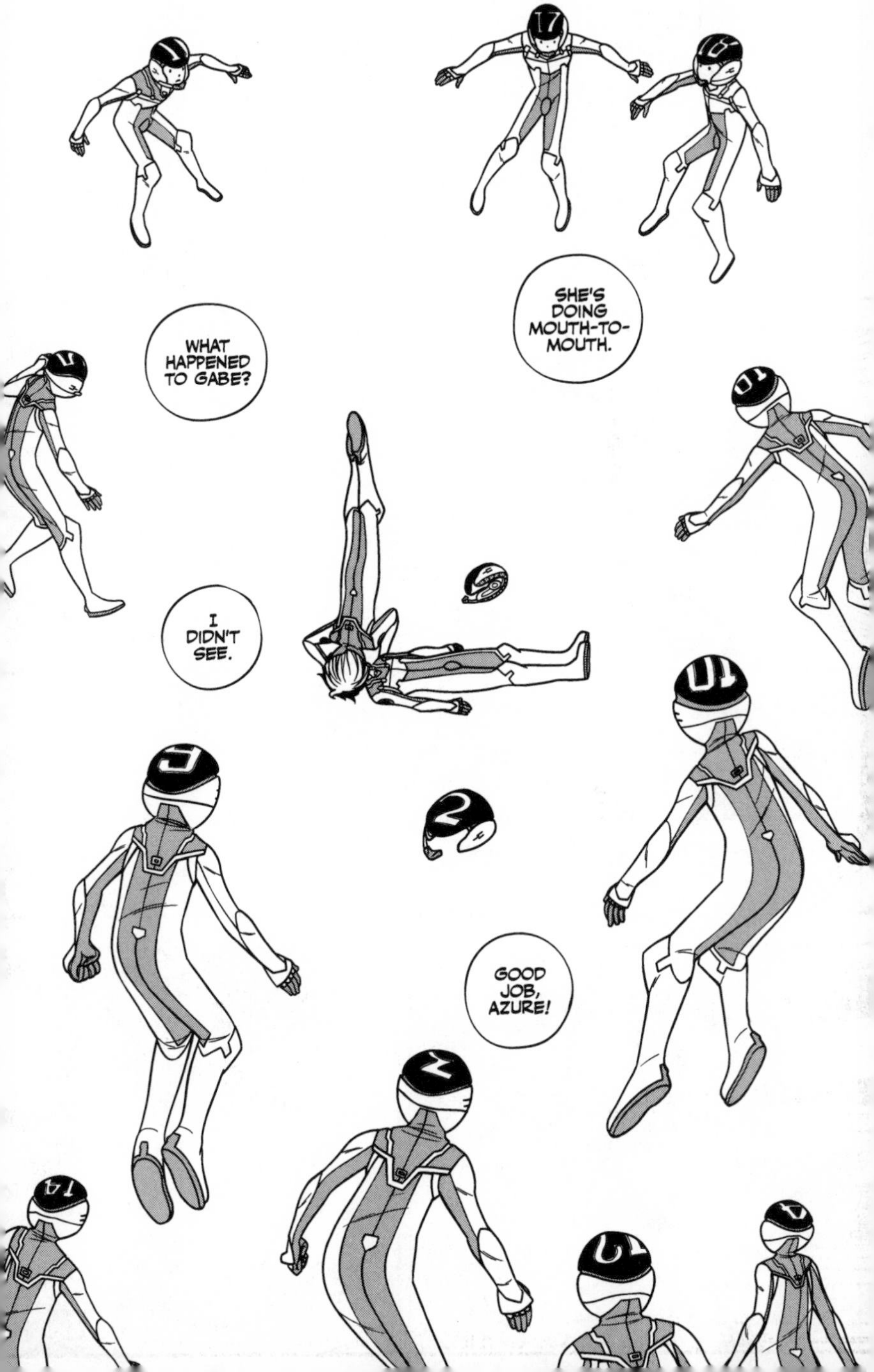
WHAT HAPPENED TO GABE?
SHE'S DOING MOUTH-TO-MOUTH.
I DIDN'T SEE.
GOOD JOB, AZURE!

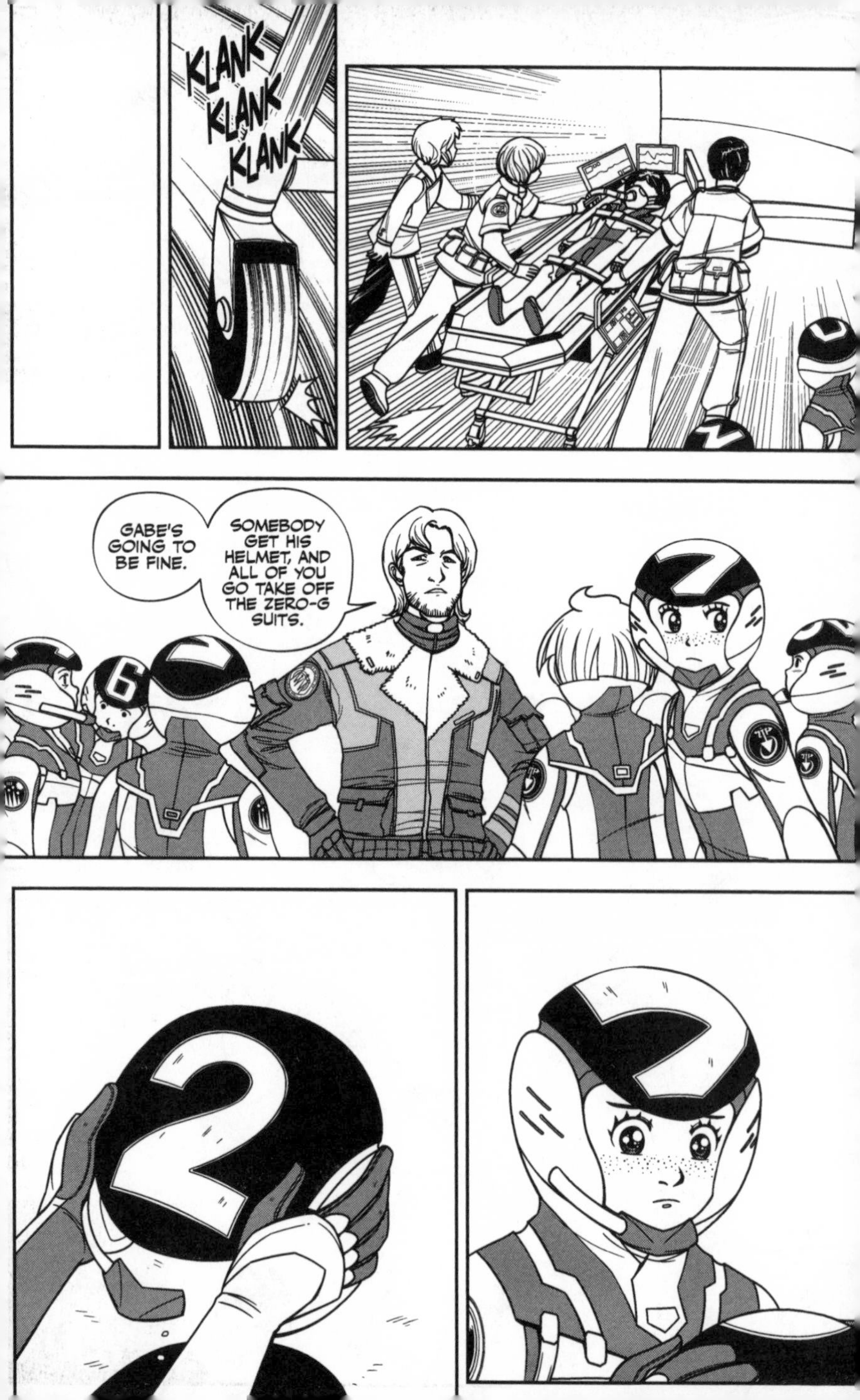
KLANK
KLANK
KLANK
GABE'S GOING TO BE FINE.
SOMEBODY GET HIS HELMET, AND ALL OF YOU GO TAKE OFF THE ZERO-G SUITS.

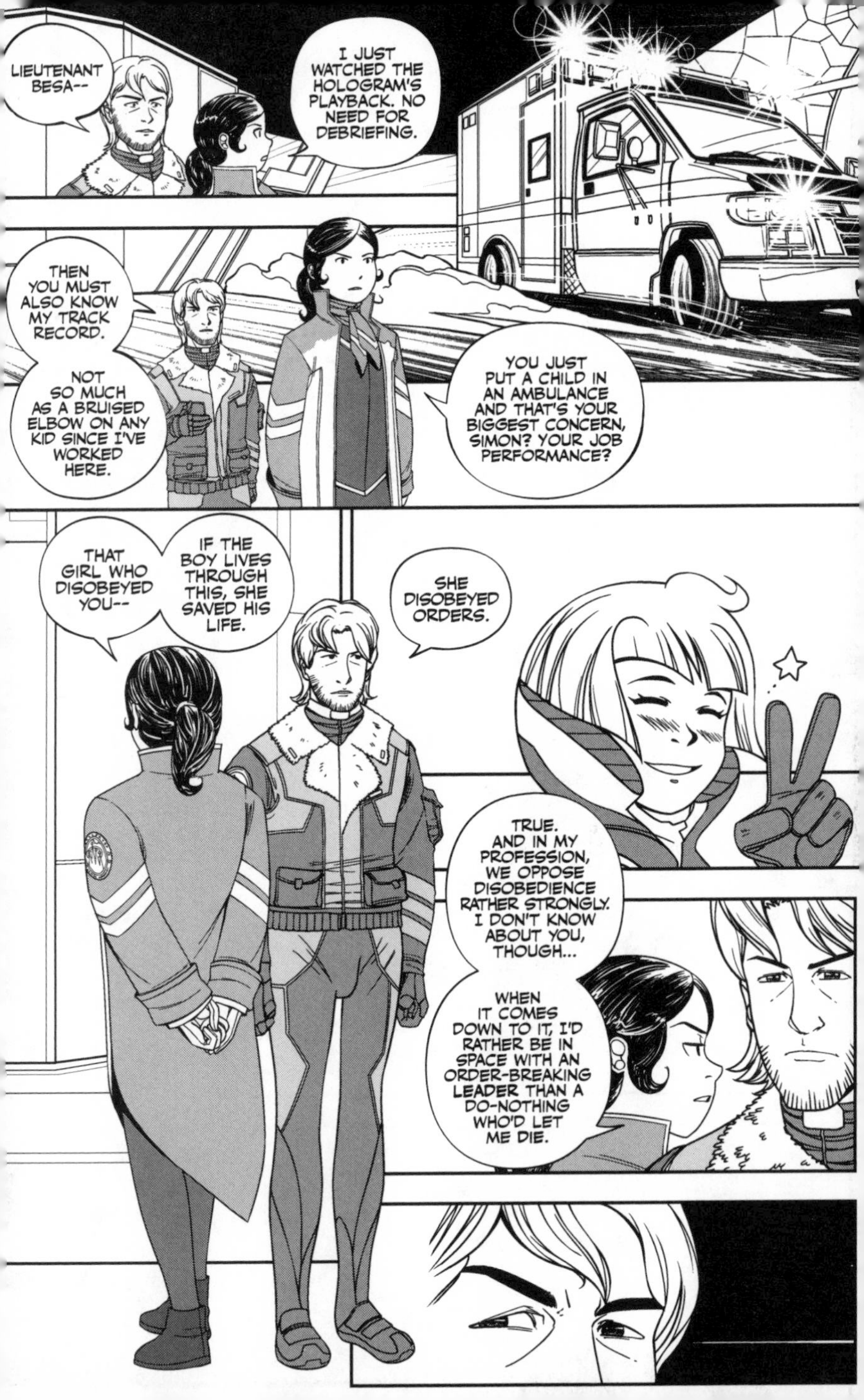
LIEUTENANT BESA--
I JUST WATCHED THE HOLOGRAM'S PLAYBACK. NO NEED FOR DEBRIEFING.
THEN YOU MUST ALSO KNOW MY TRACK RECORD.
NOT SO MUCH AS A BRUISED ELBOW ON ANY KID SINCE I'VE WORKED HERE.
YOU JUST PUT A CHILD IN AN AMBULANCE AND THAT'S YOUR BIGGEST CONCERN, SIMON? YOUR JOB PERFORMANCE?
THAT GIRL WHO DISOBEYED YOU--
IF THE BOY LIVES THROUGH THIS, SHE SAVED HIS LIFE.
SHE DISOBEYED ORDERS.
TRUE. AND IN MY PROFESSION, WE OPPOSE DISOBEDIENCE RATHER STRONGLY. I DON'T KNOW ABOUT YOU, THOUGH...
WHEN IT COMES DOWN TO IT, I'D RATHER BE IN SPACE WITH AN ORDER-BREAKING LEADER THAN A DO-NOTHING WHO'D LET ME DIE.

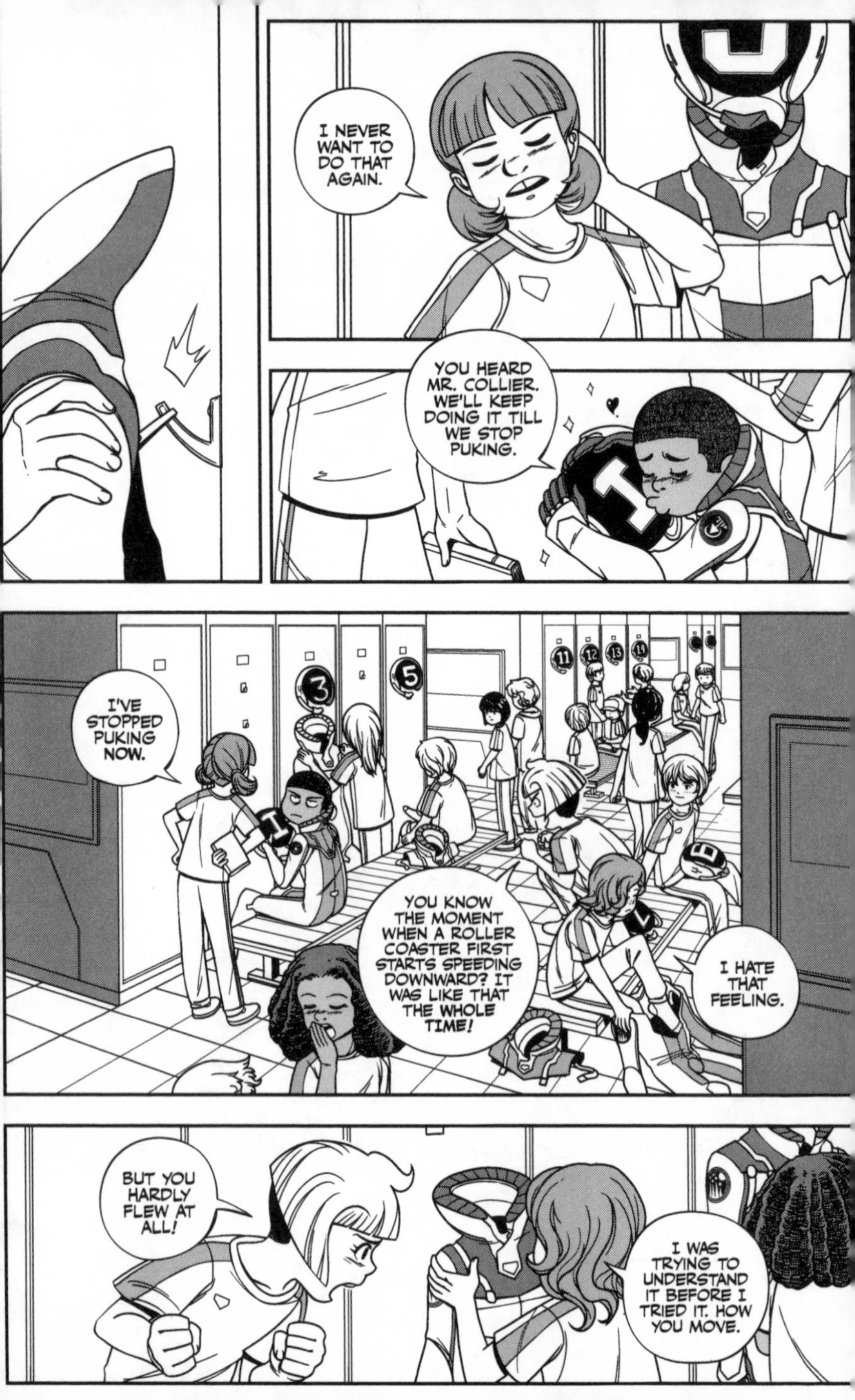
I NEVER WANT TO DO THAT AGAIN.
YOU HEARD MR. COLLIER. WE'LL KEEP DOING IT TILL WE STOP PUKING.
I'VE STOPPED PUKING NOW.
YOU KNOW THE MOMENT WHEN A ROLLER COASTER FIRST STARTS SPEEDING DOWNWARD? IT WAS LIKE THAT THE WHOLE TIME!
I HATE THAT FEELING.
BUT YOU HARDLY FLEW AT ALL!
I WAS TRYING TO UNDERSTAND IT BEFORE I TRIED IT. HOW YOU MOVE.

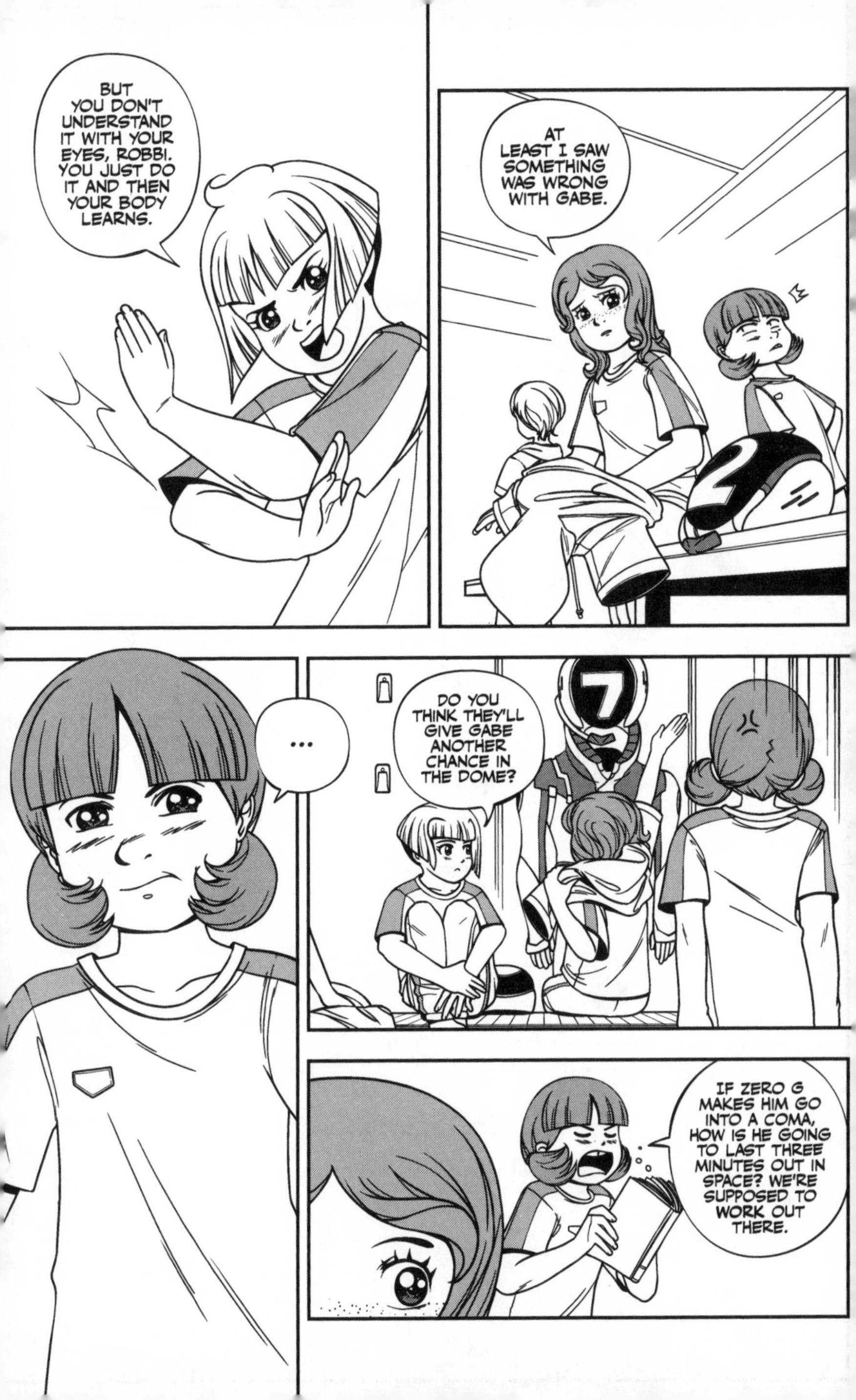
BUT YOU DON'T UNDERSTAND IT WITH YOUR EYES, ROBBI. YOU JUST DO IT AND THEN YOUR BODY LEARNS.
AT LEAST I SAW SOMETHING WAS WRONG WITH GABE.
...
DO YOU THINK THEY'LL GIVE GABE ANOTHER CHANCE IN THE DOME?
IF ZERO G MAKES HIM GO INTO A COMA, HOW IS HE GOING TO LAST THREE MINUTES OUT IN SPACE? WE'RE SUPPOSED TO WORK OUT THERE.

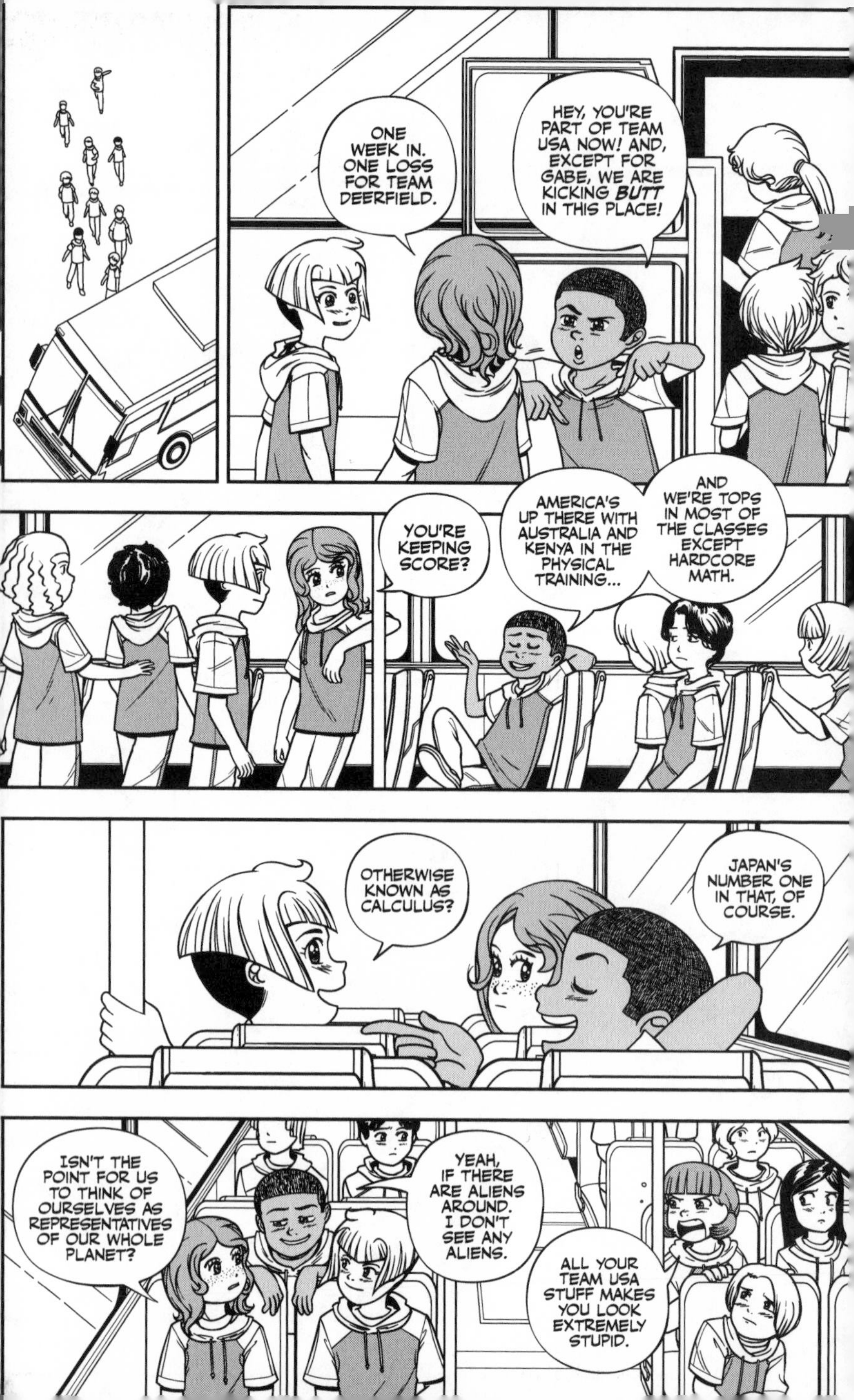
ONE WEEK IN. ONE LOSS FOR TEAM DEERFIELD.
HEY, YOU'RE PART OF TEAM USA NOW! AND, EXCEPT FOR GABE, WE ARE KICKING *BUTT* IN THIS PLACE!
YOU'RE KEEPING SCORE?
AMERICA'S UP THERE WITH AUSTRALIA AND KENYA IN THE PHYSICAL TRAINING...
AND WE'RE TOPS IN MOST OF THE CLASSES EXCEPT HARDCORE MATH.
OTHERWISE KNOWN AS CALCULUS?
JAPAN'S NUMBER ONE IN THAT, OF COURSE.
ISN'T THE POINT FOR US TO THINK OF OURSELVES AS REPRESENTATIVES OF OUR WHOLE PLANET?
YEAH, IF THERE ARE ALIENS AROUND. I DON'T SEE ANY ALIENS.
ALL YOUR TEAM USA STUFF MAKES YOU LOOK EXTREMELY STUPID.

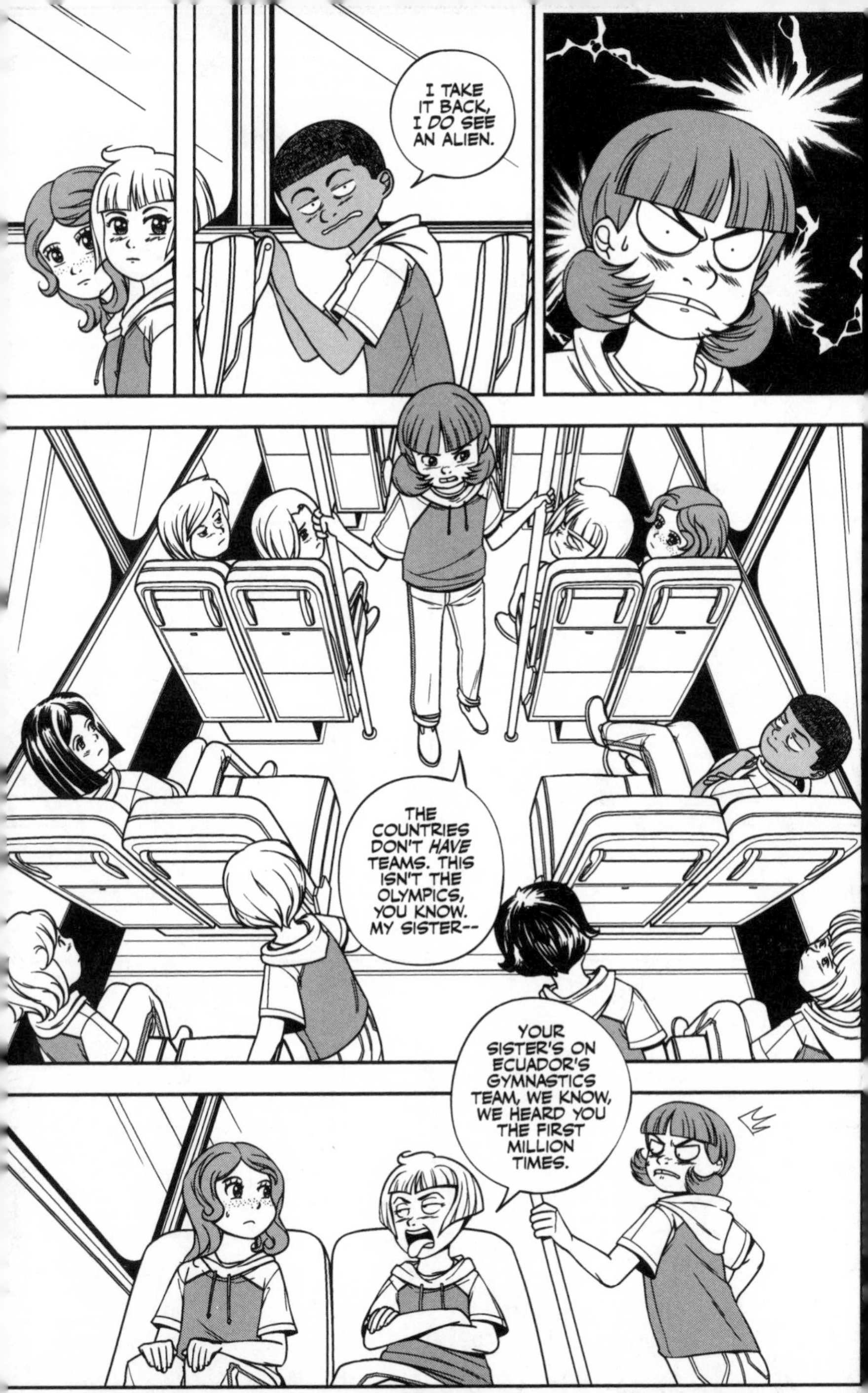
I TAKE IT BACK, I *DO* SEE AN ALIEN.
THE COUNTRIES DON'T *HAVE* TEAMS. THIS ISN'T THE OLYMPICS, YOU KNOW. MY SISTER--
YOUR SISTER'S ON ECUADOR'S GYMNASTICS TEAM, WE KNOW, WE HEARD YOU THE FIRST MILLION TIMES.

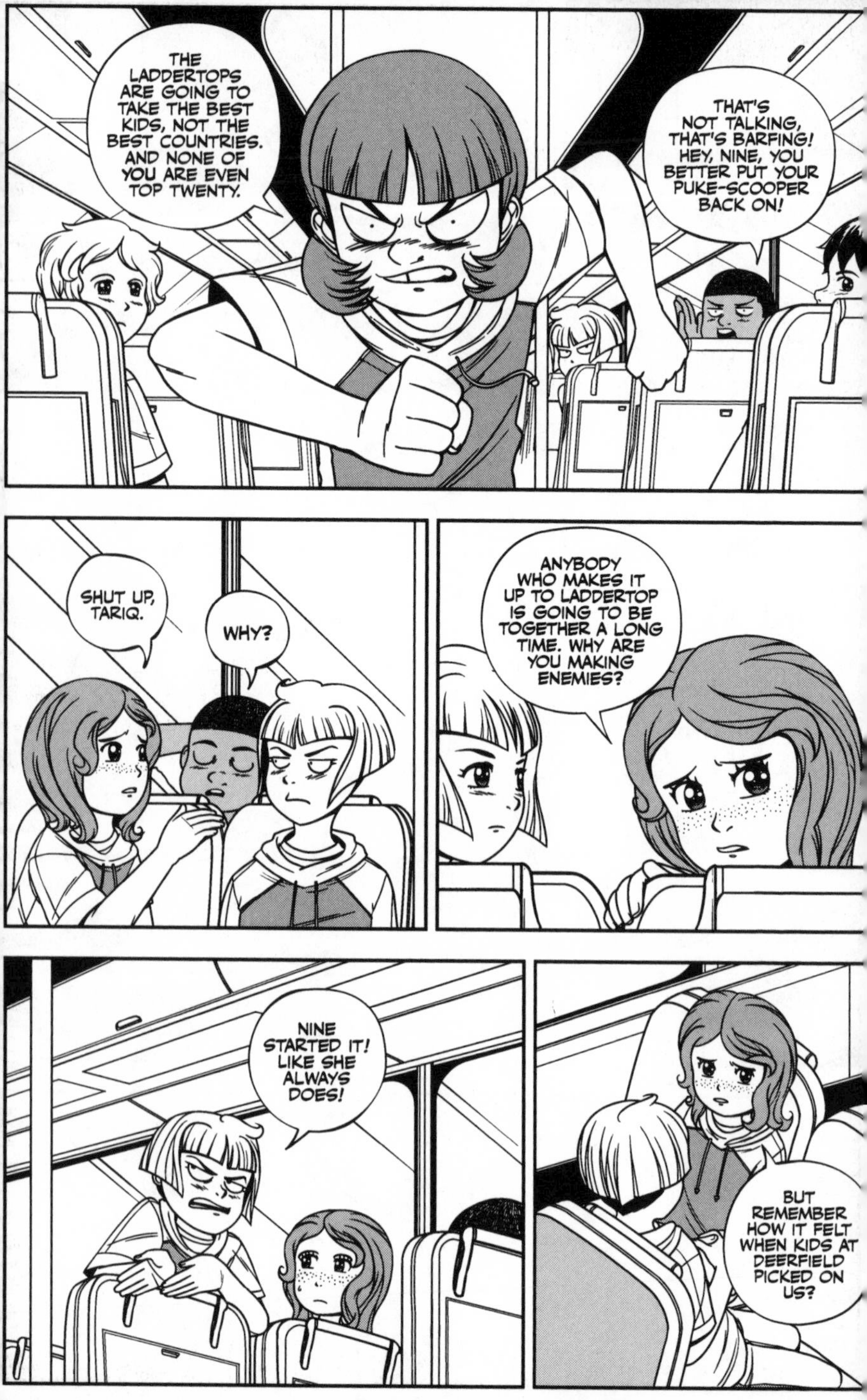
THE LADDERTOPS ARE GOING TO TAKE THE BEST KIDS, NOT THE BEST COUNTRIES. AND NONE OF YOU ARE EVEN TOP TWENTY.
THAT'S NOT TALKING, THAT'S BARFING! HEY, NINE, YOU BETTER PUT YOUR PUKE-SCOOPER BACK ON!
SHUT UP, TARIQ.
WHY?
ANYBODY WHO MAKES IT UP TO LADDERTOP IS GOING TO BE TOGETHER A LONG TIME. WHY ARE YOU MAKING ENEMIES?
NINE STARTED IT! LIKE SHE ALWAYS DOES!
BUT REMEMBER HOW IT FELT WHEN KIDS AT DEERFIELD PICKED ON US?

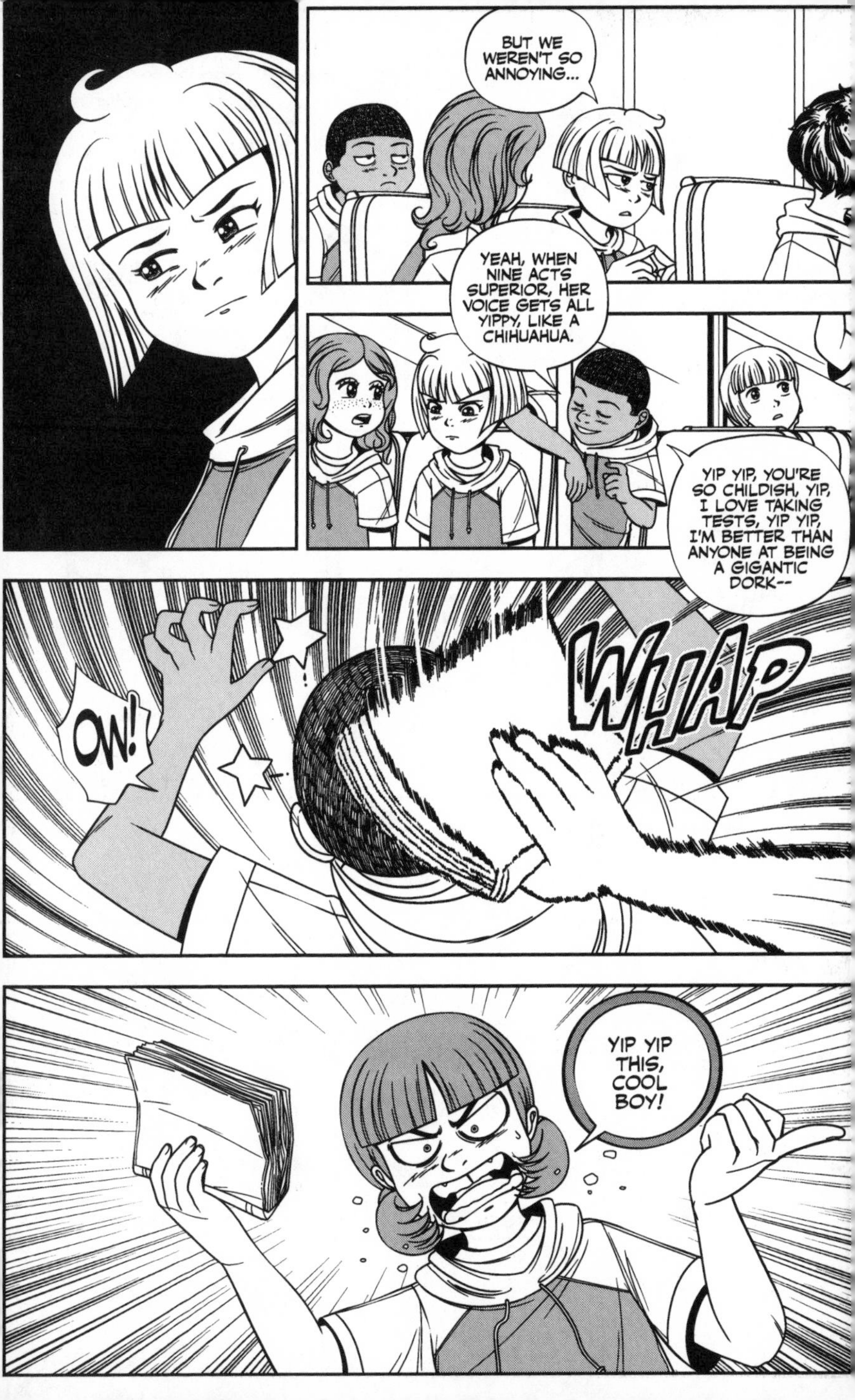
BUT WE WEREN'T SO ANNOYING...
YEAH, WHEN NINE ACTS SUPERIOR, HER VOICE GETS ALL YIPPY, LIKE A CHIHUAHUA.
YIP YIP, YOU'RE SO CHILDISH, YIP, I LOVE TAKING TESTS, YIP YIP, I'M BETTER THAN ANYONE AT BEING A GIGANTIC DORK--
OW!
WHAP
YIP YIP THIS, COOL BOY!

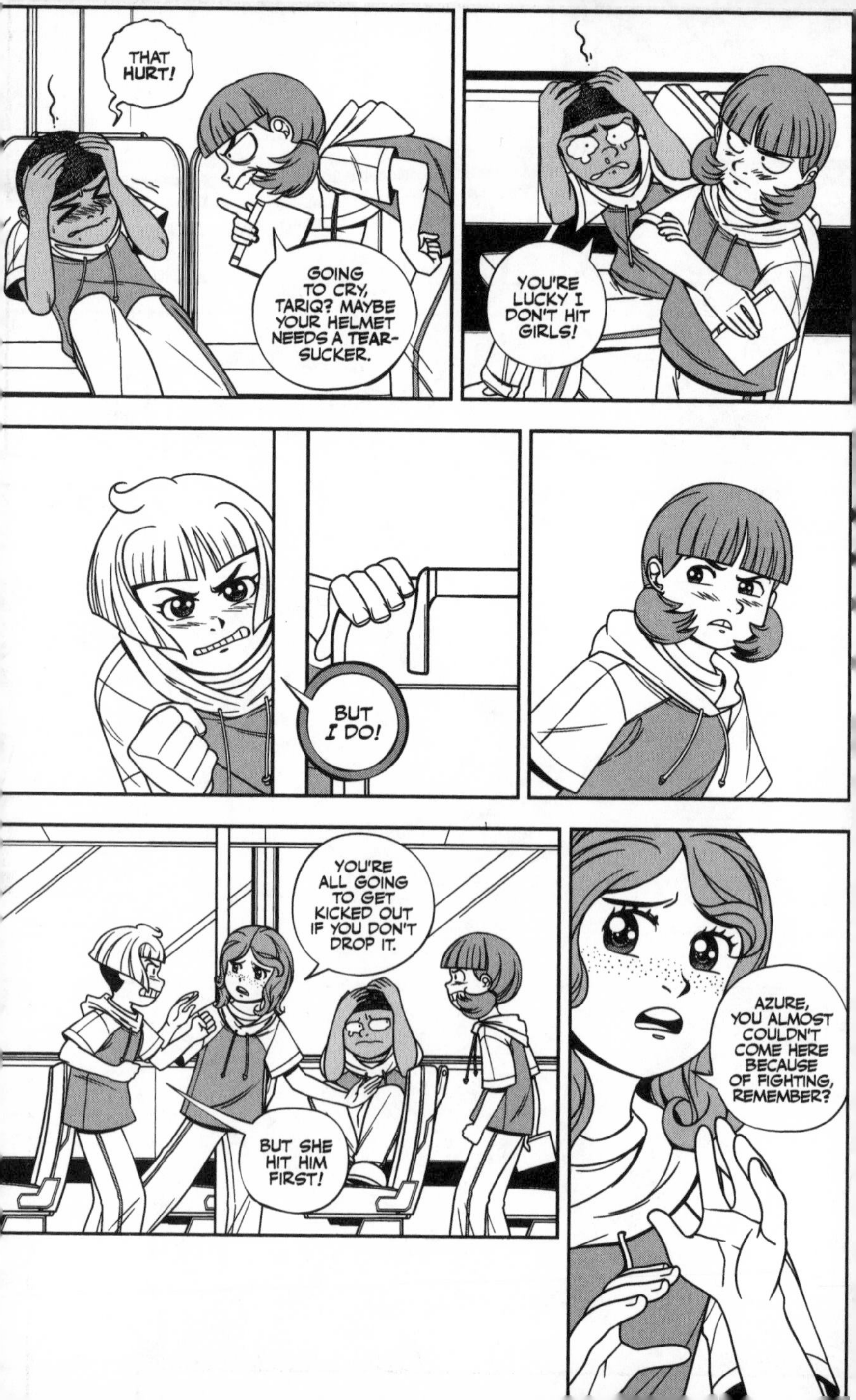
THAT HURT!
GOING TO CRY, TARIQ? MAYBE YOUR HELMET NEEDS A TEAR-SUCKER.
YOU'RE LUCKY I DON'T HIT GIRLS!
BUT *I* DO!
YOU'RE ALL GOING TO GET KICKED OUT IF YOU DON'T DROP IT.
BUT SHE HIT HIM FIRST!
AZURE, YOU ALMOST COULDN'T COME HERE BECAUSE OF FIGHTING, REMEMBER?

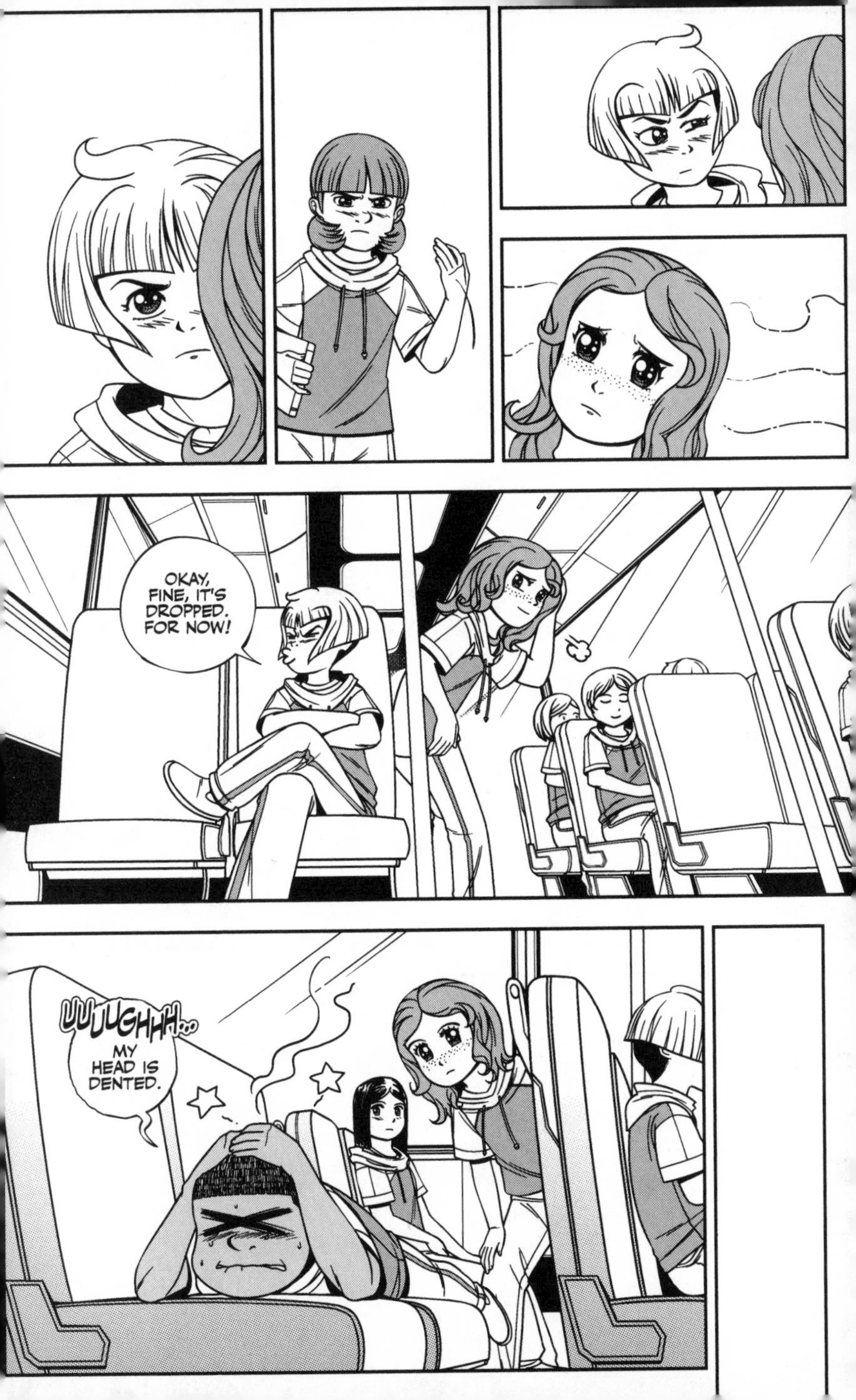
OKAY, FINE, IT'S DROPPED. FOR NOW!
UUUUGHHH...
MY HEAD IS DENTED.

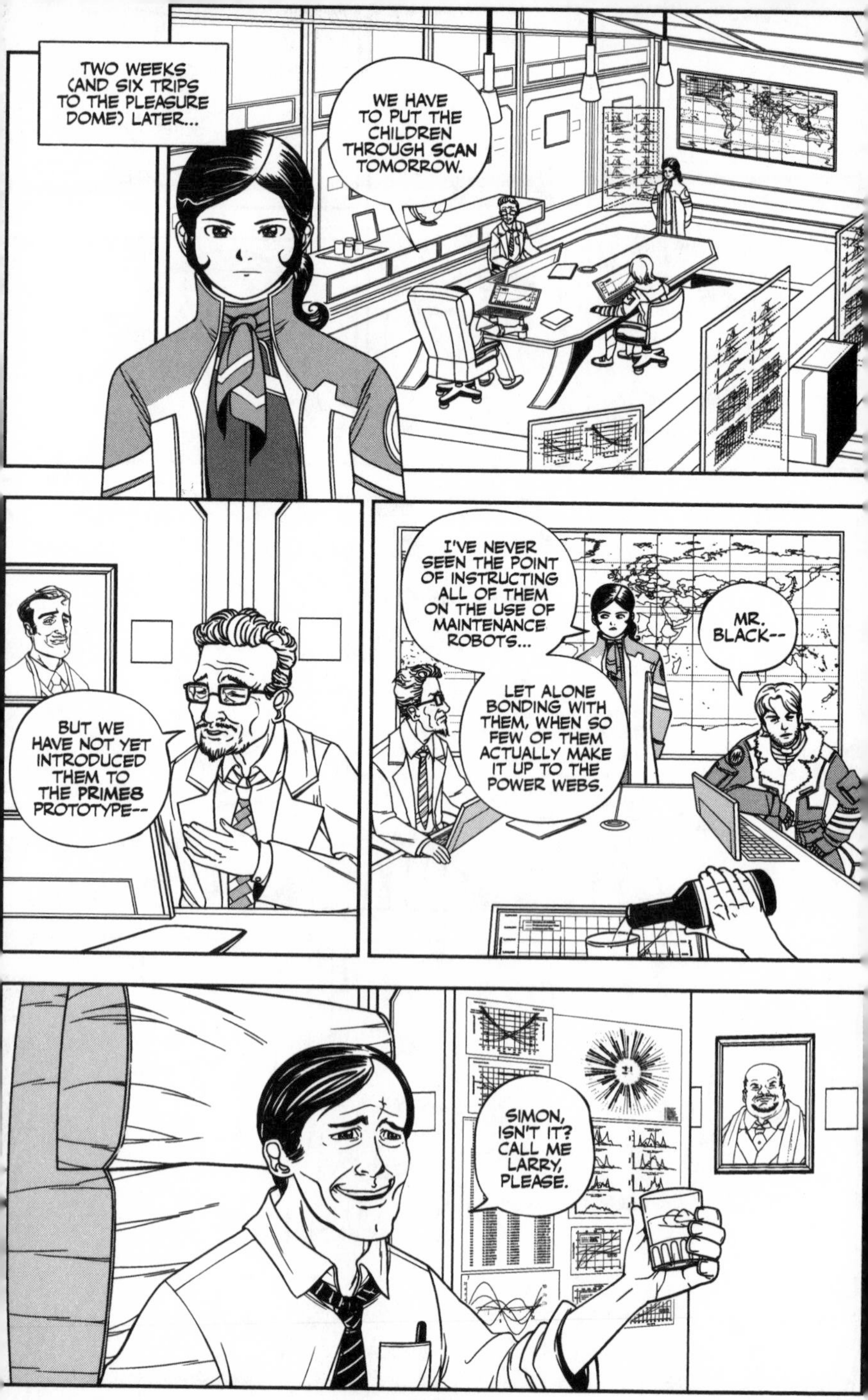
TWO WEEKS (AND SIX TRIPS TO THE PLEASURE DOME) LATER...
WE HAVE TO PUT THE CHILDREN THROUGH SCAN TOMORROW.
BUT WE HAVE NOT YET INTRODUCED THEM TO THE PRIME8 PROTOTYPE--
I'VE NEVER SEEN THE POINT OF INSTRUCTING ALL OF THEM ON THE USE OF MAINTENANCE ROBOTS...
LET ALONE BONDING WITH THEM, WHEN SO FEW OF THEM ACTUALLY MAKE IT UP TO THE POWER WEBS.
MR. BLACK--
SIMON, ISN'T IT? CALL ME LARRY, PLEASE.

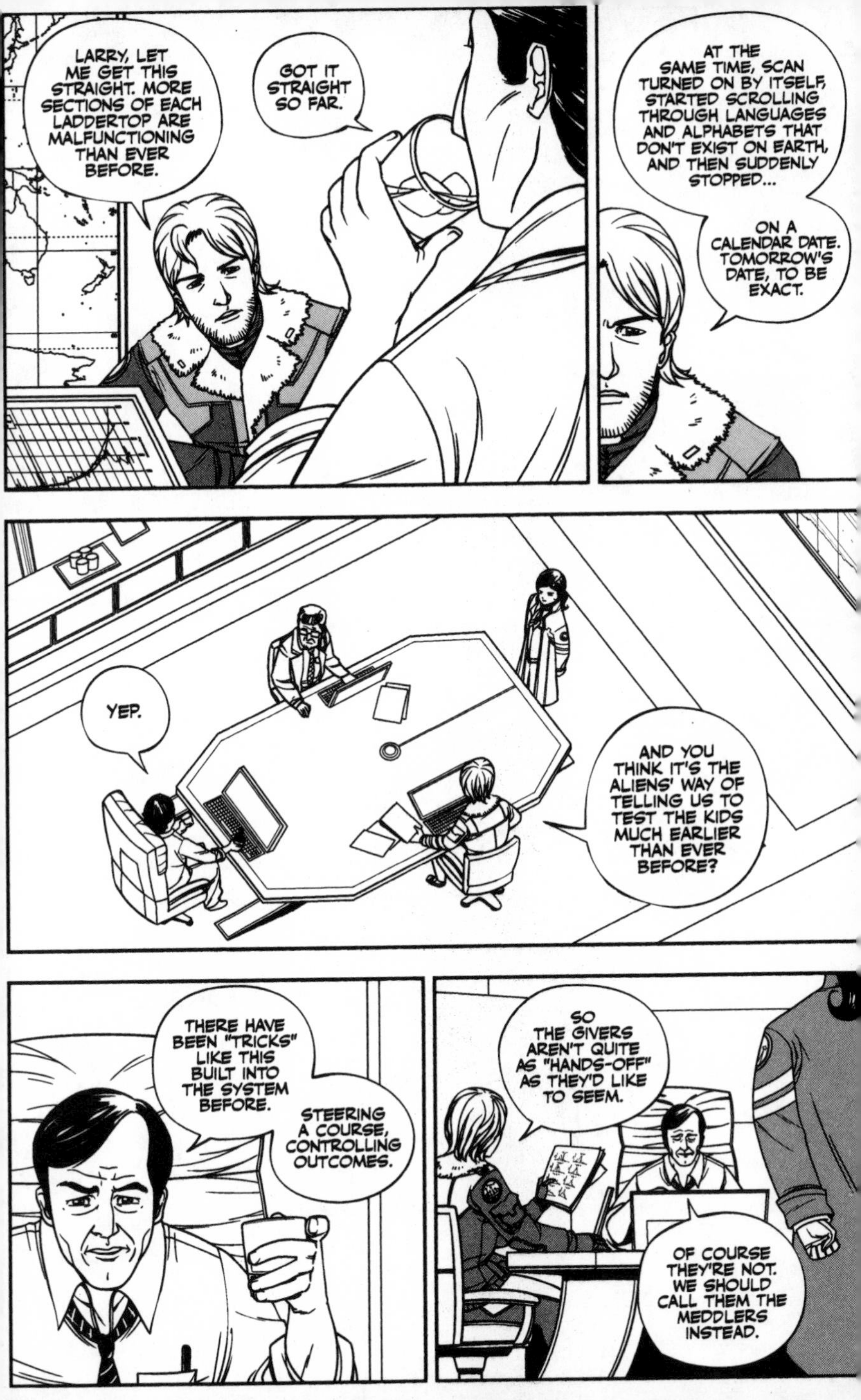
LARRY, LET ME GET THIS STRAIGHT. MORE SECTIONS OF EACH LADDERTOP ARE MALFUNCTIONING THAN EVER BEFORE.
GOT IT STRAIGHT SO FAR.
AT THE SAME TIME, SCAN TURNED ON BY ITSELF, STARTED SCROLLING THROUGH LANGUAGES AND ALPHABETS THAT DON'T EXIST ON EARTH, AND THEN SUDDENLY STOPPED...
ON A CALENDAR DATE. TOMORROW'S DATE, TO BE EXACT.
YEP.
AND YOU THINK IT'S THE ALIENS' WAY OF TELLING US TO TEST THE KIDS MUCH EARLIER THAN EVER BEFORE?
THERE HAVE BEEN "TRICKS" LIKE THIS BUILT INTO THE SYSTEM BEFORE.
STEERING A COURSE, CONTROLLING OUTCOMES.
SO THE GIVERS AREN'T QUITE AS "HANDS-OFF" AS THEY'D LIKE TO SEEM.
OF COURSE THEY'RE NOT. WE SHOULD CALL THEM THE MEDDLERS INSTEAD.

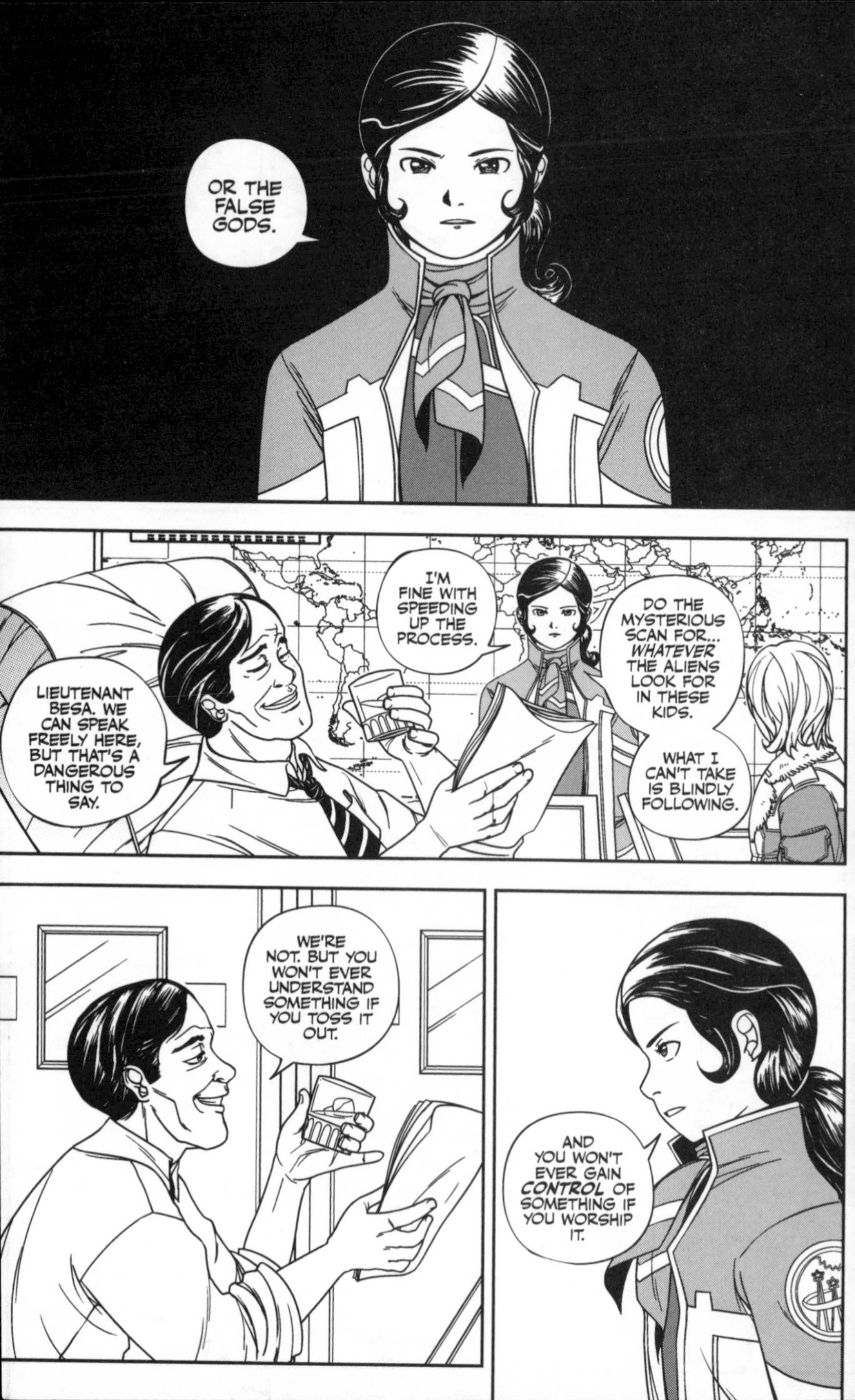
OR THE FALSE GODS.
LIEUTENANT BESA. WE CAN SPEAK FREELY HERE, BUT THAT'S A DANGEROUS THING TO SAY.
I'M FINE WITH SPEEDING UP THE PROCESS.
DO THE MYSTERIOUS SCAN FOR... *WHATEVER* THE ALIENS LOOK FOR IN THESE KIDS.
WHAT I CAN'T TAKE IS BLINDLY FOLLOWING.
WE'RE NOT. BUT YOU WON'T EVER UNDERSTAND SOMETHING IF YOU TOSS IT OUT.
AND YOU WON'T EVER GAIN ***CONTROL*** OF SOMETHING IF YOU WORSHIP IT.

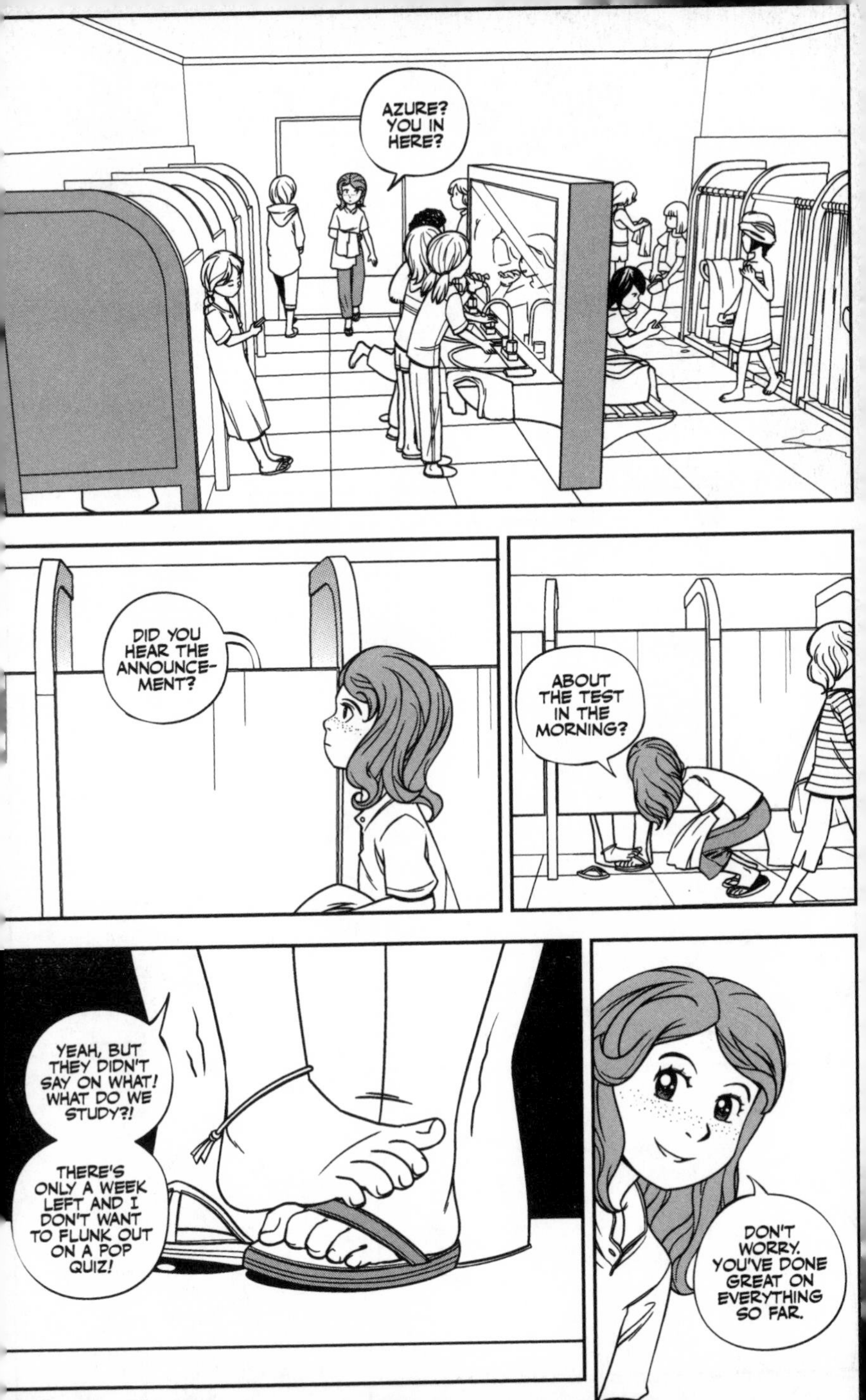
AZURE? YOU IN HERE?
DID YOU HEAR THE ANNOUNCE-MENT?
ABOUT THE TEST IN THE MORNING?
YEAH, BUT THEY DIDN'T SAY ON WHAT! WHAT DO WE STUDY?!
THERE'S ONLY A WEEK LEFT AND I DON'T WANT TO FLUNK OUT ON A POP QUIZ!
DON'T WORRY. YOU'VE DONE GREAT ON EVERYTHING SO FAR.

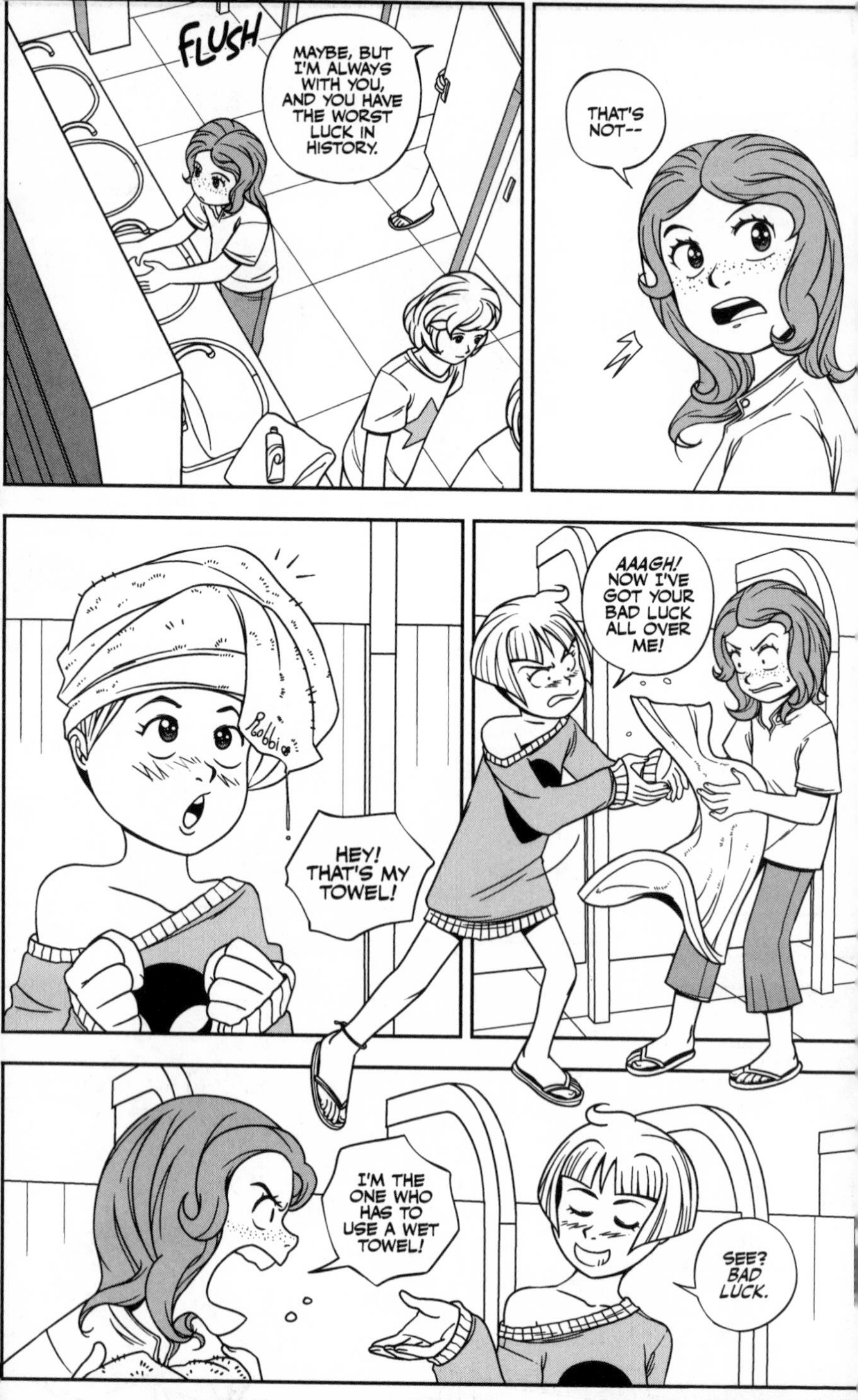
FLUSH
MAYBE, BUT I'M ALWAYS WITH YOU, AND YOU HAVE THE WORST LUCK IN HISTORY.
THAT'S NOT--
Robbi
HEY! THAT'S MY TOWEL!
AAAGH! NOW I'VE GOT YOUR BAD LUCK ALL OVER ME!
I'M THE ONE WHO HAS TO USE A WET TOWEL!
SEE? BAD LUCK.

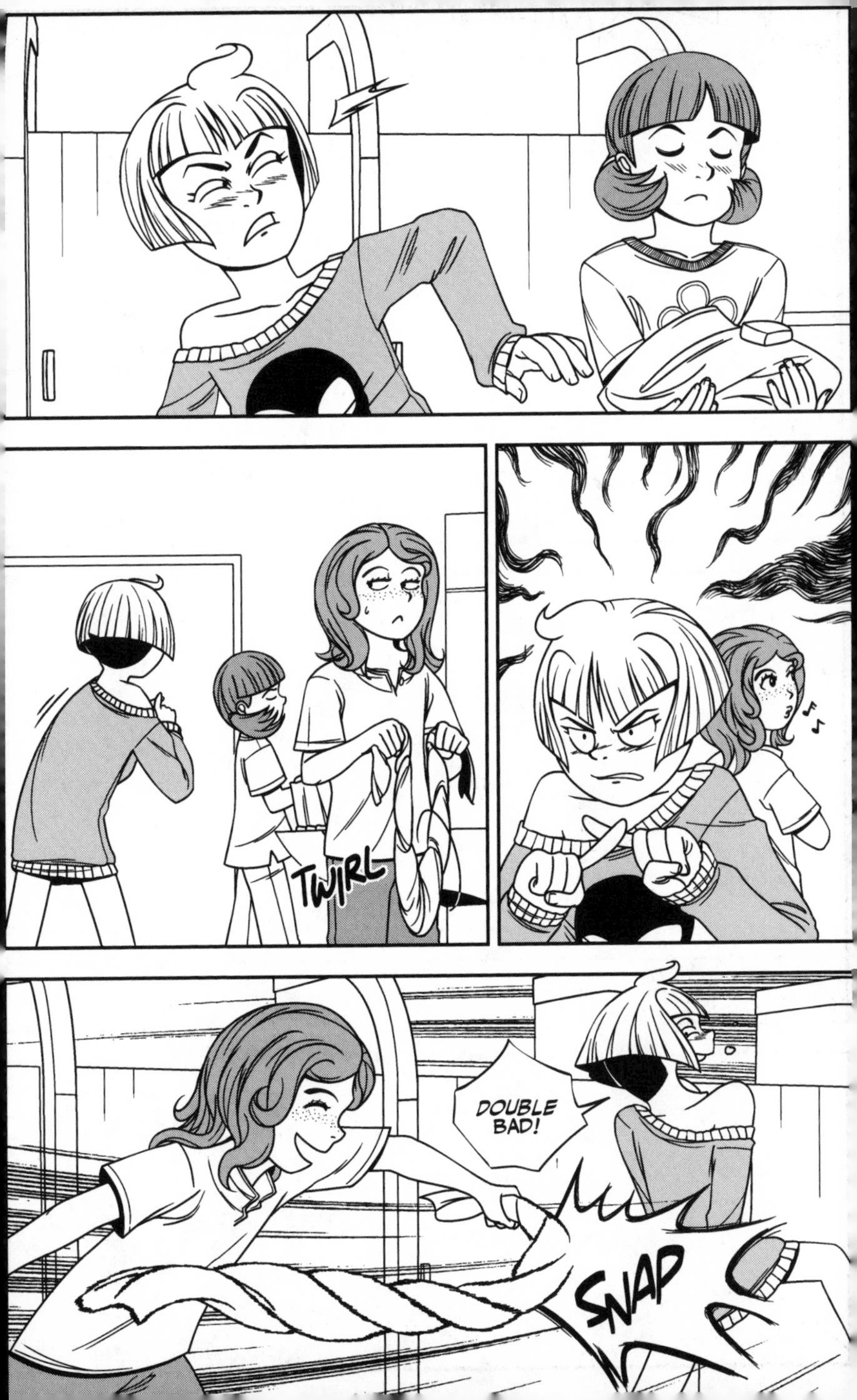
TWIRL
DOUBLE BAD!
SNAP

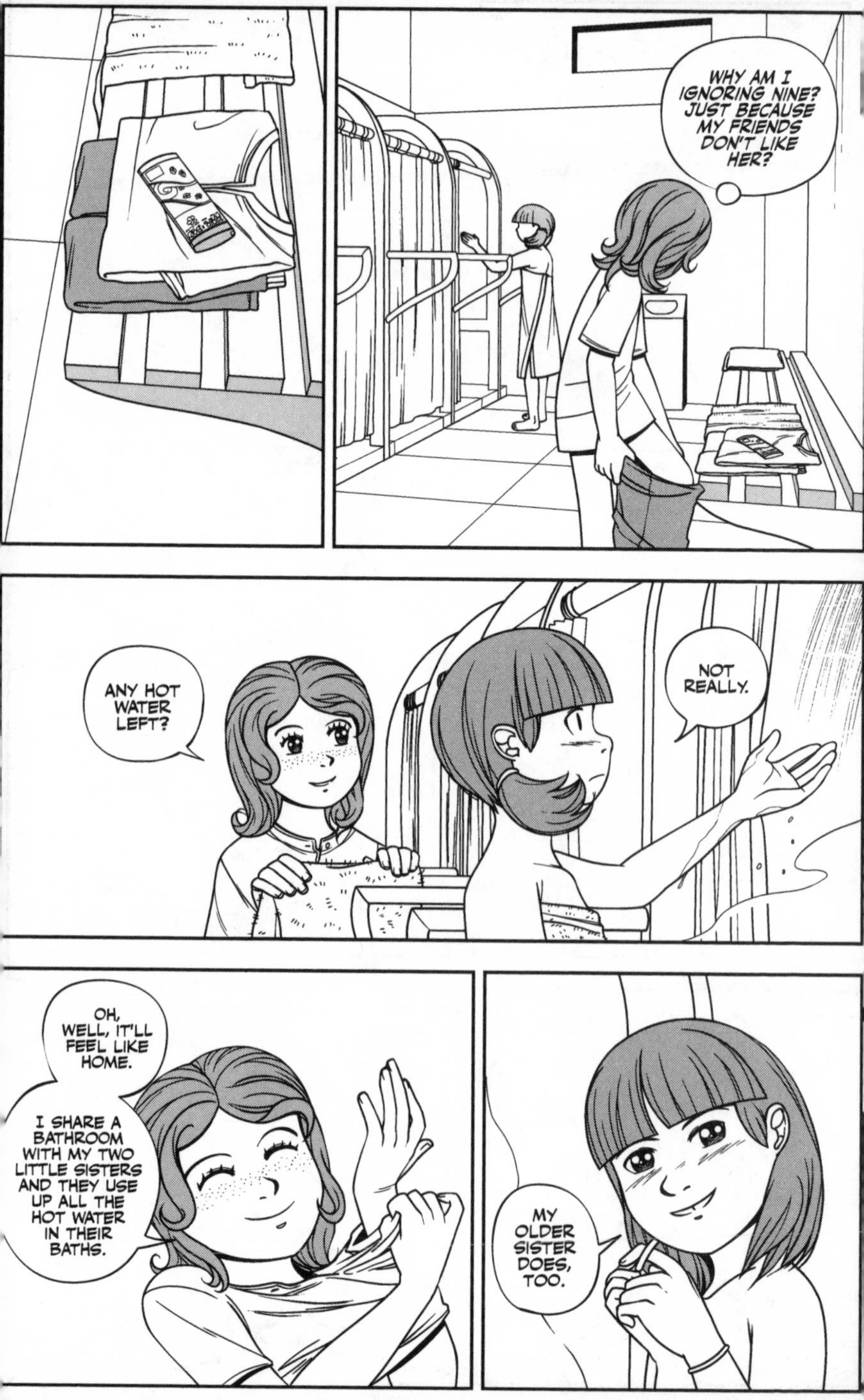
WHY AM I IGNORING NINE? JUST BECAUSE MY FRIENDS DON'T LIKE HER?
ANY HOT WATER LEFT?
NOT REALLY.
OH, WELL, IT'LL FEEL LIKE HOME.
I SHARE A BATHROOM WITH MY TWO LITTLE SISTERS AND THEY USE UP ALL THE HOT WATER IN THEIR BATHS.
MY OLDER SISTER DOES, TOO.

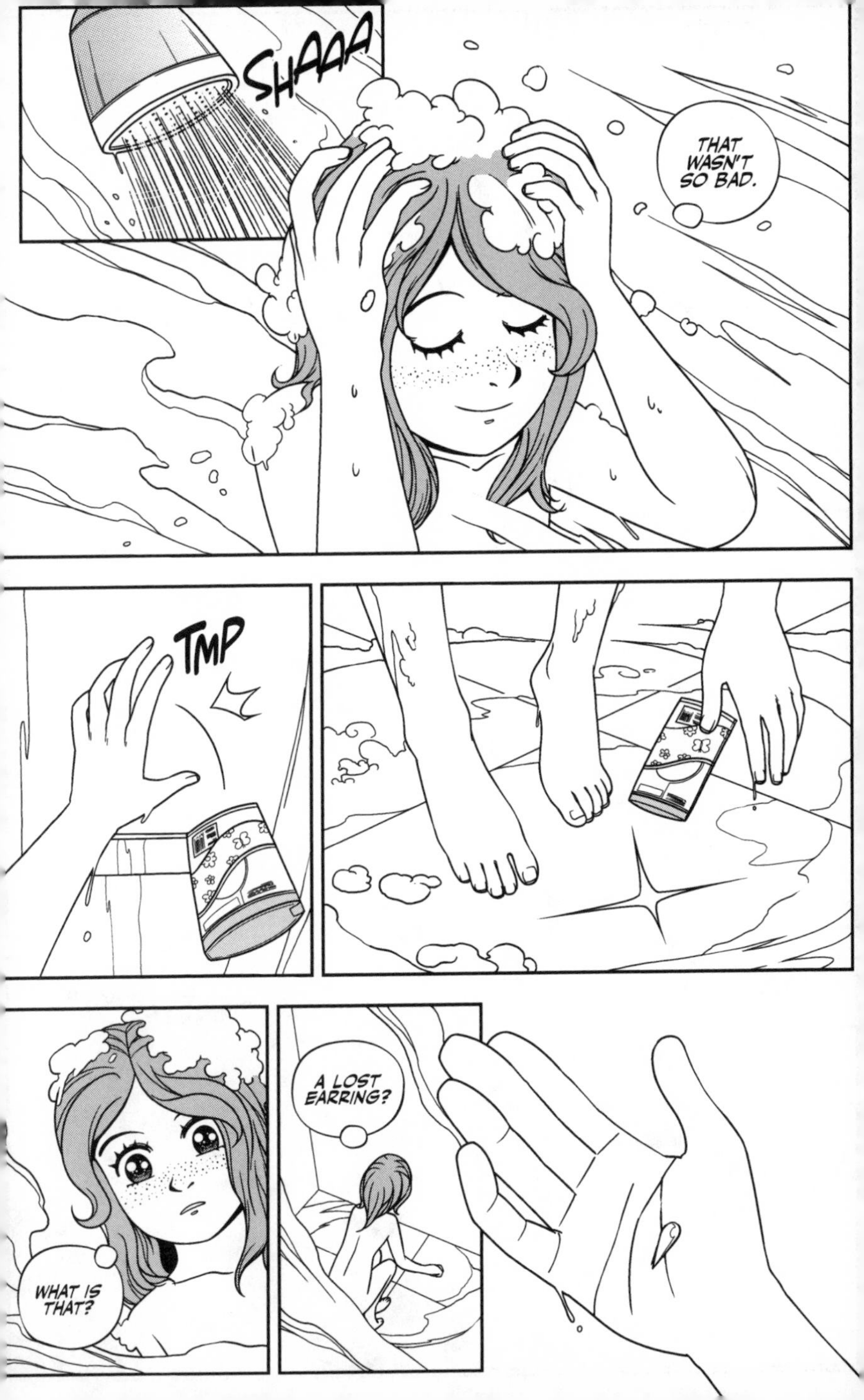
SHAAA
THAT WASN'T SO BAD.
TMP
A LOST EARRING?
WHAT IS THAT?

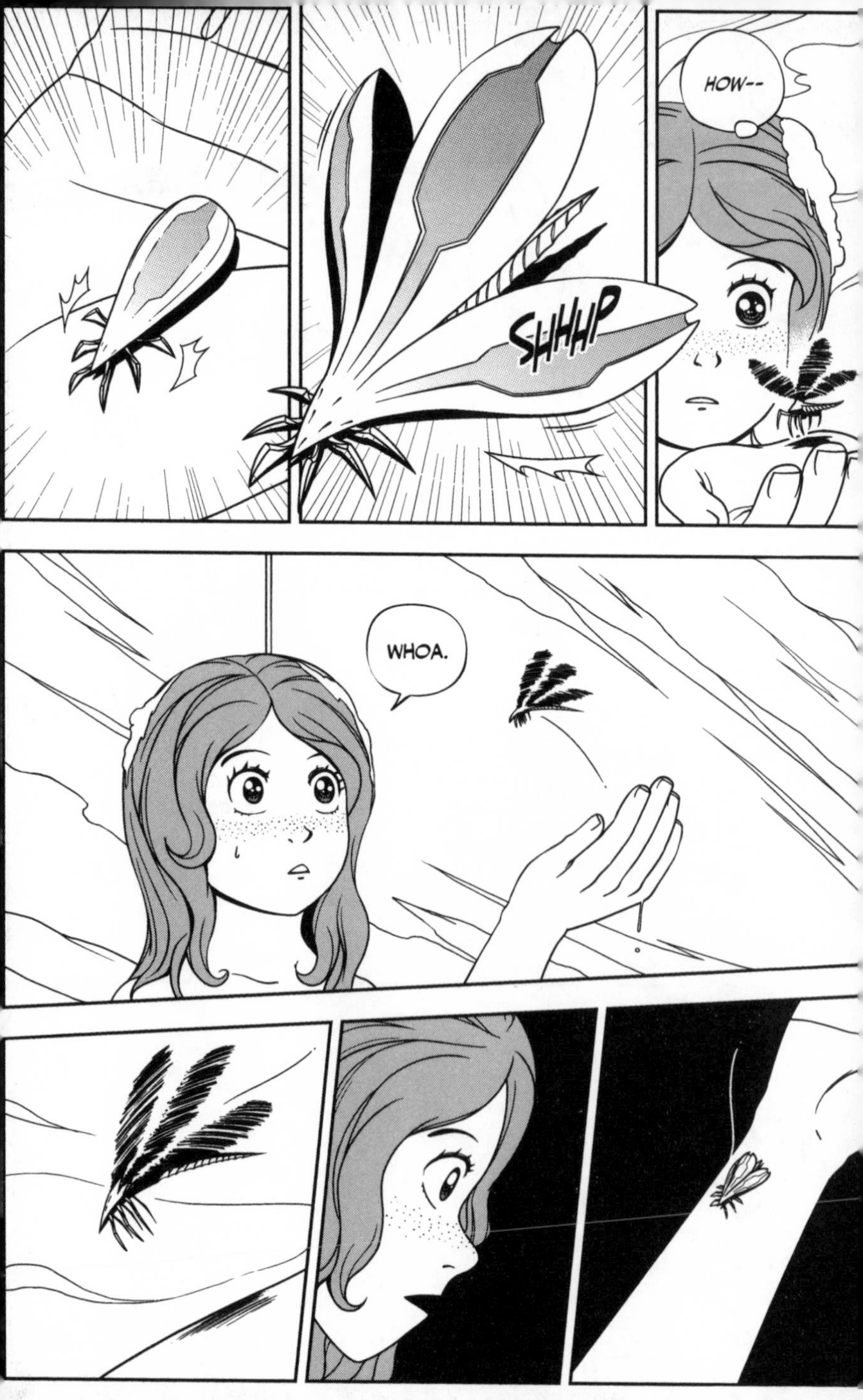
SHHHP
HOW--
WHOA.

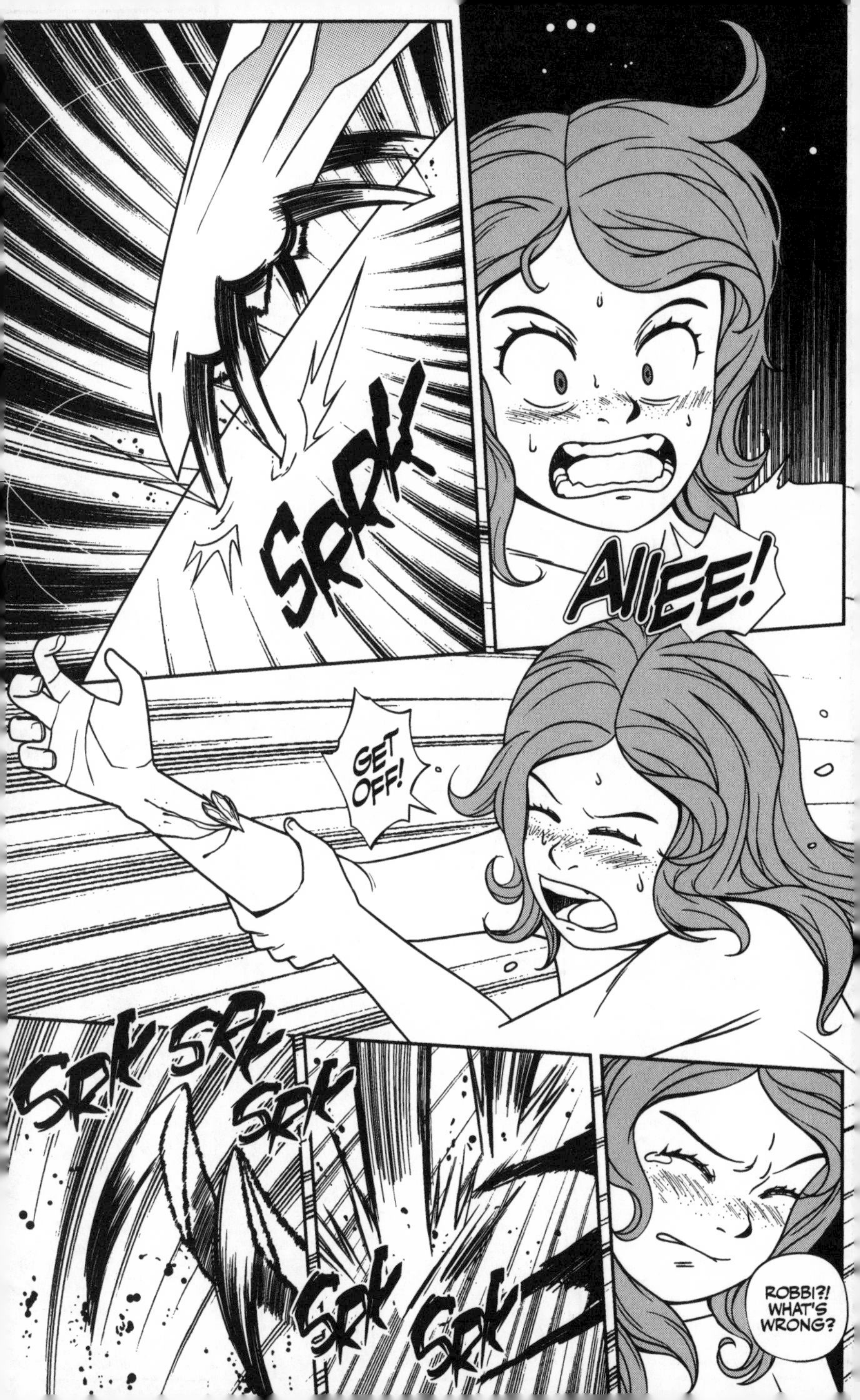
SRRK
AIIEE!
GET OFF!
SRK SRK
SRK
SRK SRK
ROBBI?! WHAT'S WRONG?

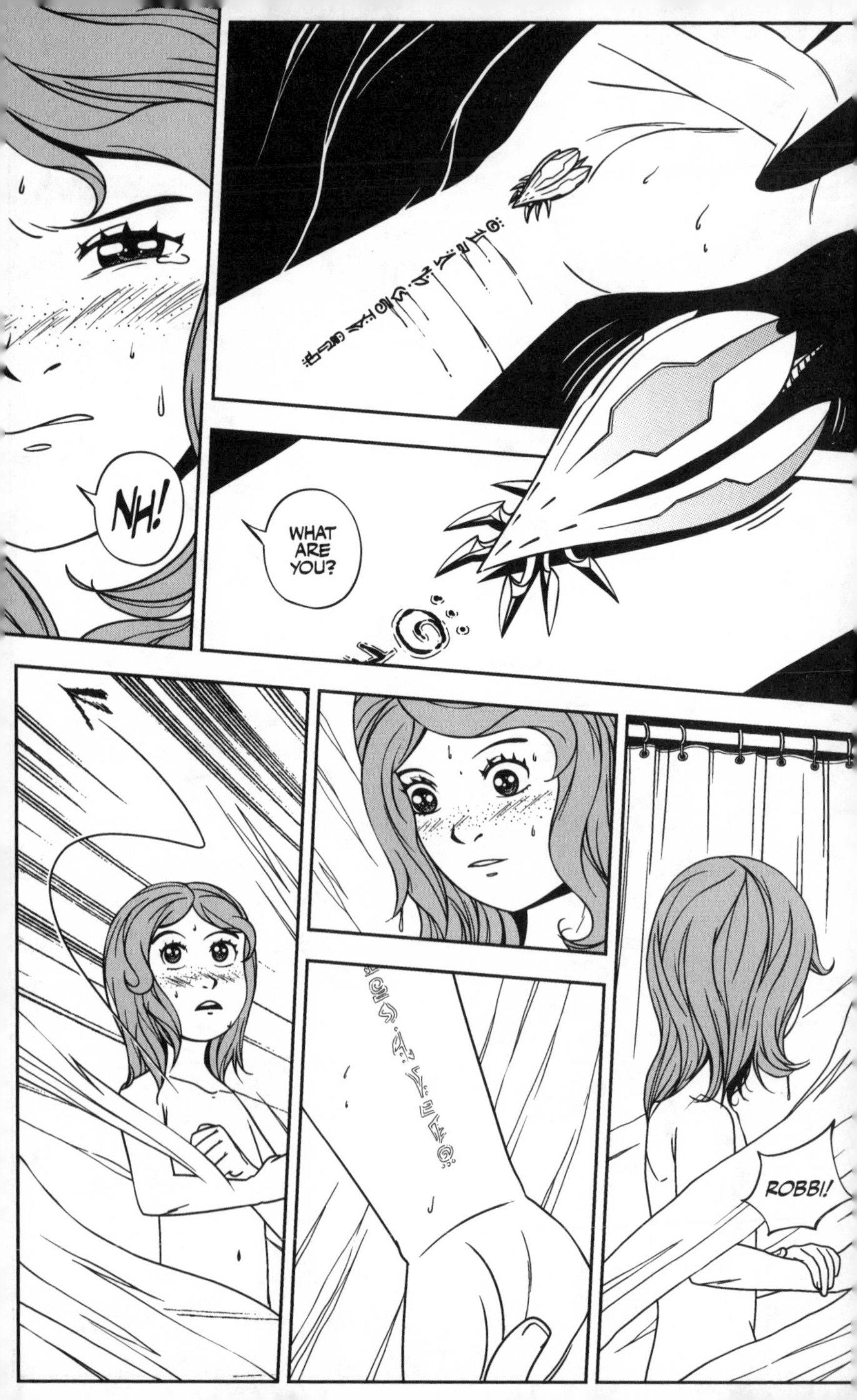
NH!
WHAT ARE YOU?
ROBBI!

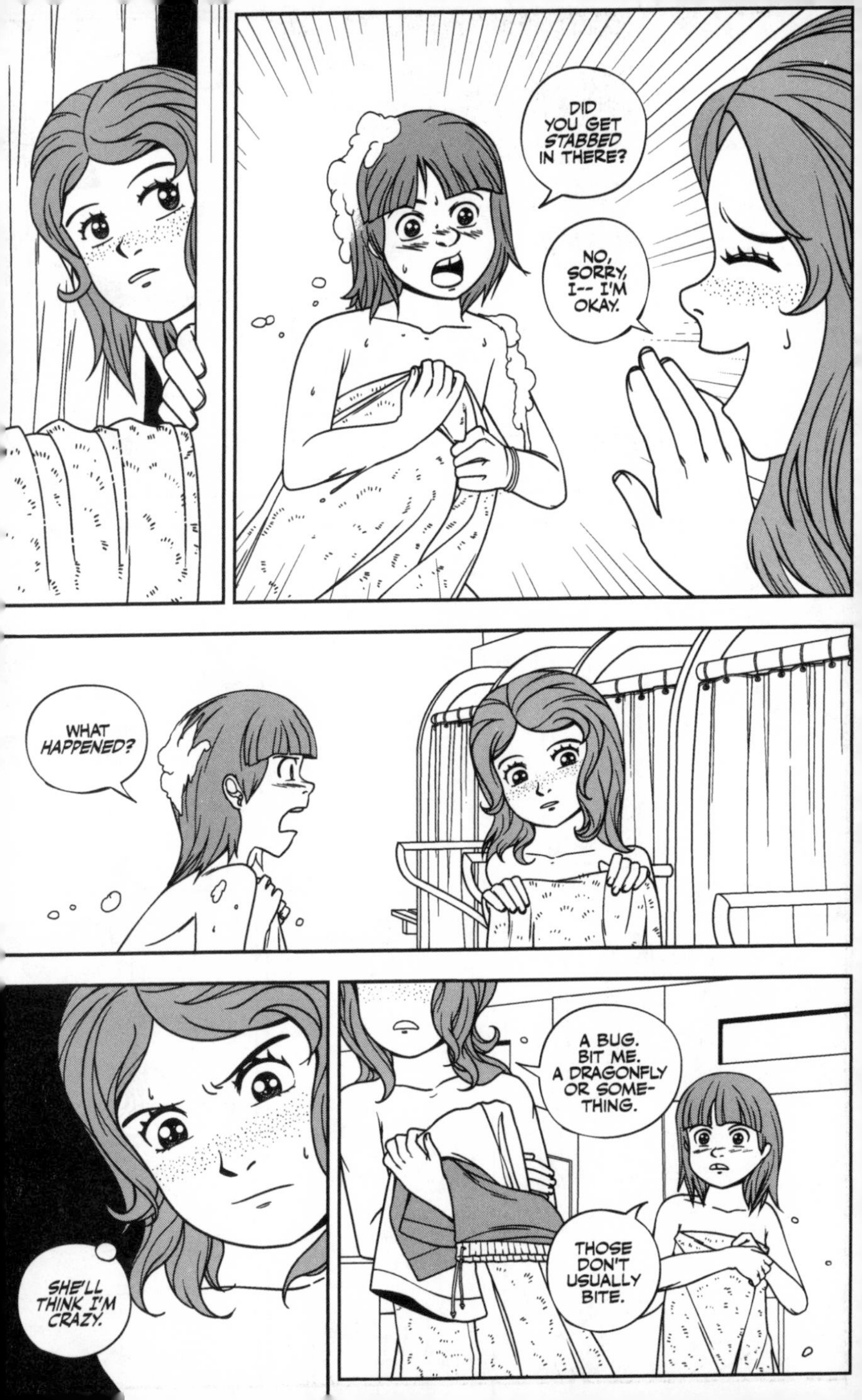
DID YOU GET STABBED IN THERE?
NO, SORRY, I-- I'M OKAY.
WHAT HAPPENED?
SHE'LL THINK I'M CRAZY.
A BUG. BIT ME. A DRAGONFLY OR SOME-THING.
THOSE DON'T USUALLY BITE.

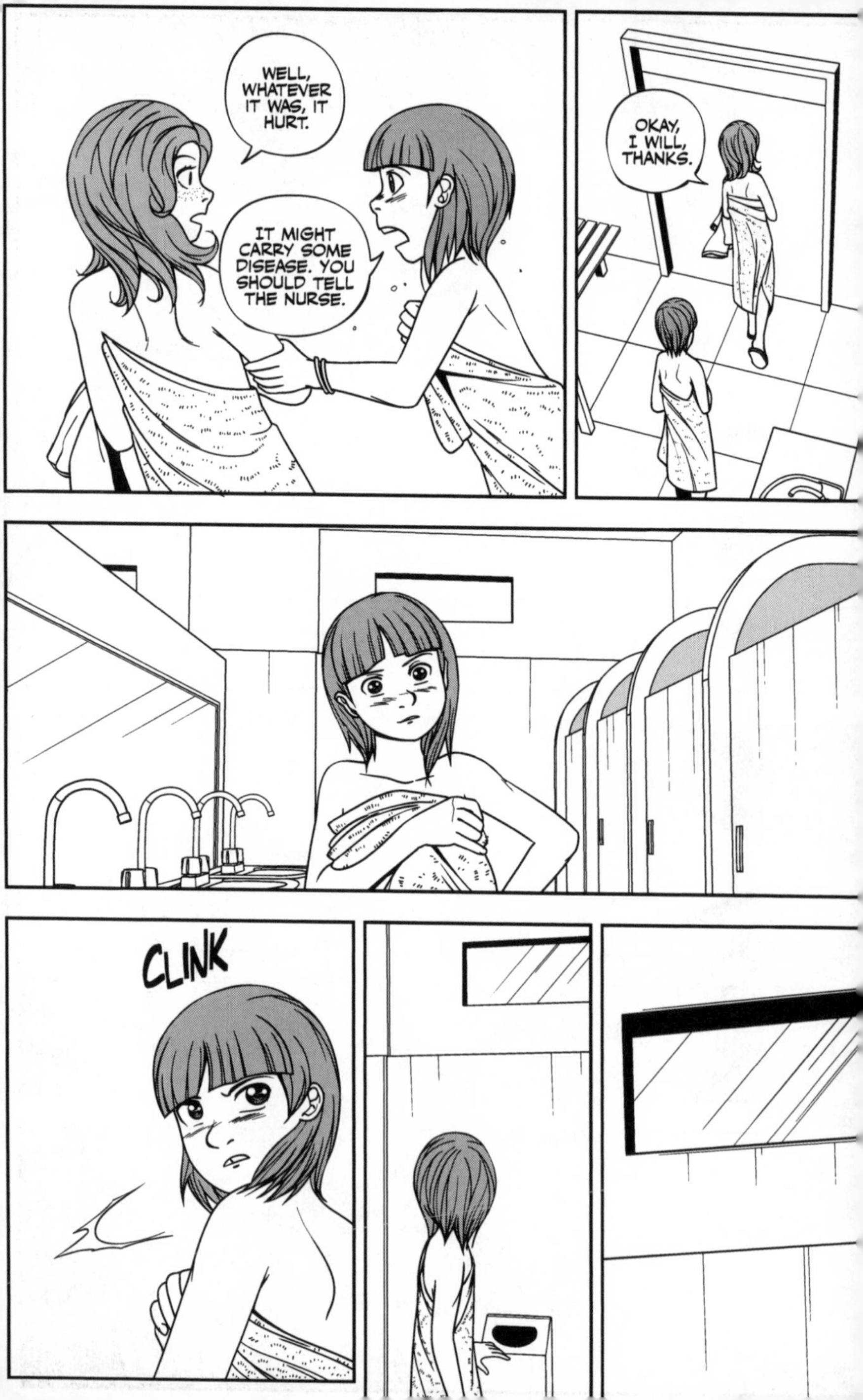
WELL, WHATEVER IT WAS, IT HURT.
IT MIGHT CARRY SOME DISEASE. YOU SHOULD TELL THE NURSE.
OKAY, I WILL, THANKS.
CLINK

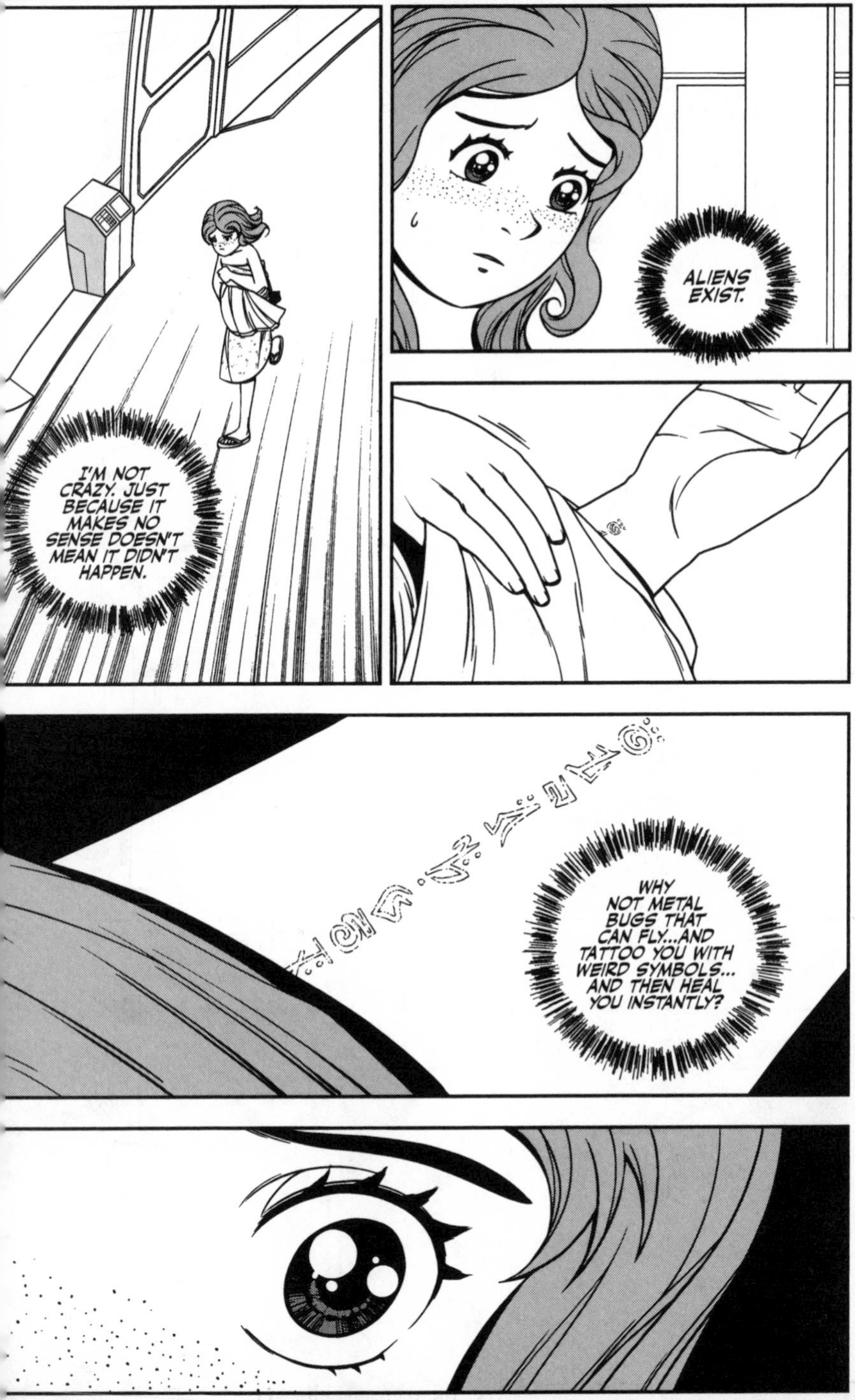
I'M NOT CRAZY. JUST BECAUSE IT MAKES NO SENSE DOESN'T MEAN IT DIDN'T HAPPEN.
ALIENS EXIST.
WHY NOT METAL BUGS THAT CAN FLY...AND TATTOO YOU WITH WEIRD SYMBOLS... AND THEN HEAL YOU INSTANTLY?

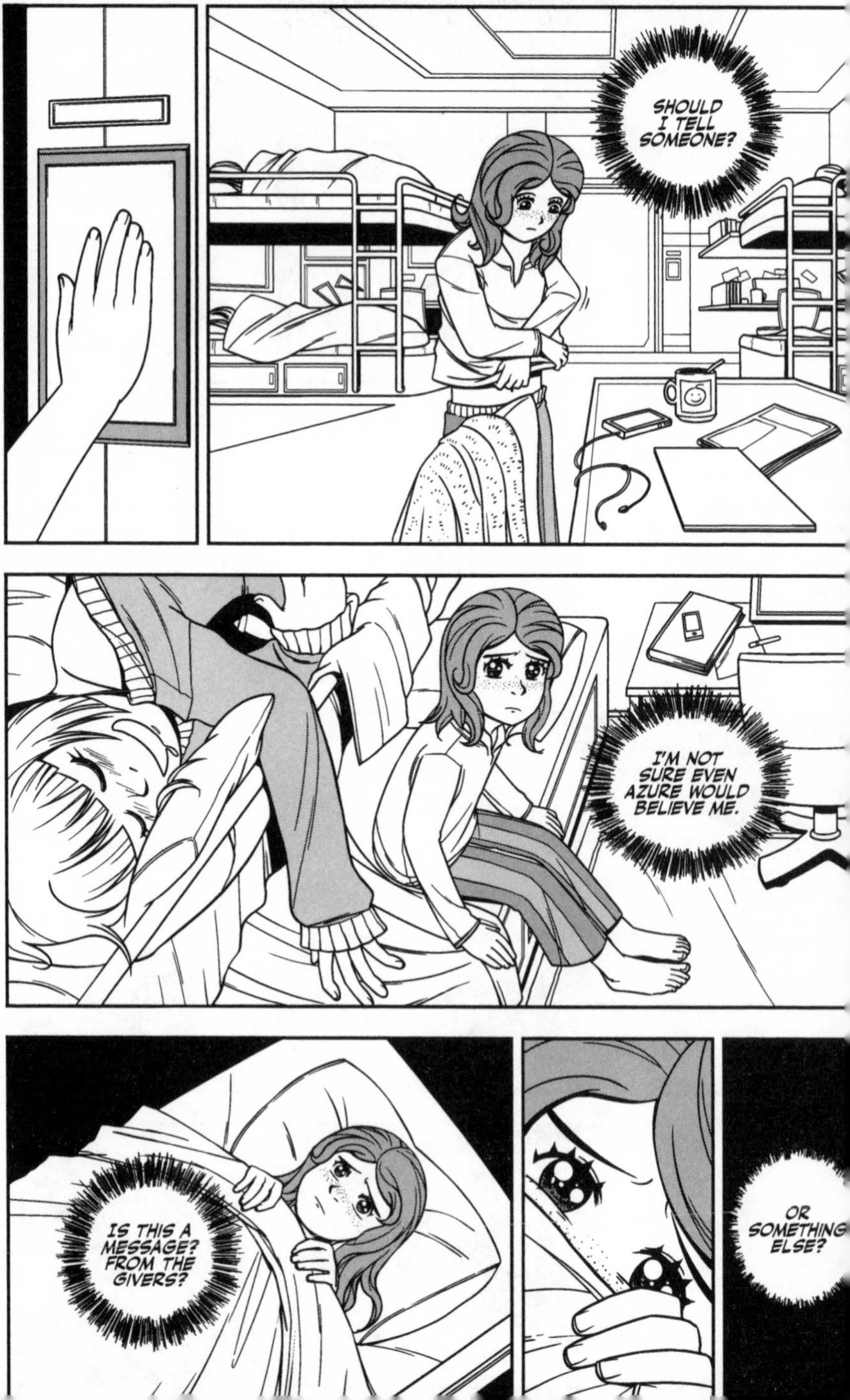
SHOULD I TELL SOMEONE?
I'M NOT SURE EVEN AZURE WOULD BELIEVE ME.
IS THIS A MESSAGE? FROM THE GIVERS?
OR SOMETHING ELSE?

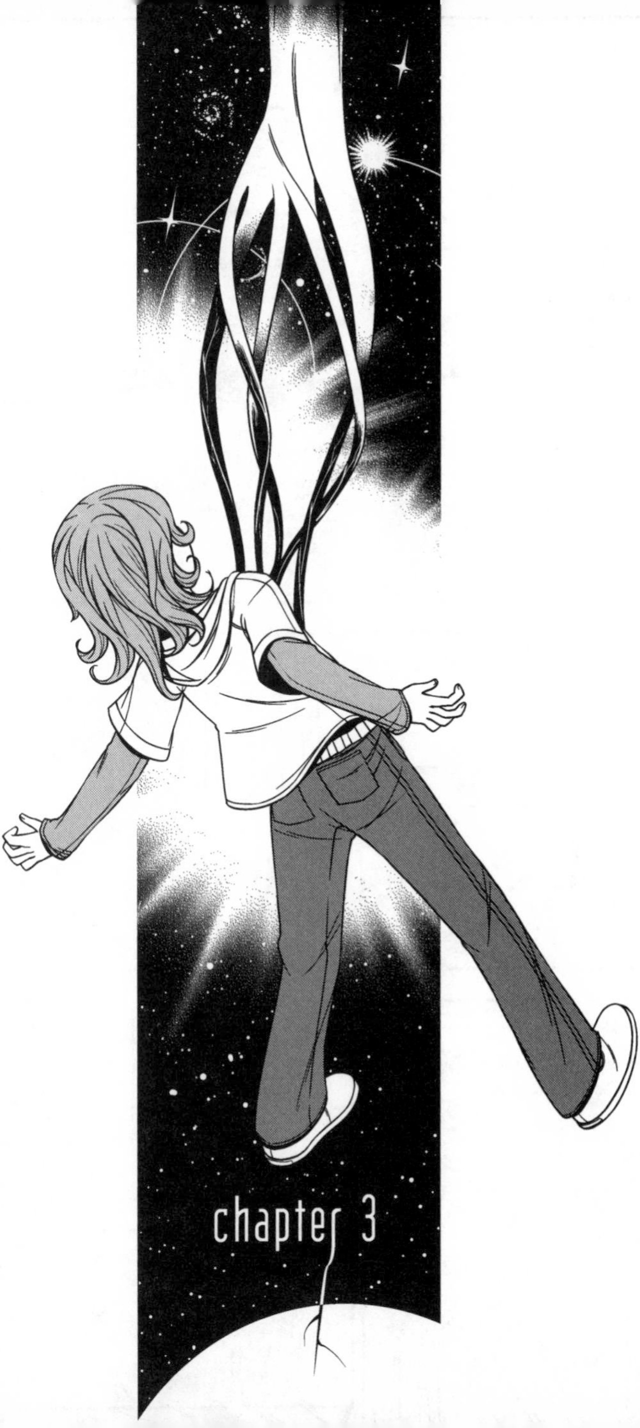
chapter 3

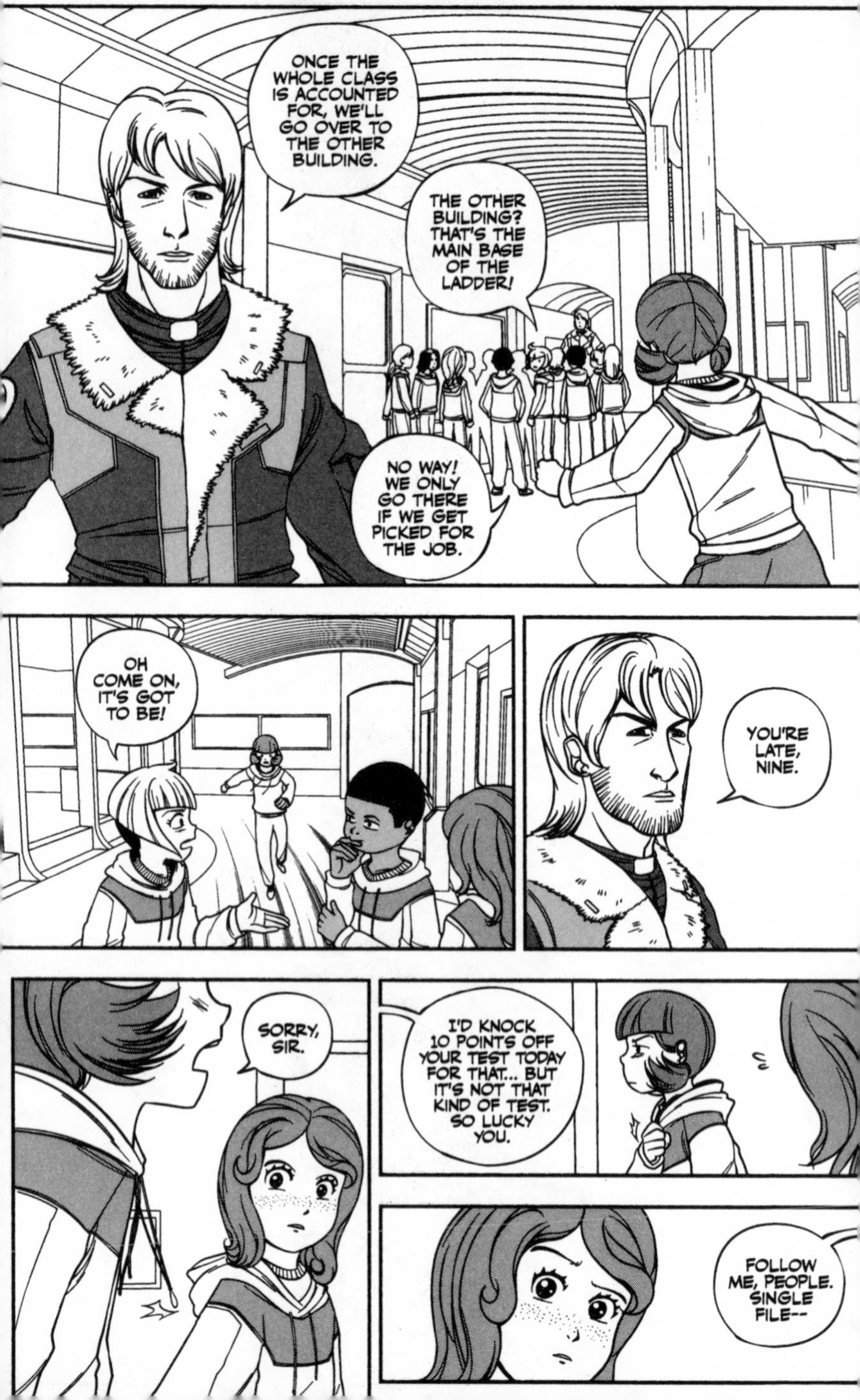
ONCE THE WHOLE CLASS IS ACCOUNTED FOR, WE'LL GO OVER TO THE OTHER BUILDING.
THE OTHER BUILDING? THAT'S THE MAIN BASE OF THE LADDER!
NO WAY! WE ONLY GO THERE IF WE GET PICKED FOR THE JOB.
OH COME ON, IT'S GOT TO BE!
YOU'RE LATE, NINE.
SORRY, SIR.
I'D KNOCK 10 POINTS OFF YOUR TEST TODAY FOR THAT... BUT IT'S NOT THAT KIND OF TEST. SO LUCKY YOU.
FOLLOW ME, PEOPLE. SINGLE FILE--

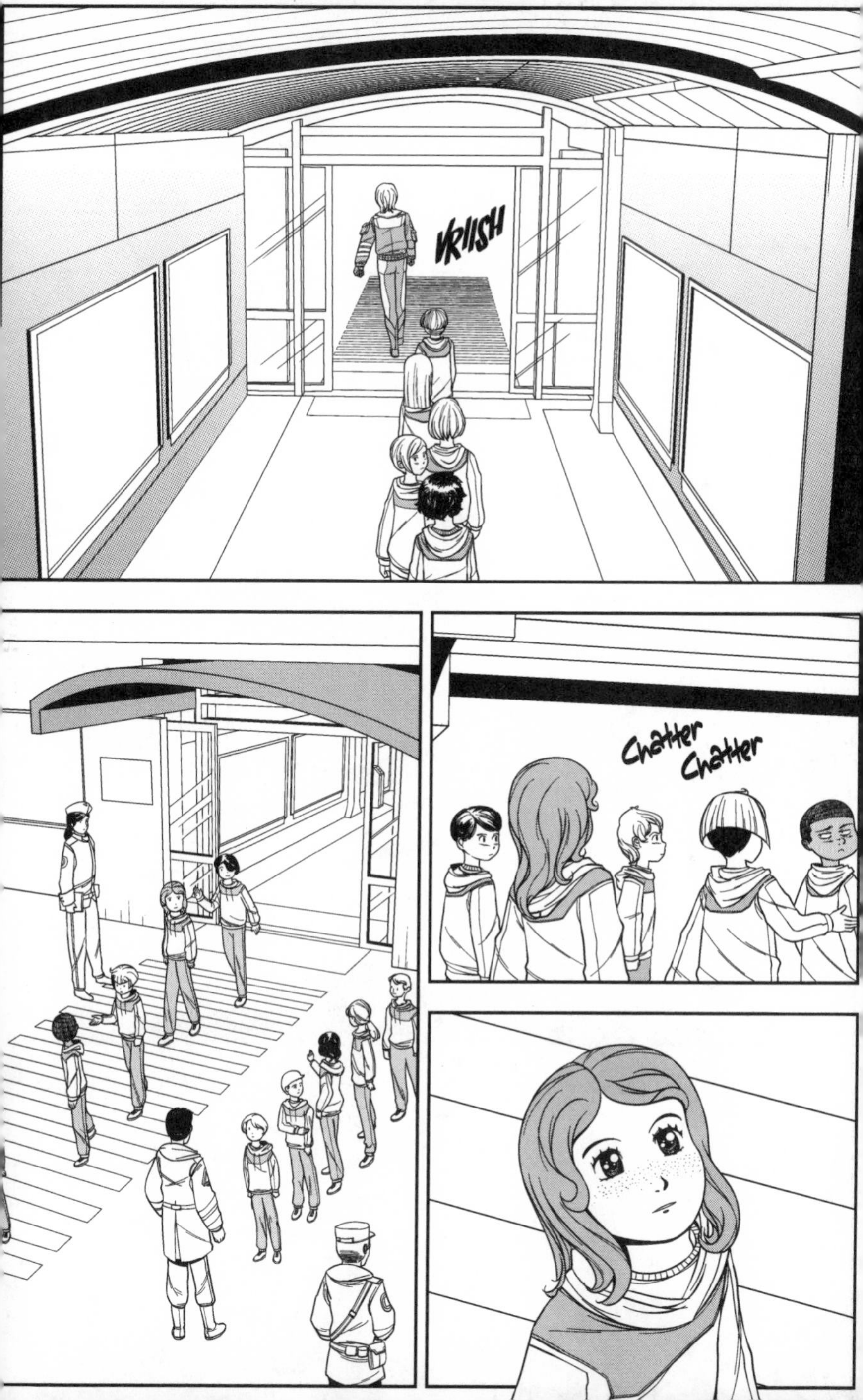
VRIISH
Chatter
Chatter

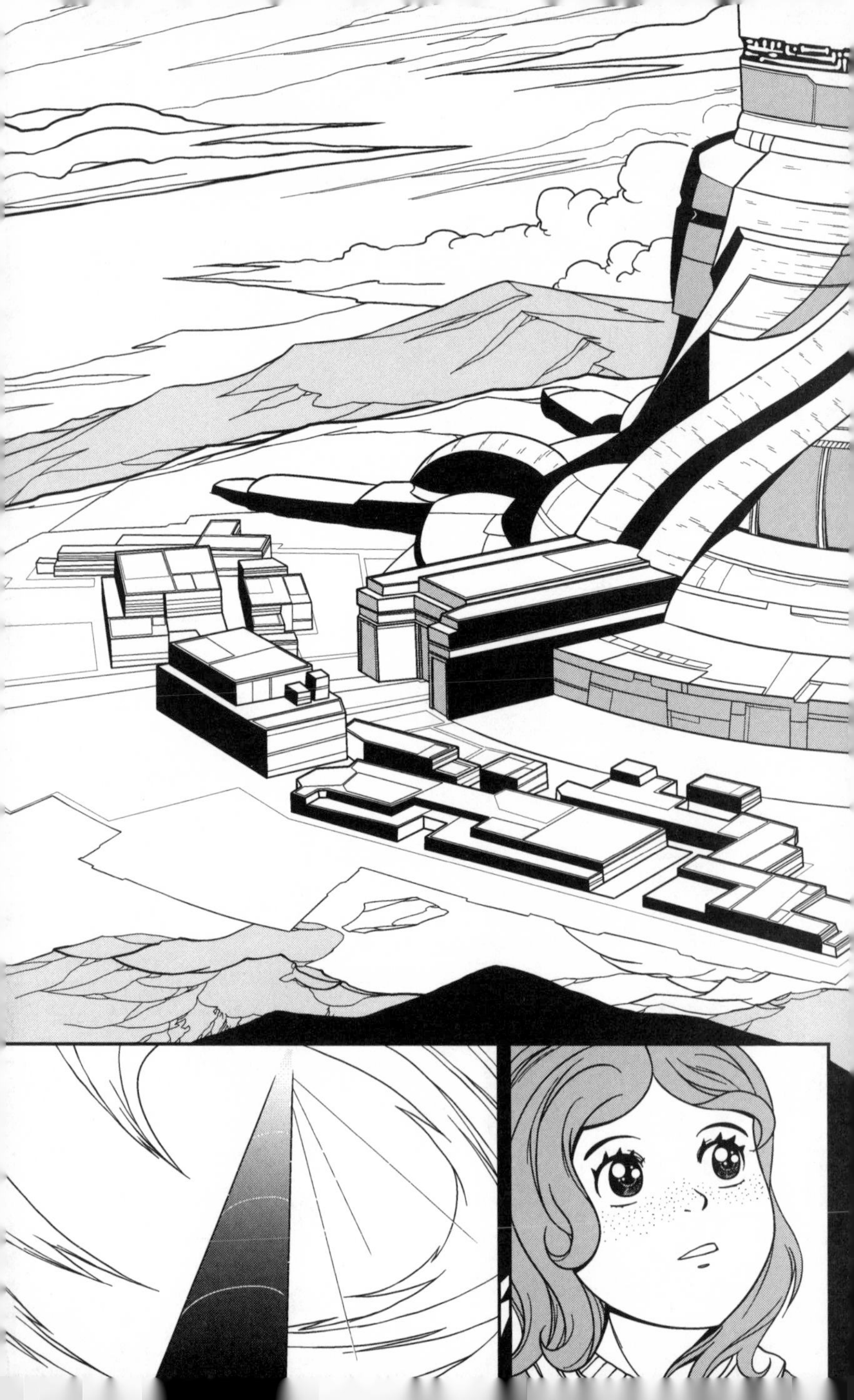

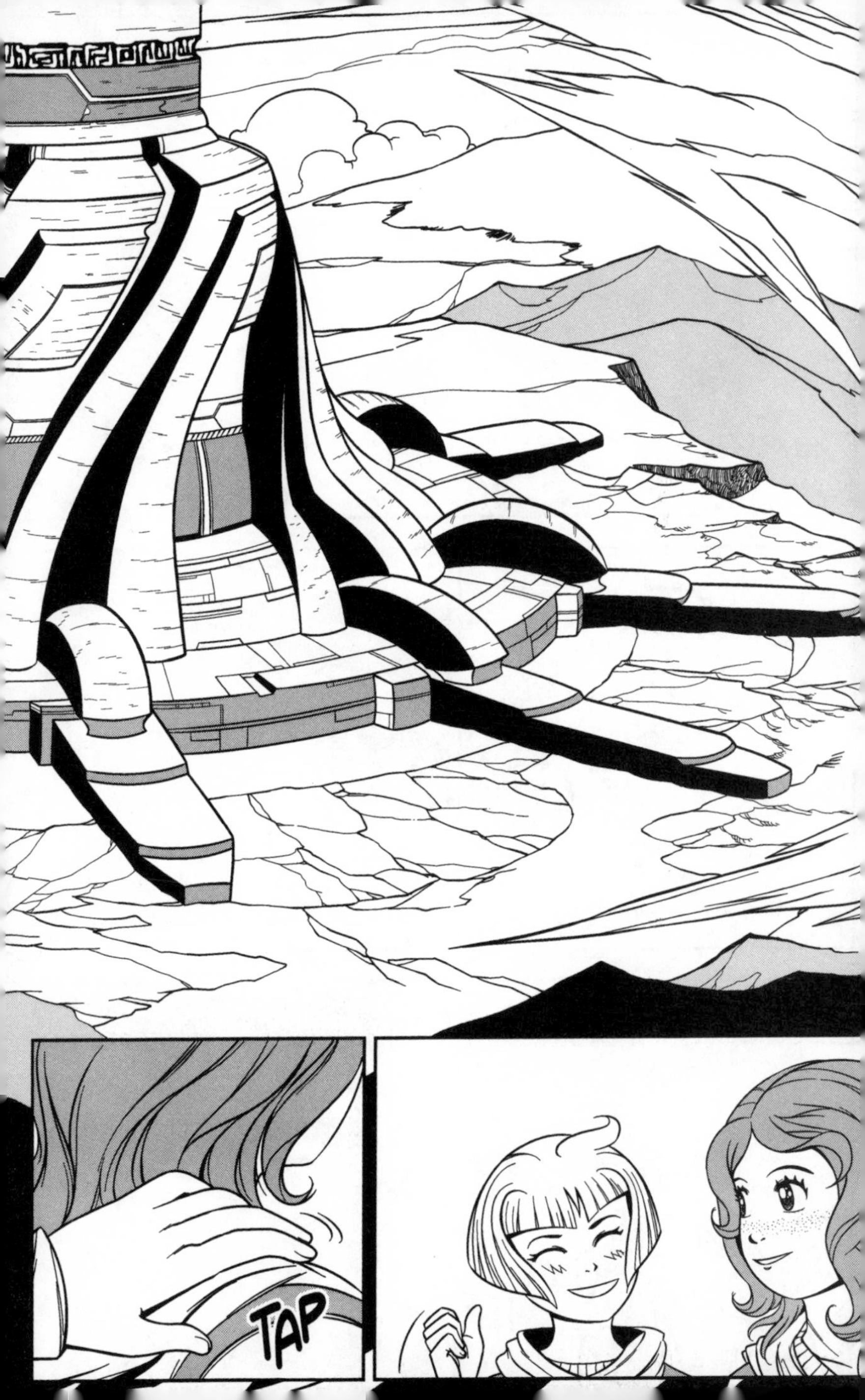
TAP

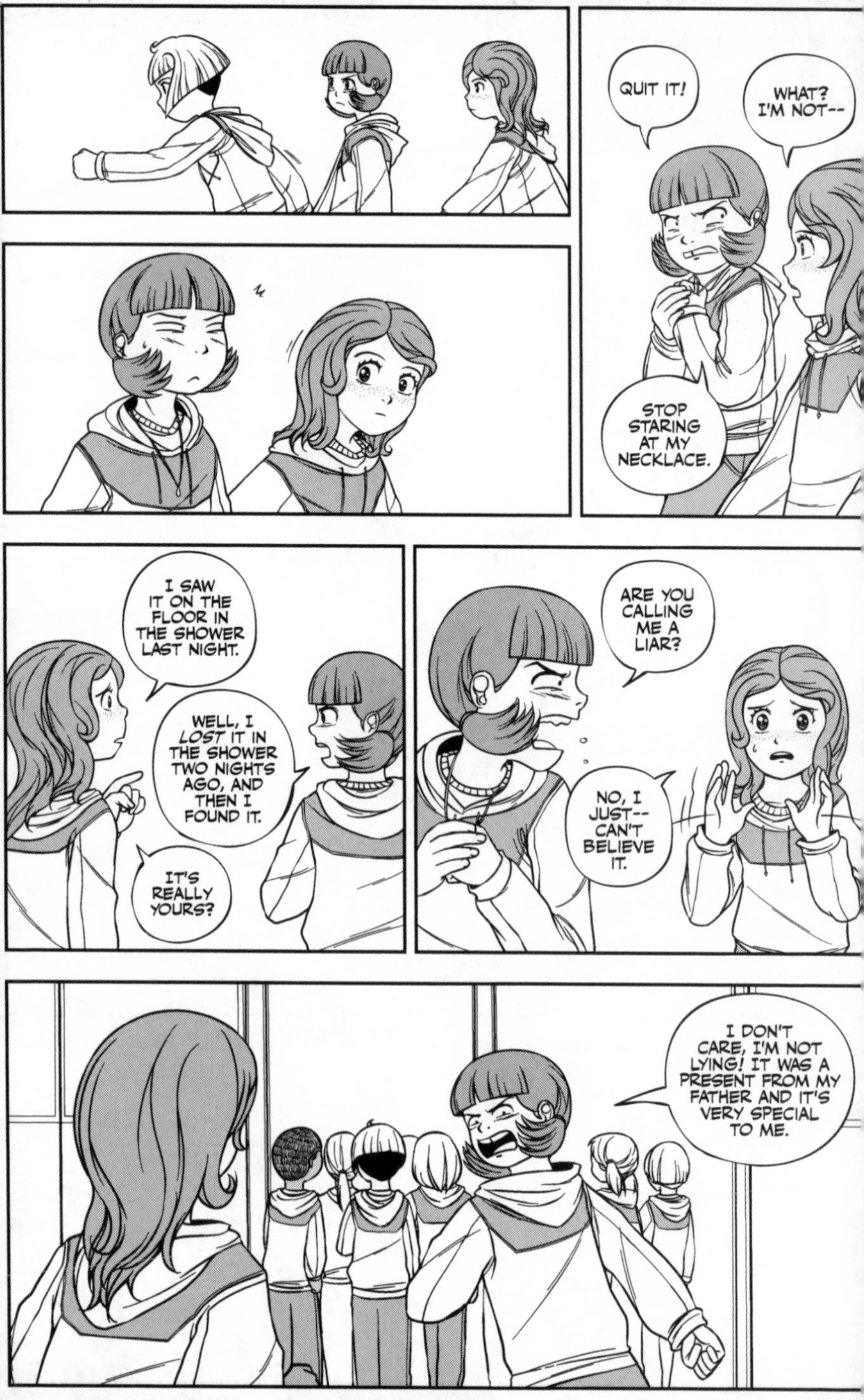

QUIT IT!
WHAT? I'M NOT--
STOP STARING AT MY NECKLACE.
I SAW IT ON THE FLOOR IN THE SHOWER LAST NIGHT.
WELL, I *LOST* IT IN THE SHOWER TWO NIGHTS AGO, AND THEN I FOUND IT.
IT'S REALLY YOURS?
ARE YOU CALLING ME A LIAR?
NO, I JUST-- CAN'T BELIEVE IT.
I DON'T CARE, I'M NOT LYING! IT WAS A PRESENT FROM MY FATHER AND IT'S VERY SPECIAL TO ME.

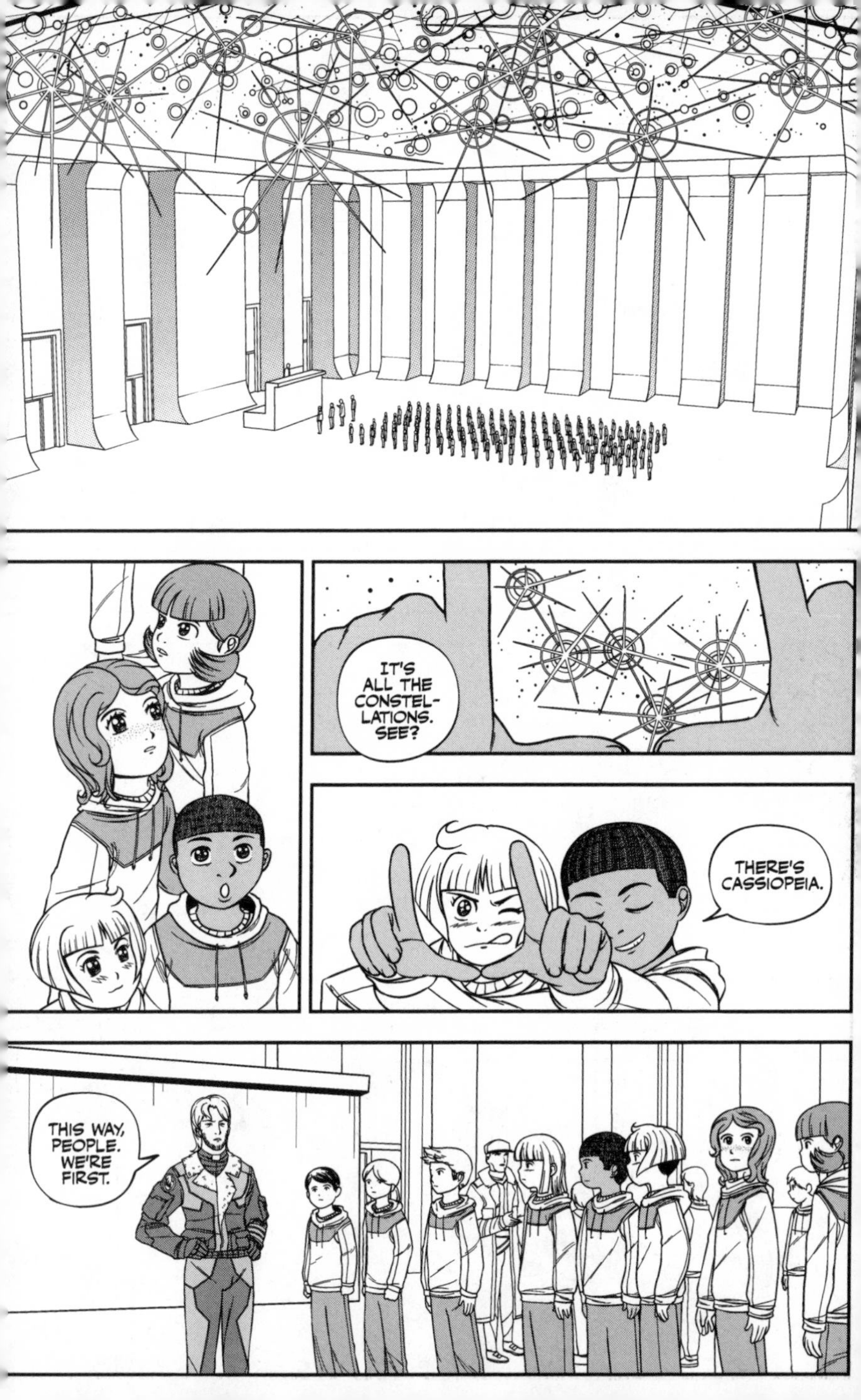
IT'S ALL THE CONSTEL-LATIONS. SEE?
THERE'S CASSIOPEIA.
THIS WAY, PEOPLE. WE'RE FIRST.

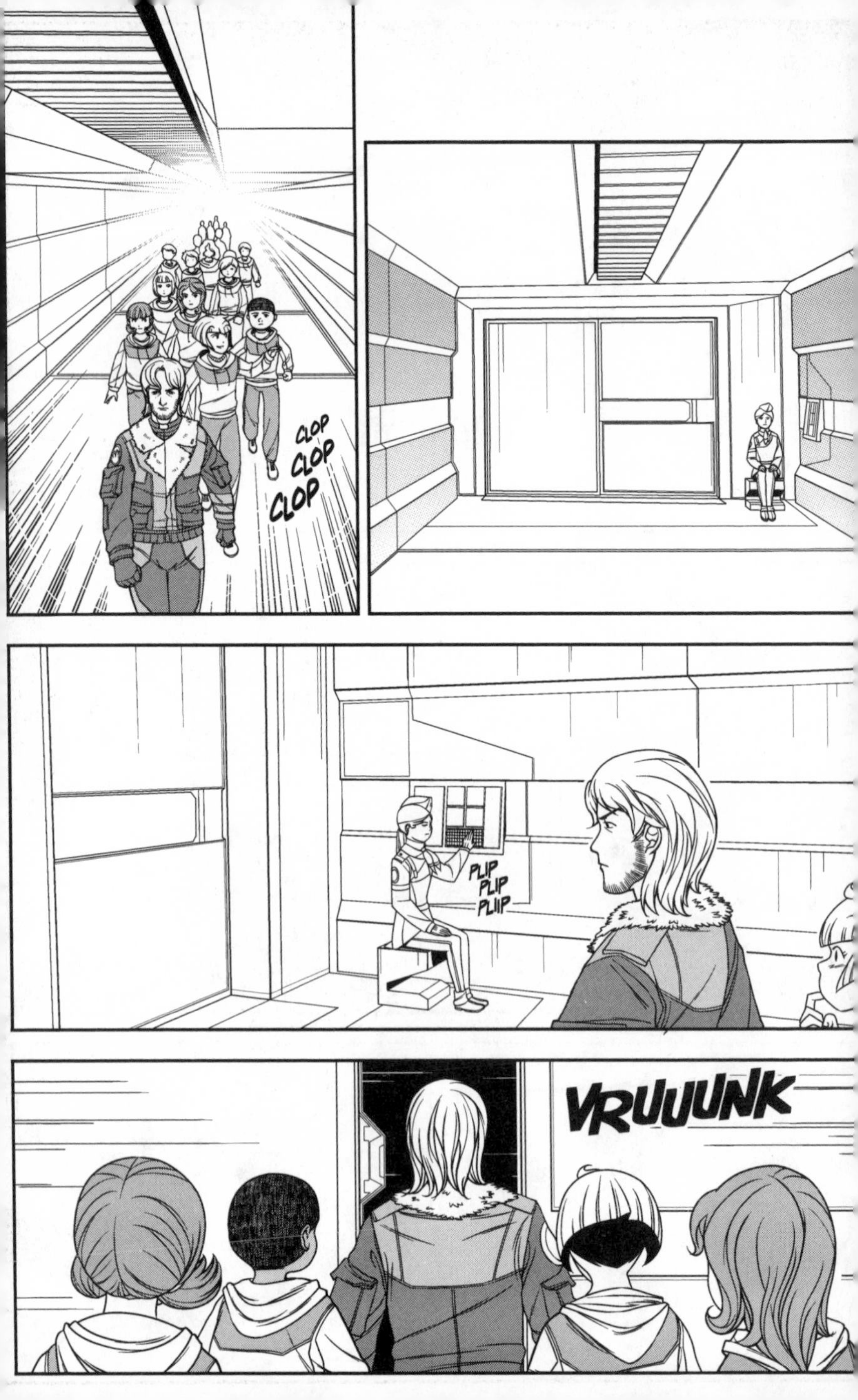
CLOP
CLOP
CLOP
PLIP
PLIP
PLIIP
VRUUUNK

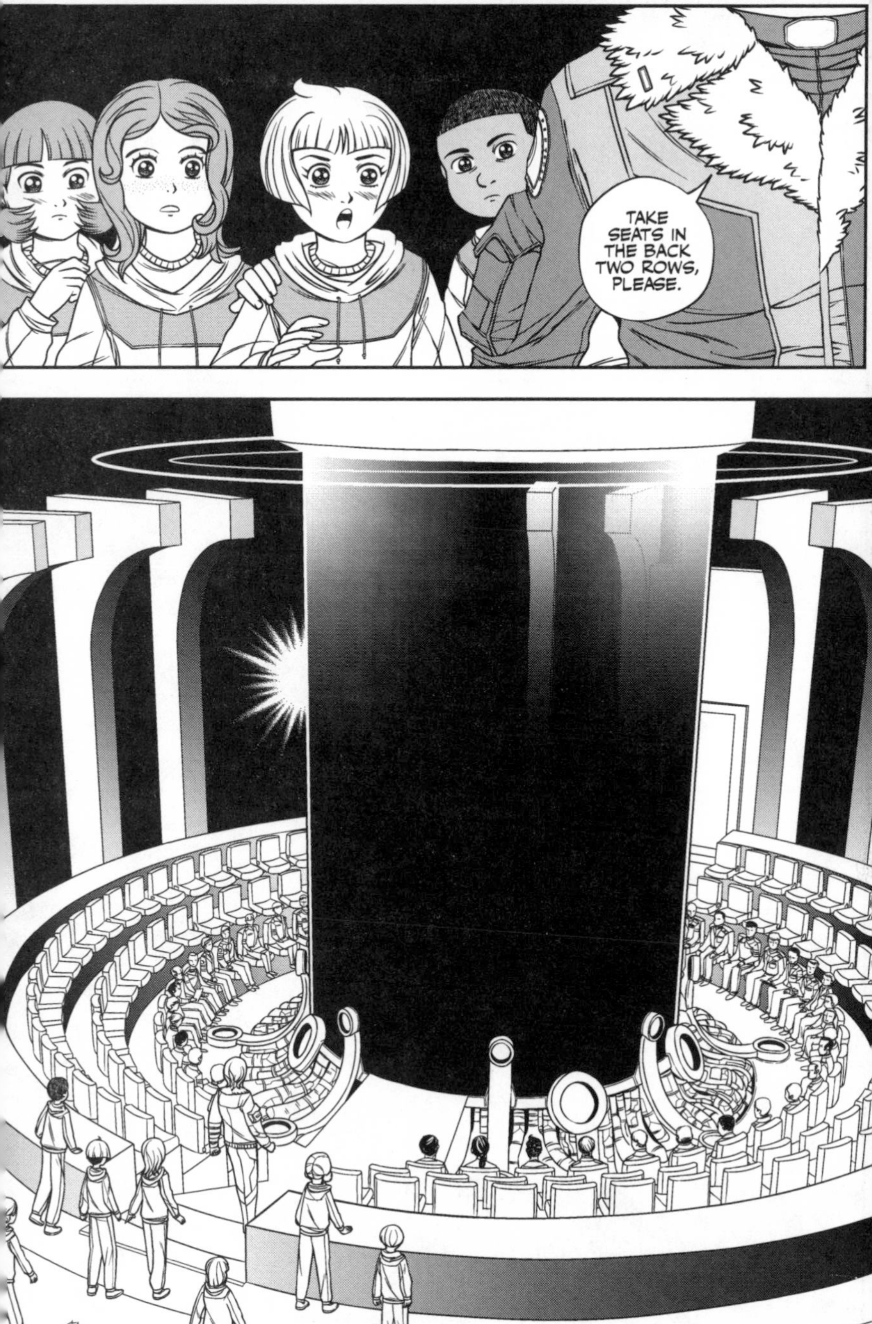
TAKE SEATS IN THE BACK TWO ROWS, PLEASE.

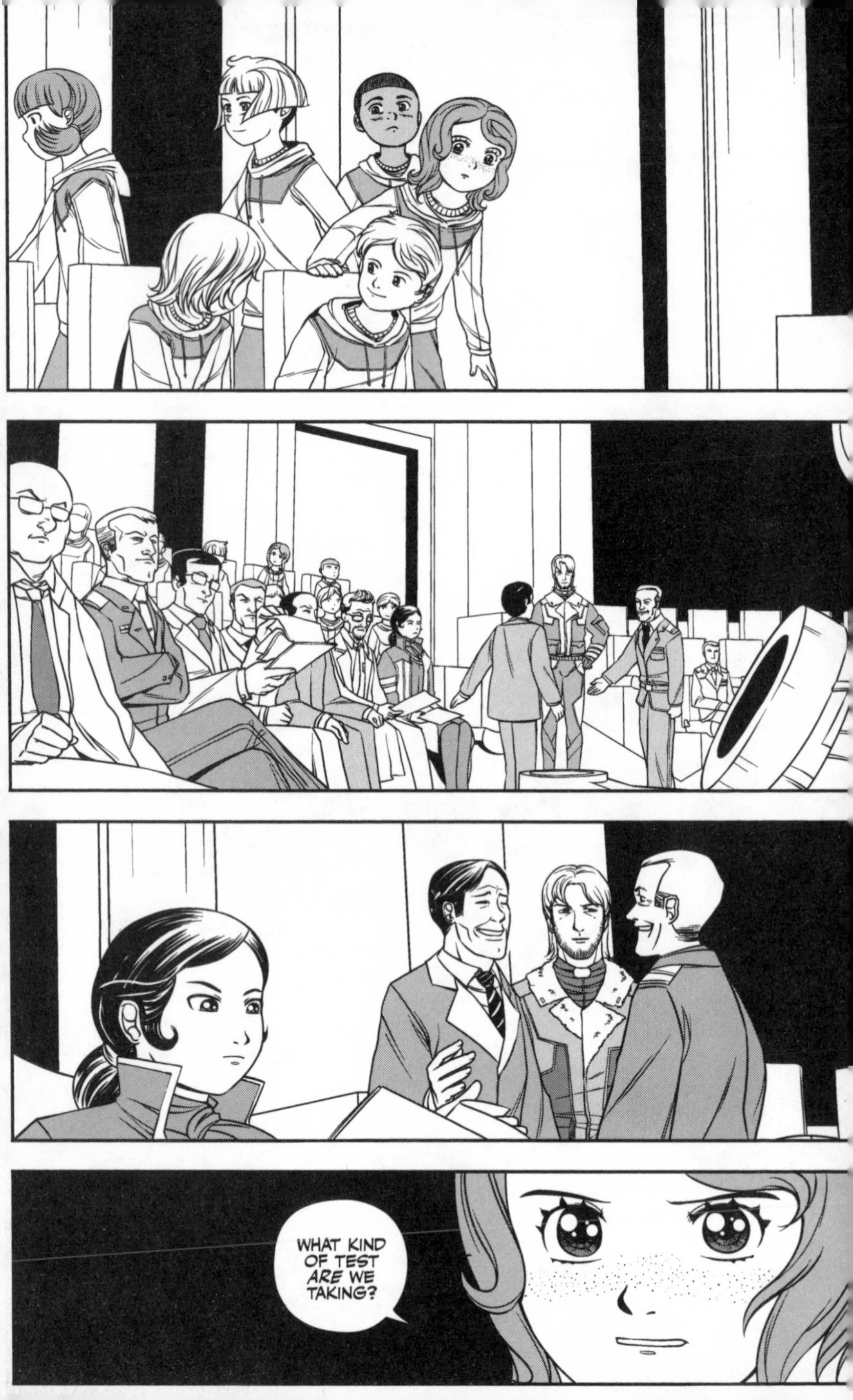
WHAT KIND OF TEST *ARE* WE TAKING?

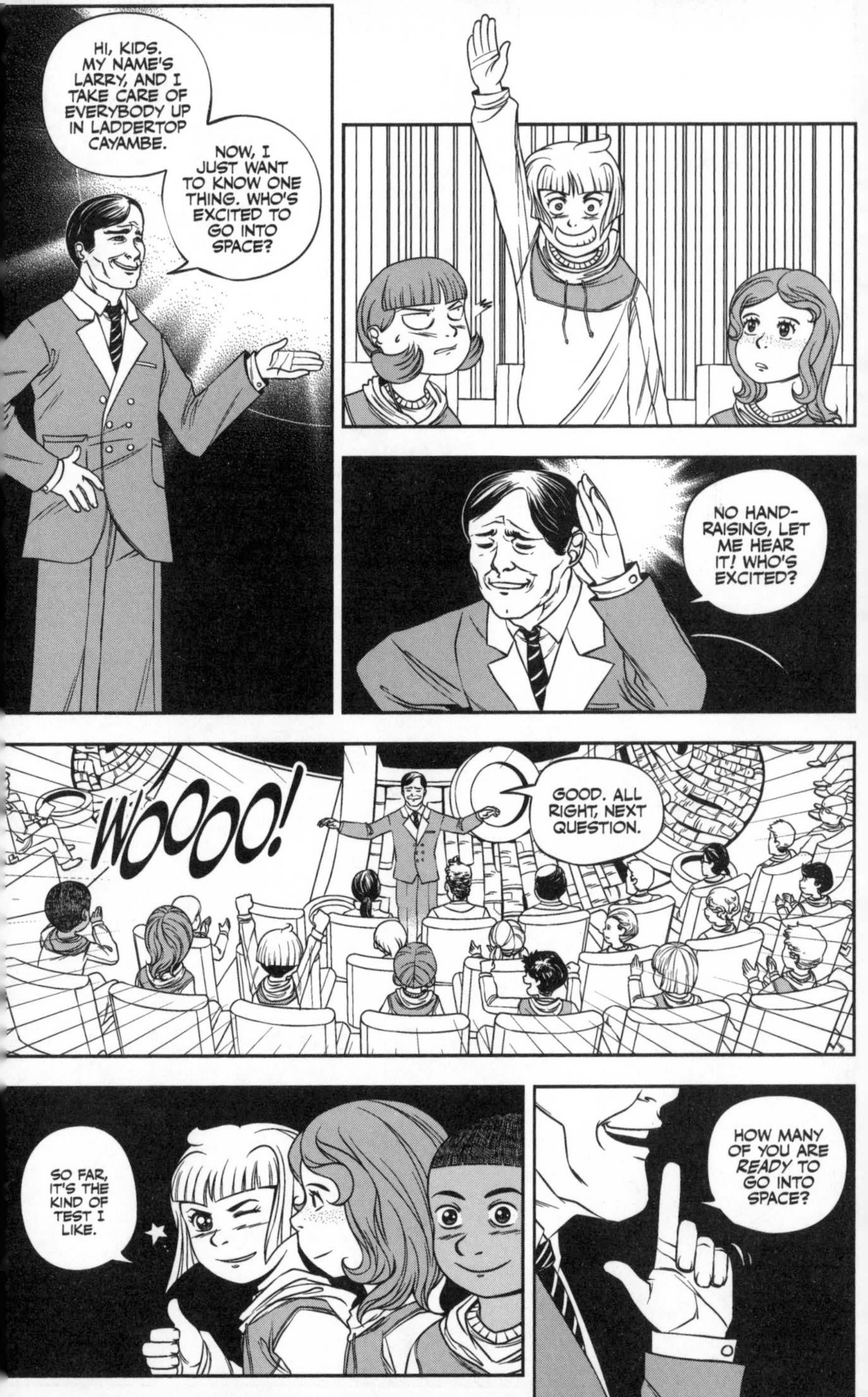
HI, KIDS. MY NAME'S LARRY, AND I TAKE CARE OF EVERYBODY UP IN LADDERTOP CAYAMBE.
NOW, I JUST WANT TO KNOW ONE THING. WHO'S EXCITED TO GO INTO SPACE?
NO HAND-RAISING, LET ME HEAR IT! WHO'S EXCITED?
WOOOO!
GOOD. ALL RIGHT, NEXT QUESTION.
SO FAR, IT'S THE KIND OF TEST I LIKE.
HOW MANY OF YOU ARE *READY* TO GO INTO SPACE?

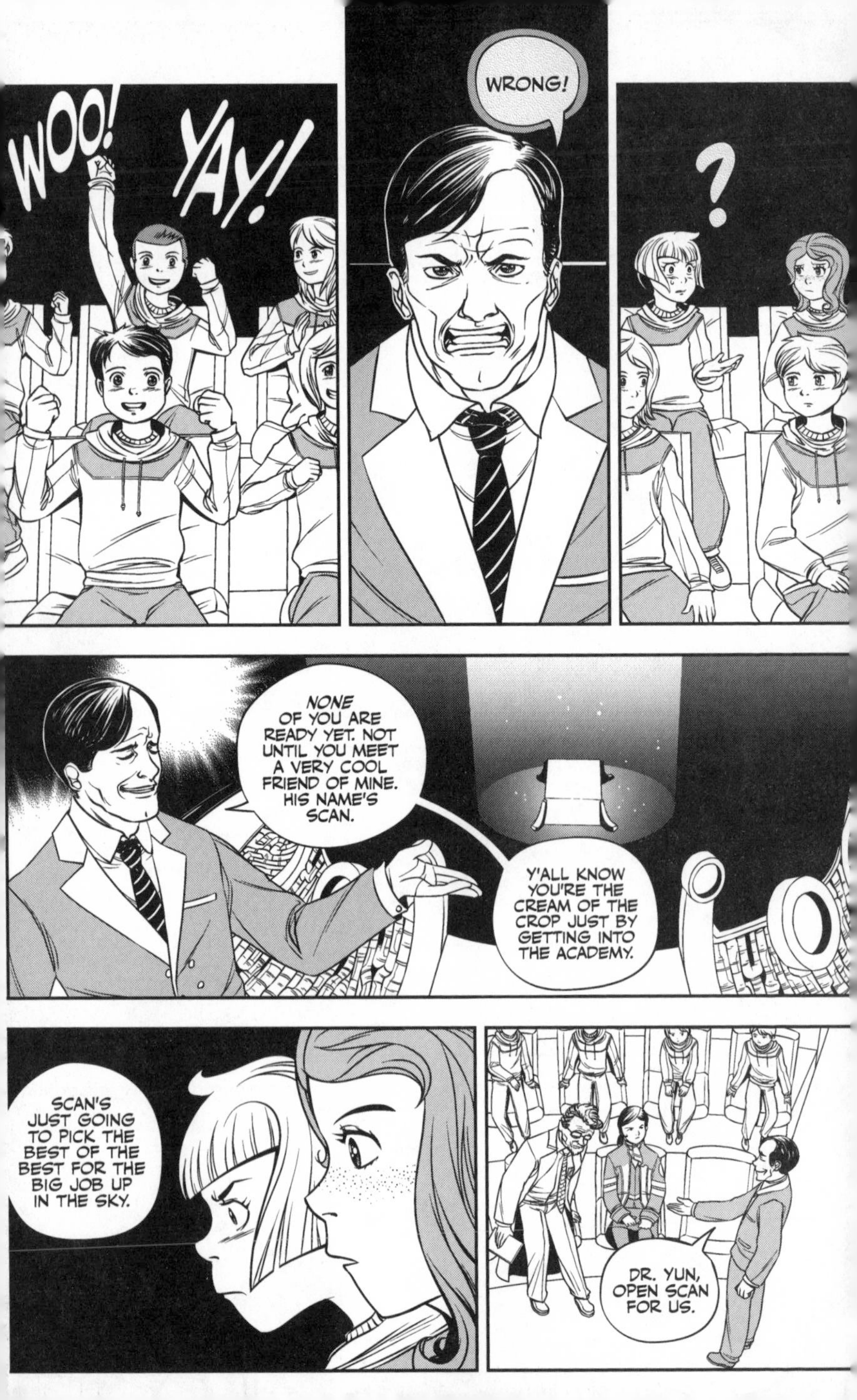
WOO!
YAY!
WRONG!
?
NONE OF YOU ARE READY YET. NOT UNTIL YOU MEET A VERY COOL FRIEND OF MINE. HIS NAME'S SCAN.
Y'ALL KNOW YOU'RE THE CREAM OF THE CROP JUST BY GETTING INTO THE ACADEMY.
SCAN'S JUST GOING TO PICK THE BEST OF THE BEST FOR THE BIG JOB UP IN THE SKY.
DR. YUN, OPEN SCAN FOR US.

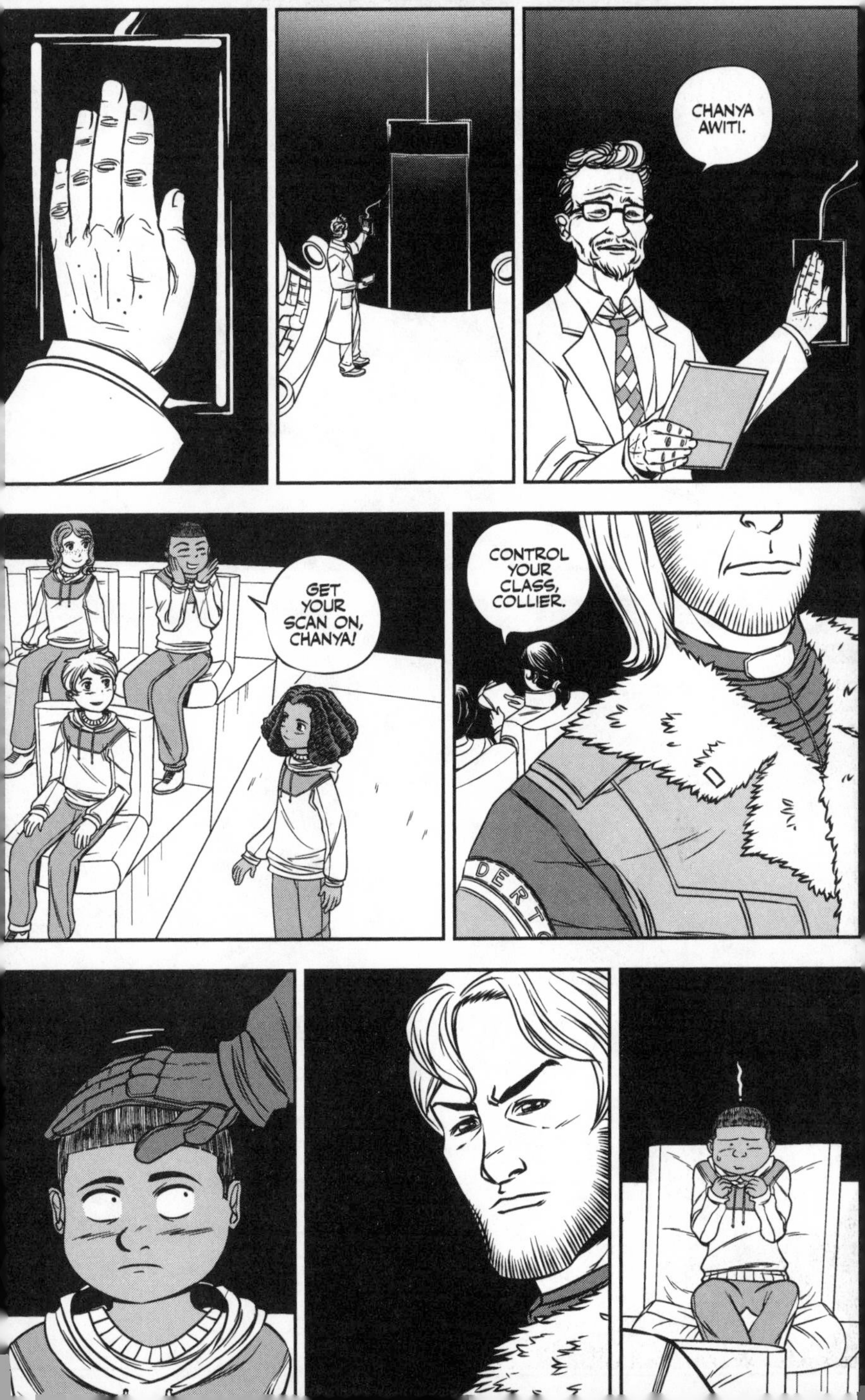
CHANYA AWITI.
GET YOUR SCAN ON, CHANYA!
CONTROL YOUR CLASS, COLLIER.

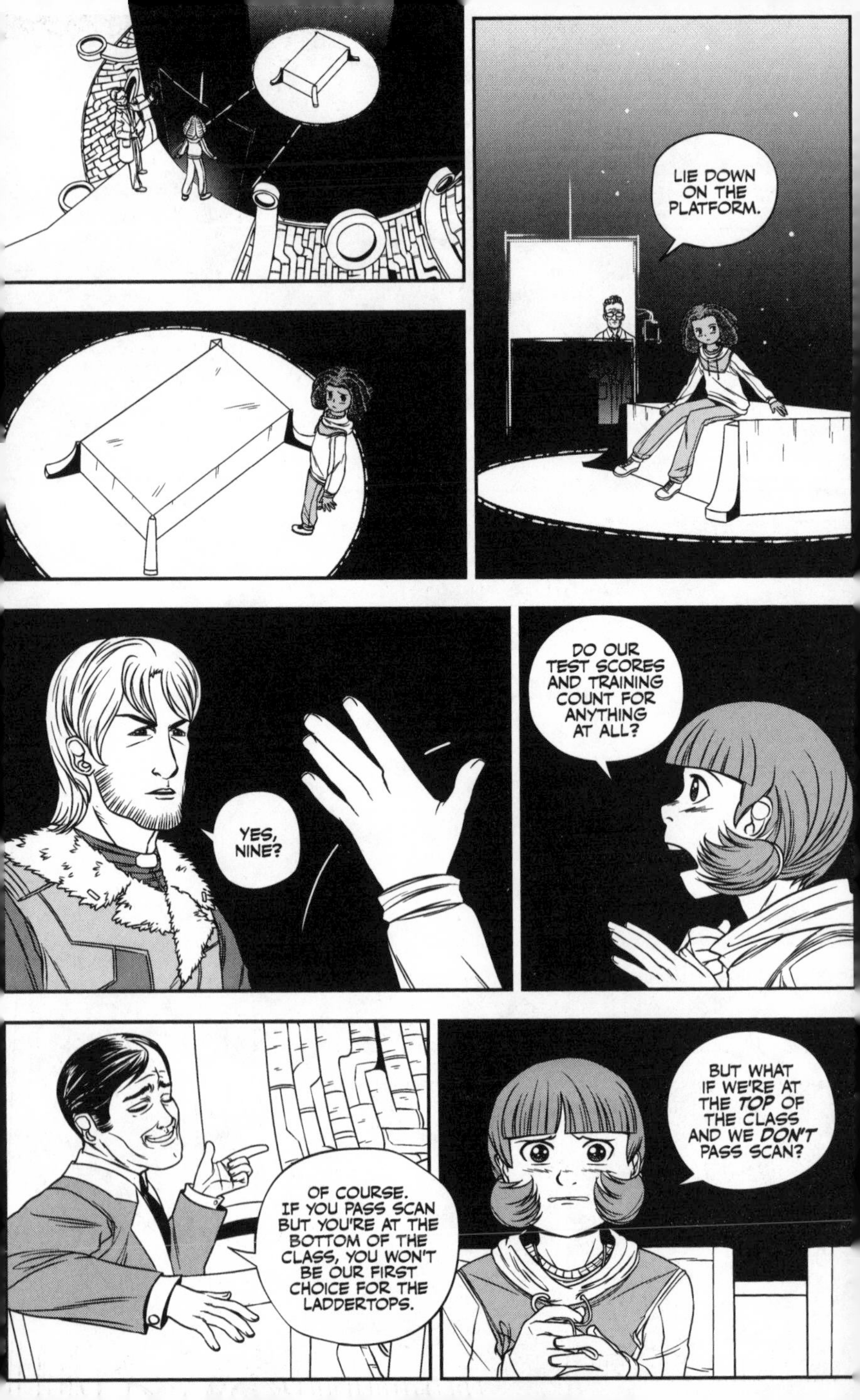
LIE DOWN ON THE PLATFORM.
YES, NINE?
DO OUR TEST SCORES AND TRAINING COUNT FOR ANYTHING AT ALL?
OF COURSE. IF YOU PASS SCAN BUT YOU'RE AT THE BOTTOM OF THE CLASS, YOU WON'T BE OUR FIRST CHOICE FOR THE LADDERTOPS.
BUT WHAT IF WE'RE AT THE *TOP* OF THE CLASS AND WE *DON'T* PASS SCAN?

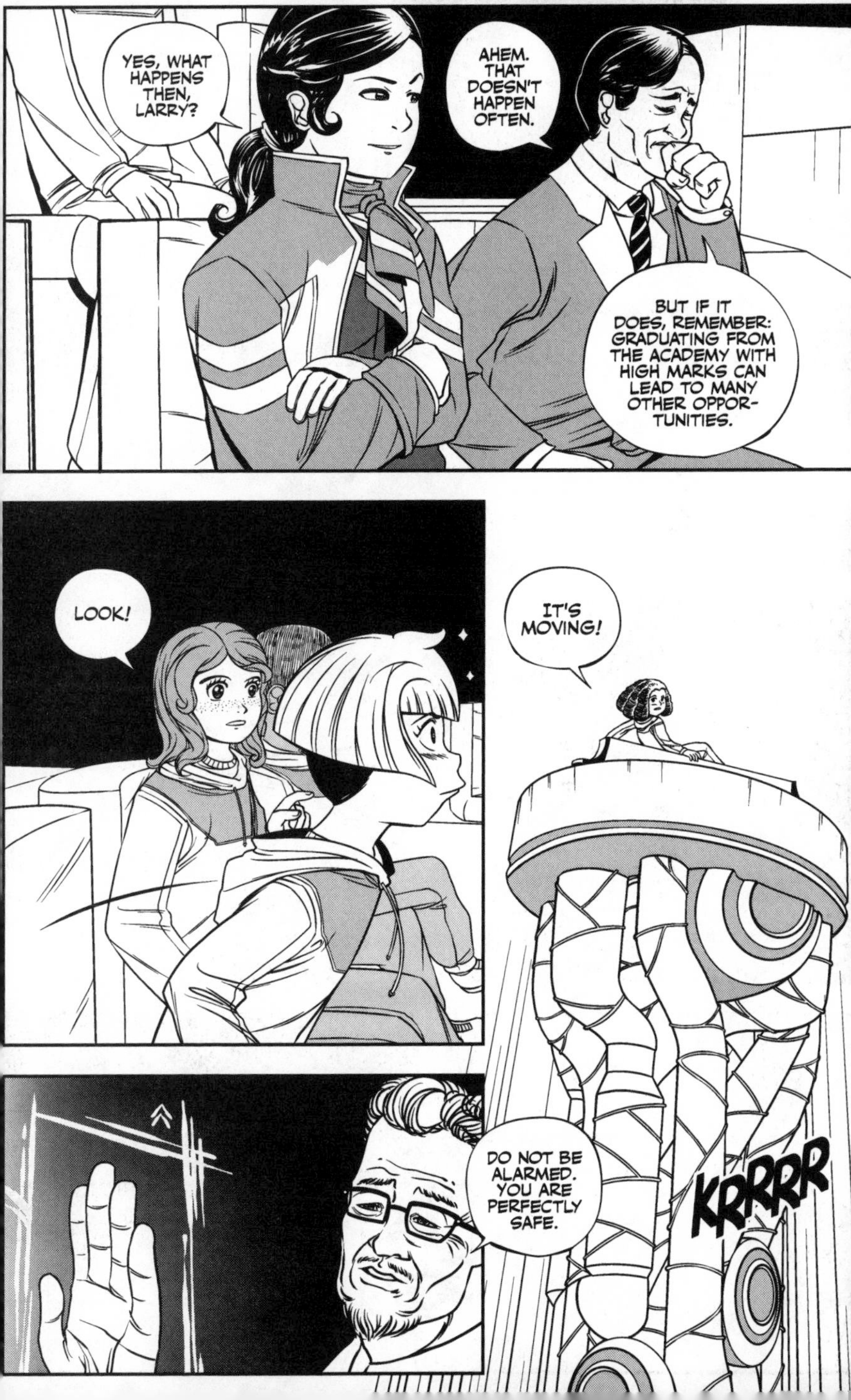
YES, WHAT HAPPENS THEN, LARRY?
AHEM. THAT DOESN'T HAPPEN OFTEN.
BUT IF IT DOES, REMEMBER: GRADUATING FROM THE ACADEMY WITH HIGH MARKS CAN LEAD TO MANY OTHER OPPOR-TUNITIES.
LOOK!
IT'S MOVING!
DO NOT BE ALARMED. YOU ARE PERFECTLY SAFE.
KRRRR

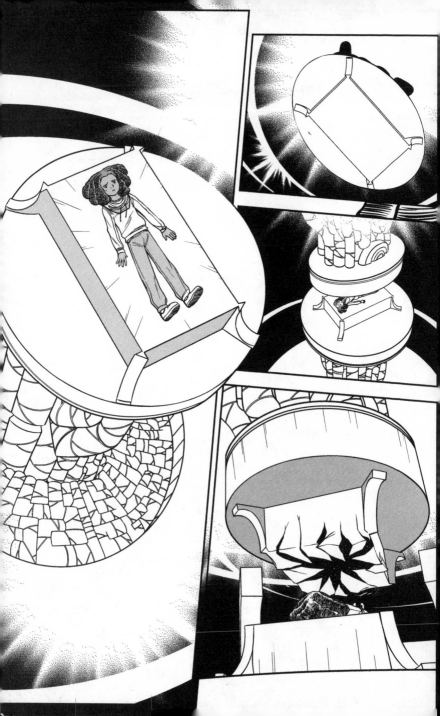

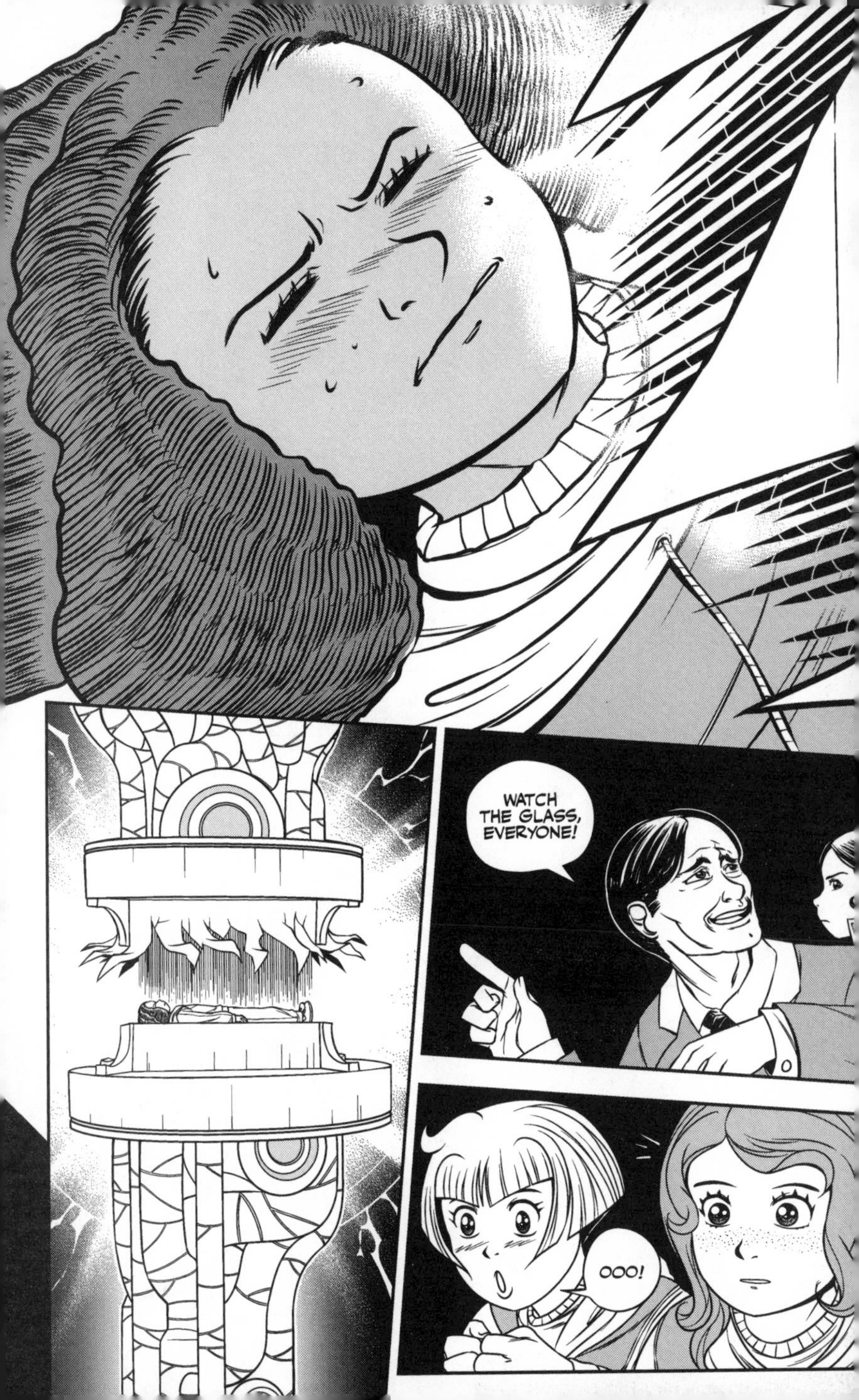
WATCH THE GLASS, EVERYONE!
OOO!

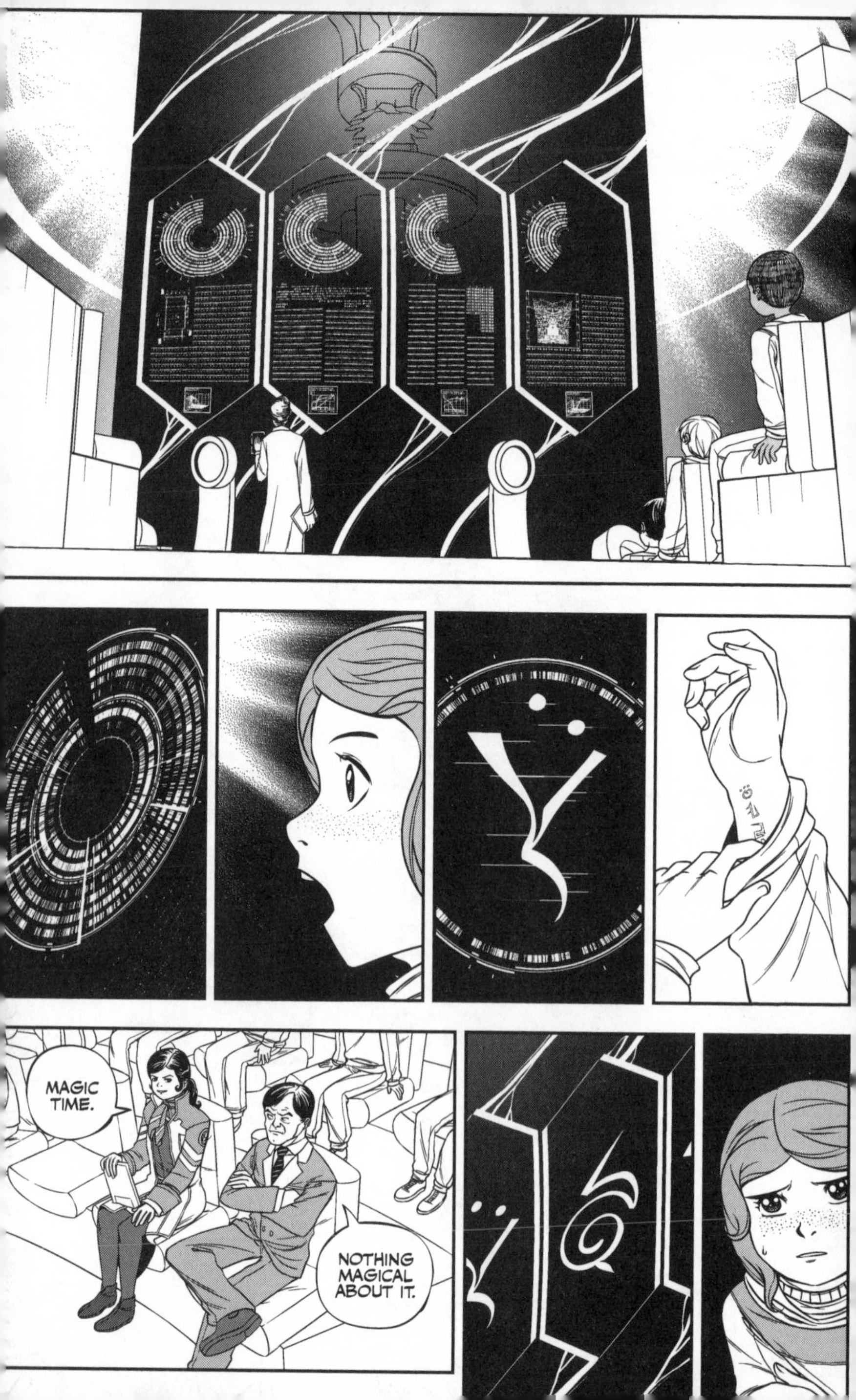
MAGIC TIME.
NOTHING MAGICAL ABOUT IT.

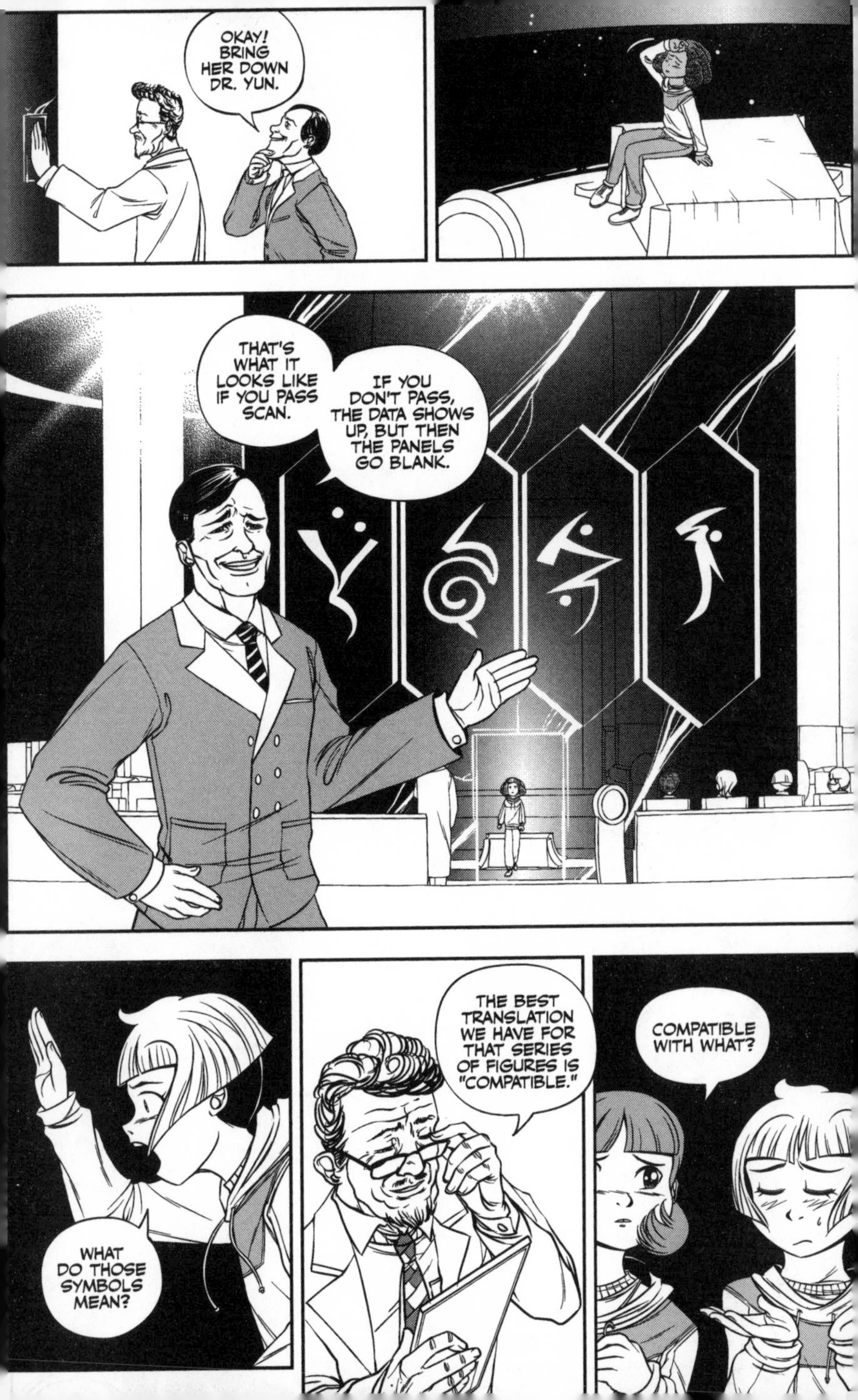
OKAY! BRING HER DOWN DR. YUN.
THAT'S WHAT IT LOOKS LIKE IF YOU PASS SCAN.
IF YOU DON'T PASS, THE DATA SHOWS UP, BUT THEN THE PANELS GO BLANK.
WHAT DO THOSE SYMBOLS MEAN?
THE BEST TRANSLATION WE HAVE FOR THAT SERIES OF FIGURES IS "COMPATIBLE."
COMPATIBLE WITH WHAT?

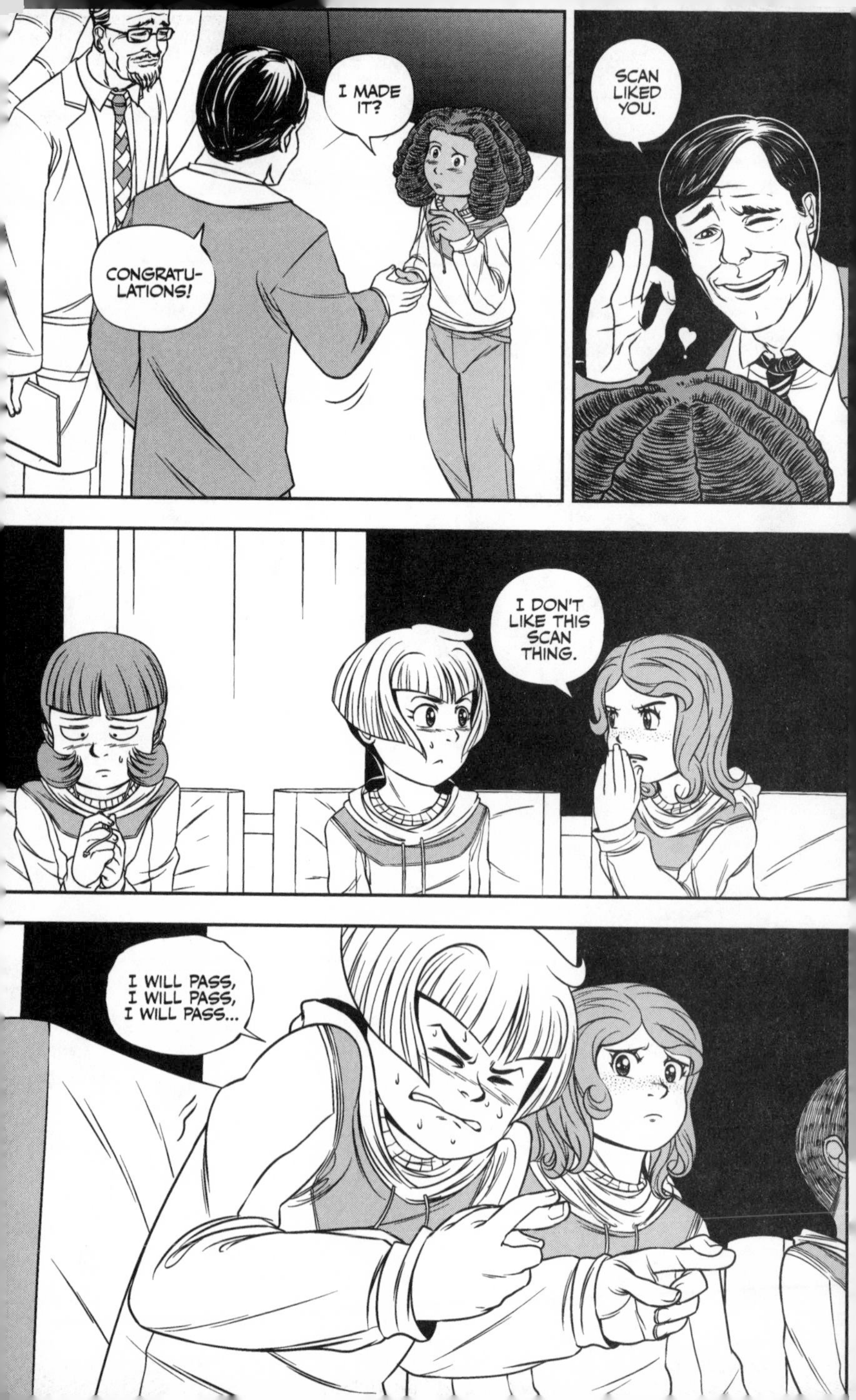
I MADE IT?
CONGRATU-LATIONS!
SCAN LIKED YOU.
I DON'T LIKE THIS SCAN THING.
I WILL PASS, I WILL PASS, I WILL PASS...

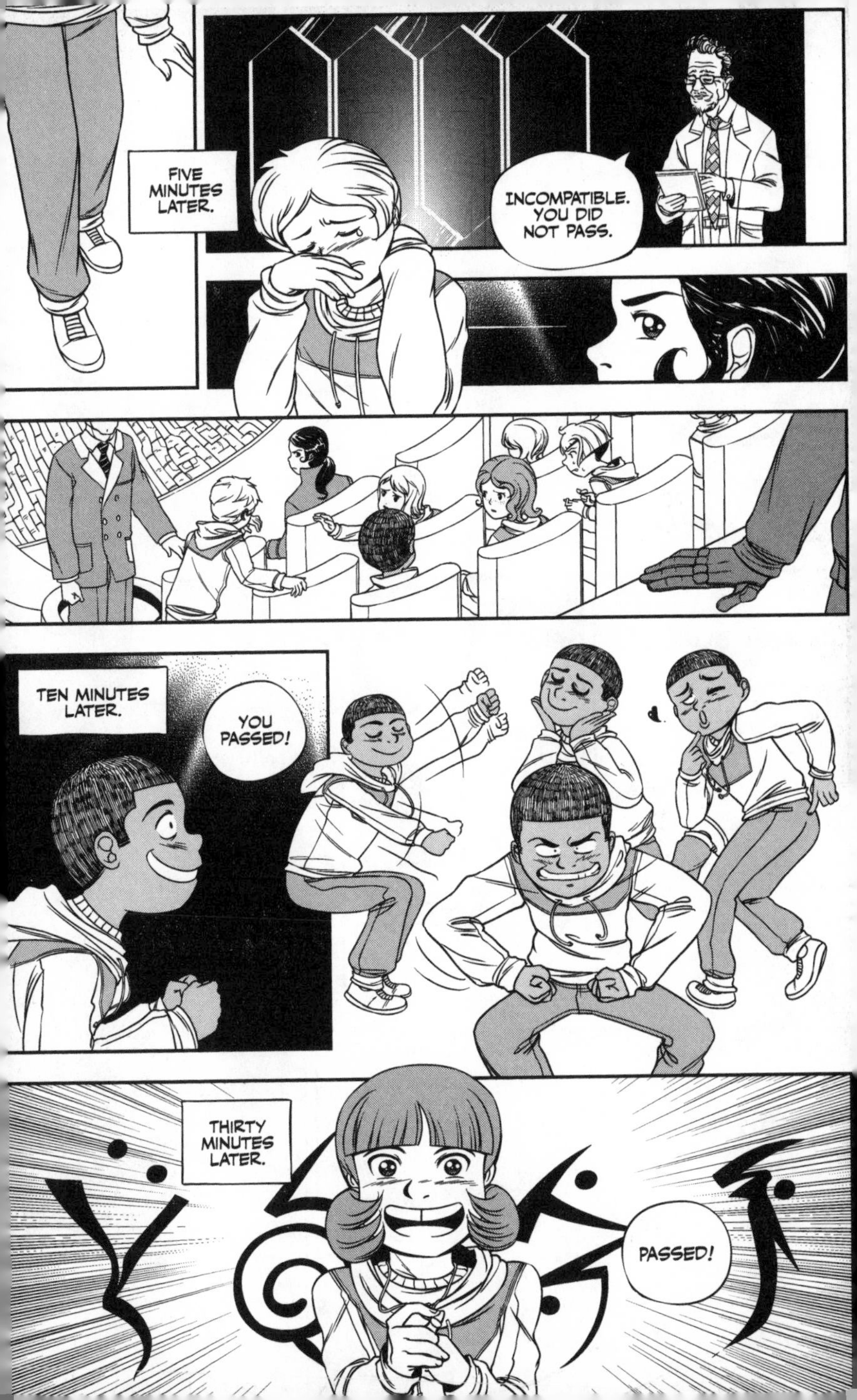
FIVE MINUTES LATER.
INCOMPATIBLE. YOU DID NOT PASS.
TEN MINUTES LATER.
YOU PASSED!
THIRTY MINUTES LATER.
PASSED!

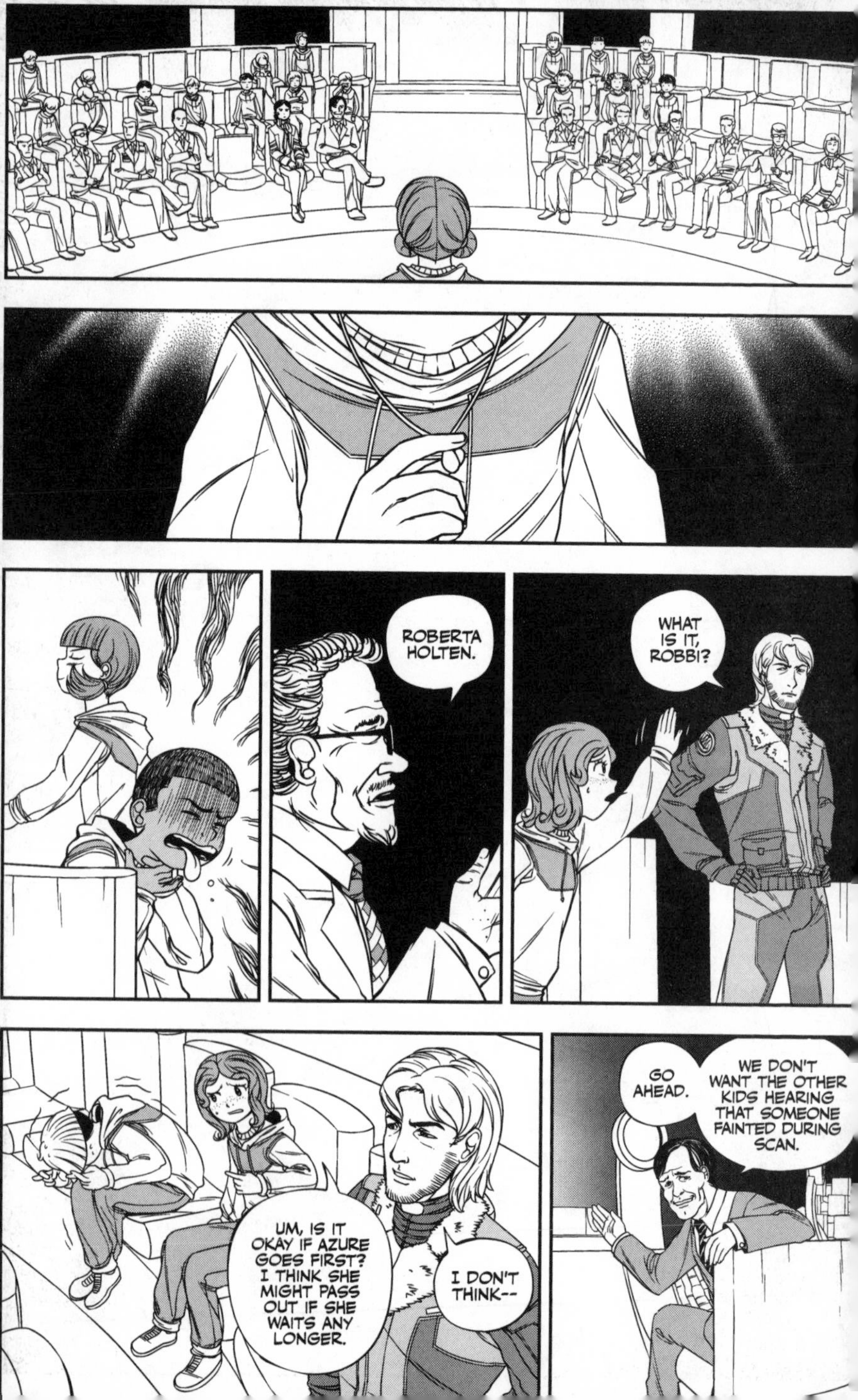
ROBERTA HOLTEN.
WHAT IS IT, ROBBI?
UM, IS IT OKAY IF AZURE GOES FIRST? I THINK SHE MIGHT PASS OUT IF SHE WAITS ANY LONGER.
I DON'T THINK--
GO AHEAD.
WE DON'T WANT THE OTHER KIDS HEARING THAT SOMEONE FAINTED DURING SCAN.

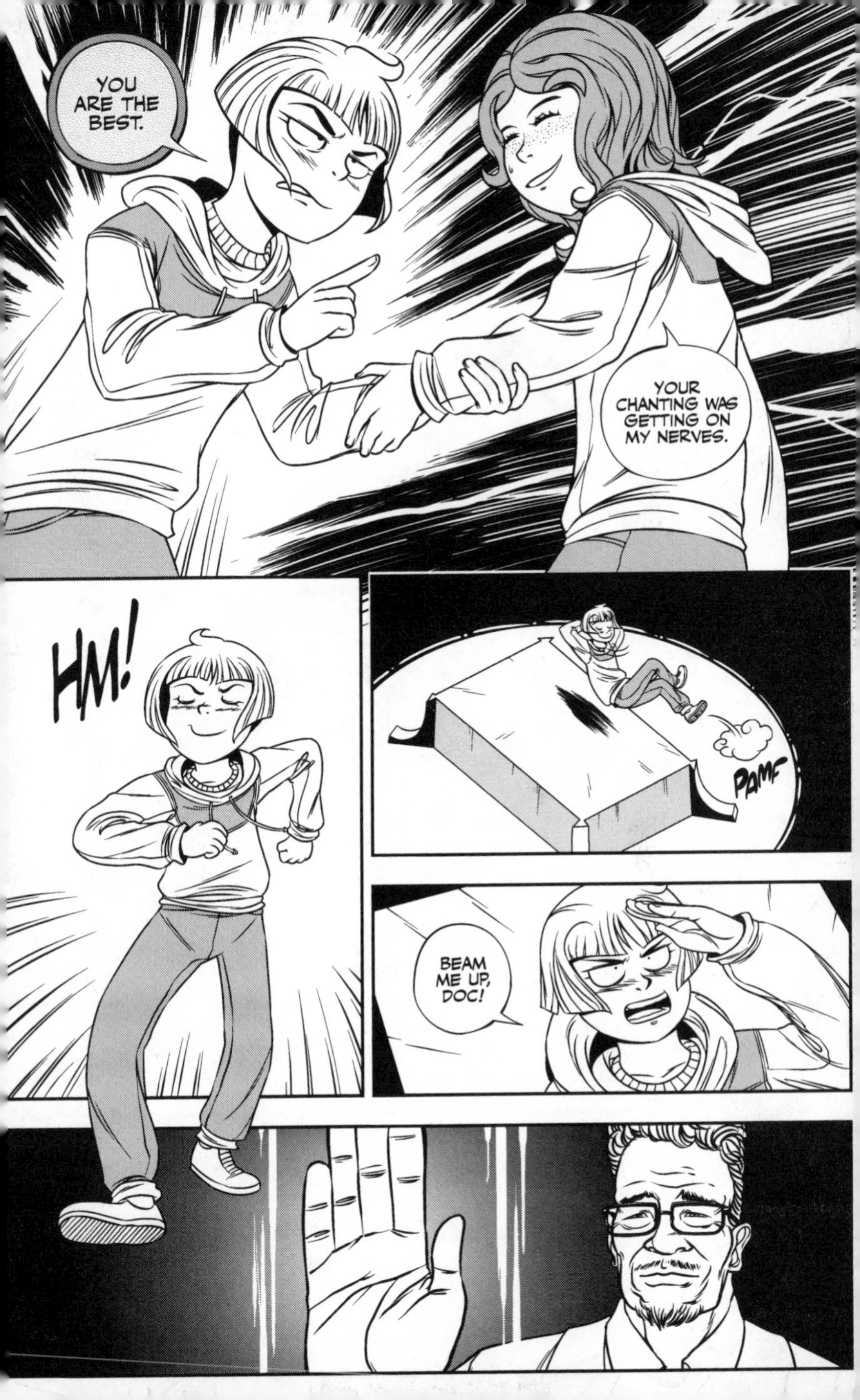

YOU ARE THE BEST.
YOUR CHANTING WAS GETTING ON MY NERVES.
HM!
PAMF
BEAM ME UP, DOC!

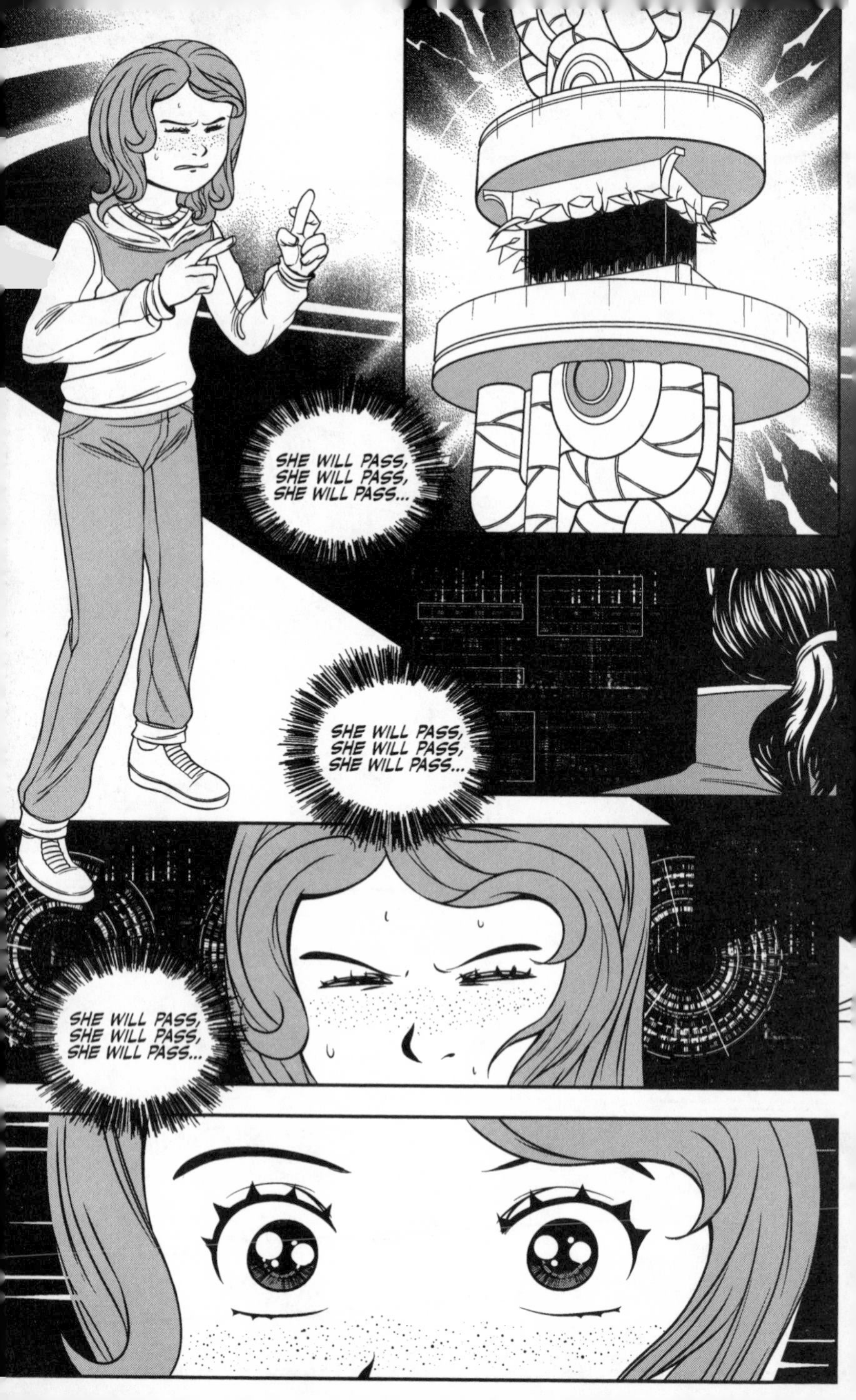
SHE WILL PASS, SHE WILL PASS, SHE WILL PASS...
SHE WILL PASS, SHE WILL PASS, SHE WILL PASS...
SHE WILL PASS, SHE WILL PASS, SHE WILL PASS...

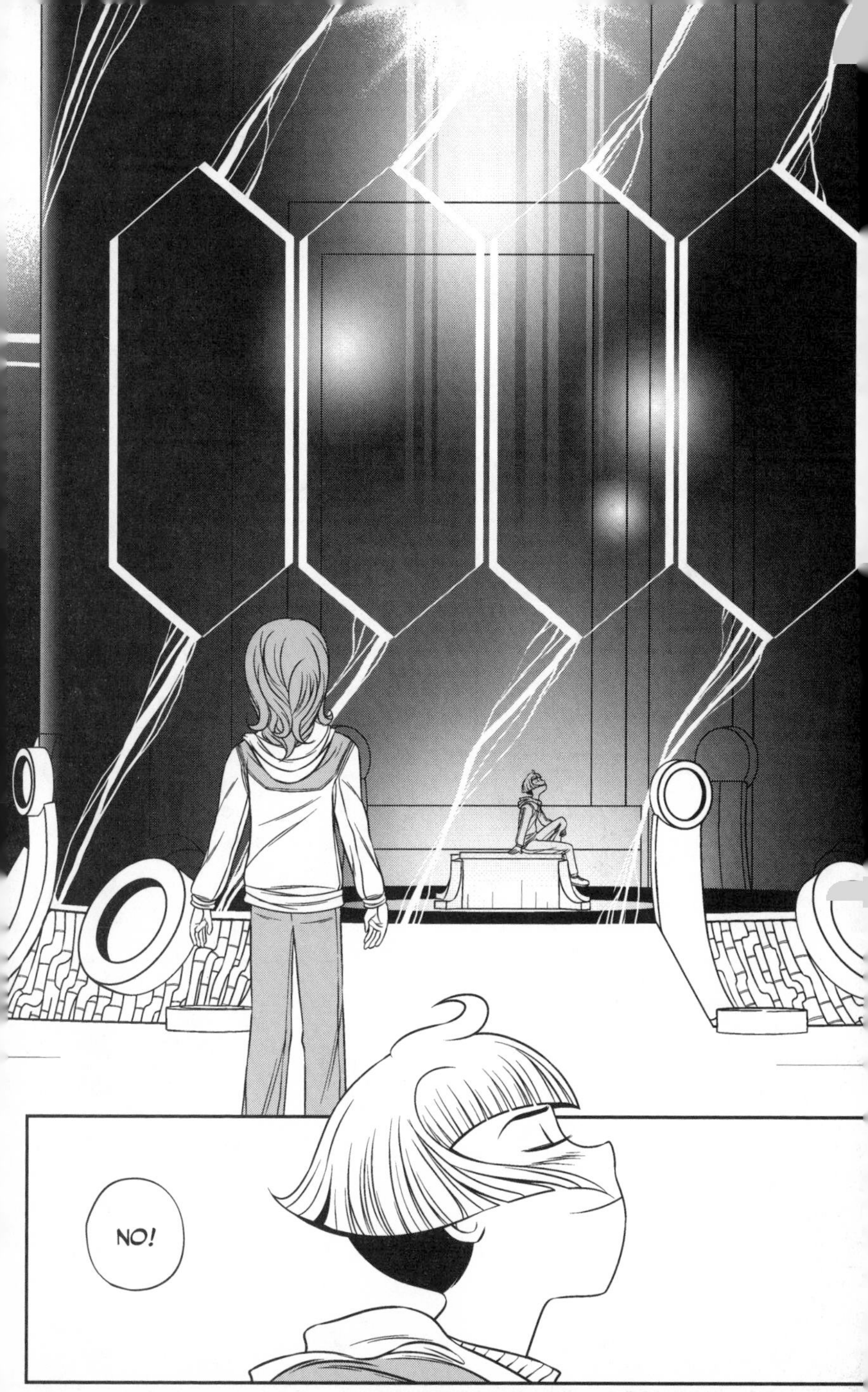
NO!

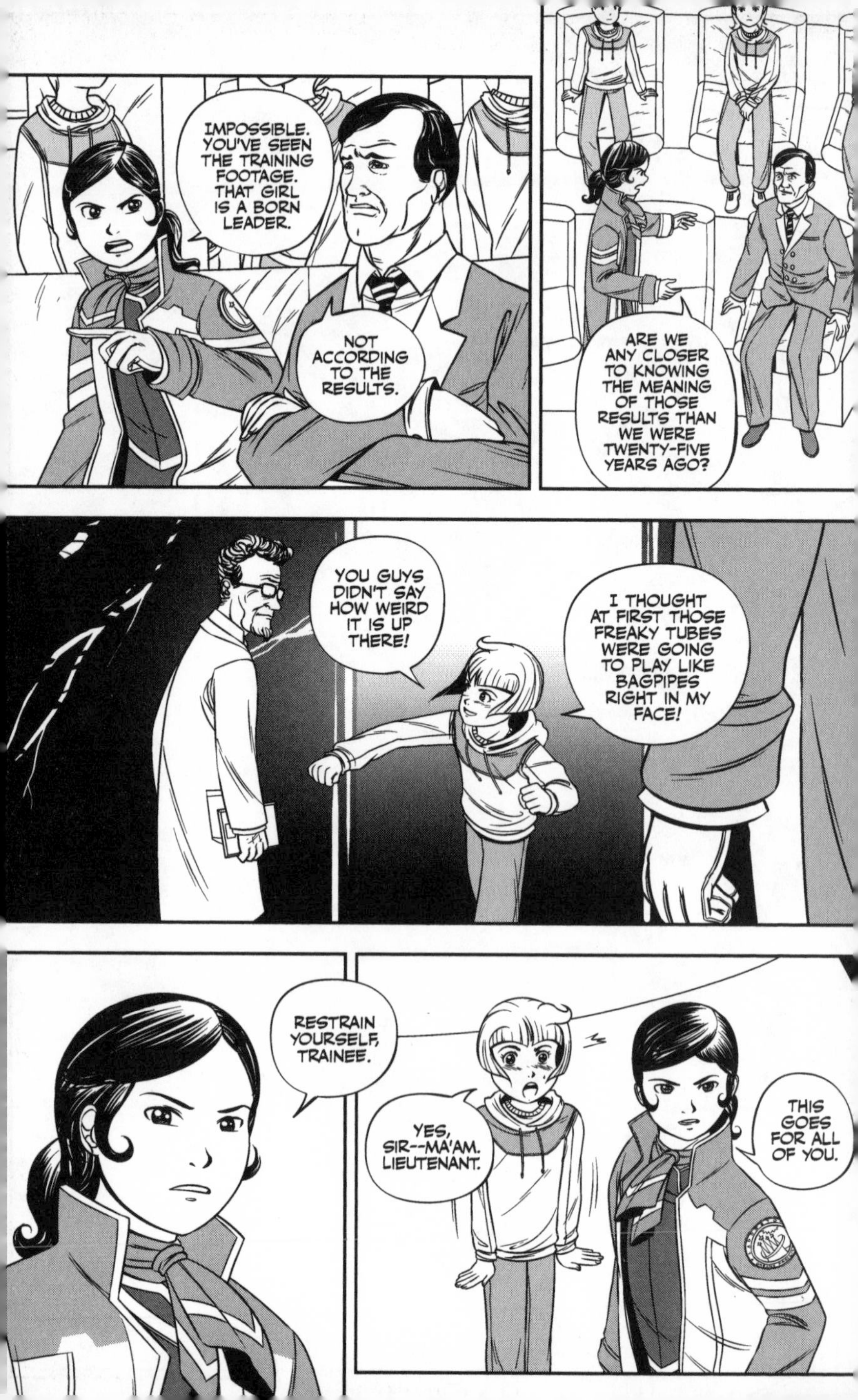
IMPOSSIBLE. YOU'VE SEEN THE TRAINING FOOTAGE. THAT GIRL IS A BORN LEADER.
NOT ACCORDING TO THE RESULTS.
ARE WE ANY CLOSER TO KNOWING THE MEANING OF THOSE RESULTS THAN WE WERE TWENTY-FIVE YEARS AGO?
YOU GUYS DIDN'T SAY HOW WEIRD IT IS UP THERE!
I THOUGHT AT FIRST THOSE FREAKY TUBES WERE GOING TO PLAY LIKE BAGPIPES RIGHT IN MY FACE!
RESTRAIN YOURSELF, TRAINEE.
YES, SIR--MA'AM. LIEUTENANT.
THIS GOES FOR ALL OF YOU.

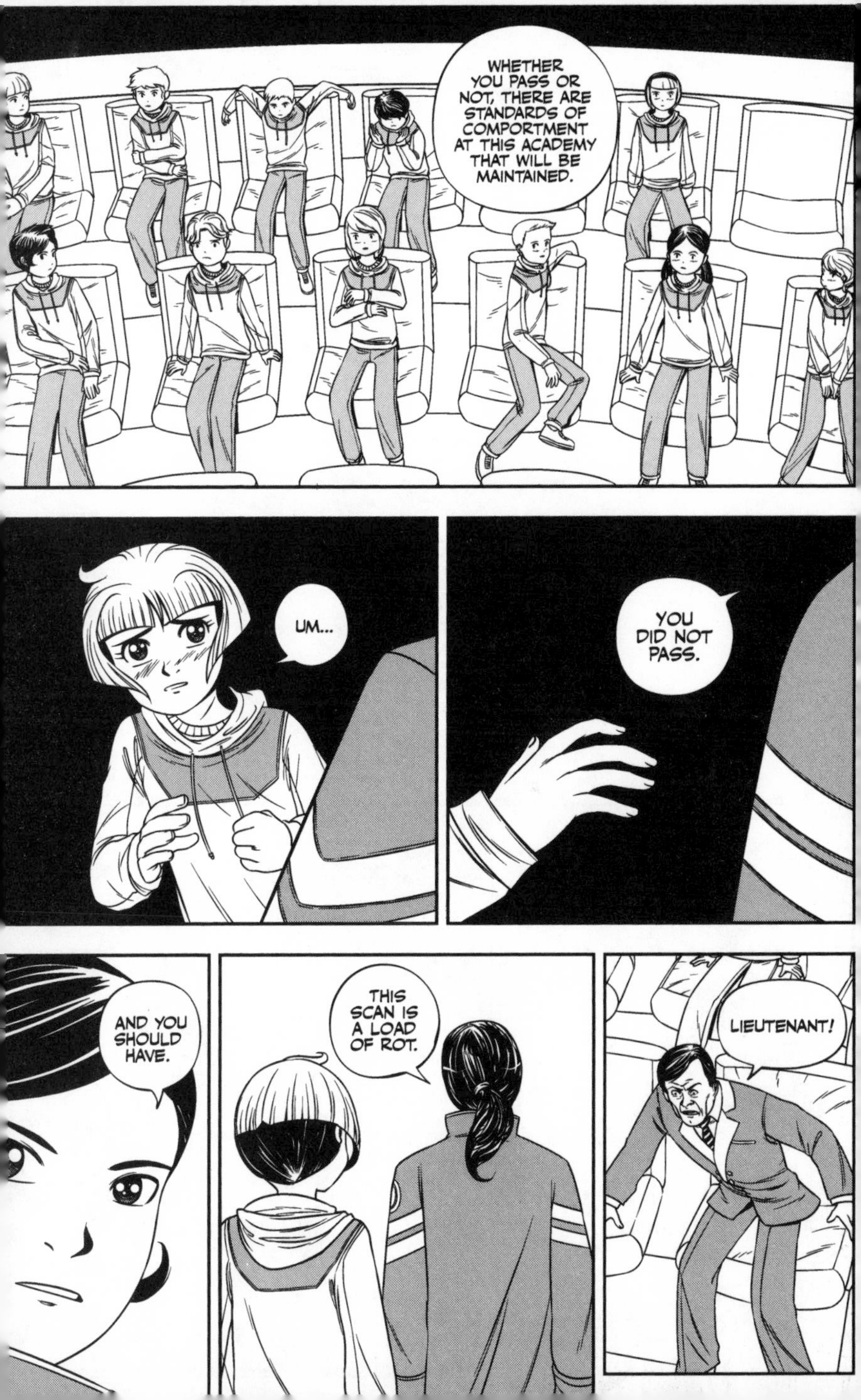
WHETHER YOU PASS OR NOT, THERE ARE STANDARDS OF COMPORTMENT AT THIS ACADEMY THAT WILL BE MAINTAINED.
UM...
YOU DID NOT PASS.
AND YOU SHOULD HAVE.
THIS SCAN IS A LOAD OF ROT.
LIEUTENANT!

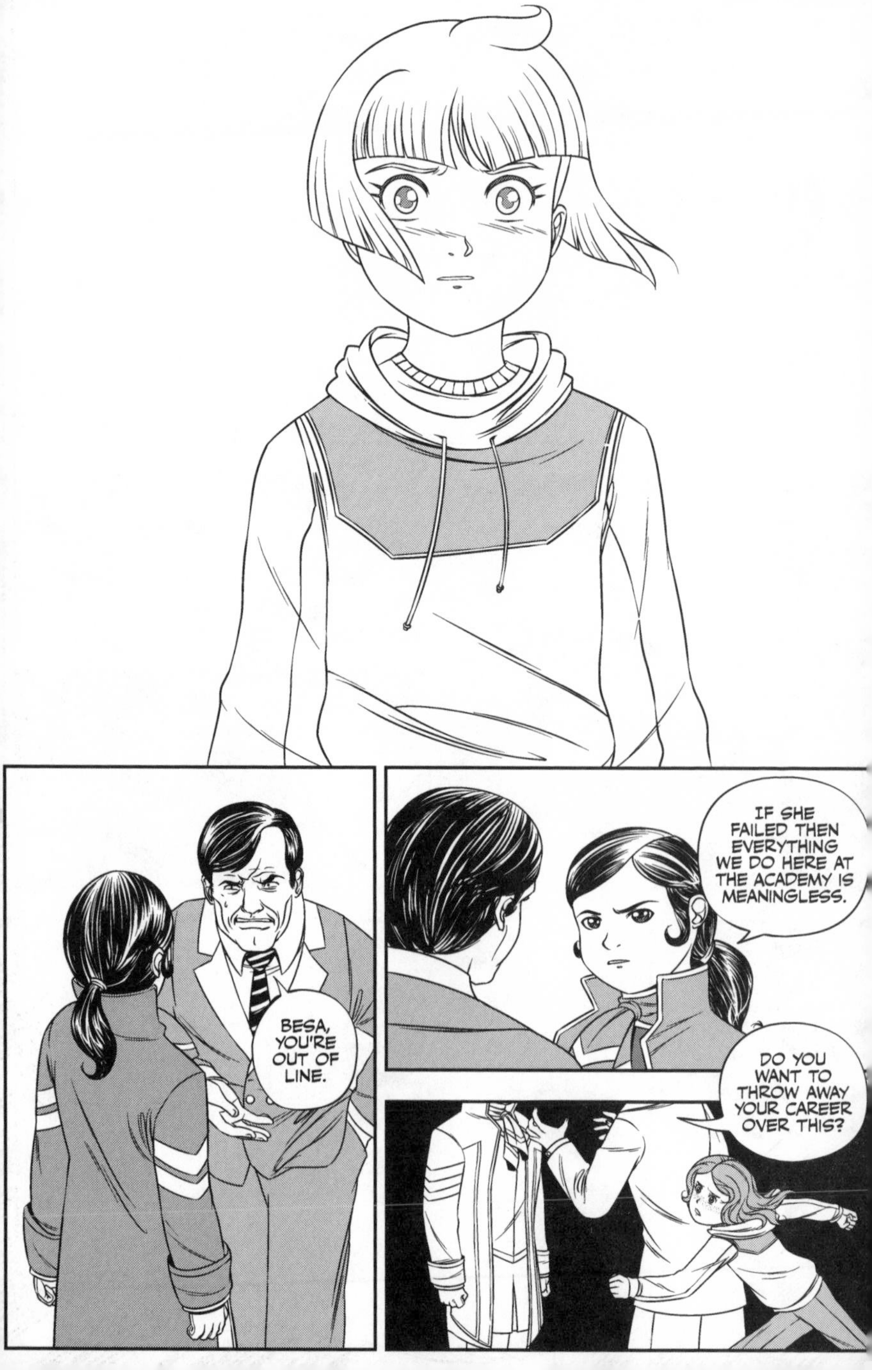
BESA, YOU'RE OUT OF LINE.
IF SHE FAILED THEN EVERYTHING WE DO HERE AT THE ACADEMY IS MEANINGLESS.
DO YOU WANT TO THROW AWAY YOUR CAREER OVER THIS?

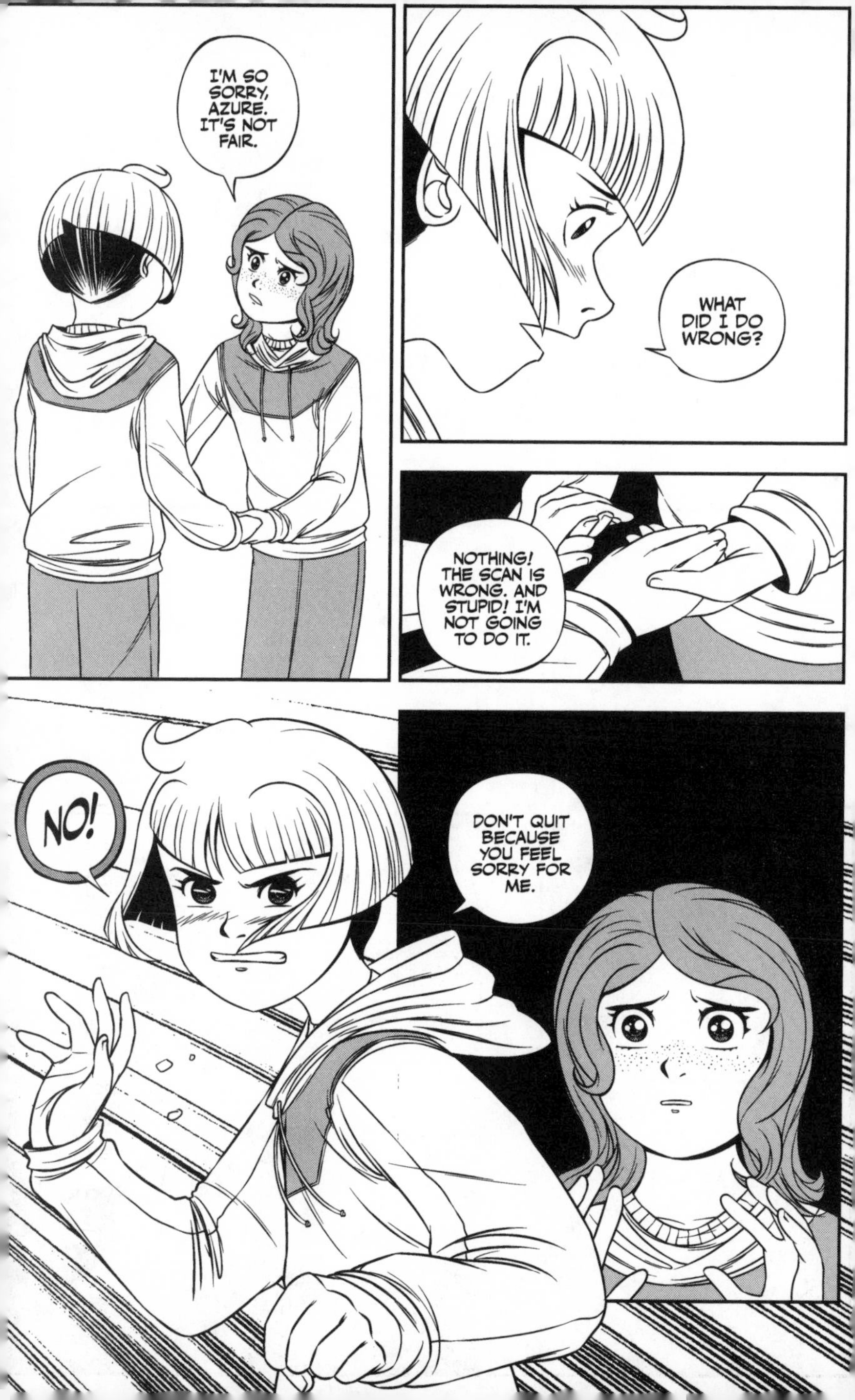
I'M SO SORRY, AZURE. IT'S NOT FAIR.
WHAT DID I DO WRONG?
NOTHING! THE SCAN IS WRONG. AND STUPID! I'M NOT GOING TO DO IT.
NO!
DON'T QUIT BECAUSE YOU FEEL SORRY FOR ME.

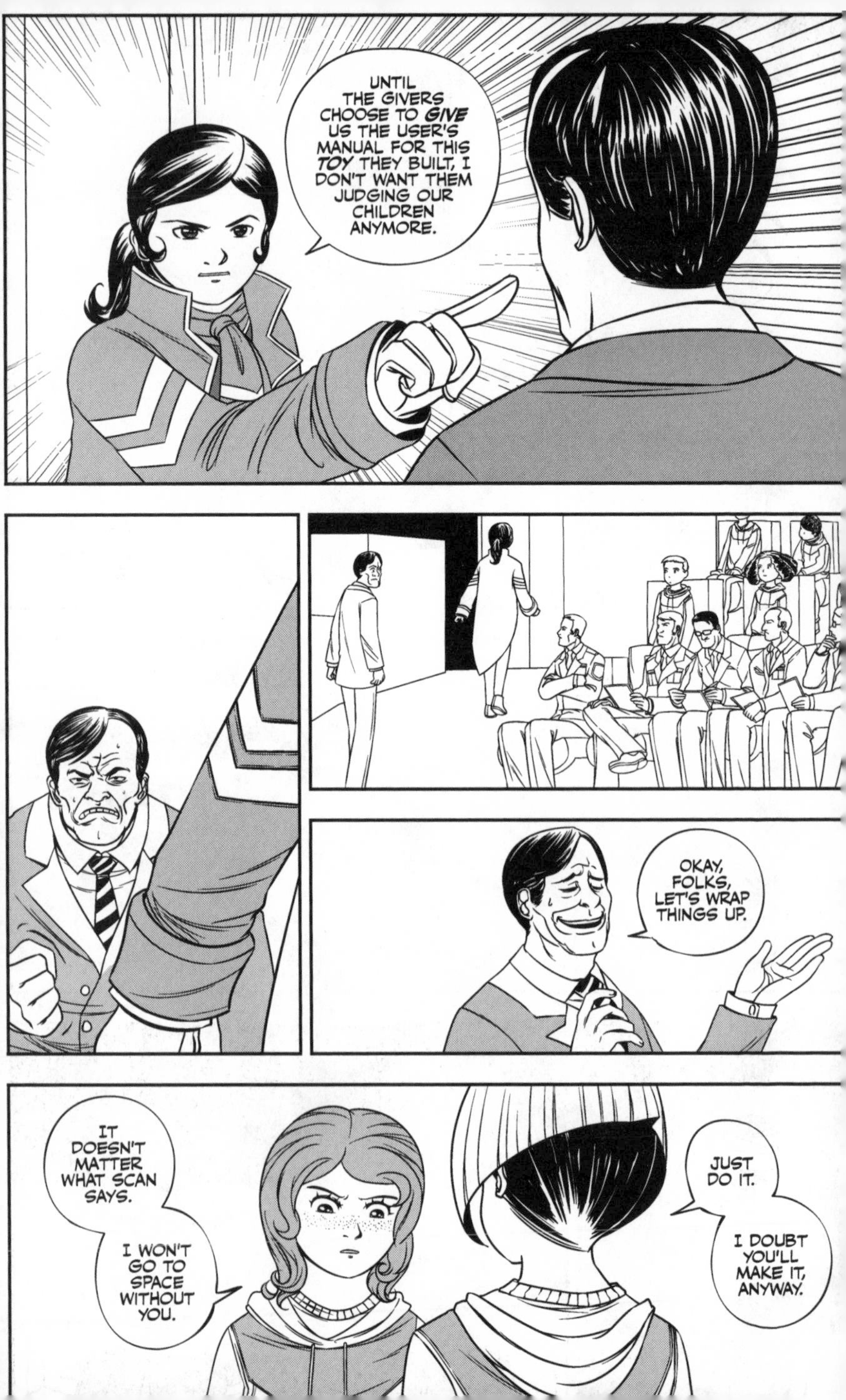
UNTIL THE GIVERS CHOOSE TO *GIVE* US THE USER'S MANUAL FOR THIS *TOY* THEY BUILT, I DON'T WANT THEM JUDGING OUR CHILDREN ANYMORE.
OKAY, FOLKS, LET'S WRAP THINGS UP.
IT DOESN'T MATTER WHAT SCAN SAYS.
I WON'T GO TO SPACE WITHOUT YOU.
JUST DO IT.
I DOUBT YOU'LL MAKE IT, ANYWAY.

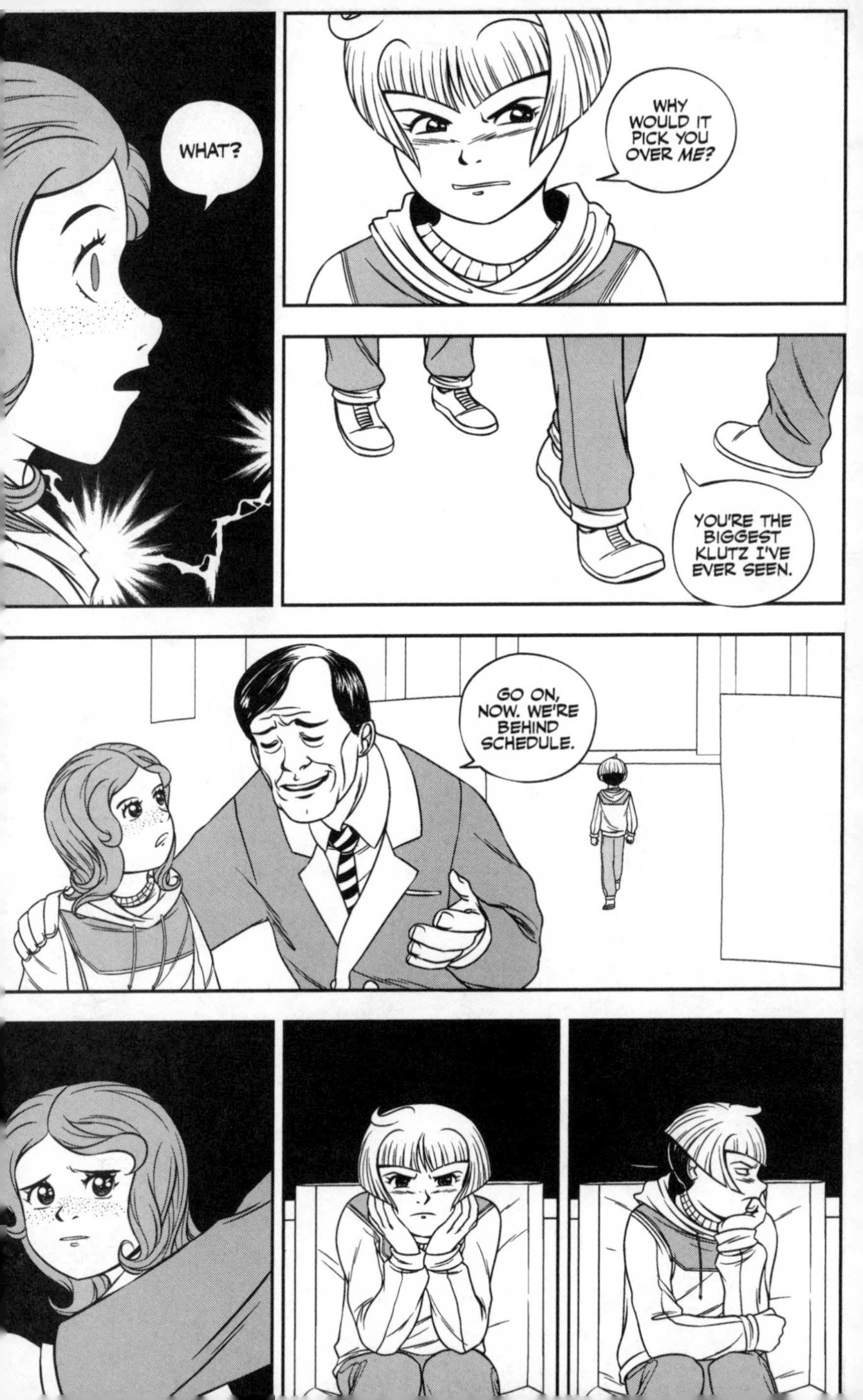
WHAT?
WHY WOULD IT PICK YOU OVER *ME*?
YOU'RE THE BIGGEST KLUTZ I'VE EVER SEEN.
GO ON, NOW. WE'RE BEHIND SCHEDULE.

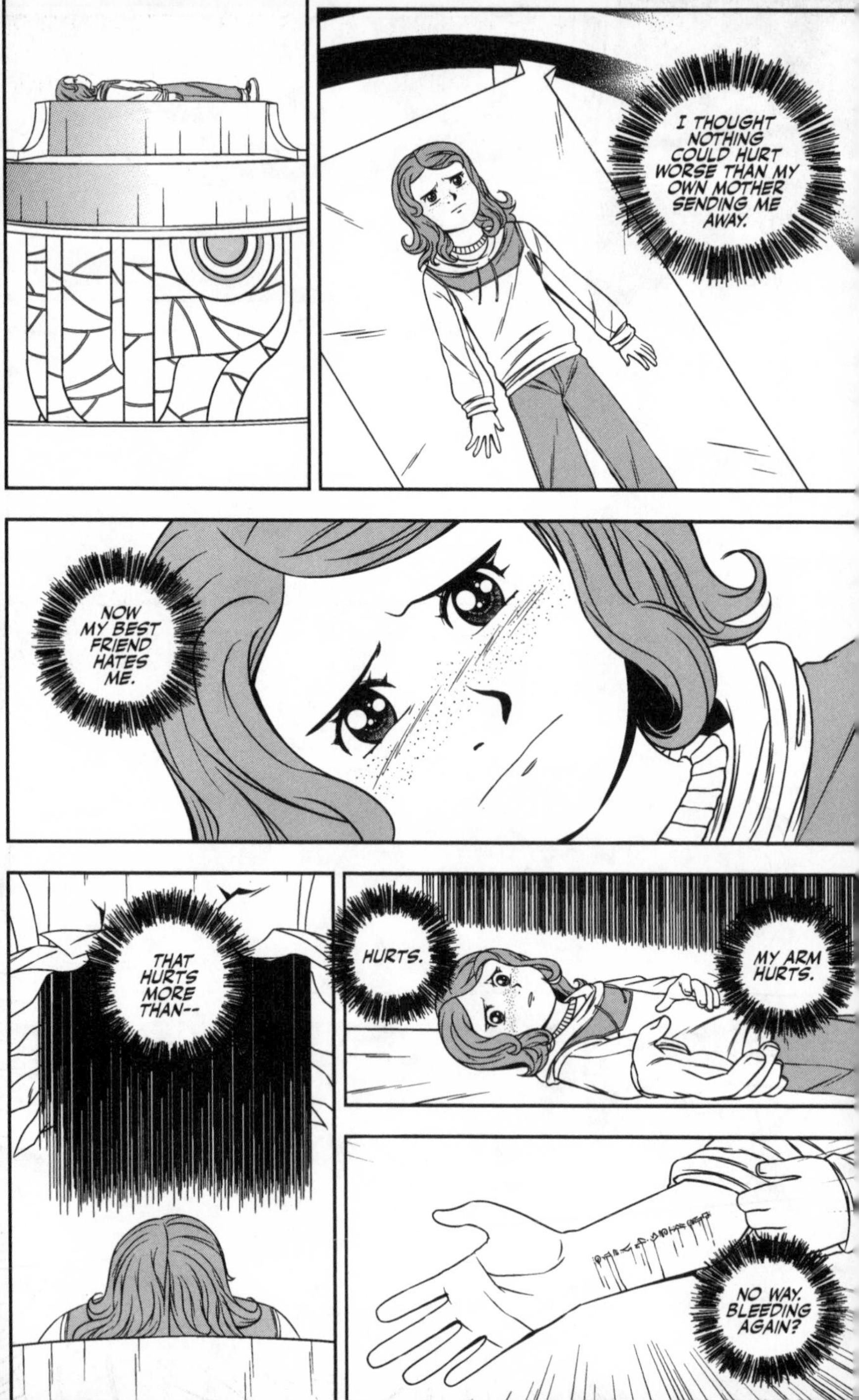
I THOUGHT NOTHING COULD HURT WORSE THAN MY OWN MOTHER SENDING ME AWAY.
NOW MY BEST FRIEND HATES ME.
THAT HURTS MORE THAN--
HURTS.
MY ARM HURTS.
NO WAY. BLEEDING AGAIN?

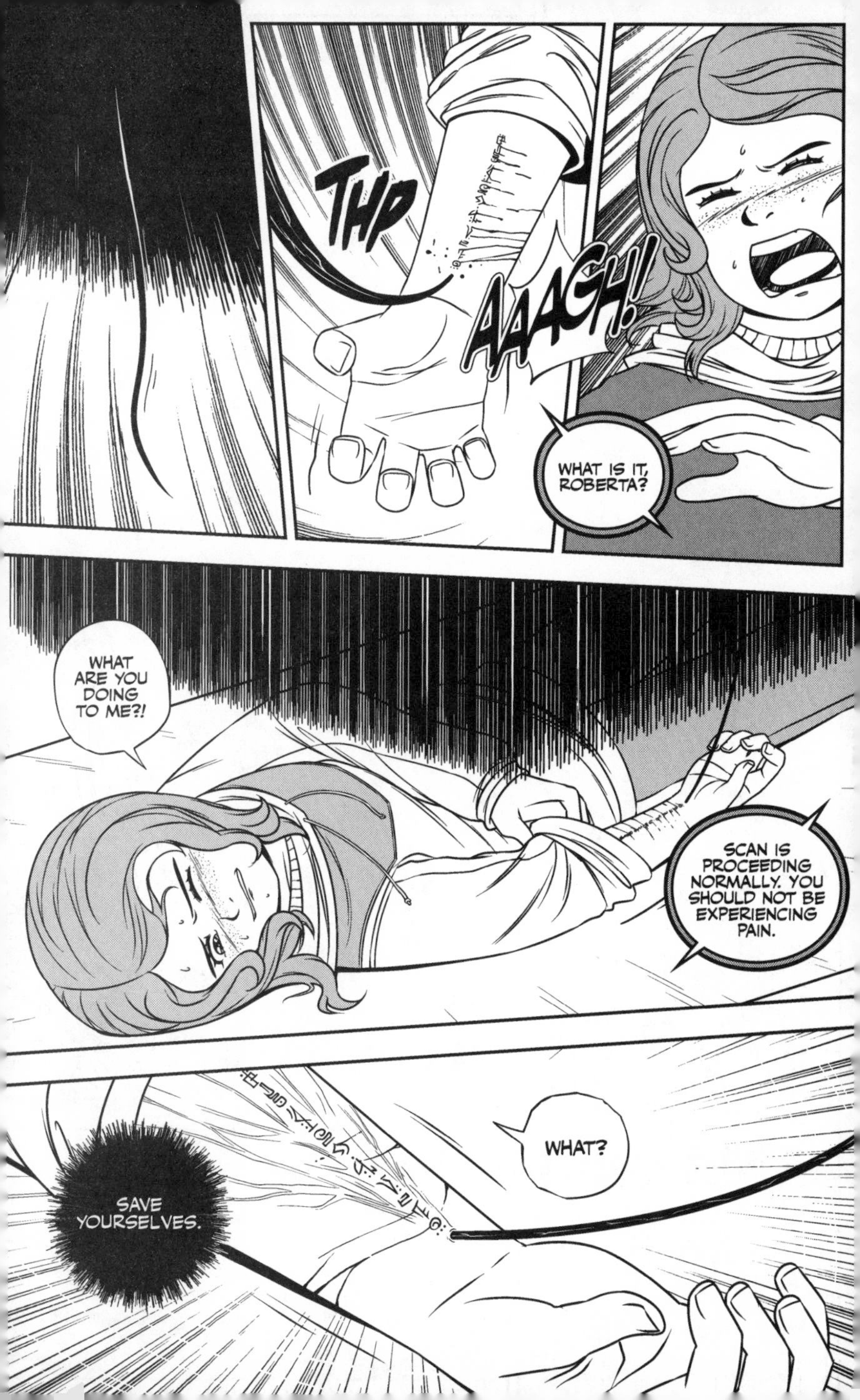
THP
AAAGH!
WHAT IS IT, ROBERTA?
WHAT ARE YOU DOING TO ME?!
SCAN IS PROCEEDING NORMALLY. YOU SHOULD NOT BE EXPERIENCING PAIN.
SAVE YOURSELVES.
WHAT?

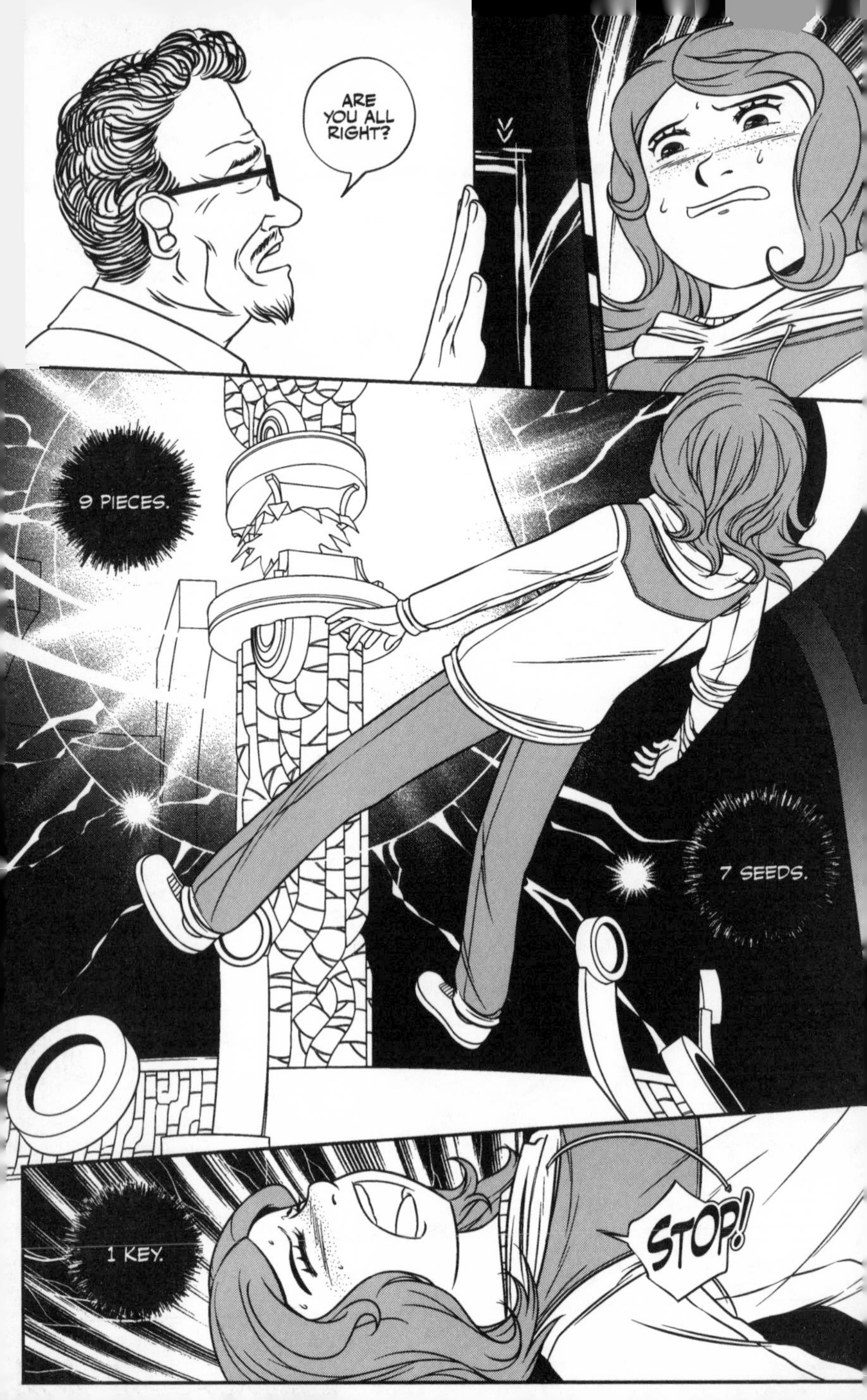
ARE YOU ALL RIGHT?
9 PIECES.
7 SEEDS.
1 KEY.
STOP!

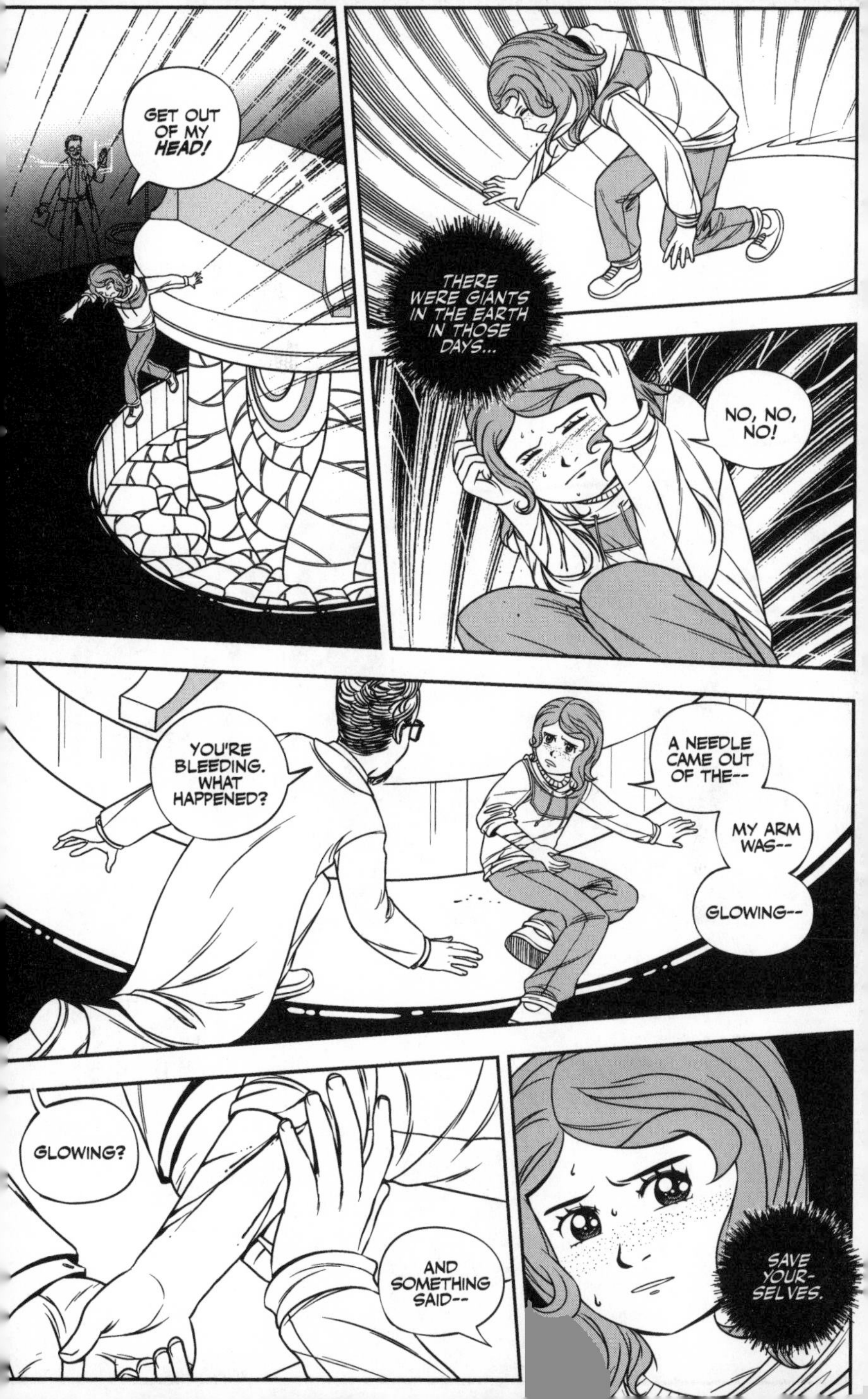
GET OUT OF MY HEAD!
THERE WERE GIANTS IN THE EARTH IN THOSE DAYS...
NO, NO, NO!
YOU'RE BLEEDING. WHAT HAPPENED?
A NEEDLE CAME OUT OF THE--
MY ARM WAS--
GLOWING--
GLOWING?
AND SOMETHING SAID--
SAVE YOUR-SELVES.

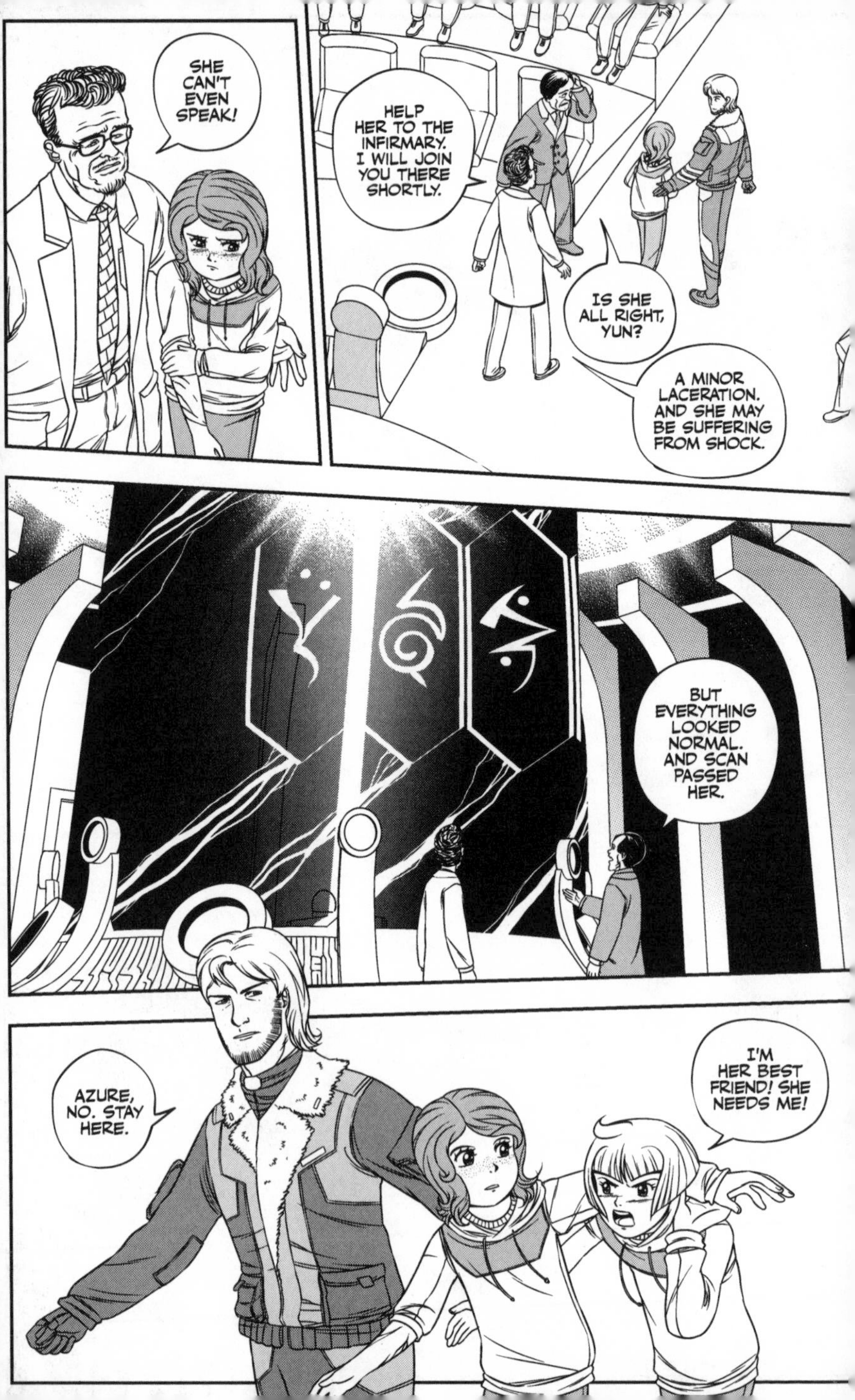
SHE CAN'T EVEN SPEAK!
HELP HER TO THE INFIRMARY. I WILL JOIN YOU THERE SHORTLY.
IS SHE ALL RIGHT, YUN?
A MINOR LACERATION. AND SHE MAY BE SUFFERING FROM SHOCK.
BUT EVERYTHING LOOKED NORMAL. AND SCAN PASSED HER.
AZURE, NO. STAY HERE.
I'M HER BEST FRIEND! SHE NEEDS ME!

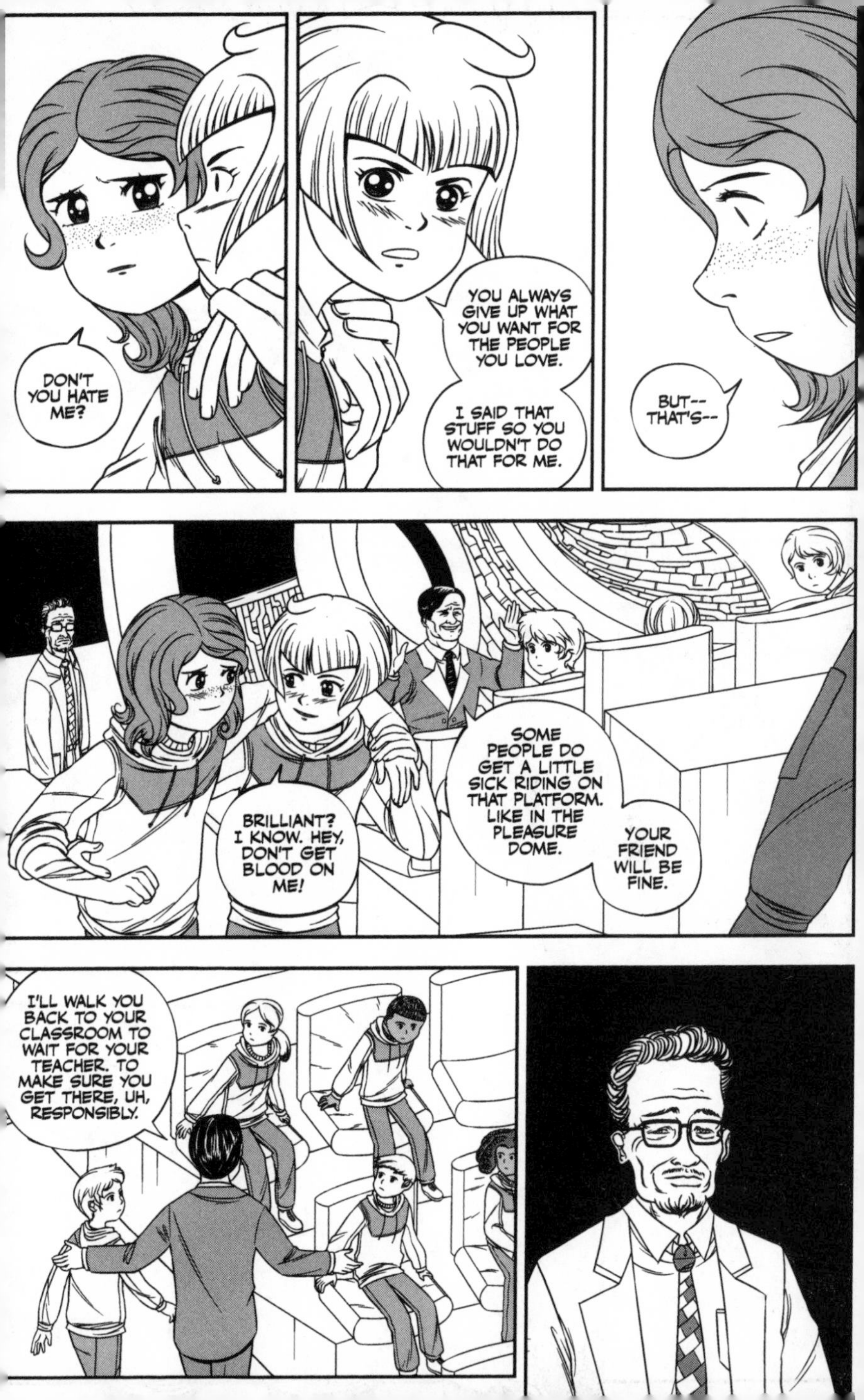
DON'T YOU HATE ME?
YOU ALWAYS GIVE UP WHAT YOU WANT FOR THE PEOPLE YOU LOVE.
I SAID THAT STUFF SO YOU WOULDN'T DO THAT FOR ME.
BUT-- THAT'S--
BRILLIANT? I KNOW. HEY, DON'T GET BLOOD ON ME!
SOME PEOPLE DO GET A LITTLE SICK RIDING ON THAT PLATFORM. LIKE IN THE PLEASURE DOME.
YOUR FRIEND WILL BE FINE.
I'LL WALK YOU BACK TO YOUR CLASSROOM TO WAIT FOR YOUR TEACHER. TO MAKE SURE YOU GET THERE, UH, RESPONSIBLY.

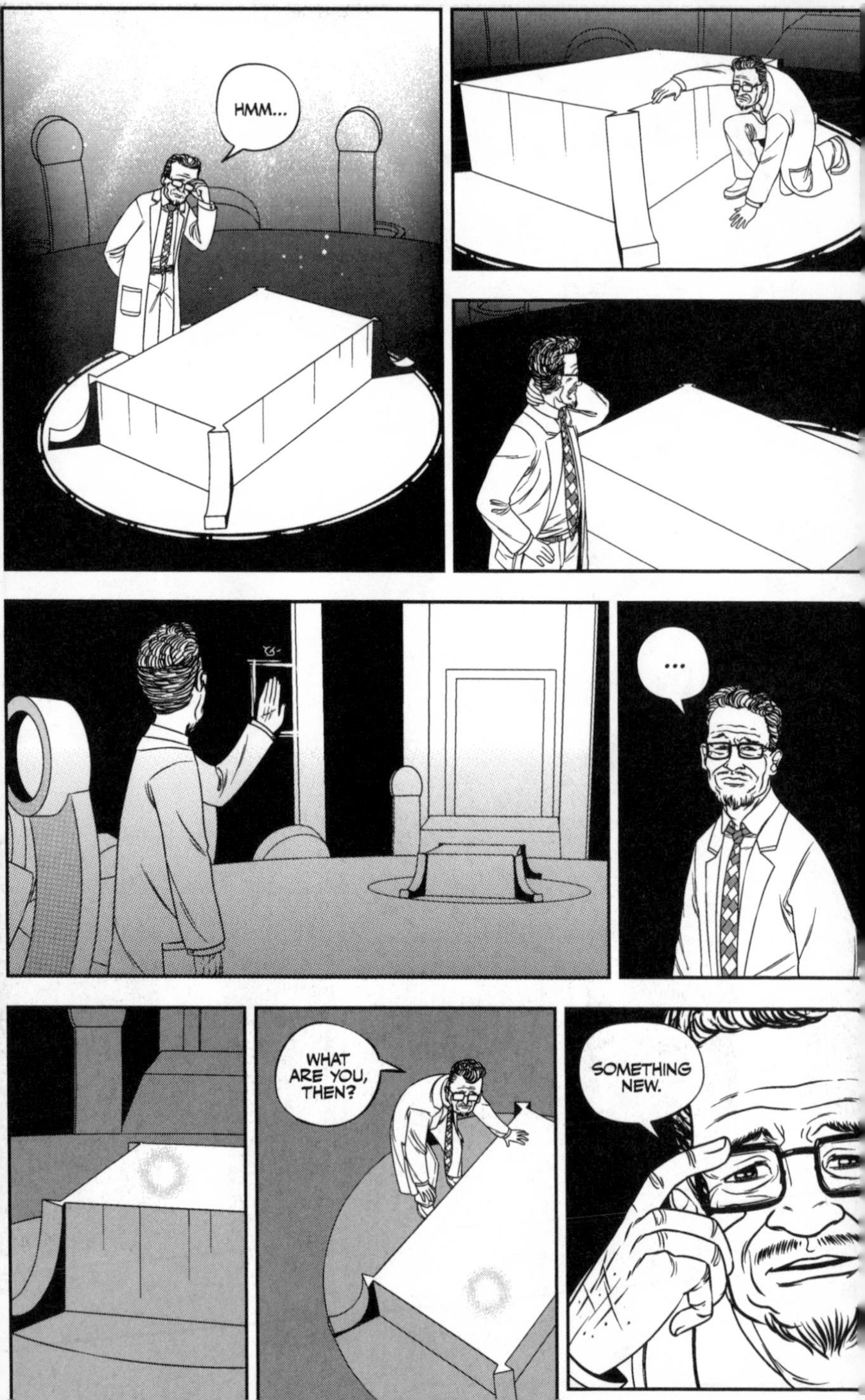
HMM...
...
WHAT ARE YOU, THEN?
SOMETHING NEW.

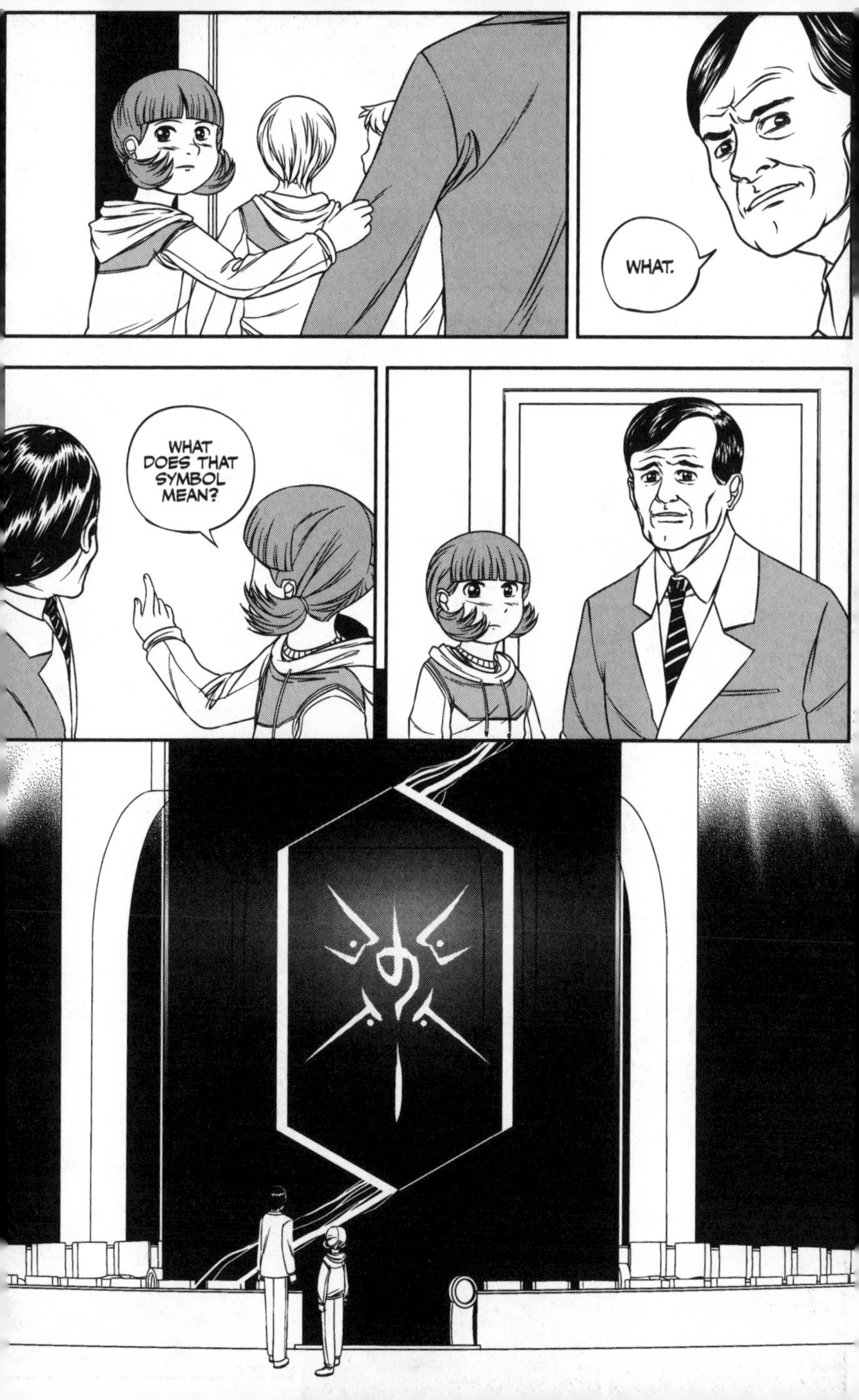
WHAT.
WHAT DOES THAT SYMBOL MEAN?

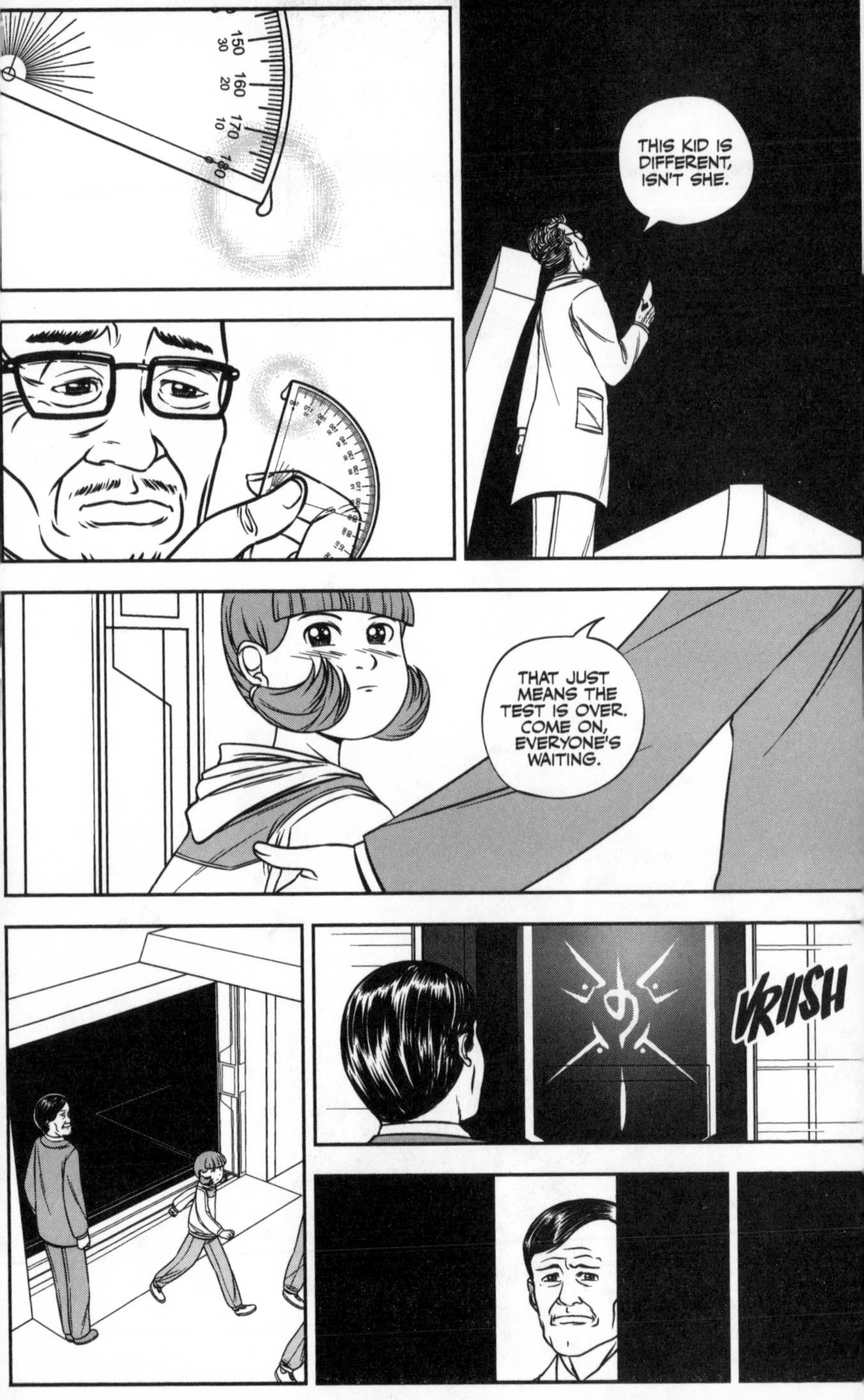
150 160 170 180
30 20 10
THIS KID IS DIFFERENT, ISN'T SHE.
THAT JUST MEANS THE TEST IS OVER. COME ON, EVERYONE'S WAITING.
VRIISH

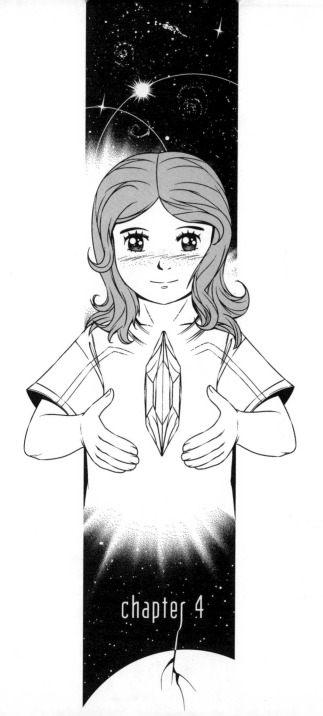

chapter 4

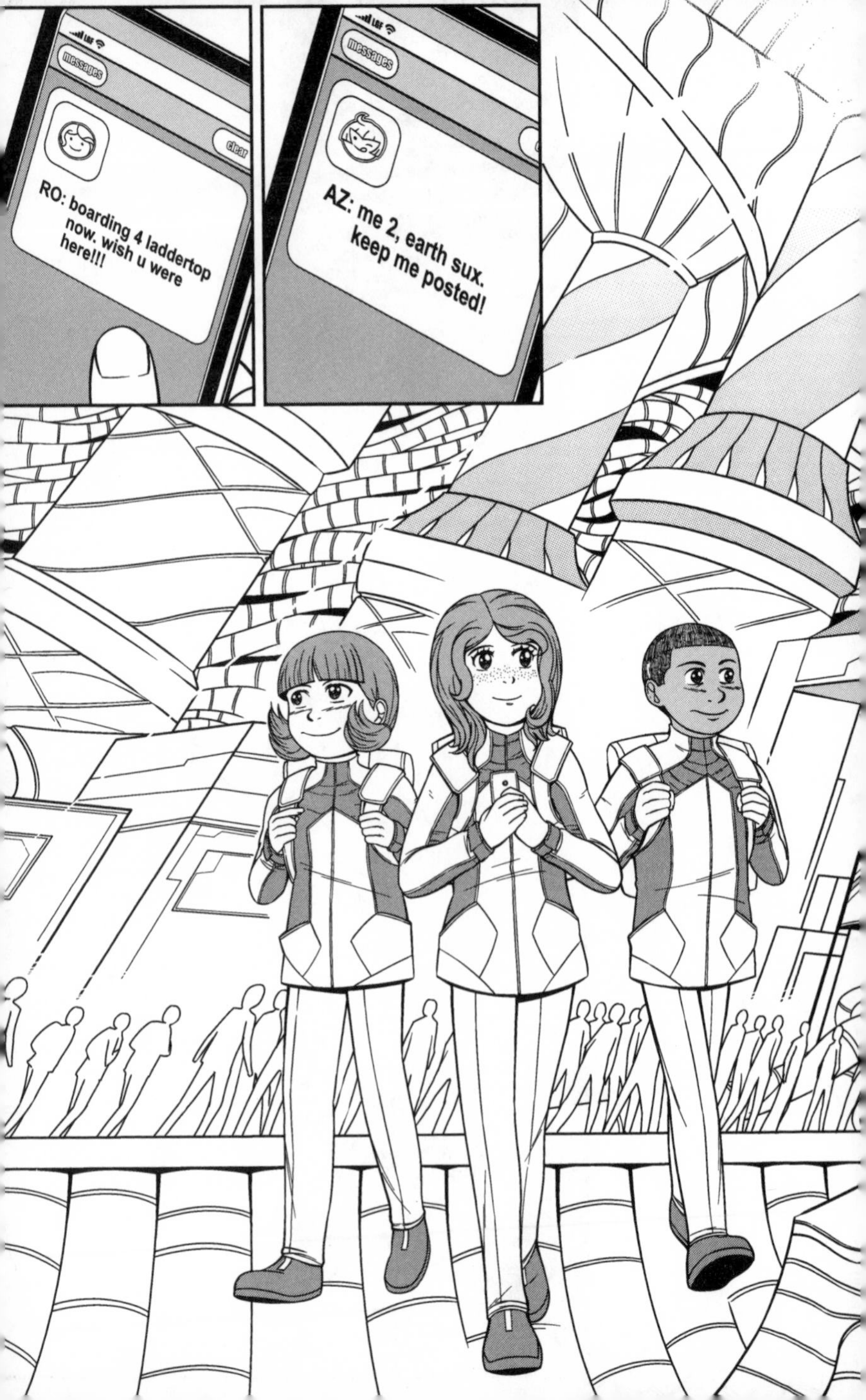
messages
clear
RO: boarding 4 laddertop now. wish u were here!!!
messages
AZ: me 2, earth sux. keep me posted!

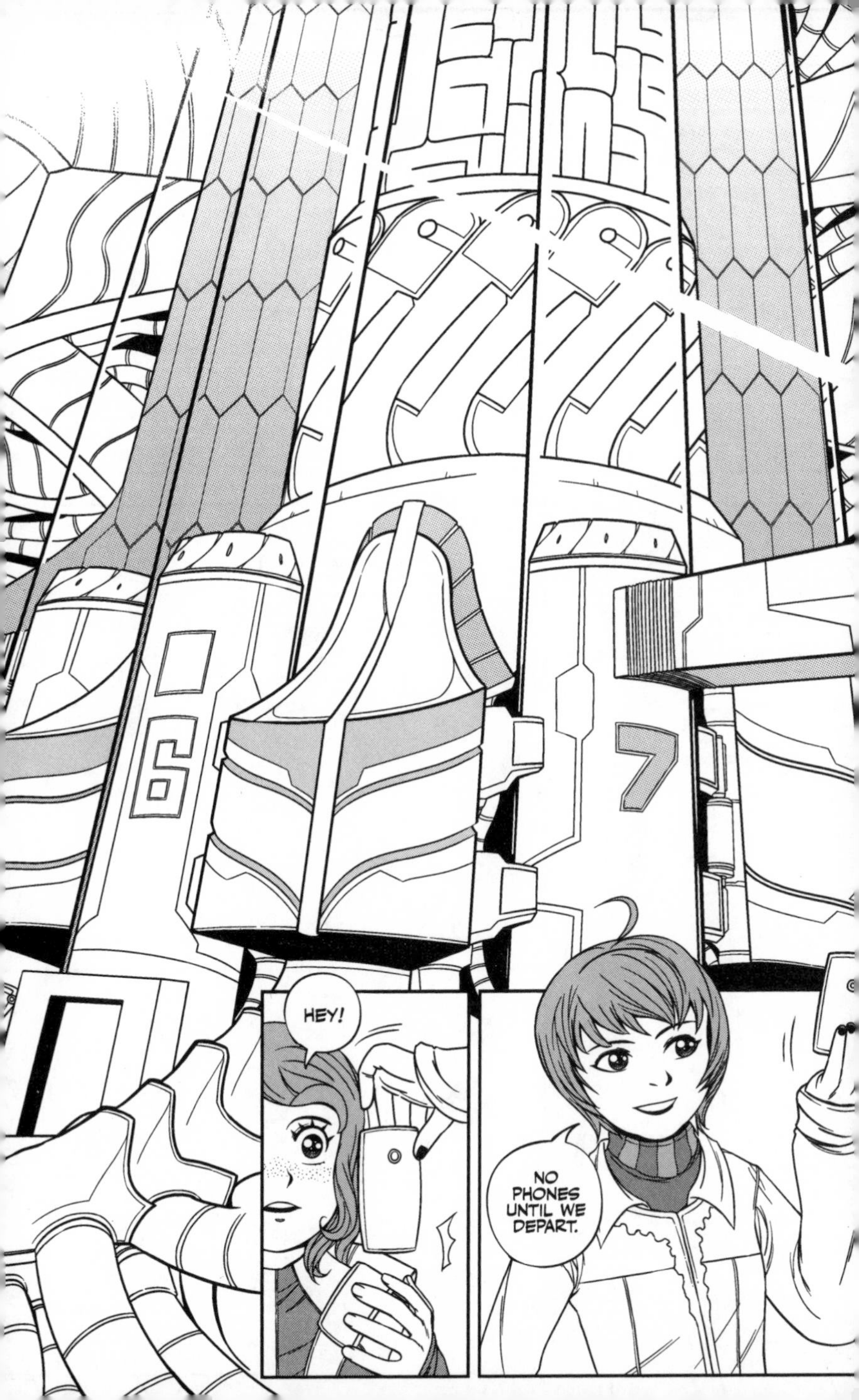
HEY!
NO PHONES UNTIL WE DEPART.

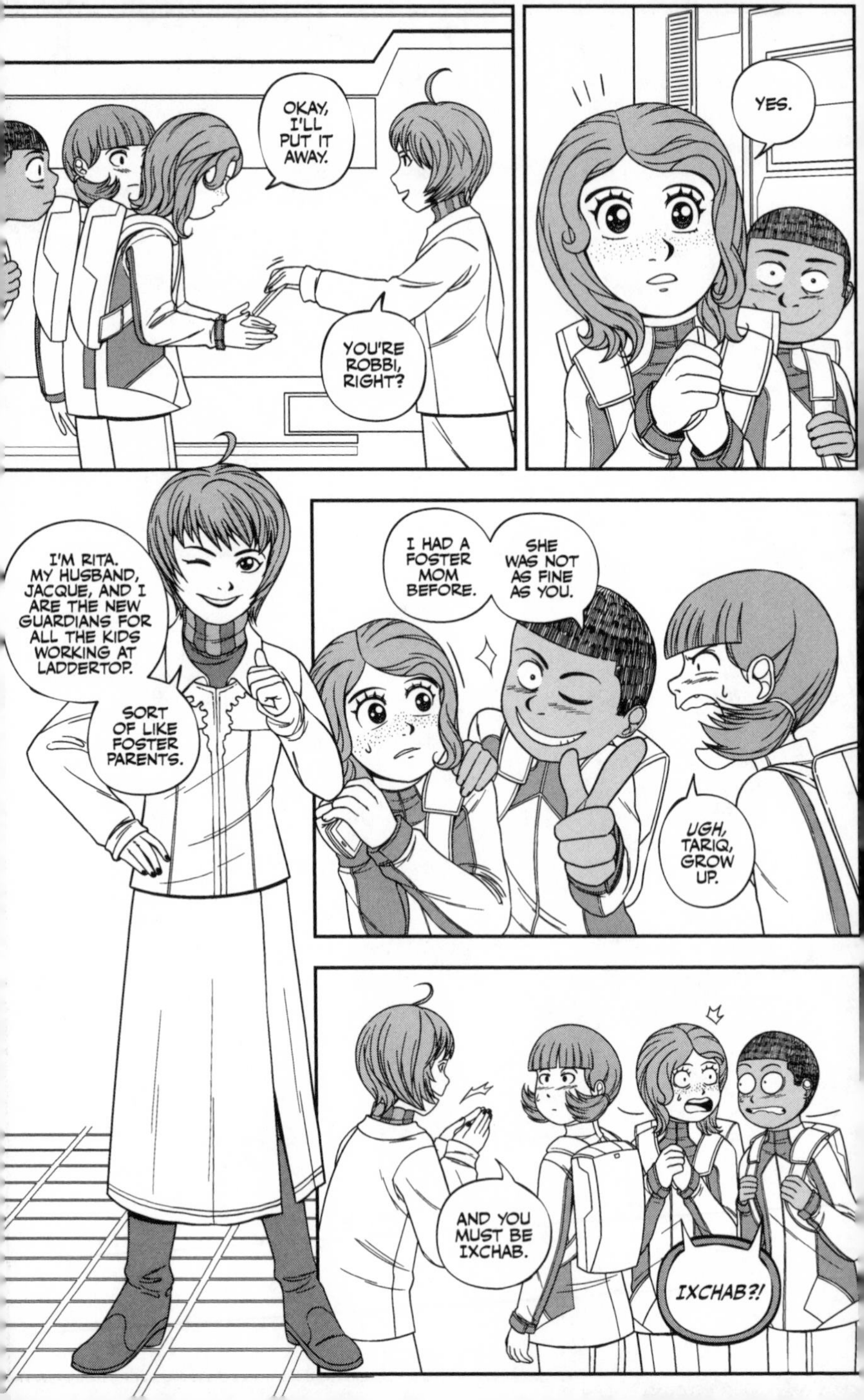
OKAY, I'LL PUT IT AWAY.
YOU'RE ROBBI, RIGHT?
YES.
I'M RITA. MY HUSBAND, JACQUE, AND I ARE THE NEW GUARDIANS FOR ALL THE KIDS WORKING AT LADDERTOP.
SORT OF LIKE FOSTER PARENTS.
I HAD A FOSTER MOM BEFORE.
SHE WAS NOT AS FINE AS YOU.
UGH, TARIQ, GROW UP.
AND YOU MUST BE IXCHAB.
IXCHAB?!

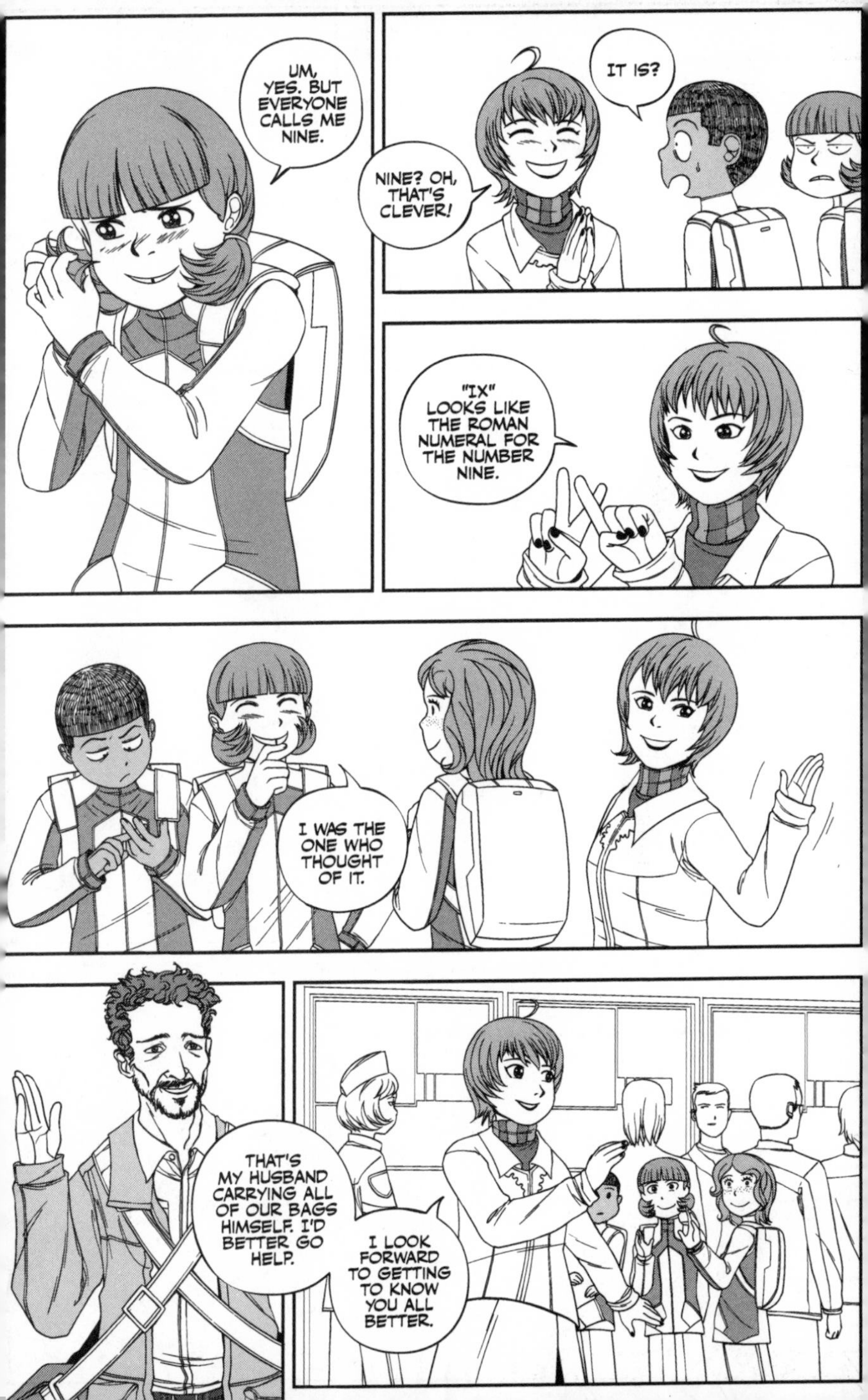
UM, YES. BUT EVERYONE CALLS ME NINE.
NINE? OH, THAT'S CLEVER!
IT IS?
"IX" LOOKS LIKE THE ROMAN NUMERAL FOR THE NUMBER NINE.
I WAS THE ONE WHO THOUGHT OF IT.
THAT'S MY HUSBAND CARRYING ALL OF OUR BAGS HIMSELF. I'D BETTER GO HELP.
I LOOK FORWARD TO GETTING TO KNOW YOU ALL BETTER.

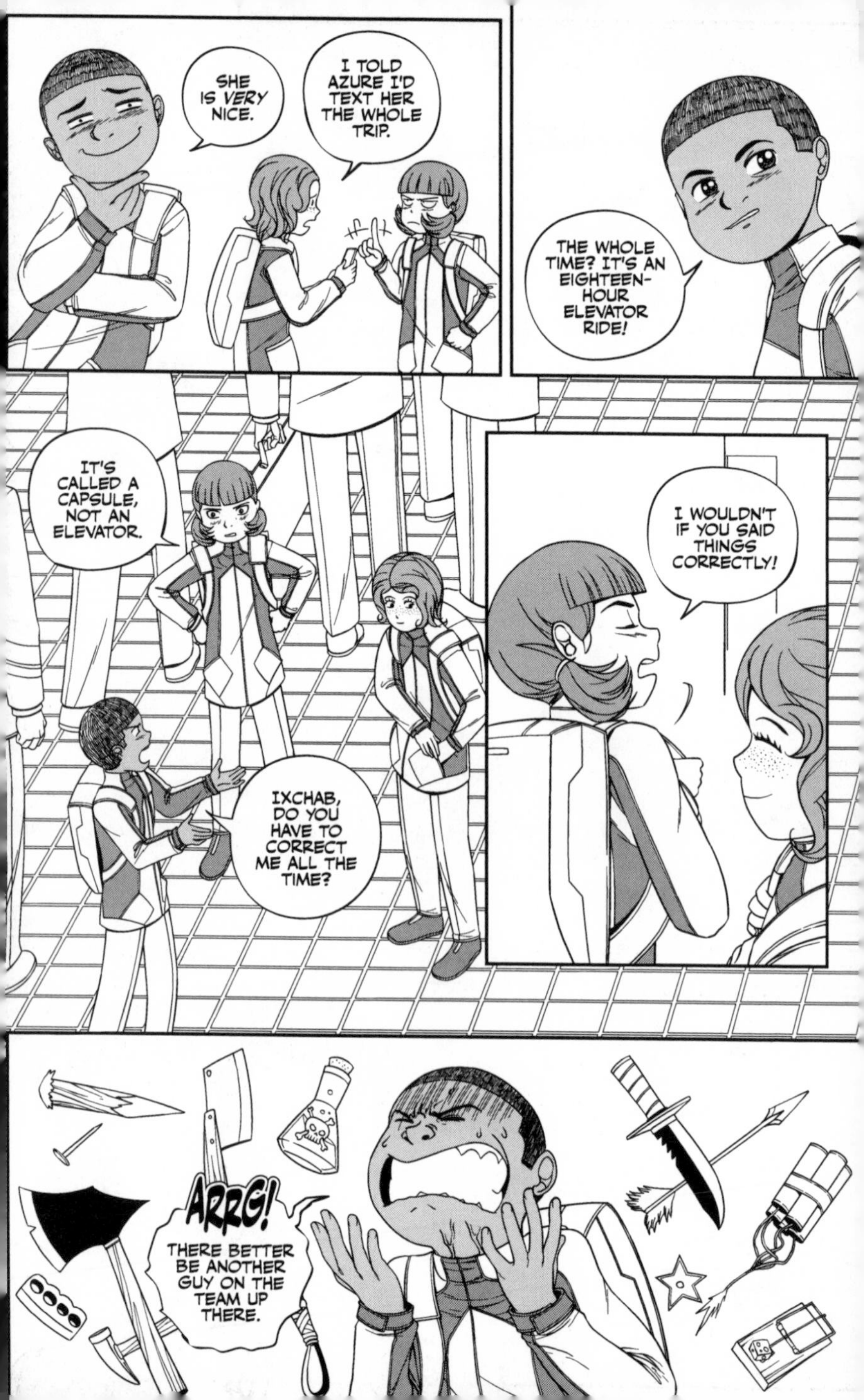
SHE IS VERY NICE.
I TOLD AZURE I'D TEXT HER THE WHOLE TRIP.
THE WHOLE TIME? IT'S AN EIGHTEEN-HOUR ELEVATOR RIDE!
IT'S CALLED A CAPSULE, NOT AN ELEVATOR.
IXCHAB, DO YOU HAVE TO CORRECT ME ALL THE TIME?
I WOULDN'T IF YOU SAID THINGS CORRECTLY!
ARRG!
THERE BETTER BE ANOTHER GUY ON THE TEAM UP THERE.

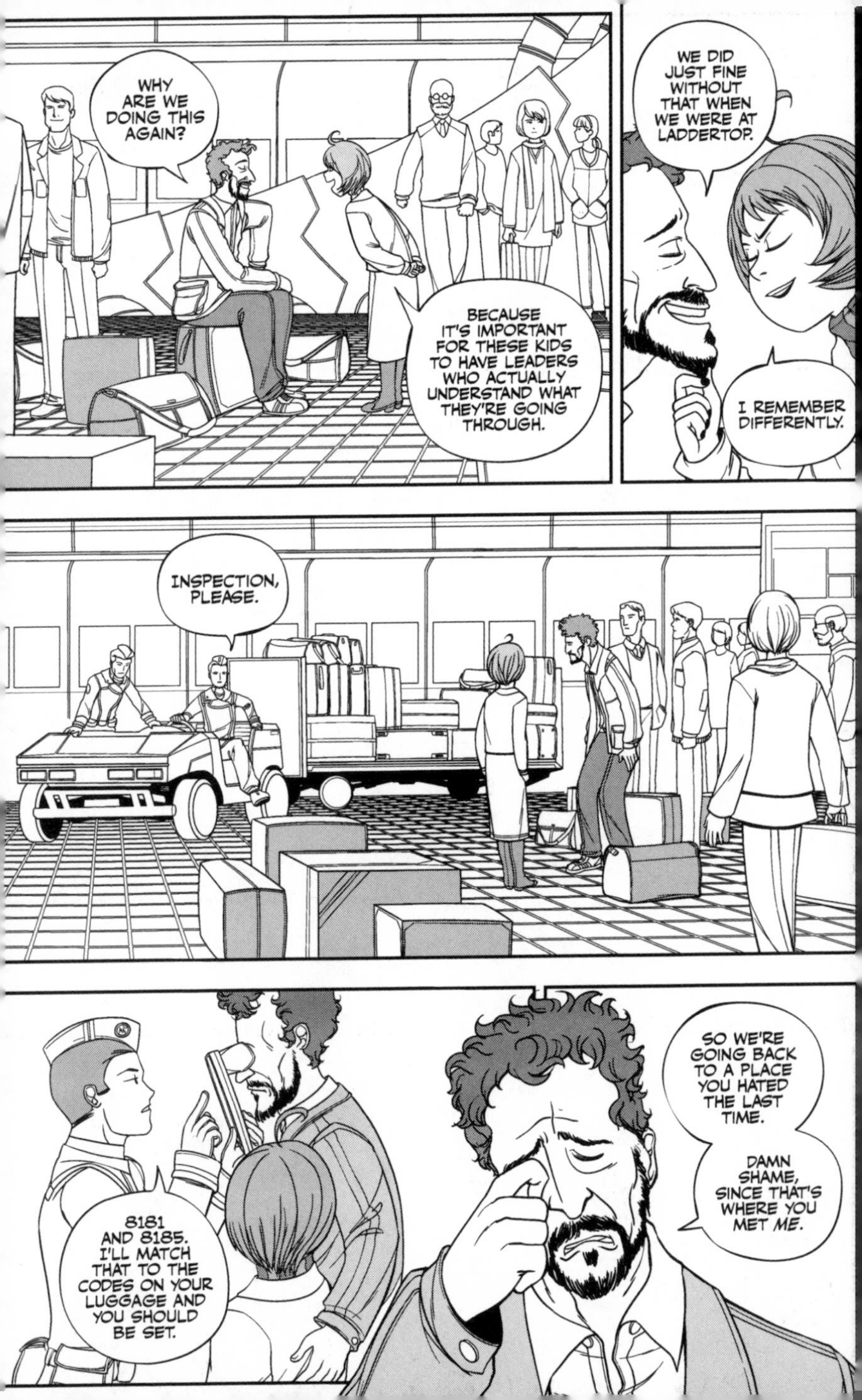
WHY ARE WE DOING THIS AGAIN?
BECAUSE IT'S IMPORTANT FOR THESE KIDS TO HAVE LEADERS WHO ACTUALLY UNDERSTAND WHAT THEY'RE GOING THROUGH.
WE DID JUST FINE WITHOUT THAT WHEN WE WERE AT LADDERTOP.
I REMEMBER DIFFERENTLY.
INSPECTION, PLEASE.
8181 AND 8185. I'LL MATCH THAT TO THE CODES ON YOUR LUGGAGE AND YOU SHOULD BE SET.
SO WE'RE GOING BACK TO A PLACE YOU HATED THE LAST TIME.
DAMN SHAME, SINCE THAT'S WHERE YOU MET *ME*.

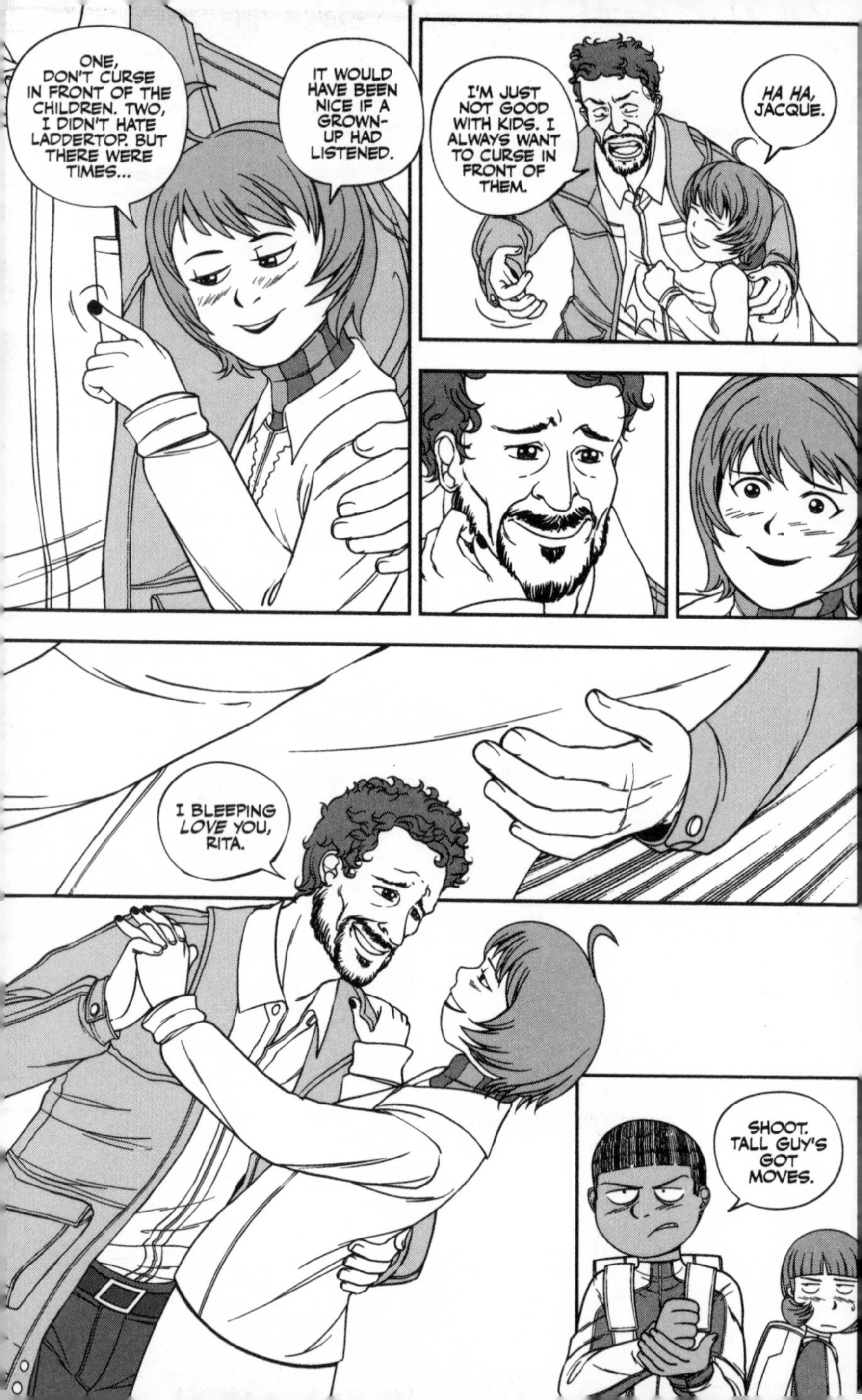
ONE, DON'T CURSE IN FRONT OF THE CHILDREN. TWO, I DIDN'T HATE LADDERTOP. BUT THERE WERE TIMES...
IT WOULD HAVE BEEN NICE IF A GROWN-UP HAD LISTENED.
I'M JUST NOT GOOD WITH KIDS. I ALWAYS WANT TO CURSE IN FRONT OF THEM.
HA HA, JACQUE.
I BLEEPING *LOVE* YOU, RITA.
SHOOT. TALL GUY'S GOT MOVES.

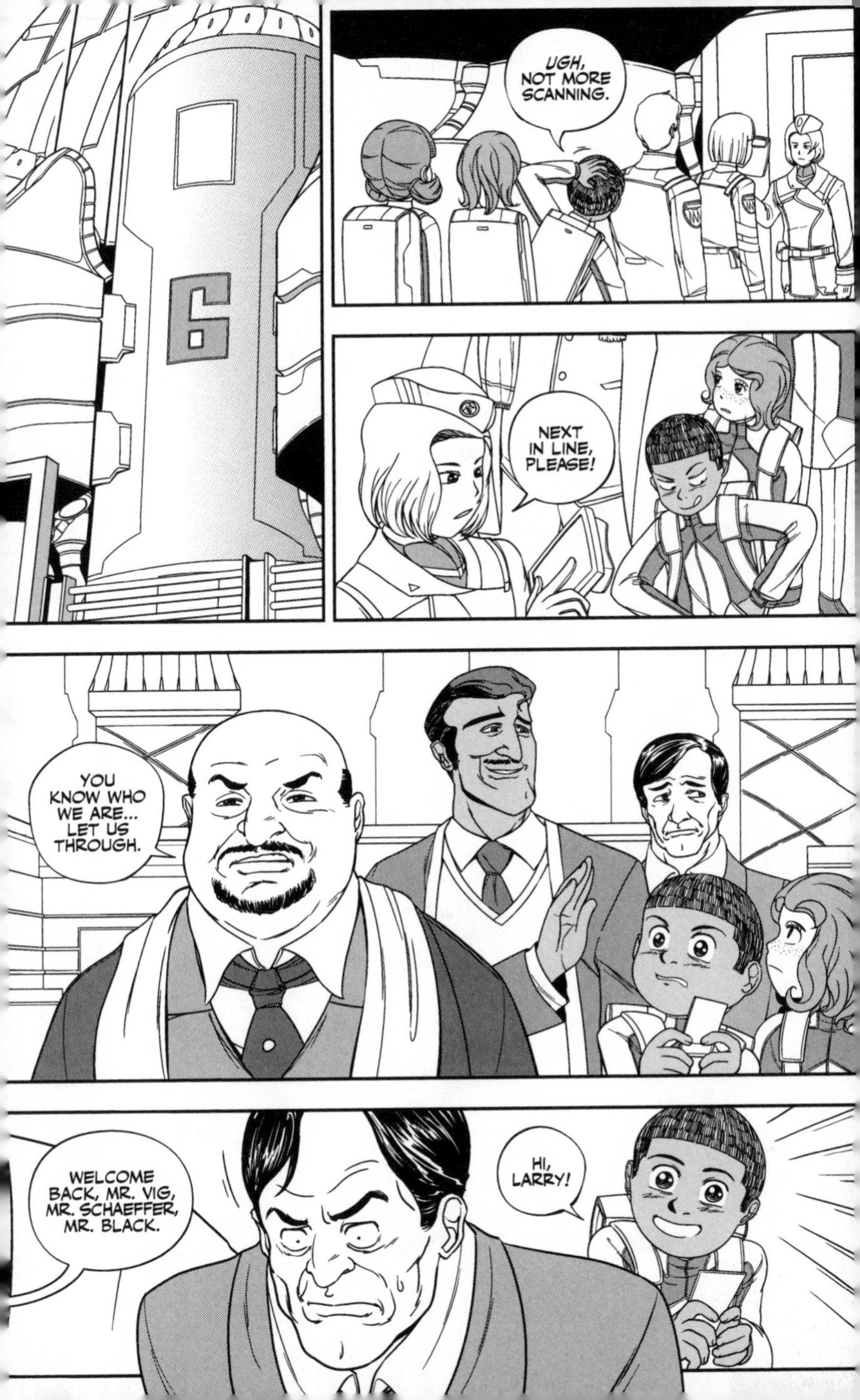
UGH, NOT MORE SCANNING.
NEXT IN LINE, PLEASE!
YOU KNOW WHO WE ARE... LET US THROUGH.
WELCOME BACK, MR. VIG, MR. SCHAEFFER, MR. BLACK.
HI, LARRY!

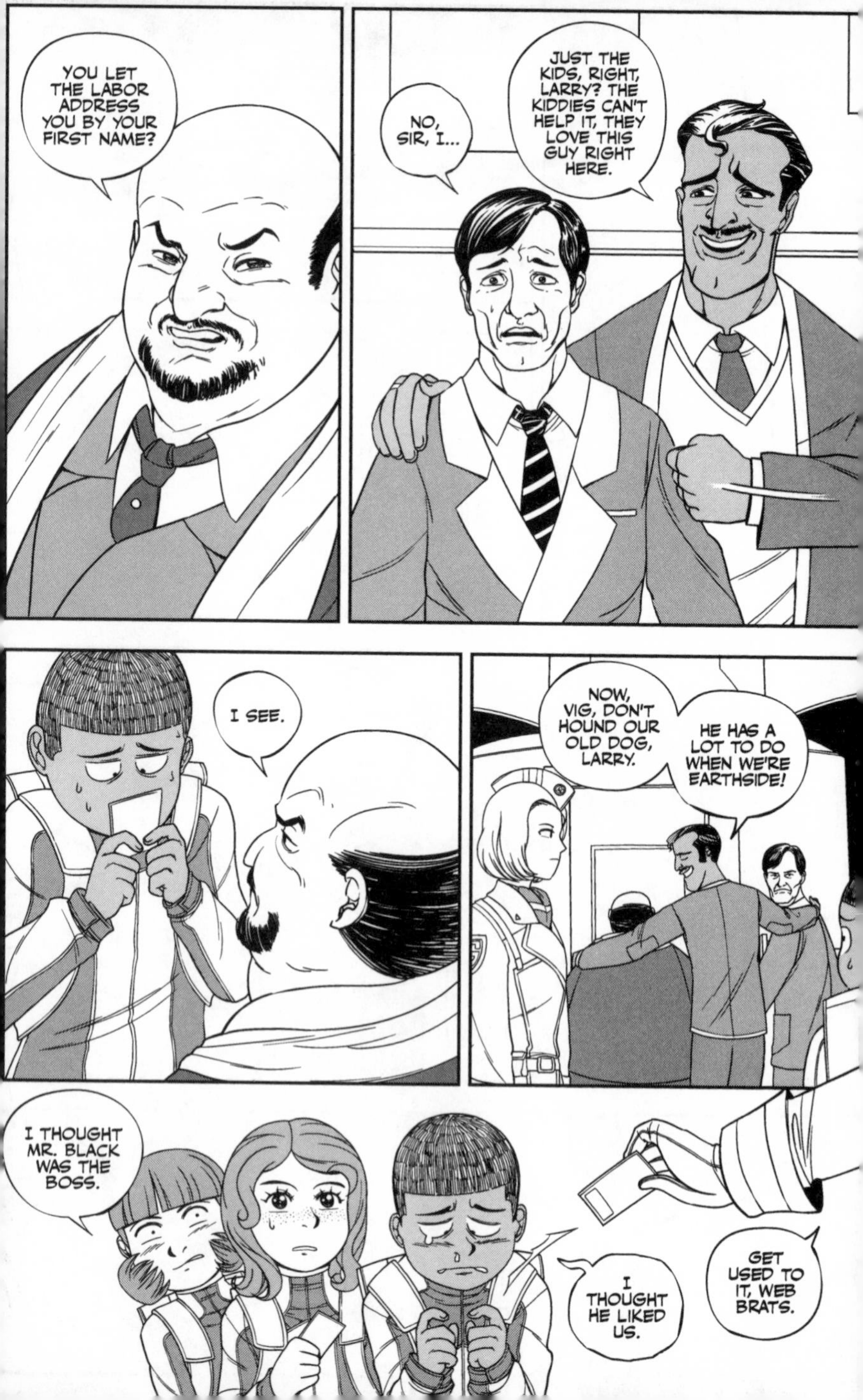
YOU LET THE LABOR ADDRESS YOU BY YOUR FIRST NAME?
NO, SIR, I...
JUST THE KIDS, RIGHT, LARRY? THE KIDDIES CAN'T HELP IT, THEY LOVE THIS GUY RIGHT HERE.
I SEE.
NOW, VIG, DON'T HOUND OUR OLD DOG, LARRY.
HE HAS A LOT TO DO WHEN WE'RE EARTHSIDE!
I THOUGHT MR. BLACK WAS THE BOSS.
I THOUGHT HE LIKED US.
GET USED TO IT, WEB BRATS.

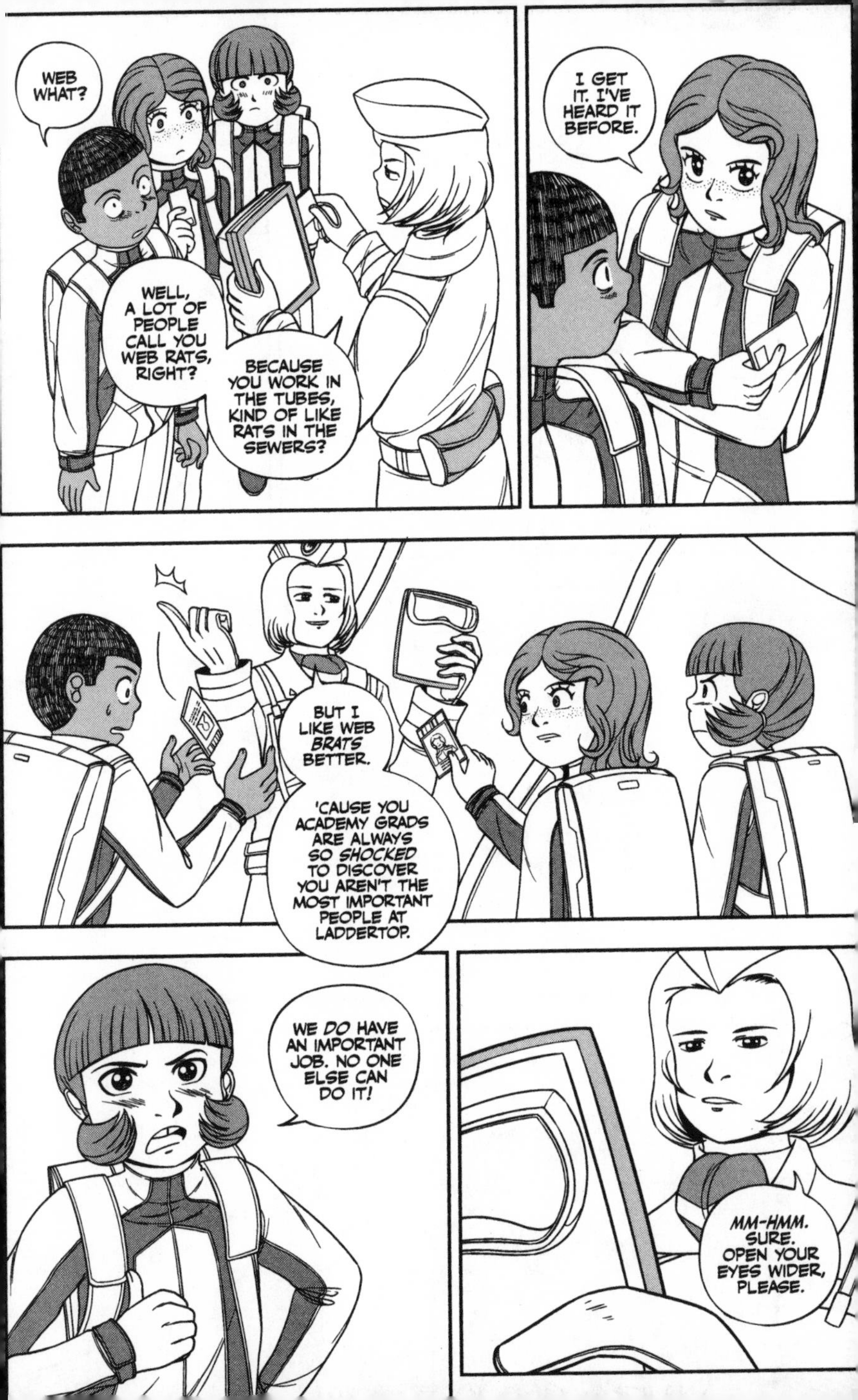
WEB WHAT?
WELL, A LOT OF PEOPLE CALL YOU WEB RATS, RIGHT?
BECAUSE YOU WORK IN THE TUBES, KIND OF LIKE RATS IN THE SEWERS?
I GET IT. I'VE HEARD IT BEFORE.
BUT I LIKE WEB *BRATS* BETTER.
'CAUSE YOU ACADEMY GRADS ARE ALWAYS *SO SHOCKED* TO DISCOVER YOU AREN'T THE MOST IMPORTANT PEOPLE AT LADDERTOP.
WE *DO* HAVE AN IMPORTANT JOB. NO ONE ELSE CAN DO IT!
MM-HMM. SURE. OPEN YOUR EYES WIDER, PLEASE.

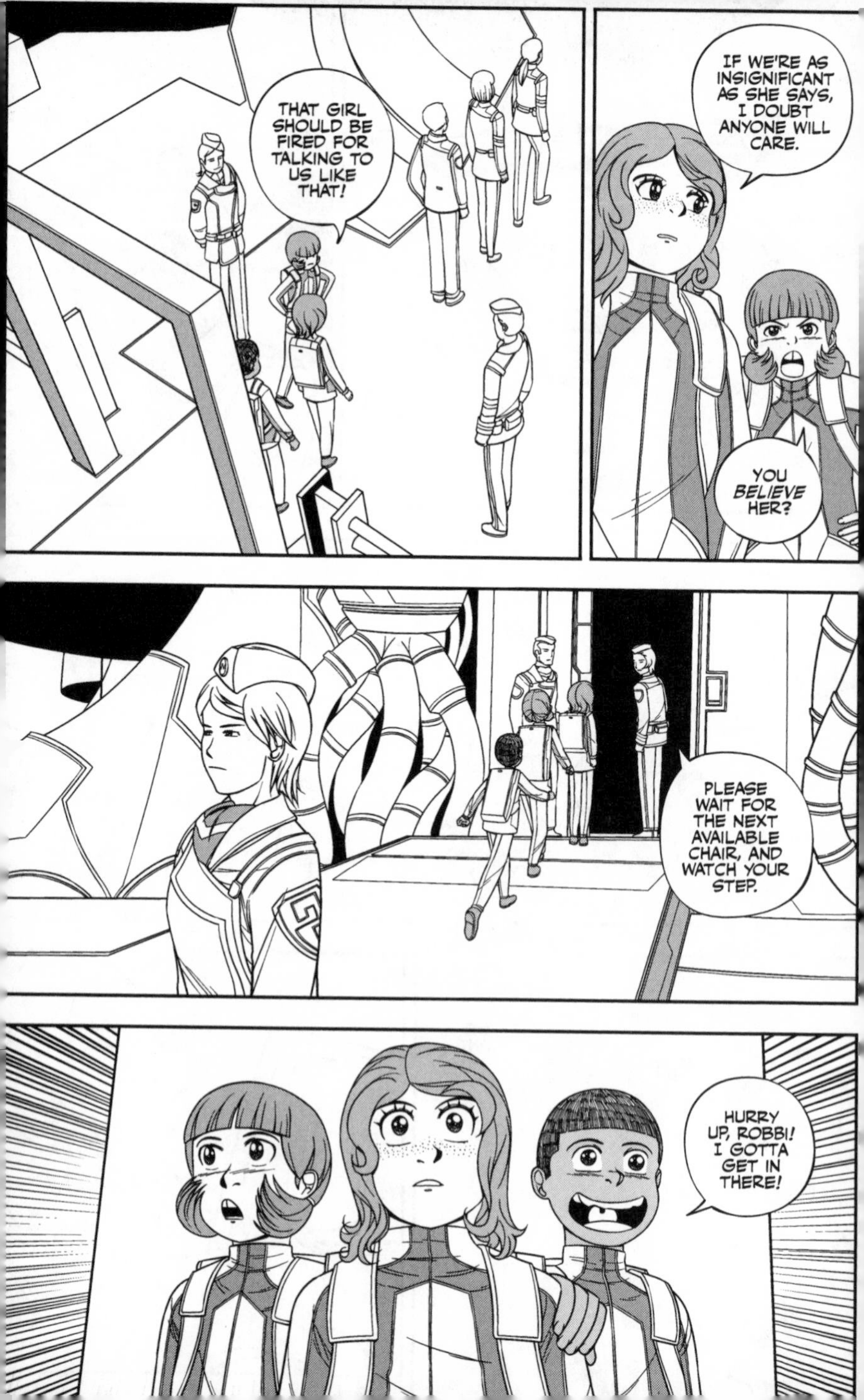
THAT GIRL SHOULD BE FIRED FOR TALKING TO US LIKE THAT!
IF WE'RE AS INSIGNIFICANT AS SHE SAYS, I DOUBT ANYONE WILL CARE.
YOU *BELIEVE* HER?
PLEASE WAIT FOR THE NEXT AVAILABLE CHAIR, AND WATCH YOUR STEP.
HURRY UP, ROBBI! I GOTTA GET IN THERE!

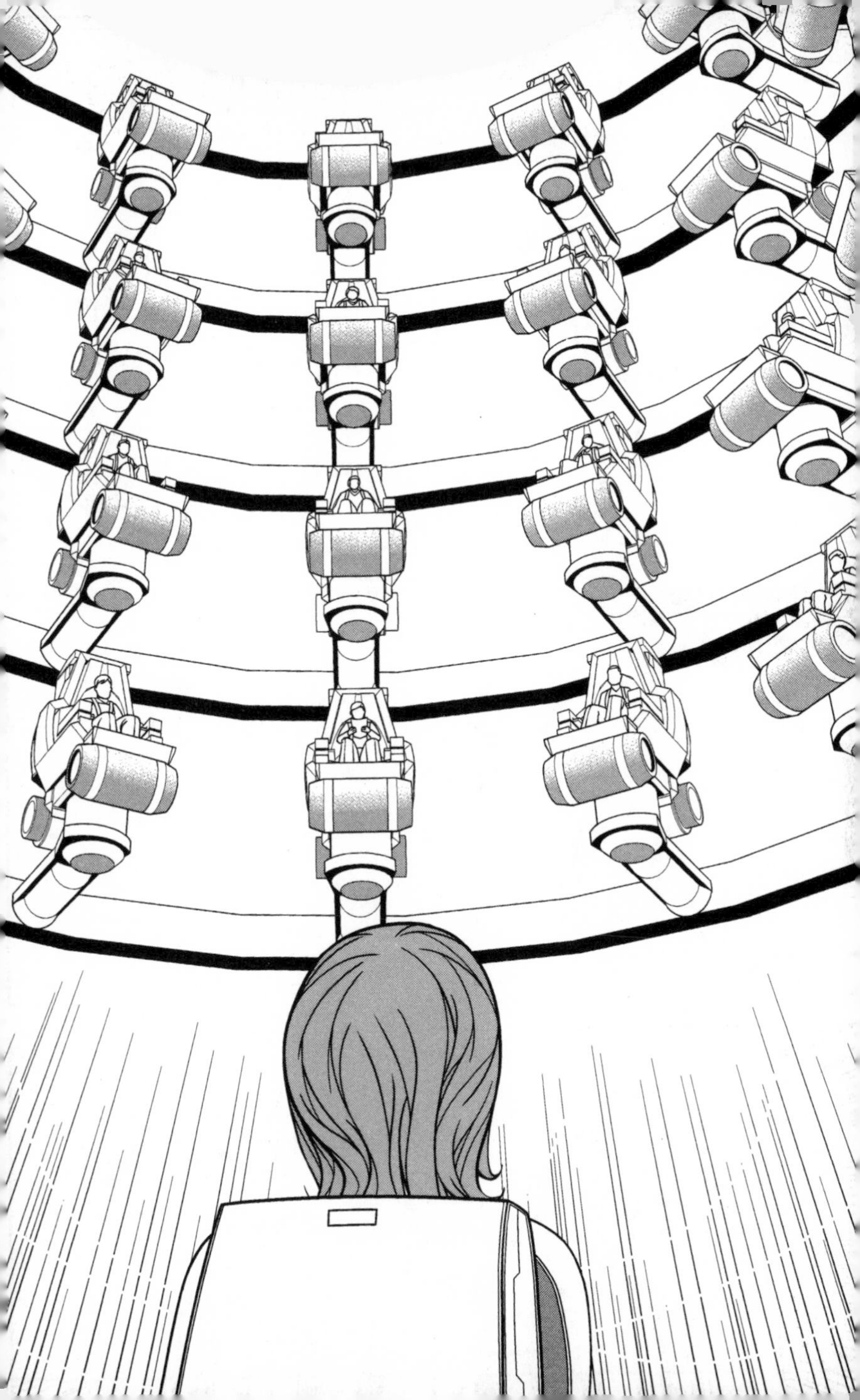

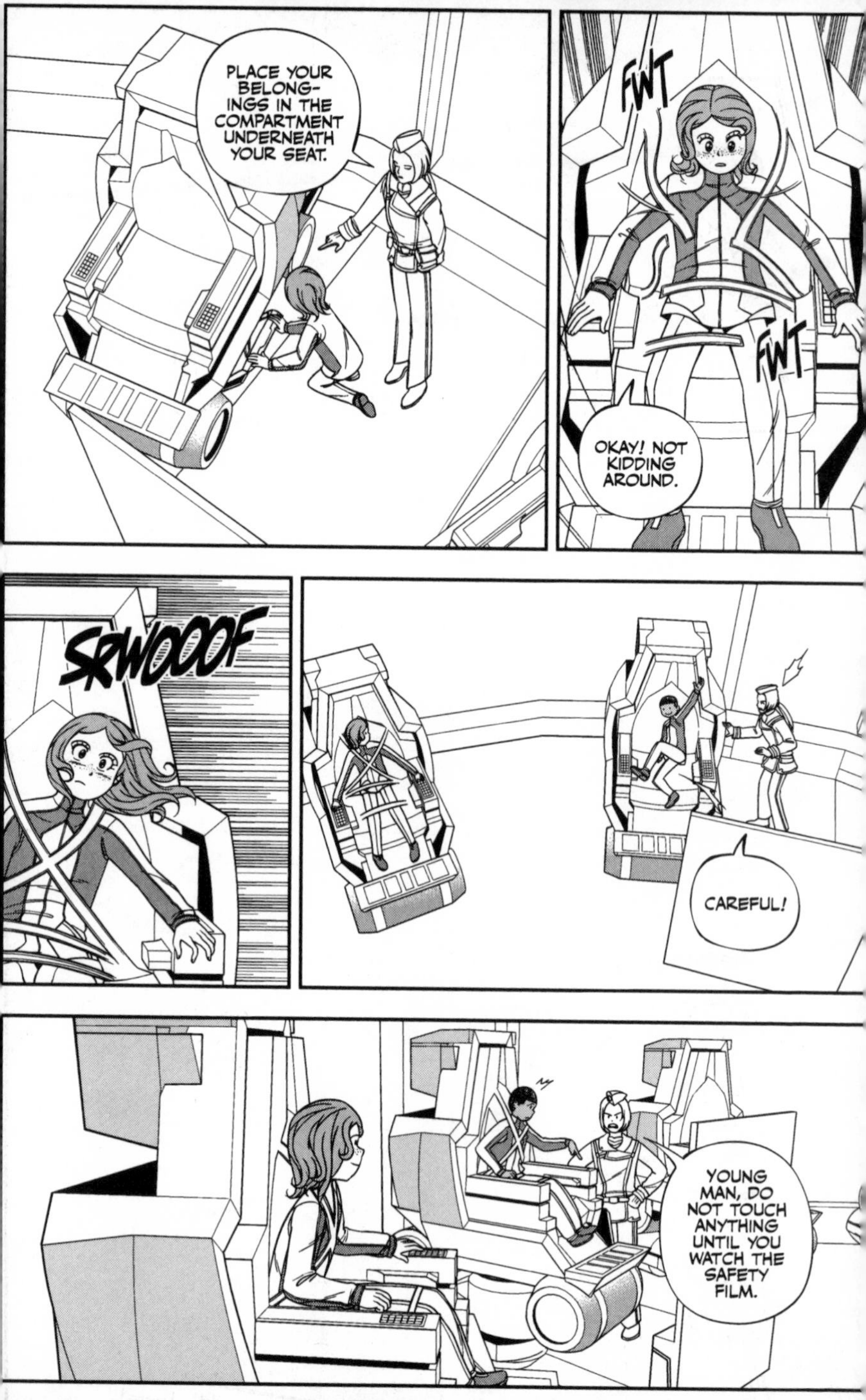
PLACE YOUR BELONGINGS IN THE COMPARTMENT UNDERNEATH YOUR SEAT.
FWT
FWT
OKAY! NOT KIDDING AROUND.
SRWOOOF
CAREFUL!
YOUNG MAN, DO NOT TOUCH ANYTHING UNTIL YOU WATCH THE SAFETY FILM.

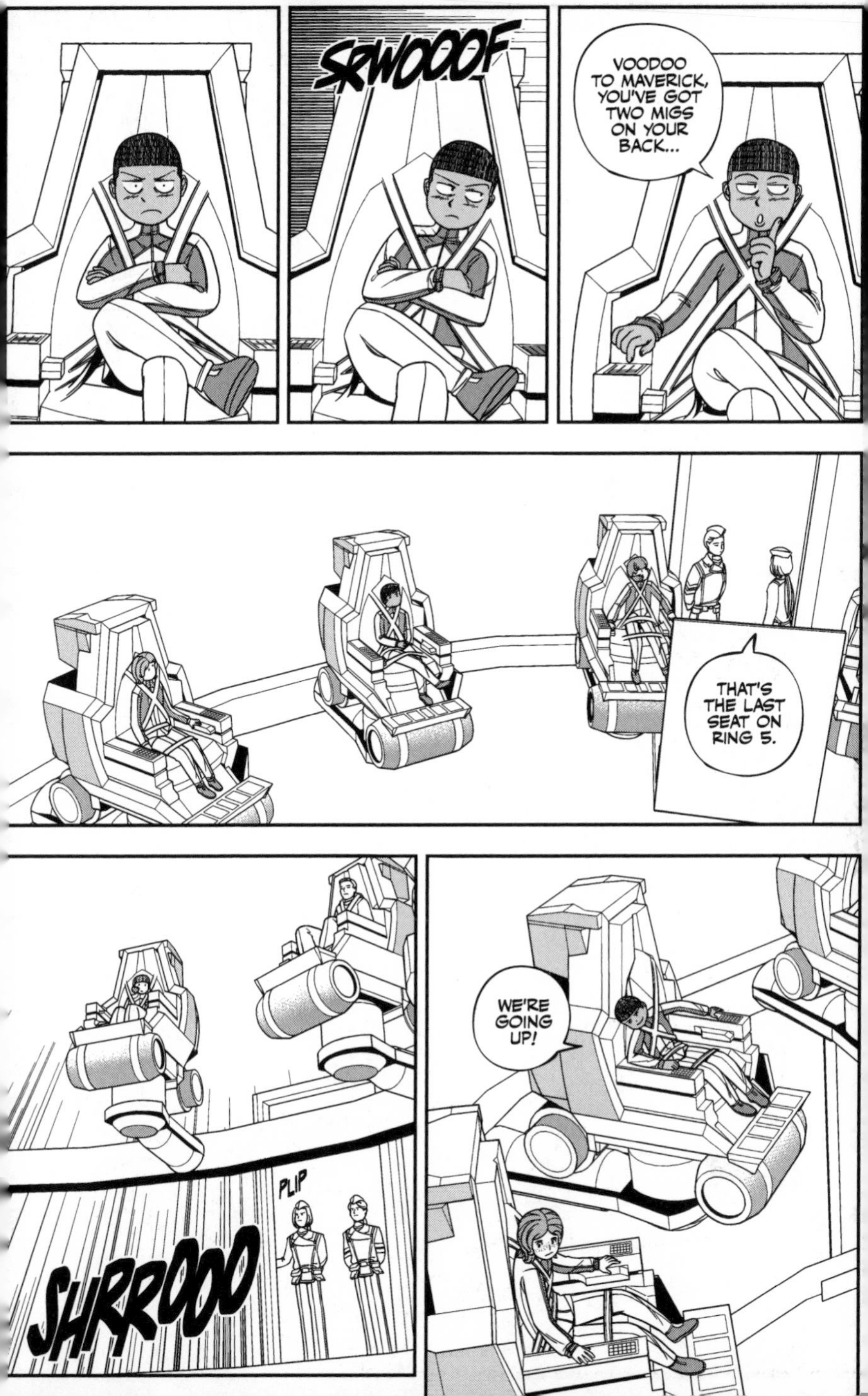
SRWOOOF
VOODOO TO MAVERICK, YOU'VE GOT TWO MIGS ON YOUR BACK...
THAT'S THE LAST SEAT ON RING 5.
PLIP
SHRROOO
WE'RE GOING UP!

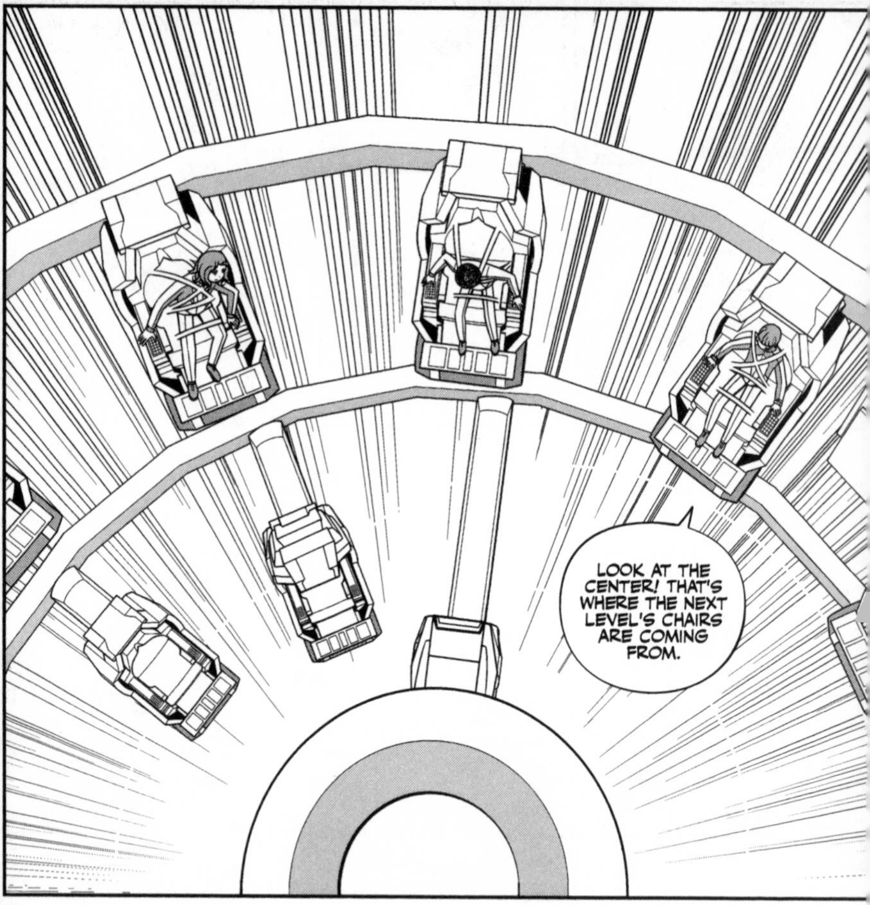
LOOK AT THE CENTER! THAT'S WHERE THE NEXT LEVEL'S CHAIRS ARE COMING FROM.
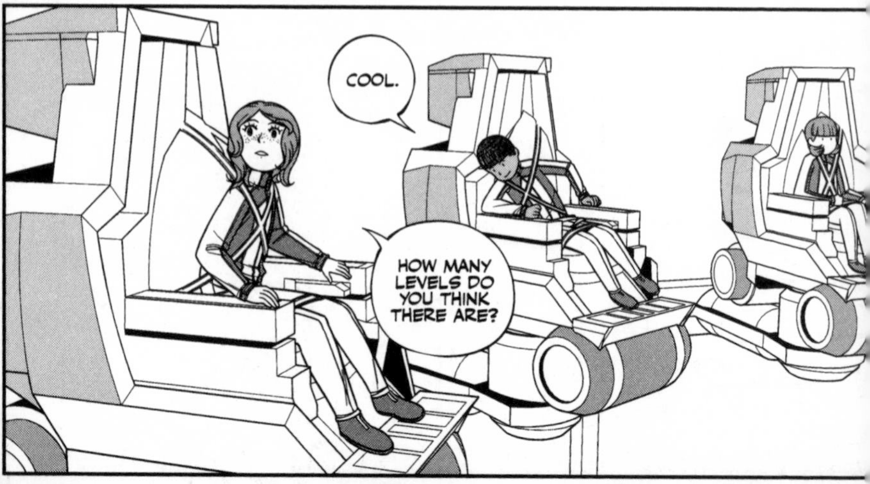
COOL.
HOW MANY LEVELS DO YOU THINK THERE ARE?

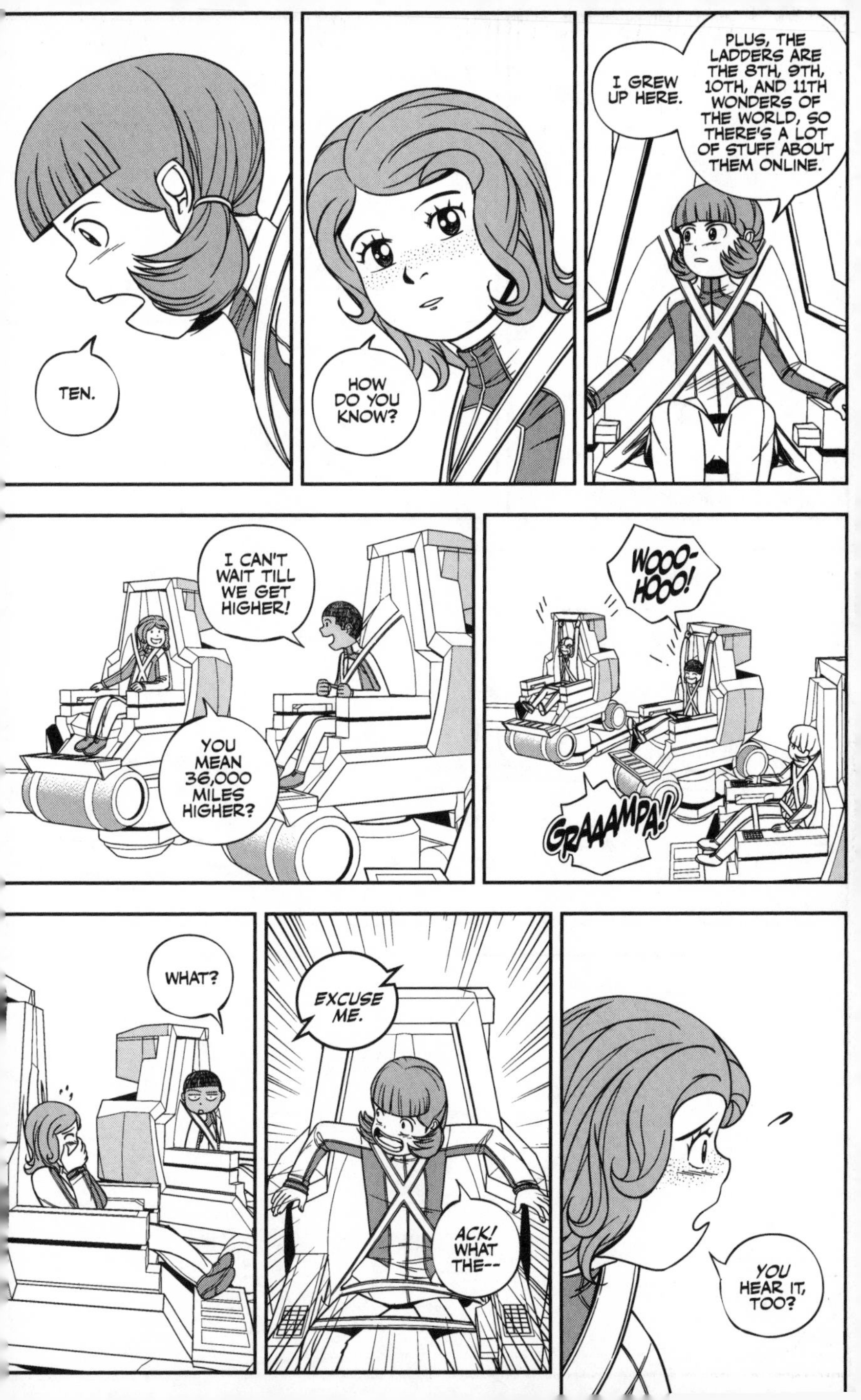
TEN.
HOW DO YOU KNOW?
I GREW UP HERE.
PLUS, THE LADDERS ARE THE 8TH, 9TH, 10TH, AND 11TH WONDERS OF THE WORLD, SO THERE'S A LOT OF STUFF ABOUT THEM ONLINE.
I CAN'T WAIT TILL WE GET HIGHER!
YOU MEAN 36,000 MILES HIGHER?
WOOO-HOOO!
GRAAAMPA!
WHAT?
EXCUSE ME.
ACK! WHAT THE--
YOU HEAR IT, TOO?

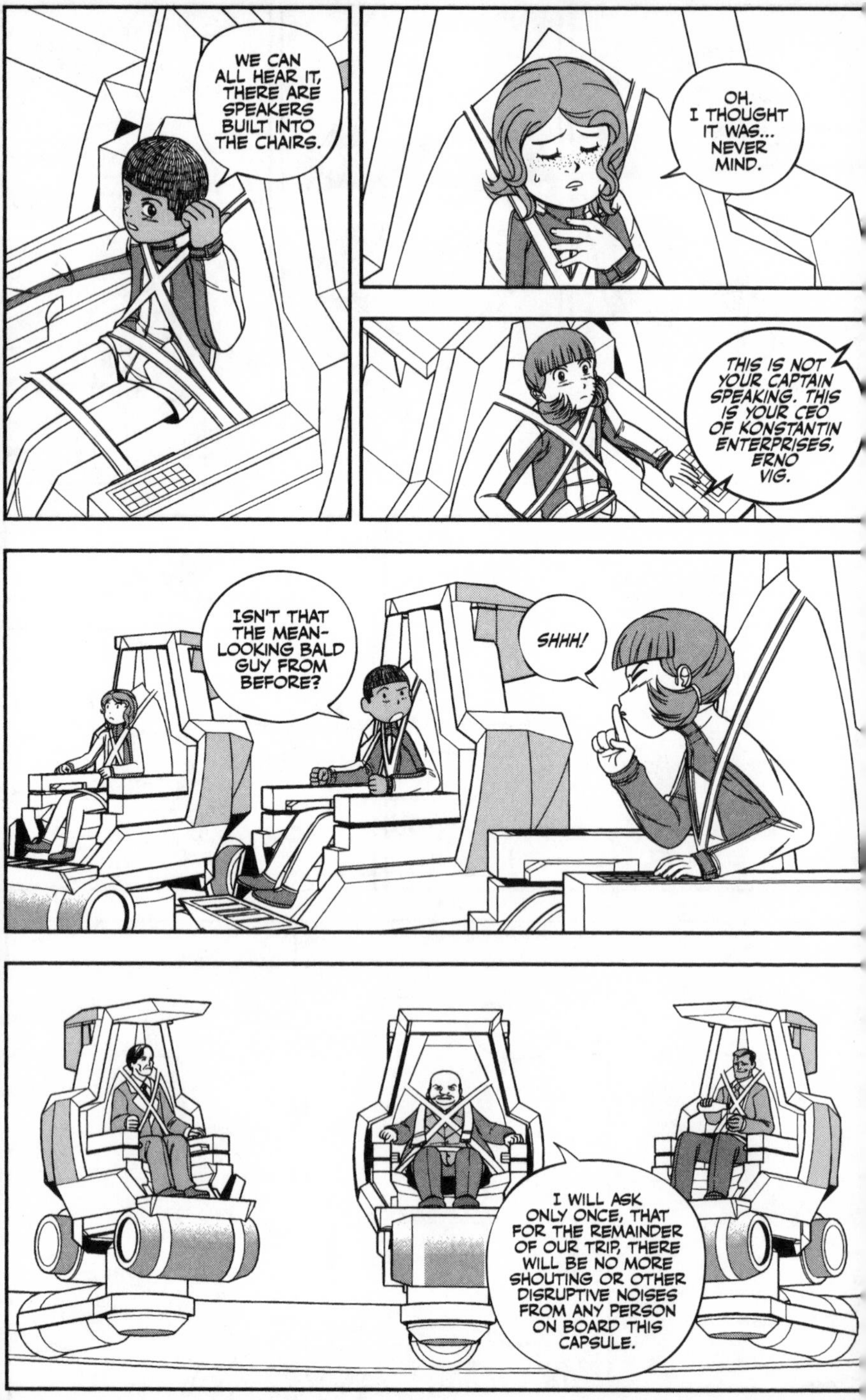
WE CAN ALL HEAR IT, THERE ARE SPEAKERS BUILT INTO THE CHAIRS.
OH. I THOUGHT IT WAS... NEVER MIND.
THIS IS NOT YOUR CAPTAIN SPEAKING. THIS IS YOUR CEO OF KONSTANTIN ENTERPRISES, ERNO VIG.
ISN'T THAT THE MEAN-LOOKING BALD GUY FROM BEFORE?
SHHH!
I WILL ASK ONLY ONCE, THAT FOR THE REMAINDER OF OUR TRIP, THERE WILL BE NO MORE SHOUTING OR OTHER DISRUPTIVE NOISES FROM ANY PERSON ON BOARD THIS CAPSULE.

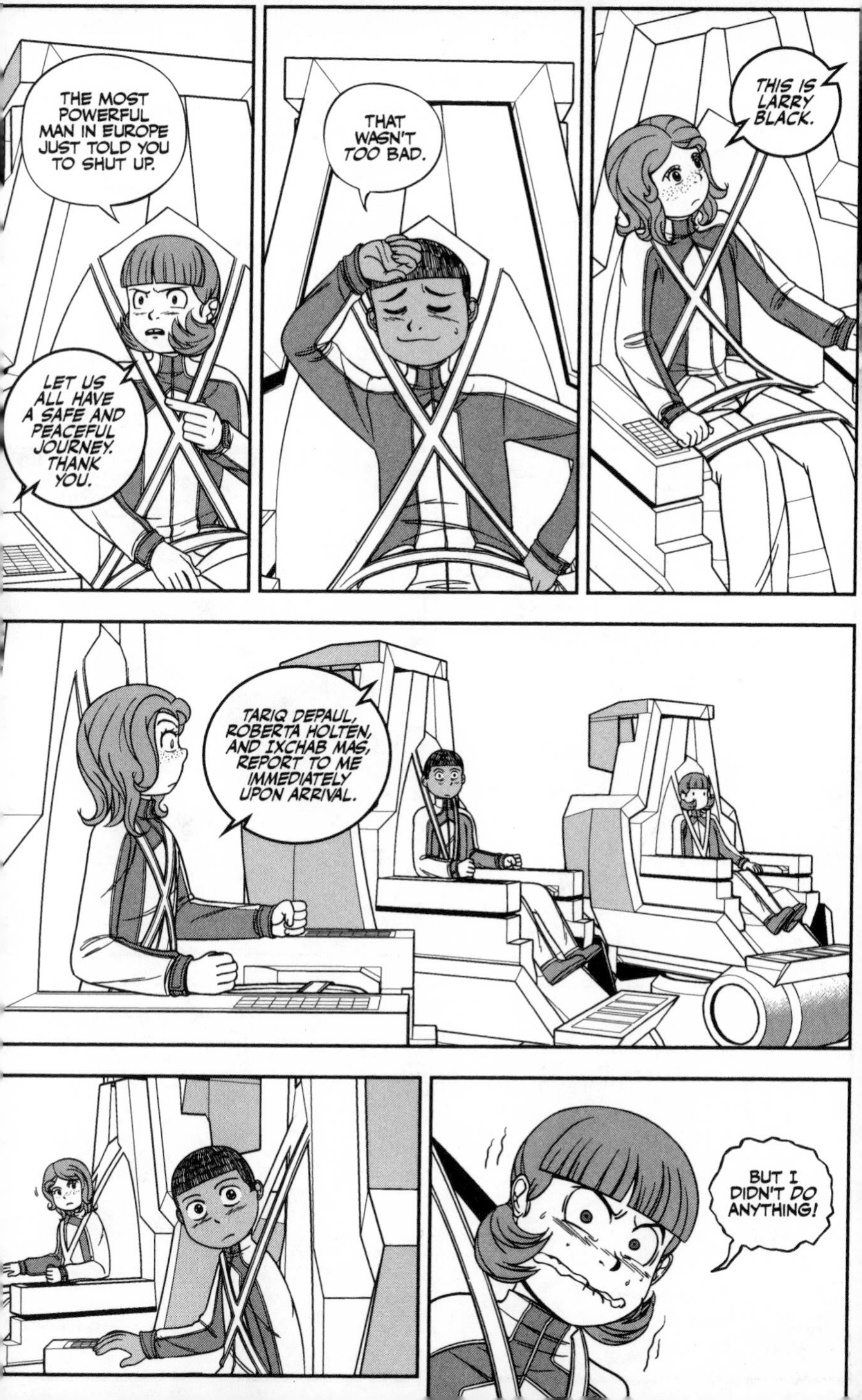
THE MOST POWERFUL MAN IN EUROPE JUST TOLD YOU TO SHUT UP.
LET US ALL HAVE A SAFE AND PEACEFUL JOURNEY. THANK YOU.
THAT WASN'T TOO BAD.
THIS IS LARRY BLACK.
TARIQ DEPAUL, ROBERTA HOLTEN, AND IXCHAB MAS, REPORT TO ME IMMEDIATELY UPON ARRIVAL.
BUT I DIDN'T DO ANYTHING!

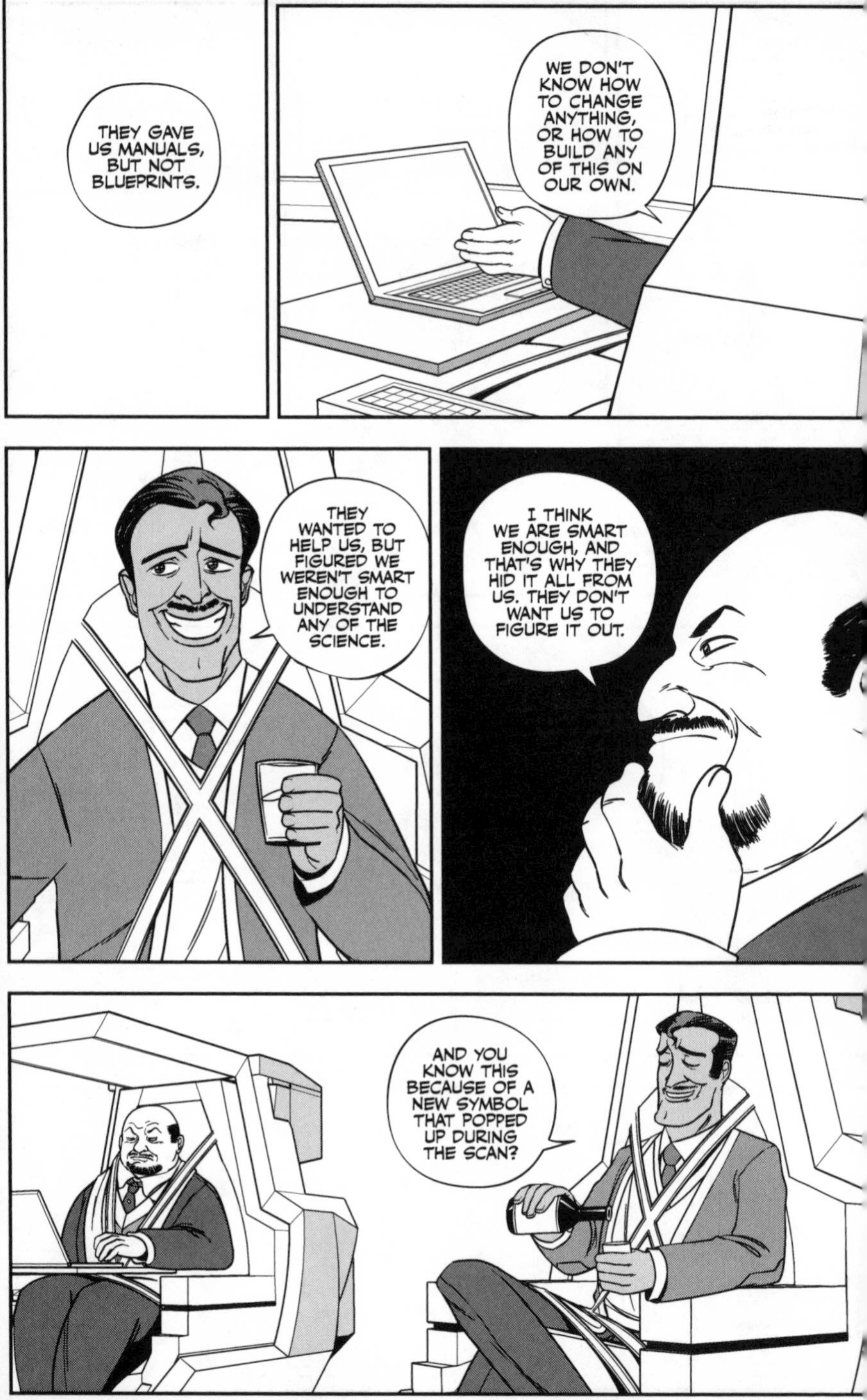
THEY GAVE US MANUALS, BUT NOT BLUEPRINTS.
WE DON'T KNOW HOW TO CHANGE ANYTHING, OR HOW TO BUILD ANY OF THIS ON OUR OWN.
THEY WANTED TO HELP US, BUT FIGURED WE WEREN'T SMART ENOUGH TO UNDERSTAND ANY OF THE SCIENCE.
I THINK WE ARE SMART ENOUGH, AND THAT'S WHY THEY HID IT ALL FROM US. THEY DON'T WANT US TO FIGURE IT OUT.
AND YOU KNOW THIS BECAUSE OF A NEW SYMBOL THAT POPPED UP DURING THE SCAN?

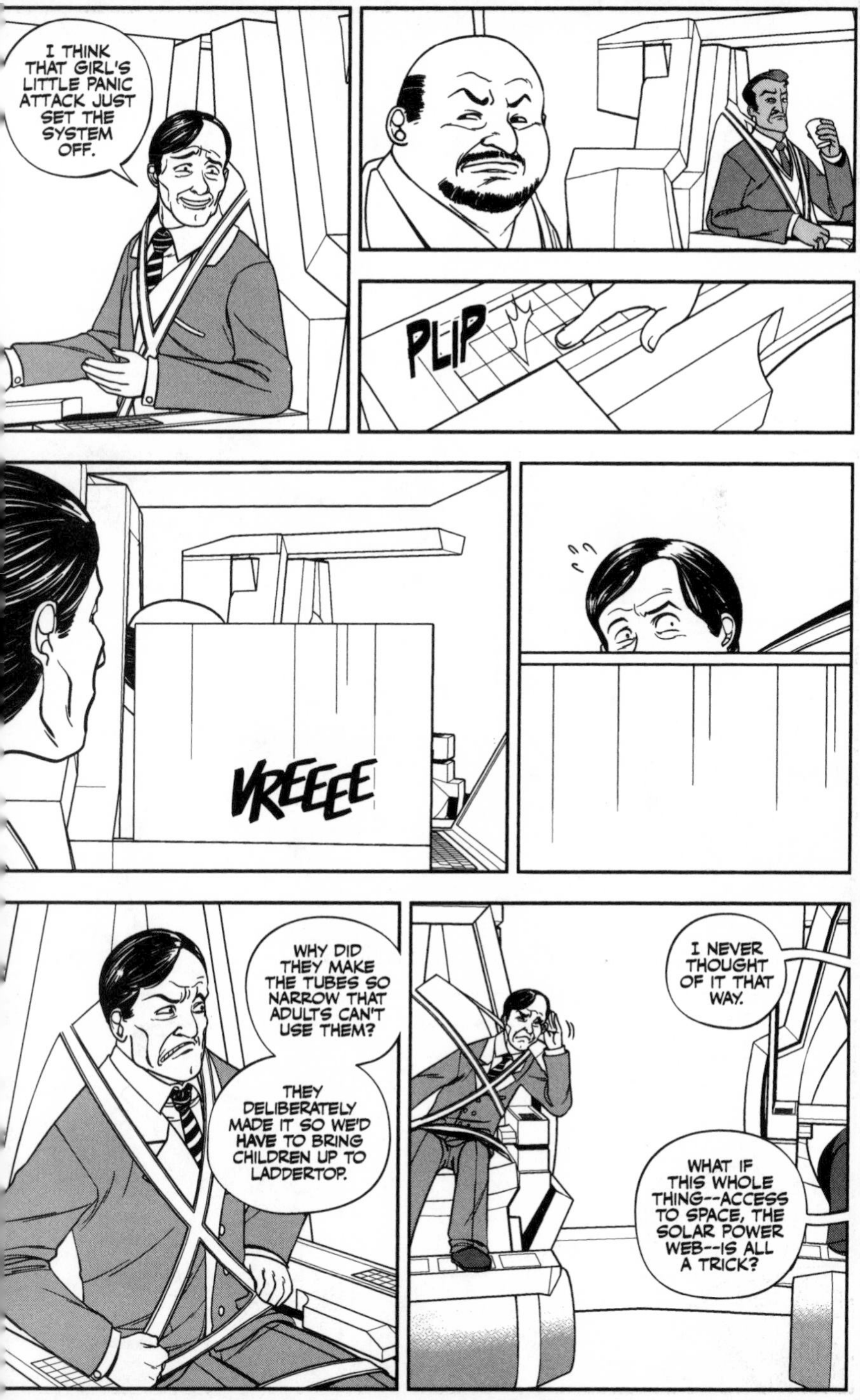
I THINK THAT GIRL'S LITTLE PANIC ATTACK JUST SET THE SYSTEM OFF.
PLIP
VREEEE
WHY DID THEY MAKE THE TUBES SO NARROW THAT ADULTS CAN'T USE THEM?
THEY DELIBERATELY MADE IT SO WE'D HAVE TO BRING CHILDREN UP TO LADDERTOP.
I NEVER THOUGHT OF IT THAT WAY.
WHAT IF THIS WHOLE THING--ACCESS TO SPACE, THE SOLAR POWER WEB--IS ALL A TRICK?

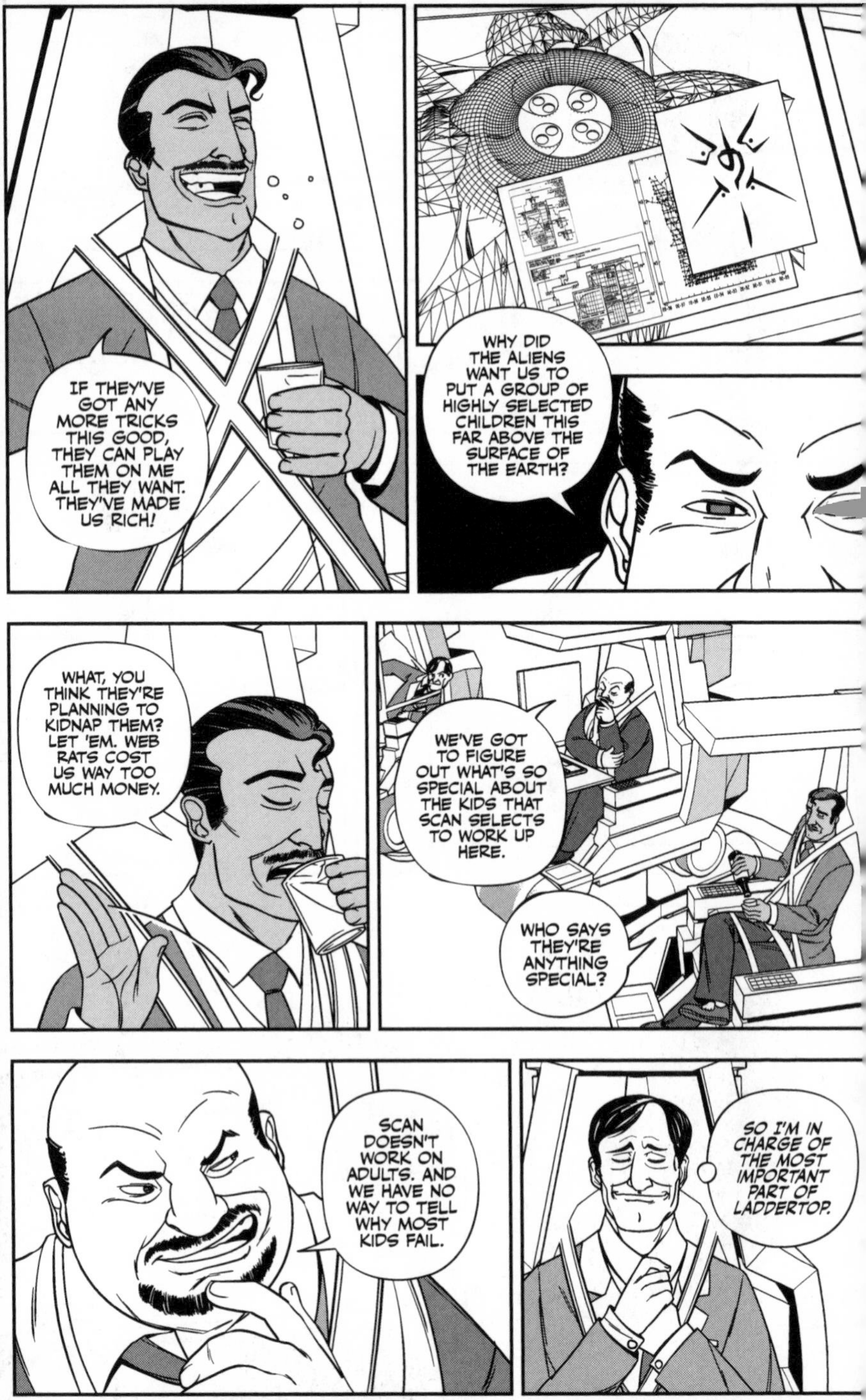
IF THEY'VE GOT ANY MORE TRICKS THIS GOOD, THEY CAN PLAY THEM ON ME ALL THEY WANT. THEY'VE MADE US RICH!
WHY DID THE ALIENS WANT US TO PUT A GROUP OF HIGHLY SELECTED CHILDREN THIS FAR ABOVE THE SURFACE OF THE EARTH?
WHAT, YOU THINK THEY'RE PLANNING TO KIDNAP THEM? LET 'EM. WEB RATS COST US WAY TOO MUCH MONEY.
WE'VE GOT TO FIGURE OUT WHAT'S SO SPECIAL ABOUT THE KIDS THAT SCAN SELECTS TO WORK UP HERE.
WHO SAYS THEY'RE ANYTHING SPECIAL?
SCAN DOESN'T WORK ON ADULTS. AND WE HAVE NO WAY TO TELL WHY MOST KIDS FAIL.
SO I'M IN CHARGE OF THE MOST IMPORTANT PART OF LADDERTOP.

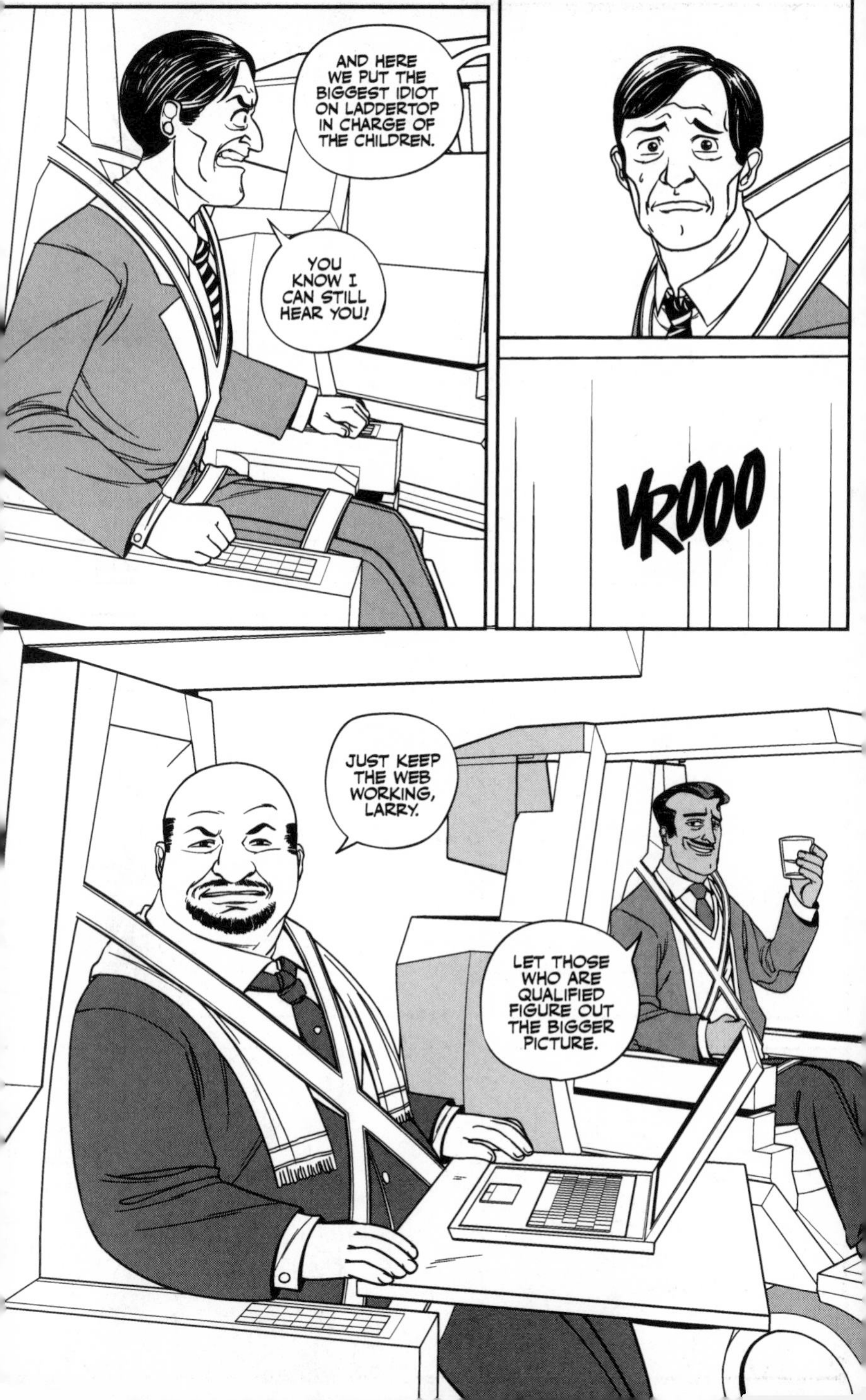
AND HERE WE PUT THE BIGGEST IDIOT ON LADDERTOP IN CHARGE OF THE CHILDREN.
YOU KNOW I CAN STILL HEAR YOU!
VROOO
JUST KEEP THE WEB WORKING, LARRY.
LET THOSE WHO ARE QUALIFIED FIGURE OUT THE BIGGER PICTURE.

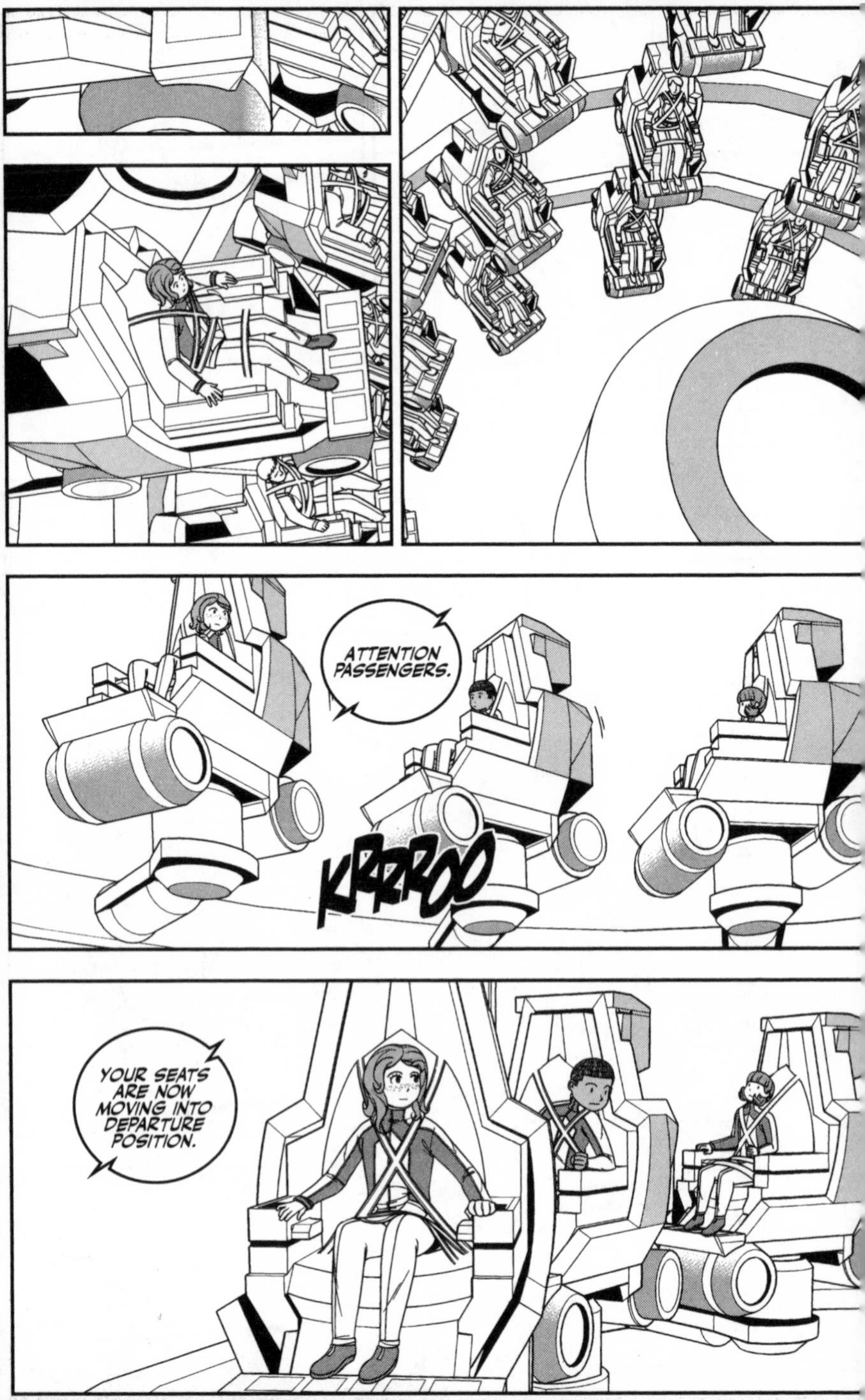
ATTENTION PASSENGERS.
KRRROO
YOUR SEATS ARE NOW MOVING INTO DEPARTURE POSITION.

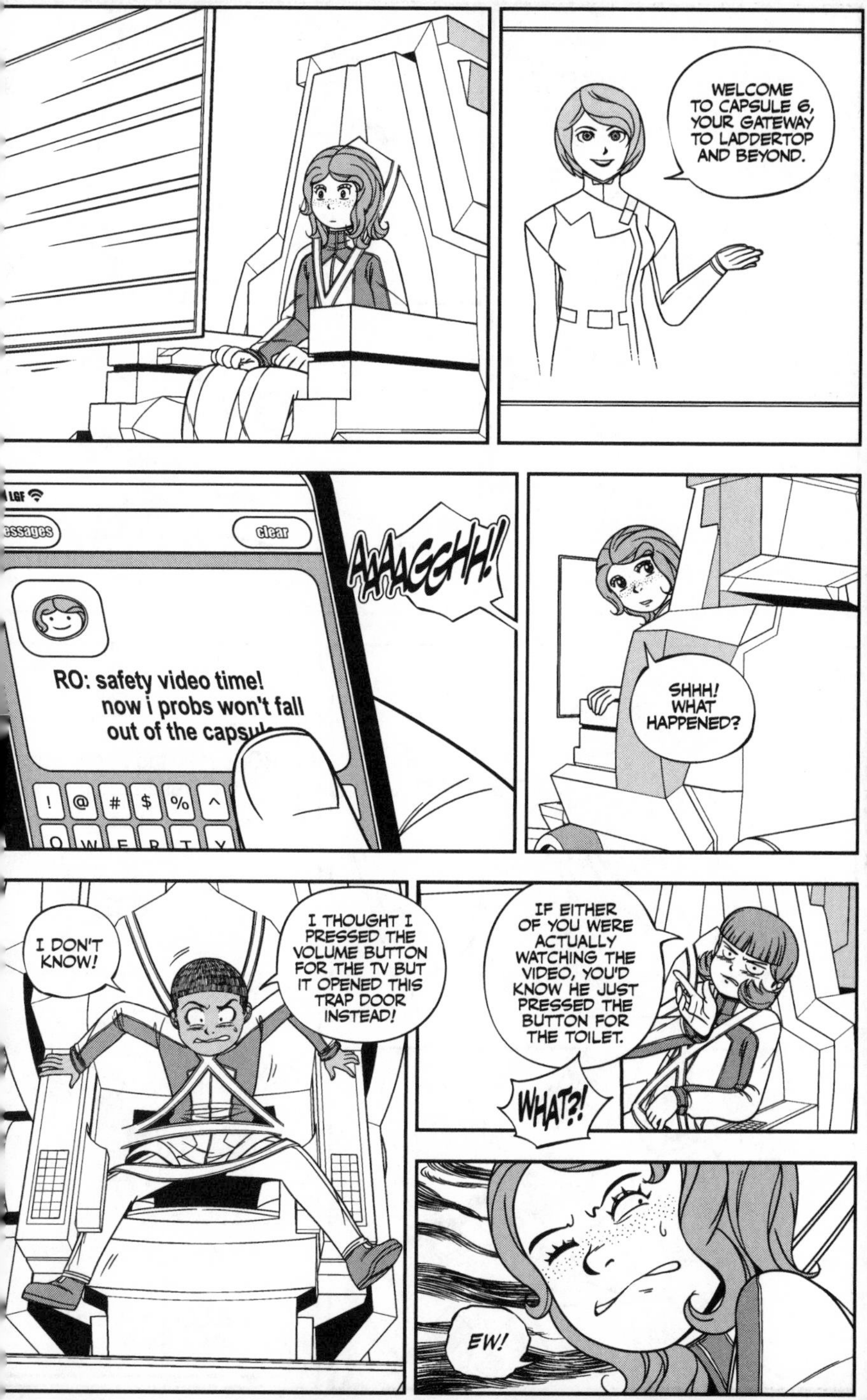
WELCOME TO CAPSULE 6, YOUR GATEWAY TO LADDERTOP AND BEYOND.
LGF
essages
clear
RO: safety video time! now i probs won't fall out of the capsul
AAAAGGHH!
SHHH! WHAT HAPPENED?
I DON'T KNOW!
I THOUGHT I PRESSED THE VOLUME BUTTON FOR THE TV BUT IT OPENED THIS TRAP DOOR INSTEAD!
IF EITHER OF YOU WERE ACTUALLY WATCHING THE VIDEO, YOU'D KNOW HE JUST PRESSED THE BUTTON FOR THE TOILET.
WHAT?!
EW!

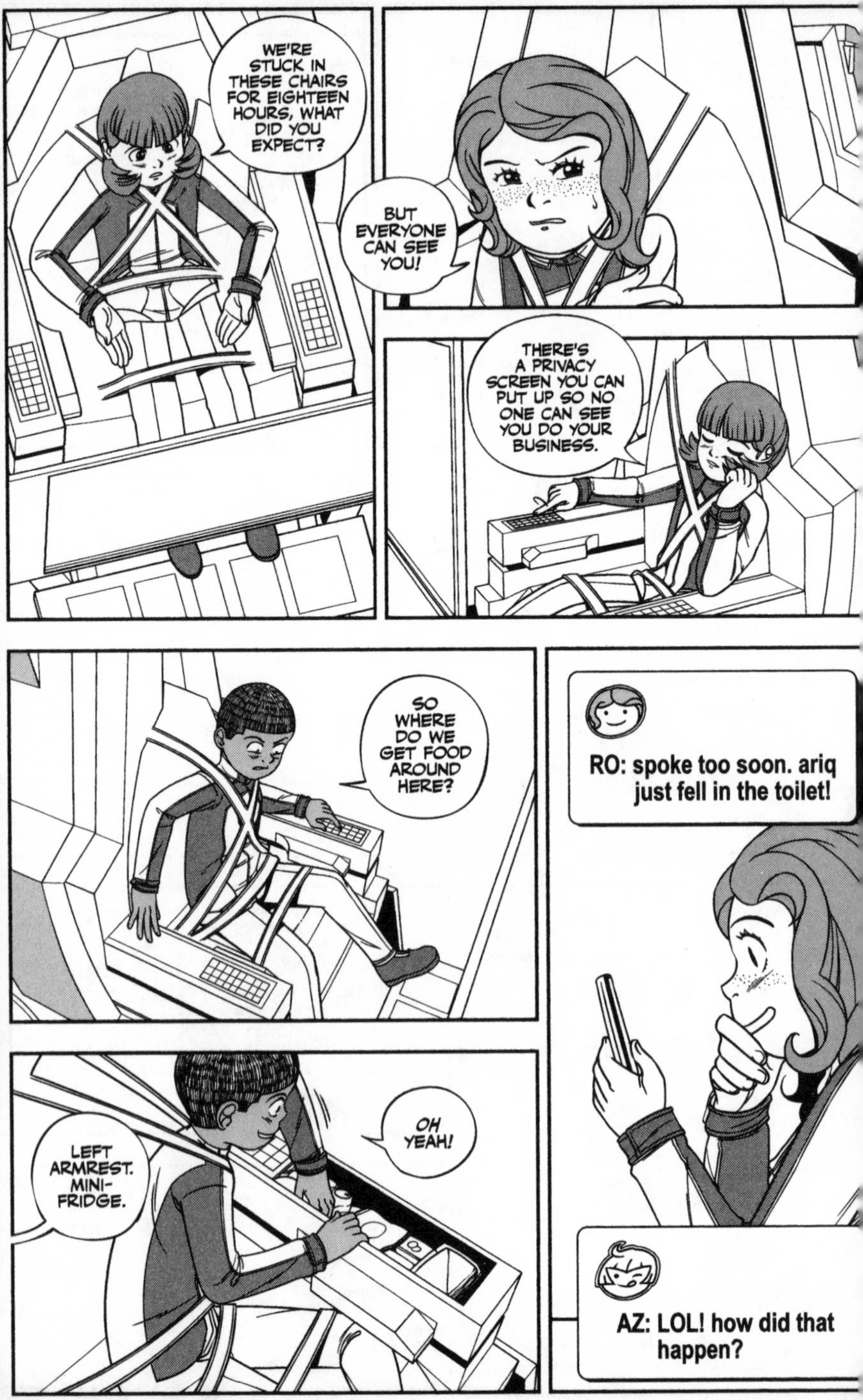
WE'RE STUCK IN THESE CHAIRS FOR EIGHTEEN HOURS, WHAT DID YOU EXPECT?
BUT EVERYONE CAN SEE YOU!
THERE'S A PRIVACY SCREEN YOU CAN PUT UP SO NO ONE CAN SEE YOU DO YOUR BUSINESS.
SO WHERE DO WE GET FOOD AROUND HERE?
LEFT ARMREST. MINI-FRIDGE.
OH YEAH!
RO: spoke too soon. ariq just fell in the toilet!
AZ: LOL! how did that happen?

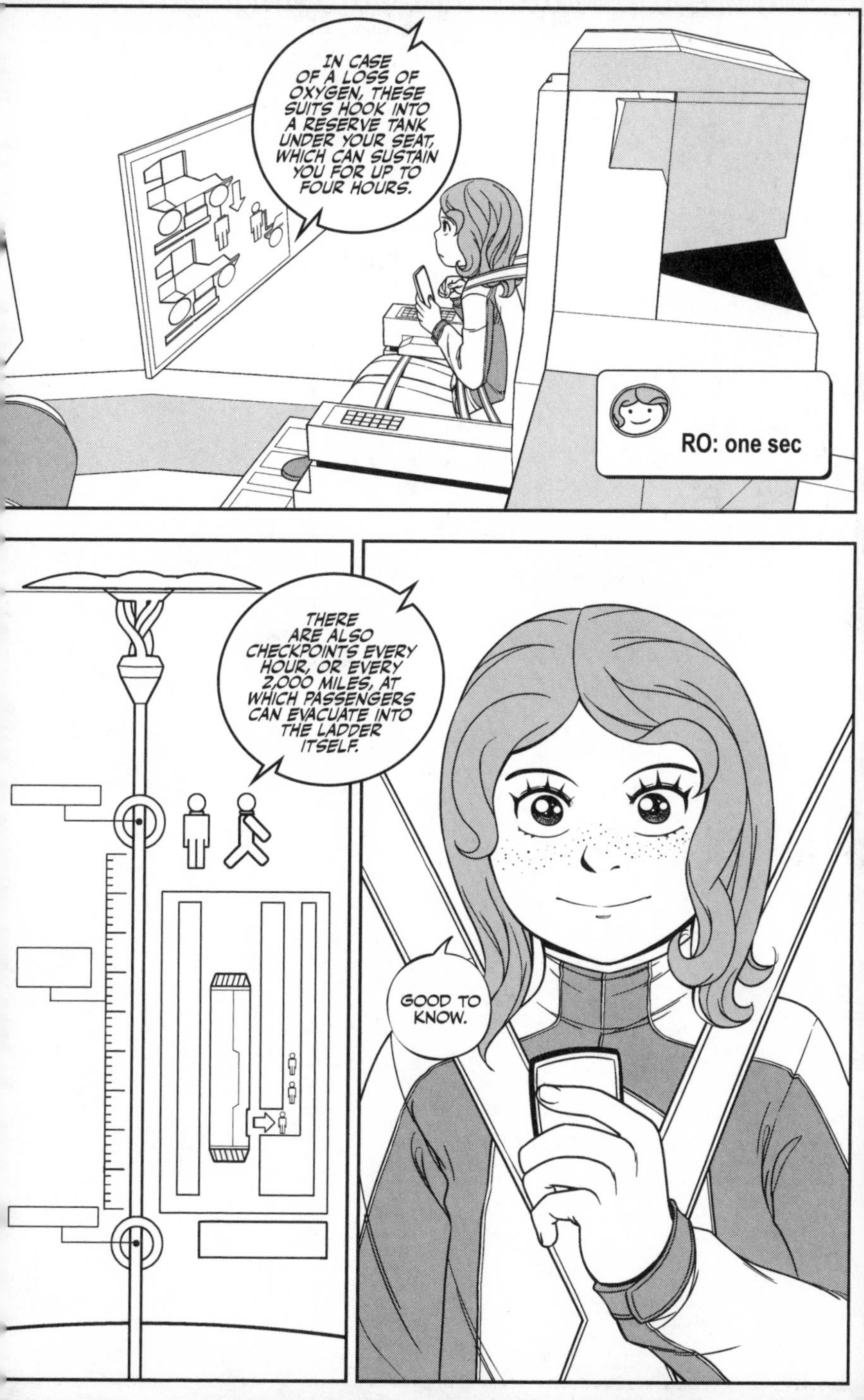

IN CASE OF A LOSS OF OXYGEN, THESE SUITS HOOK INTO A RESERVE TANK UNDER YOUR SEAT, WHICH CAN SUSTAIN YOU FOR UP TO FOUR HOURS.
RO: one sec
THERE ARE ALSO CHECKPOINTS EVERY HOUR, OR EVERY 2,000 MILES, AT WHICH PASSENGERS CAN EVACUATE INTO THE LADDER ITSELF.
GOOD TO KNOW.

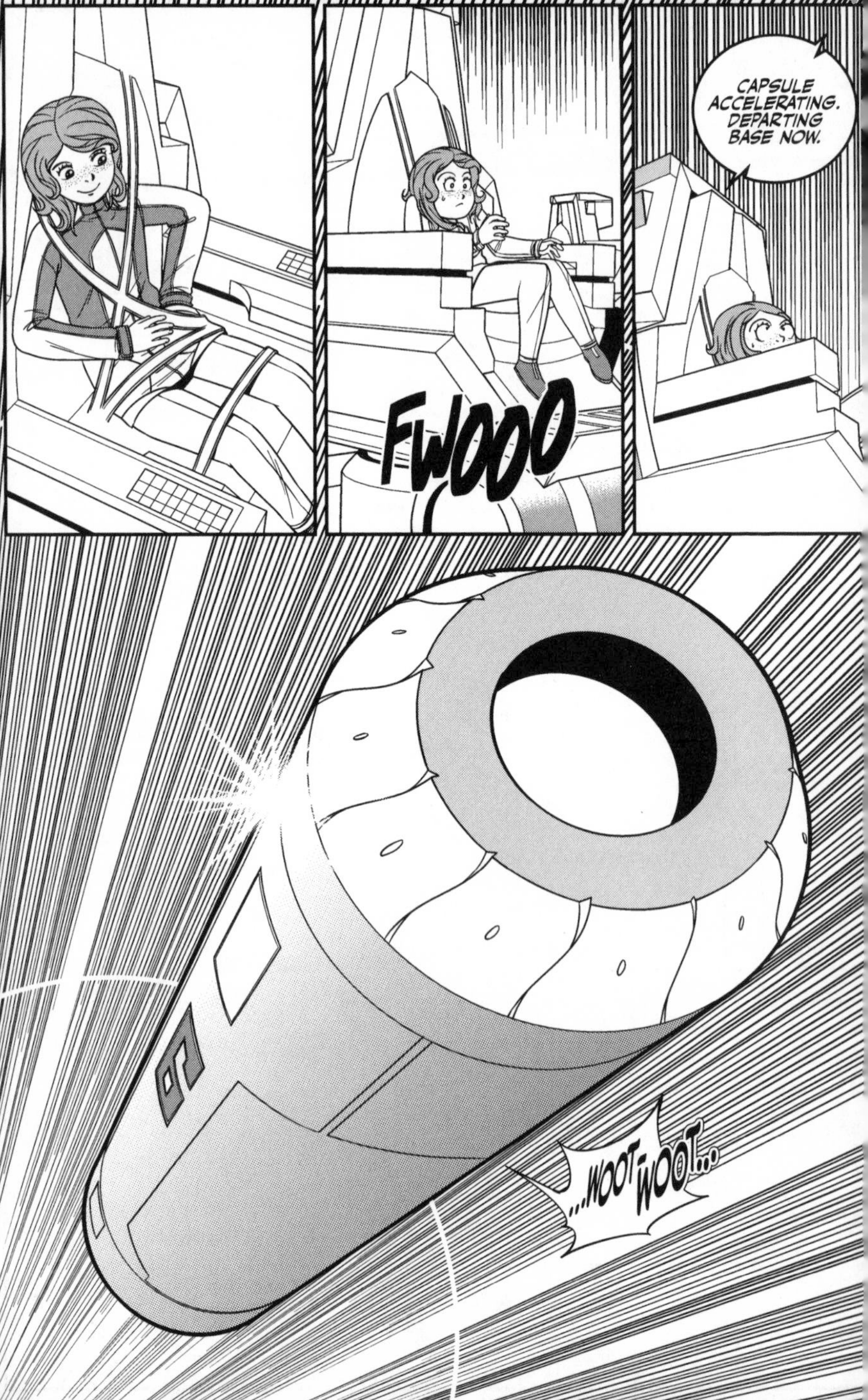
FWOOO
CAPSULE ACCELERATING. DEPARTING BASE NOW.
...WOOT-WOOT...

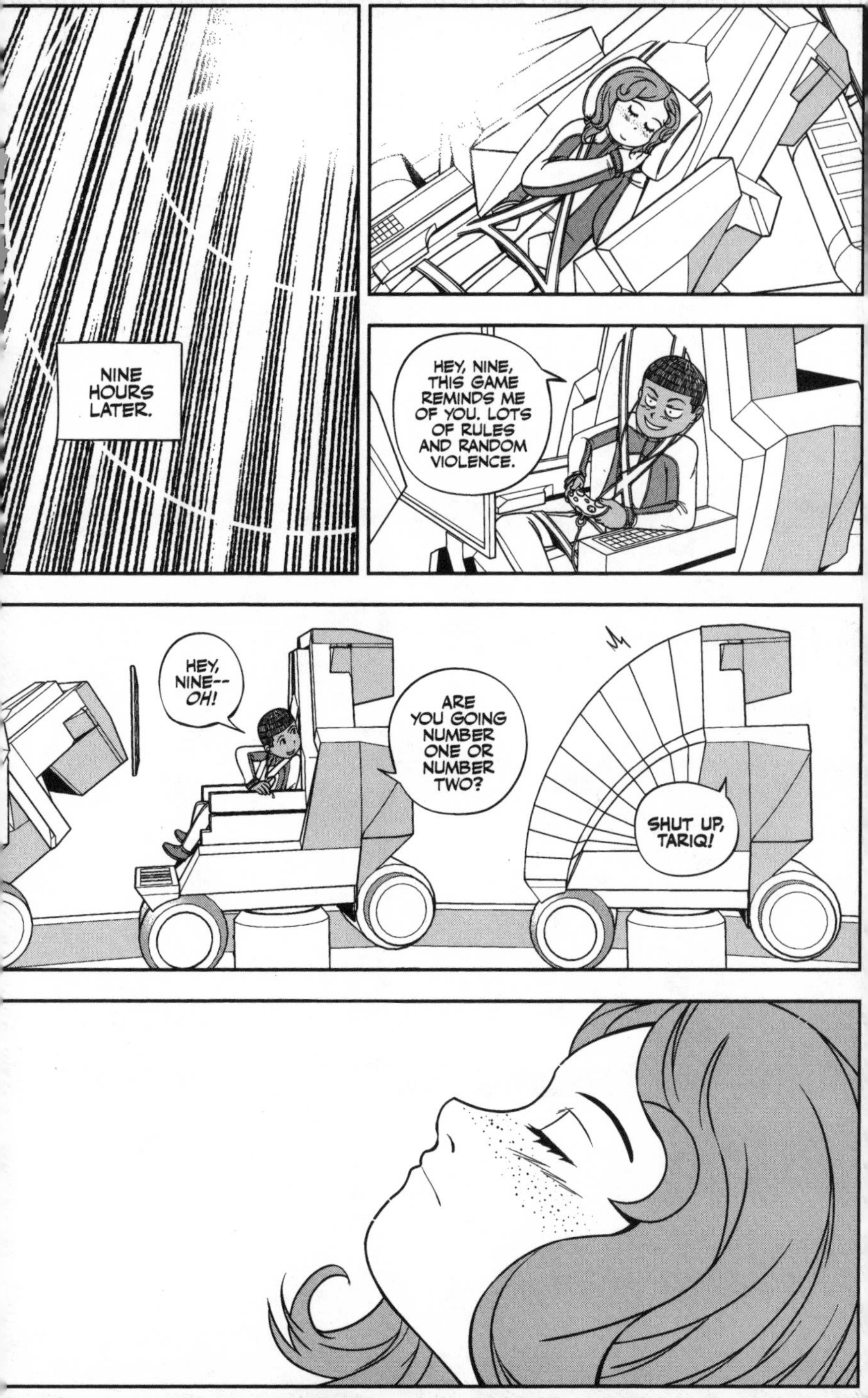
NINE HOURS LATER.
HEY, NINE, THIS GAME REMINDS ME OF YOU. LOTS OF RULES AND RANDOM VIOLENCE.
HEY, NINE-- OH!
ARE YOU GOING NUMBER ONE OR NUMBER TWO?
SHUT UP, TARIQ!

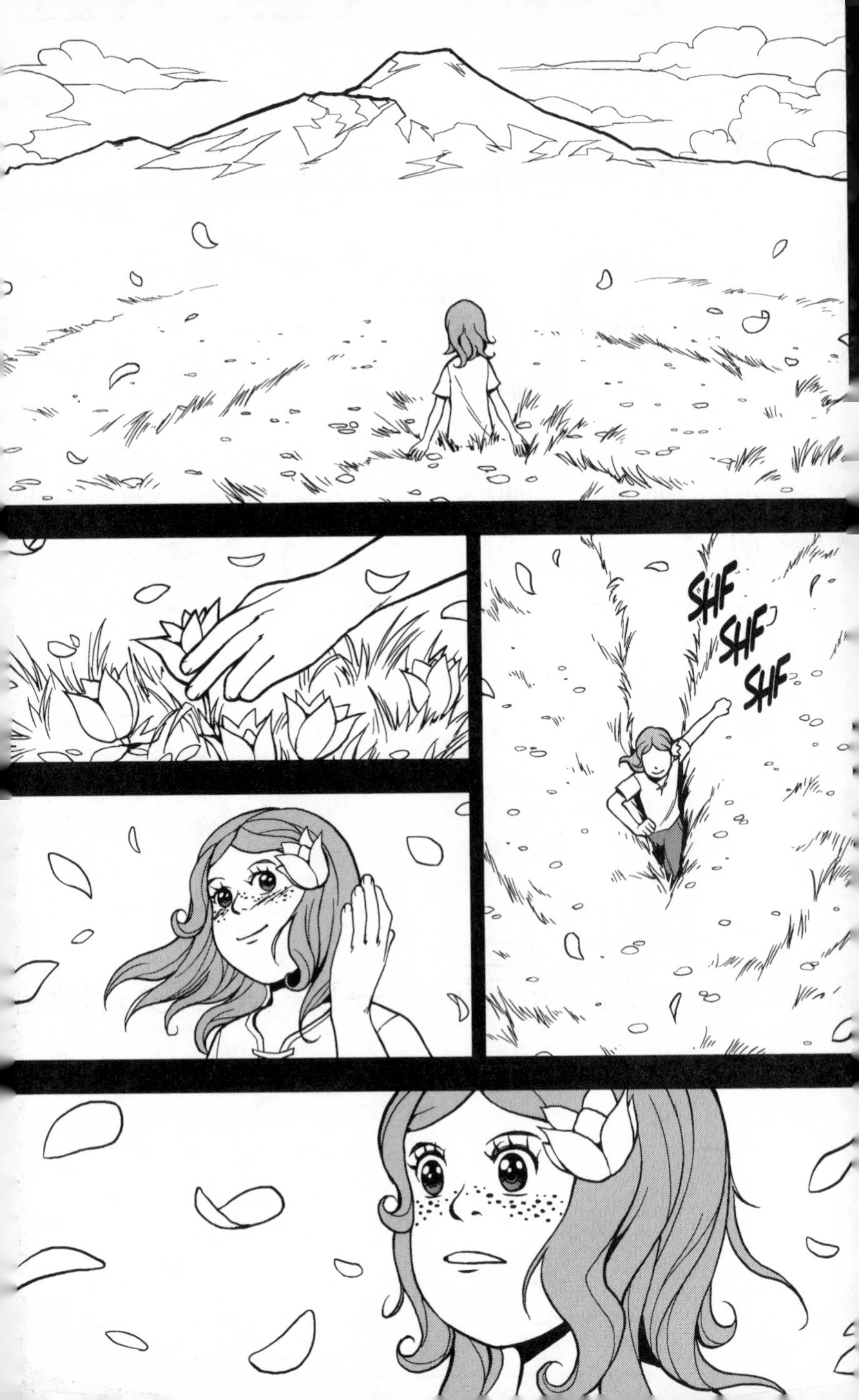
SHF
SHF
SHF

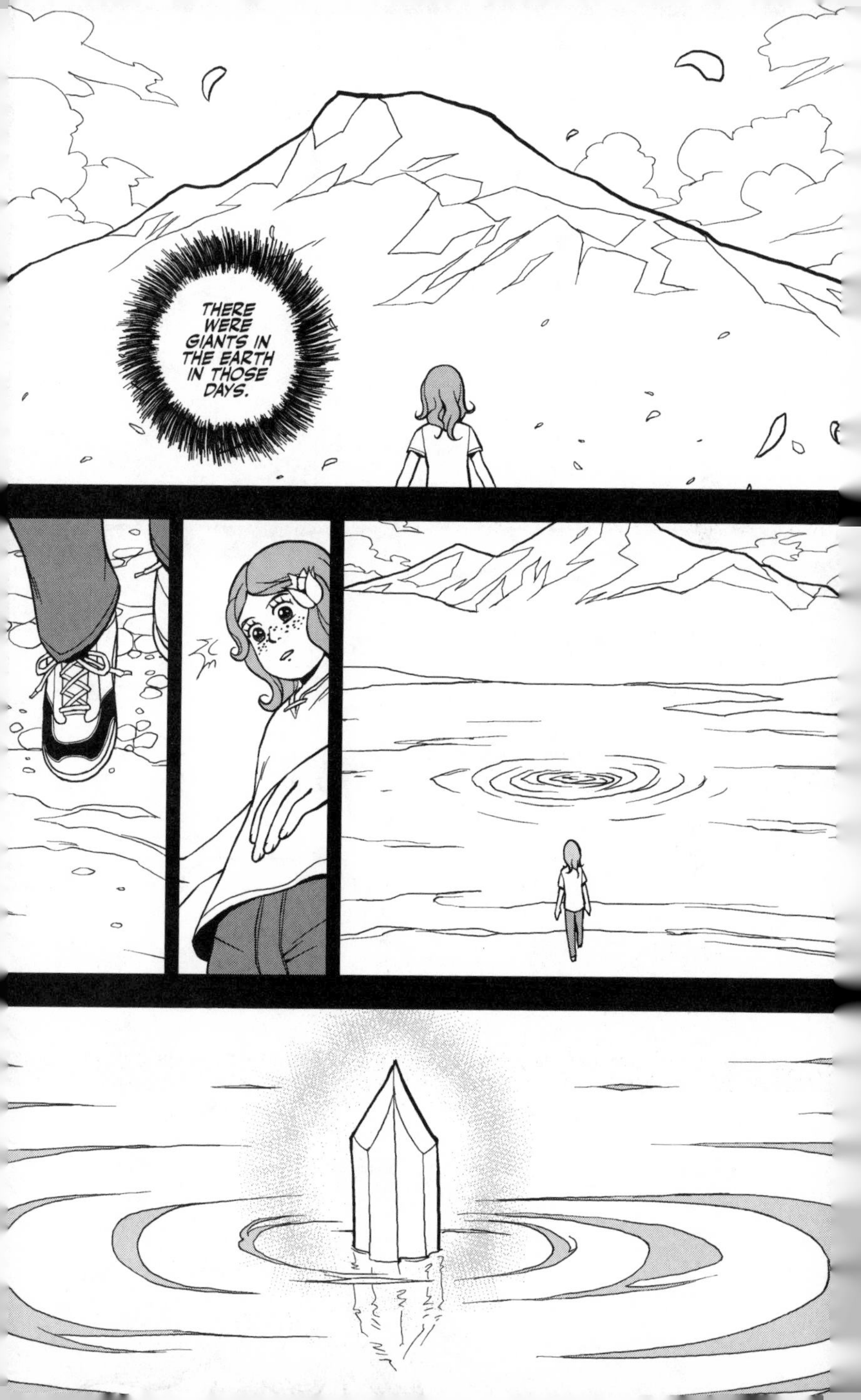
THERE WERE GIANTS IN THE EARTH IN THOSE DAYS.

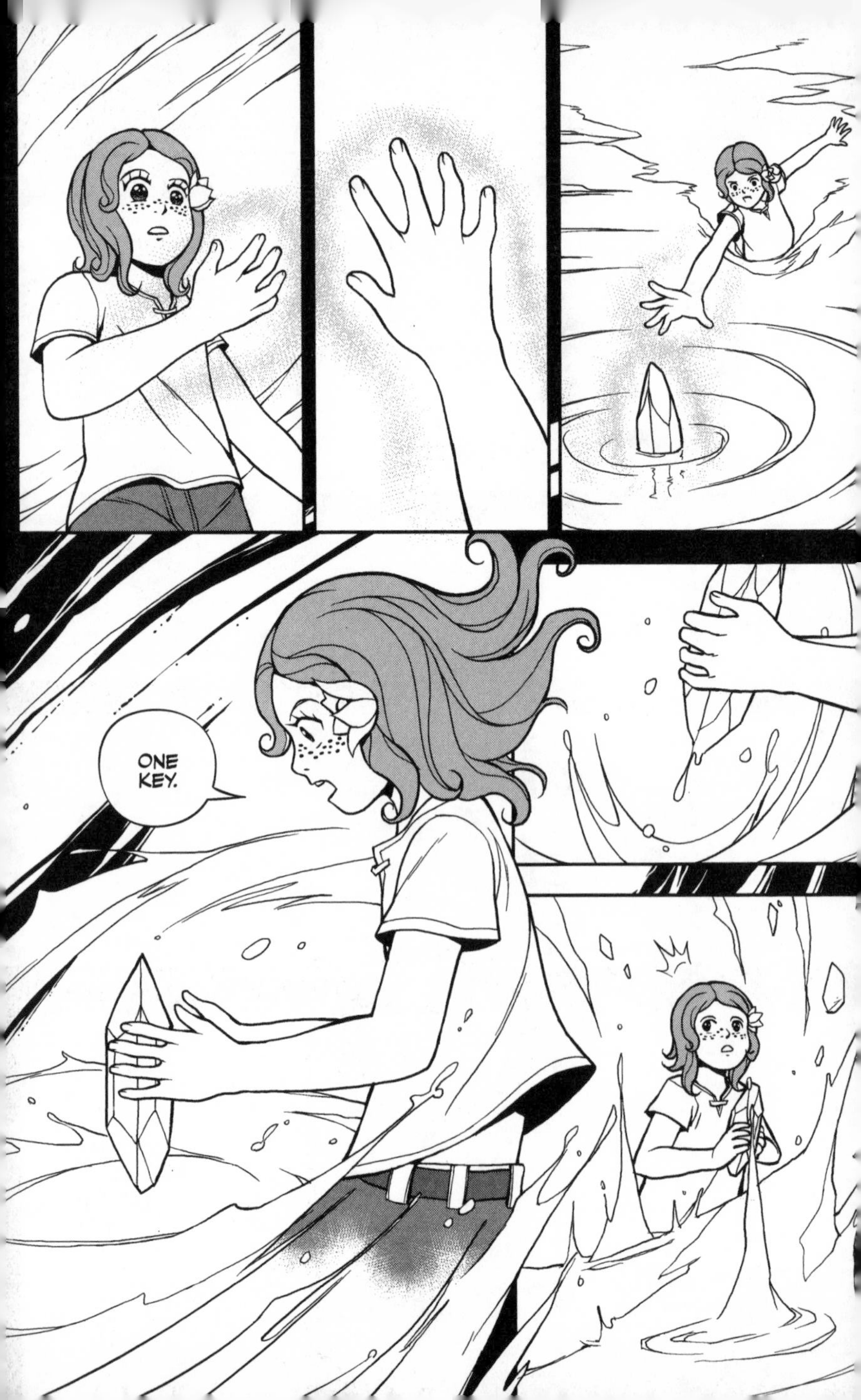
ONE KEY.

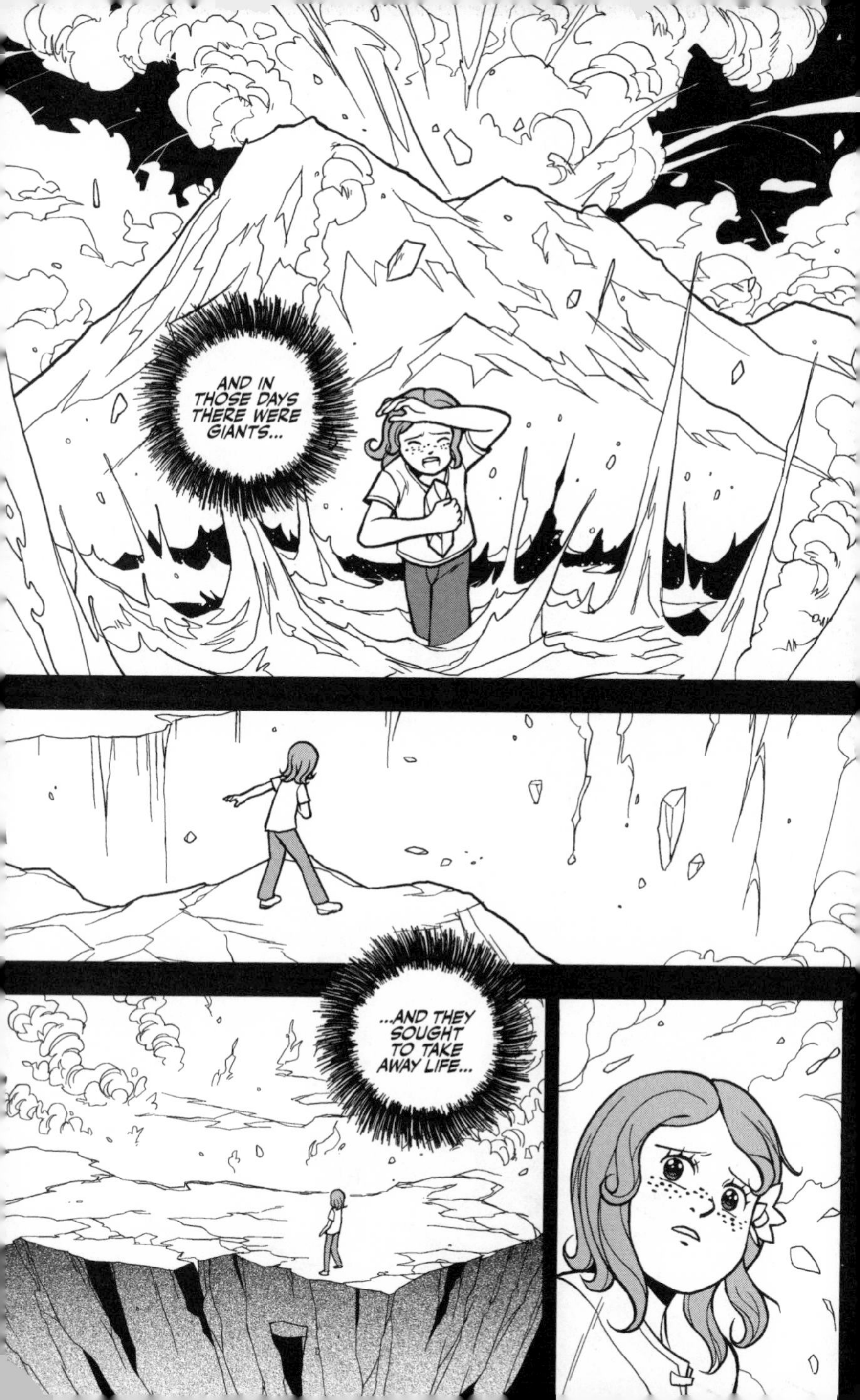
AND IN THOSE DAYS THERE WERE GIANTS...
...AND THEY SOUGHT TO TAKE AWAY LIFE...

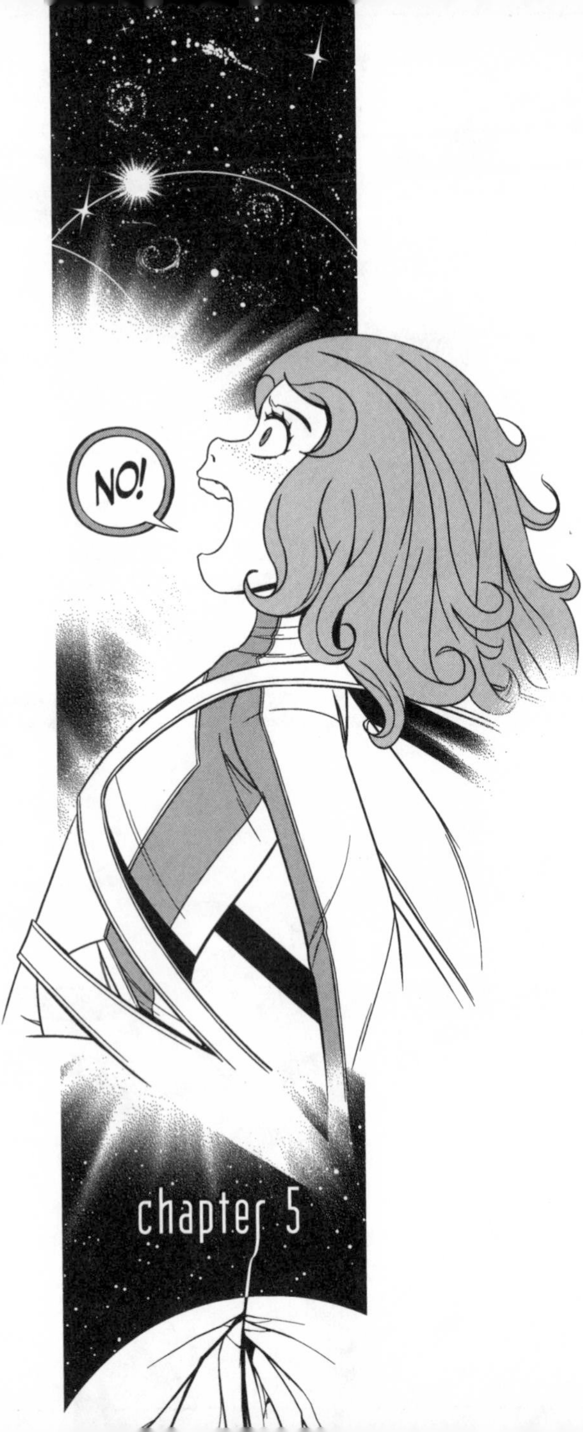
NO!
chapter 5

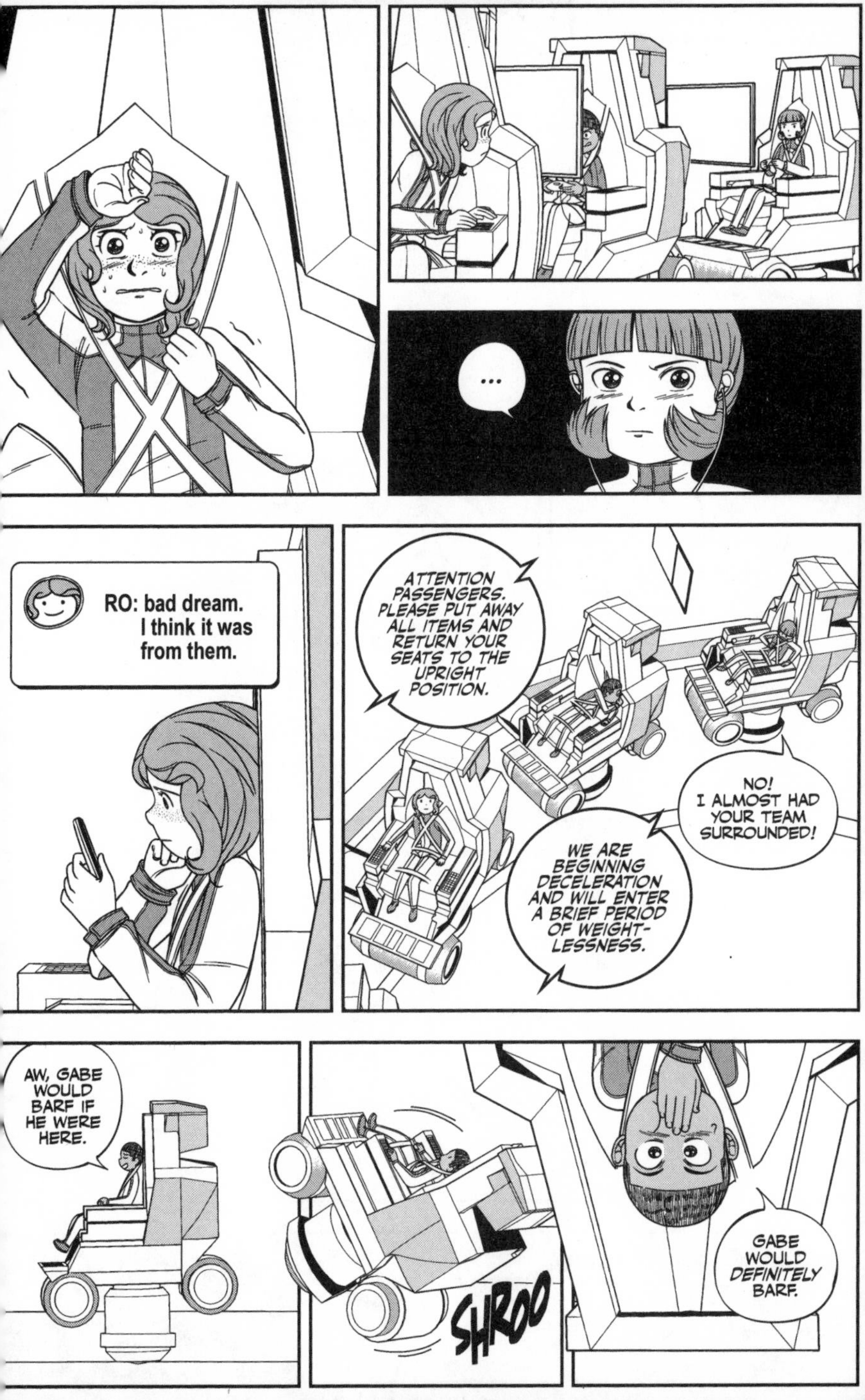
...
RO: bad dream. I think it was from them.
ATTENTION PASSENGERS. PLEASE PUT AWAY ALL ITEMS AND RETURN YOUR SEATS TO THE UPRIGHT POSITION.
NO! I ALMOST HAD YOUR TEAM SURROUNDED!
WE ARE BEGINNING DECELERATION AND WILL ENTER A BRIEF PERIOD OF WEIGHT-LESSNESS.
AW, GABE WOULD BARF IF HE WERE HERE.
SHROO
GABE WOULD DEFINITELY BARF.

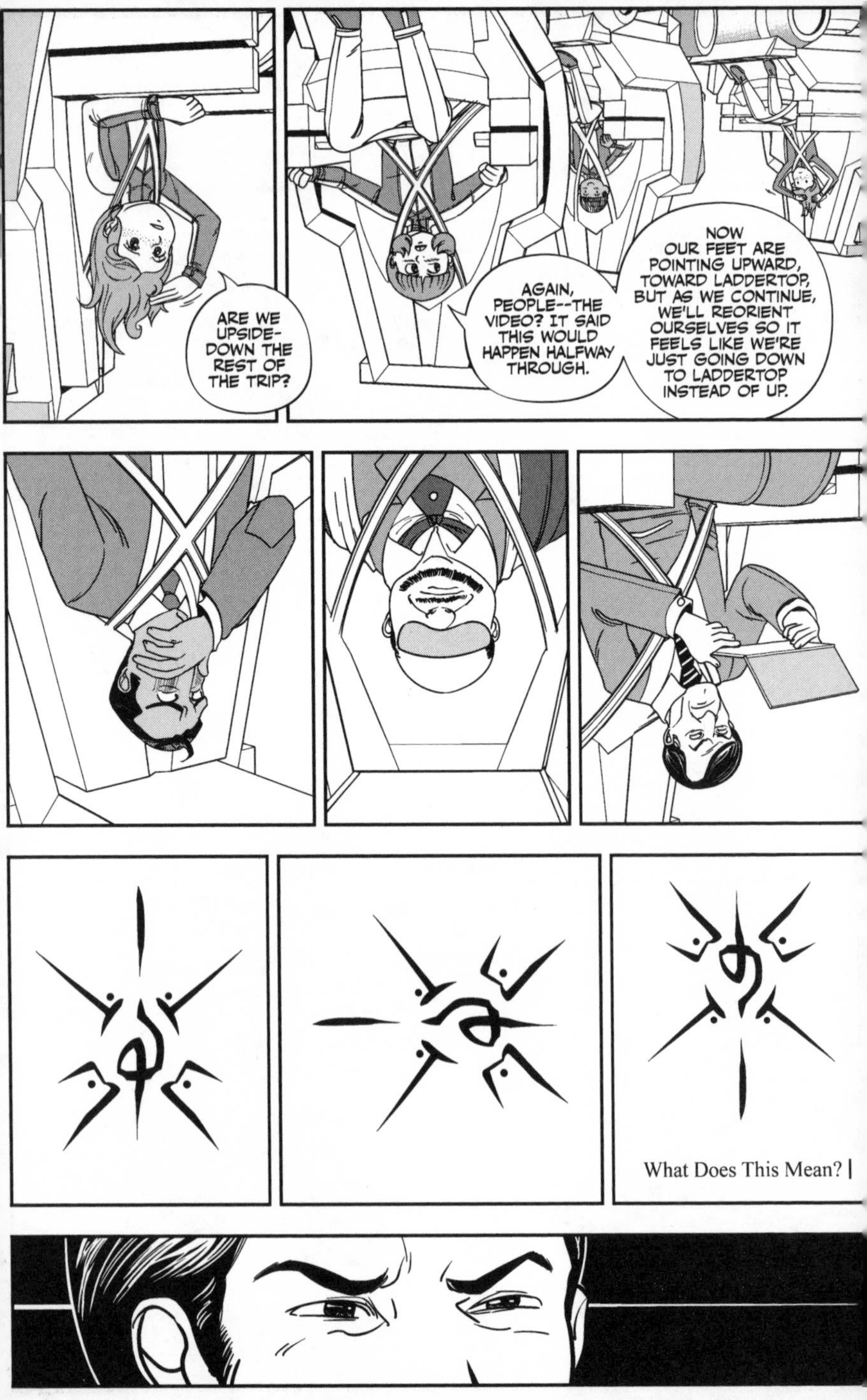
ARE WE UPSIDE-DOWN THE REST OF THE TRIP?
AGAIN, PEOPLE--THE VIDEO? IT SAID THIS WOULD HAPPEN HALFWAY THROUGH.
NOW OUR FEET ARE POINTING UPWARD, TOWARD LADDERTOP, BUT AS WE CONTINUE, WE'LL REORIENT OURSELVES SO IT FEELS LIKE WE'RE JUST GOING DOWN TO LADDERTOP INSTEAD OF UP.
What Does This Mean? |

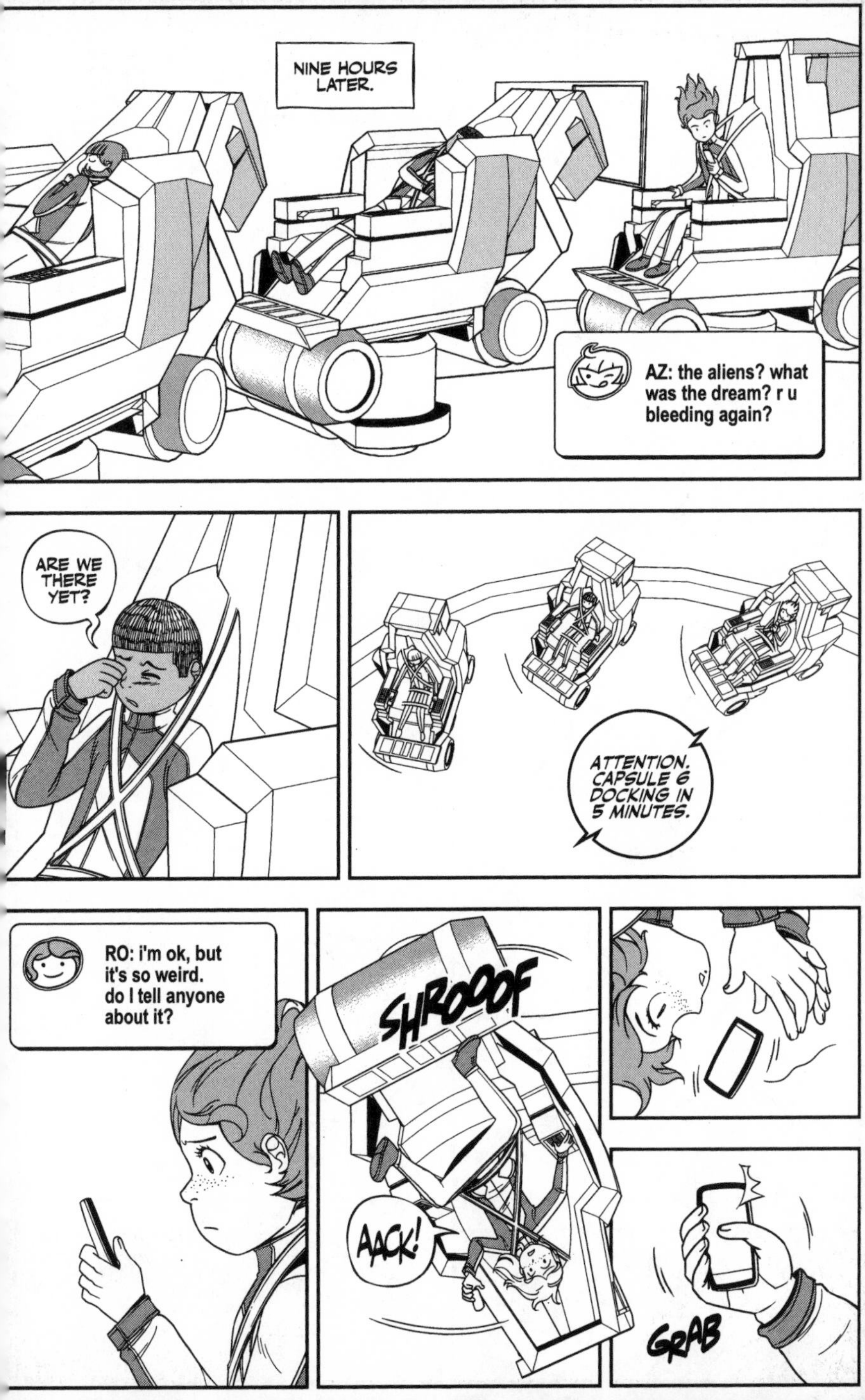
NINE HOURS LATER.
AZ: the aliens? what was the dream? r u bleeding again?
ARE WE THERE YET?
ATTENTION. CAPSULE 6 DOCKING IN 5 MINUTES.
RO: i'm ok, but it's so weird. do I tell anyone about it?
SHROOOF
AACK!
GRAB

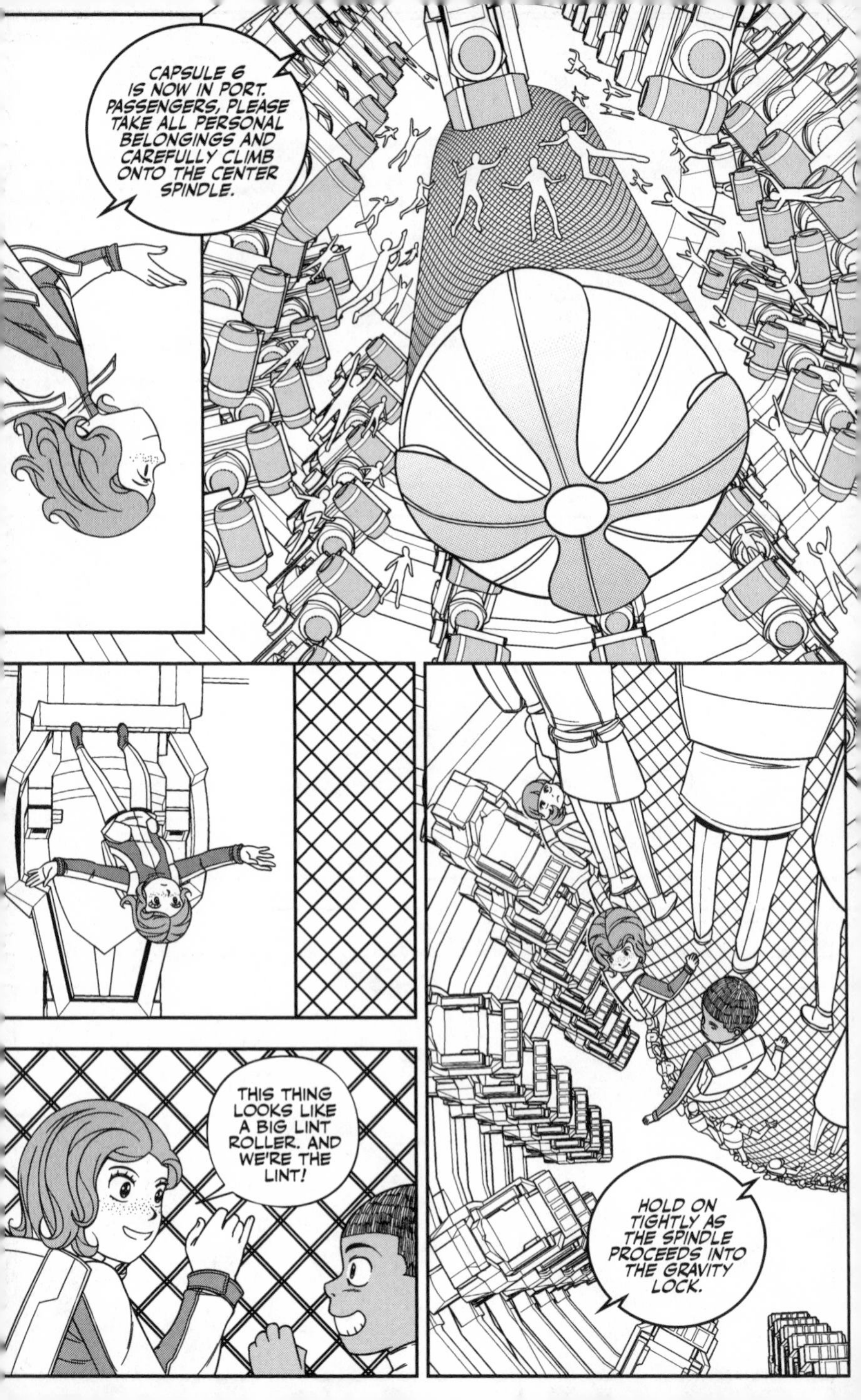
CAPSULE 6 IS NOW IN PORT. PASSENGERS, PLEASE TAKE ALL PERSONAL BELONGINGS AND CAREFULLY CLIMB ONTO THE CENTER SPINDLE.
THIS THING LOOKS LIKE A BIG LINT ROLLER. AND WE'RE THE LINT!
HOLD ON TIGHTLY AS THE SPINDLE PROCEEDS INTO THE GRAVITY LOCK.

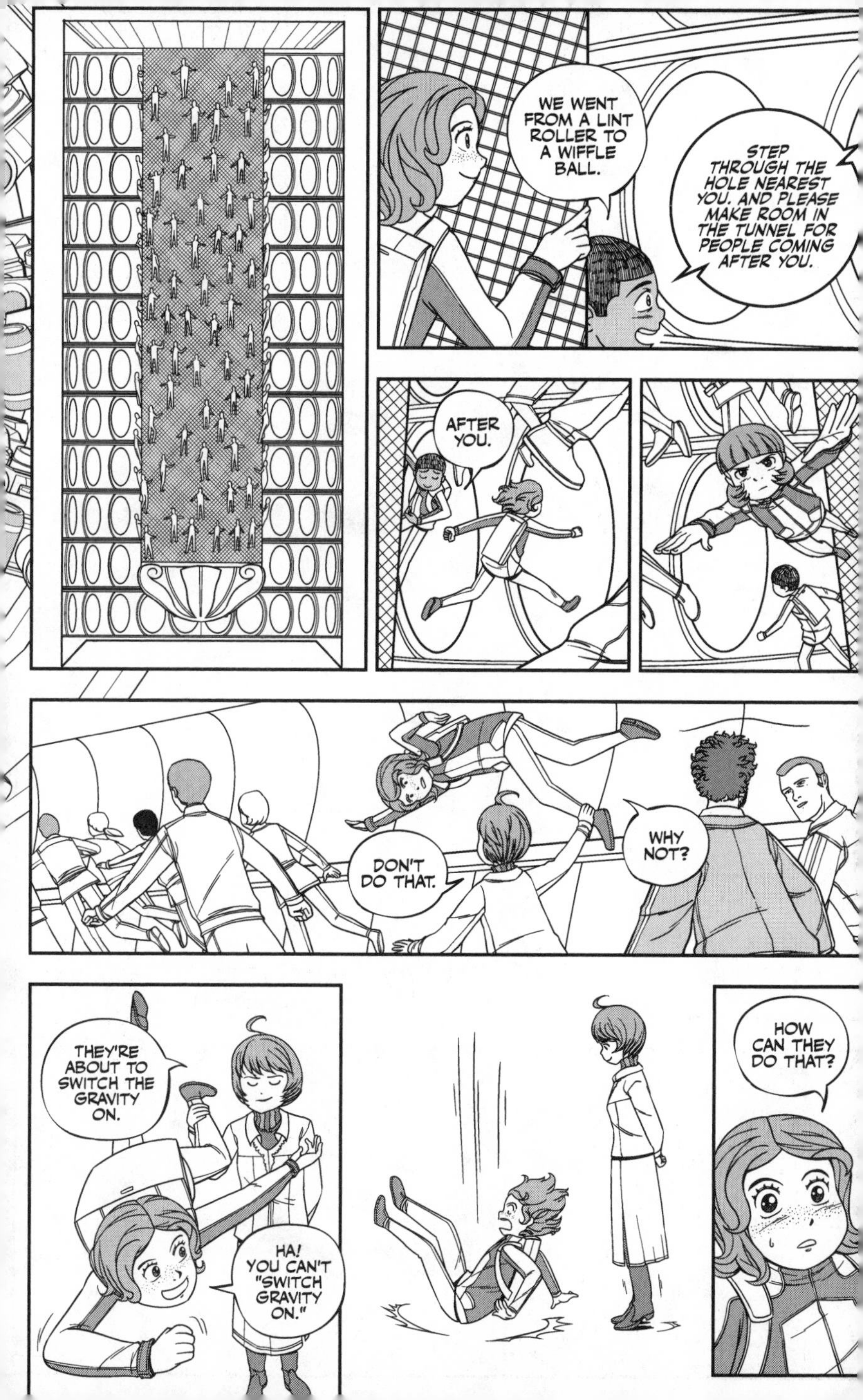
WE WENT FROM A LINT ROLLER TO A WIFFLE BALL.
STEP THROUGH THE HOLE NEAREST YOU. AND PLEASE MAKE ROOM IN THE TUNNEL FOR PEOPLE COMING AFTER YOU.
AFTER YOU.
DON'T DO THAT.
WHY NOT?
THEY'RE ABOUT TO SWITCH THE GRAVITY ON.
HA! YOU CAN'T "SWITCH GRAVITY ON."
HOW CAN THEY DO THAT?

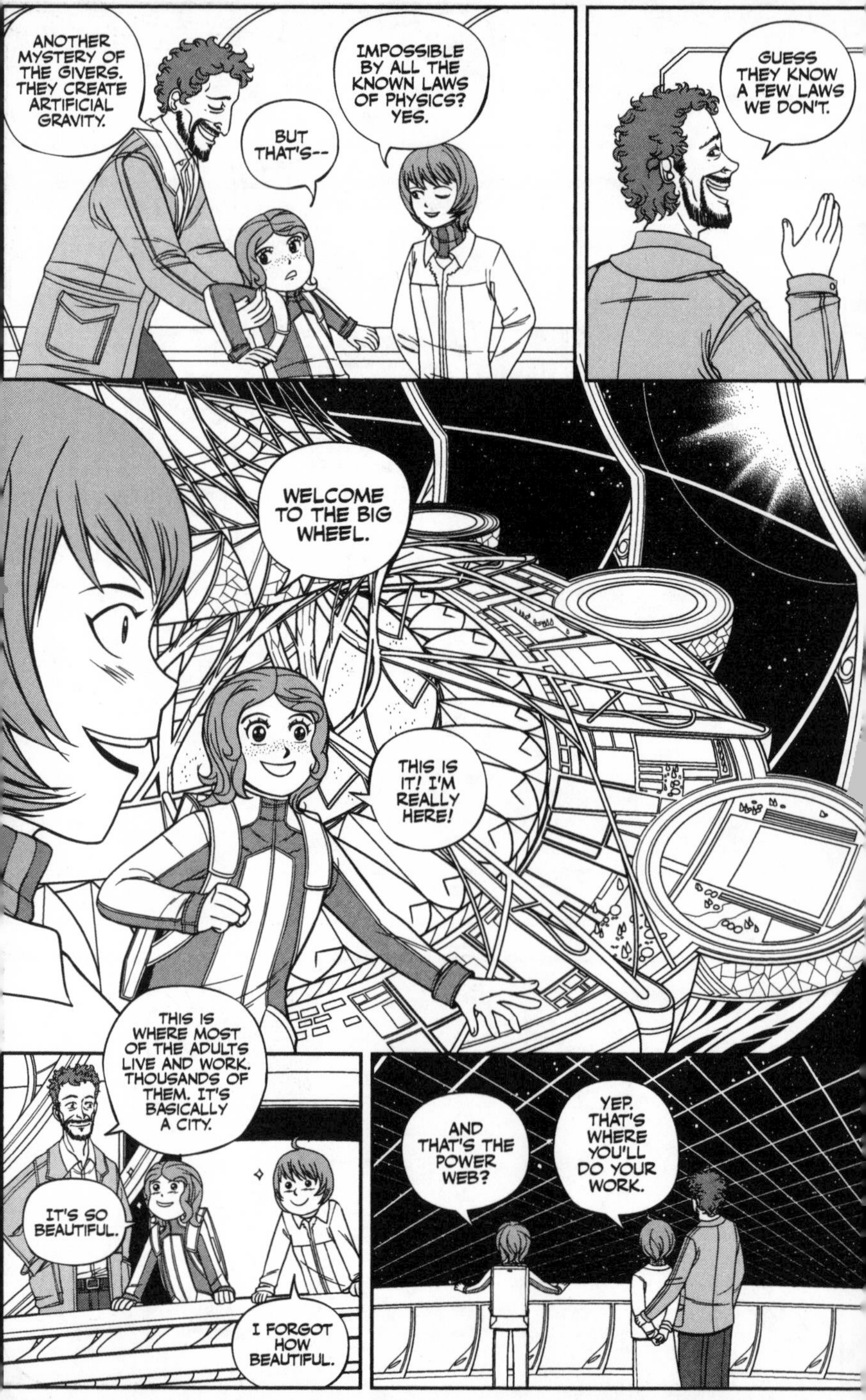
ANOTHER MYSTERY OF THE GIVERS. THEY CREATE ARTIFICIAL GRAVITY.
BUT THAT'S--
IMPOSSIBLE BY ALL THE KNOWN LAWS OF PHYSICS? YES.
GUESS THEY KNOW A FEW LAWS WE DON'T.
WELCOME TO THE BIG WHEEL.
THIS IS IT! I'M REALLY HERE!
THIS IS WHERE MOST OF THE ADULTS LIVE AND WORK. THOUSANDS OF THEM. IT'S BASICALLY A CITY.
IT'S SO BEAUTIFUL.
I FORGOT HOW BEAUTIFUL.
AND THAT'S THE POWER WEB?
YEP. THAT'S WHERE YOU'LL DO YOUR WORK.

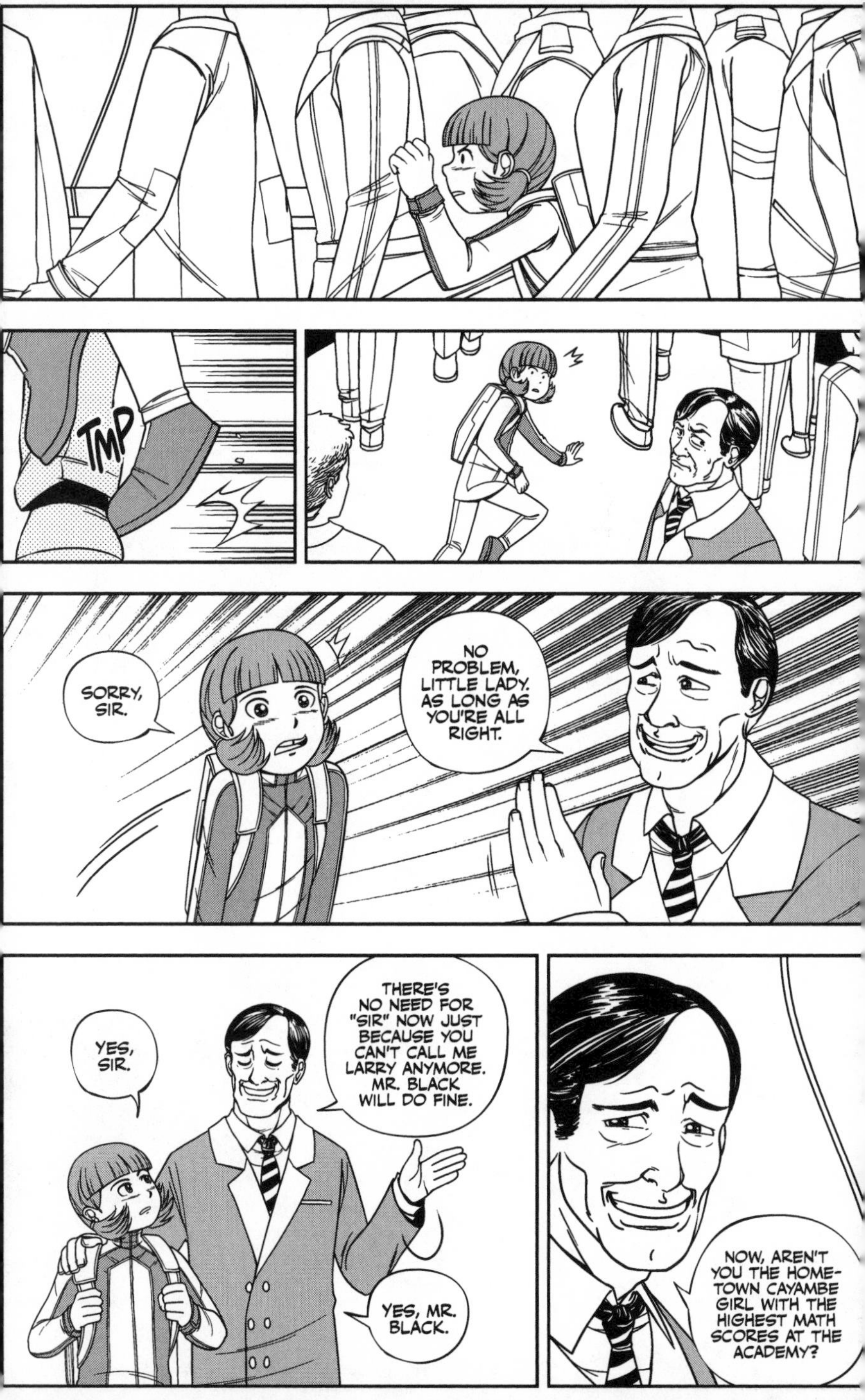
TMP
SORRY, SIR.
NO PROBLEM, LITTLE LADY. AS LONG AS YOU'RE ALL RIGHT.
YES, SIR.
THERE'S NO NEED FOR "SIR" NOW JUST BECAUSE YOU CAN'T CALL ME LARRY ANYMORE. MR. BLACK WILL DO FINE.
YES, MR. BLACK.
NOW, AREN'T YOU THE HOME-TOWN CAYAMBE GIRL WITH THE HIGHEST MATH SCORES AT THE ACADEMY?

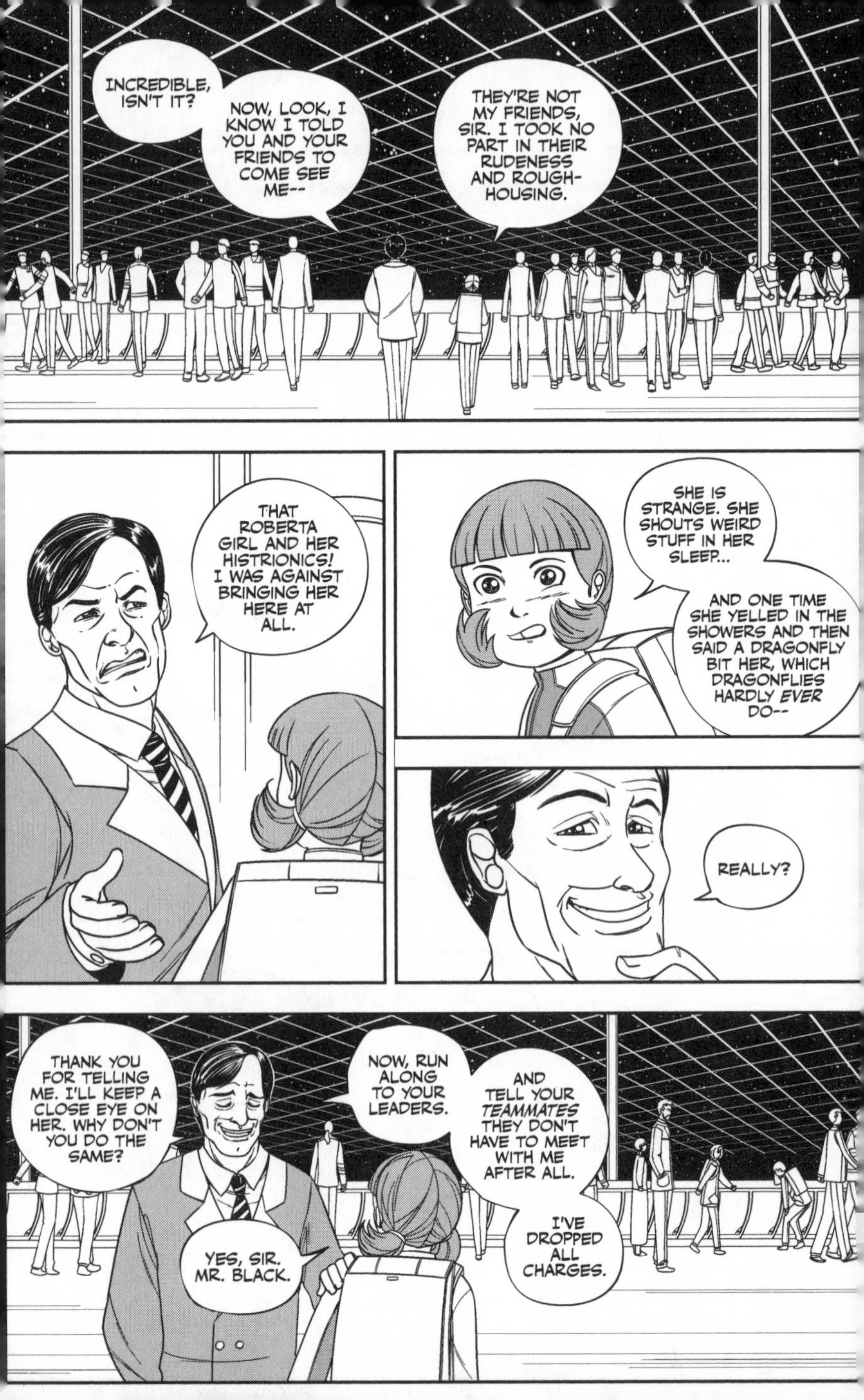
INCREDIBLE, ISN'T IT?
NOW, LOOK, I KNOW I TOLD YOU AND YOUR FRIENDS TO COME SEE ME--
THEY'RE NOT MY FRIENDS, SIR. I TOOK NO PART IN THEIR RUDENESS AND ROUGH-HOUSING.
THAT ROBERTA GIRL AND HER HISTRIONICS! I WAS AGAINST BRINGING HER HERE AT ALL.
SHE IS STRANGE. SHE SHOUTS WEIRD STUFF IN HER SLEEP...
AND ONE TIME SHE YELLED IN THE SHOWERS AND THEN SAID A DRAGONFLY BIT HER, WHICH DRAGONFLIES HARDLY *EVER* DO--
REALLY?
THANK YOU FOR TELLING ME. I'LL KEEP A CLOSE EYE ON HER. WHY DON'T YOU DO THE SAME?
YES, SIR. MR. BLACK.
NOW, RUN ALONG TO YOUR LEADERS.
AND TELL YOUR *TEAMMATES* THEY DON'T HAVE TO MEET WITH ME AFTER ALL.
I'VE DROPPED ALL CHARGES.

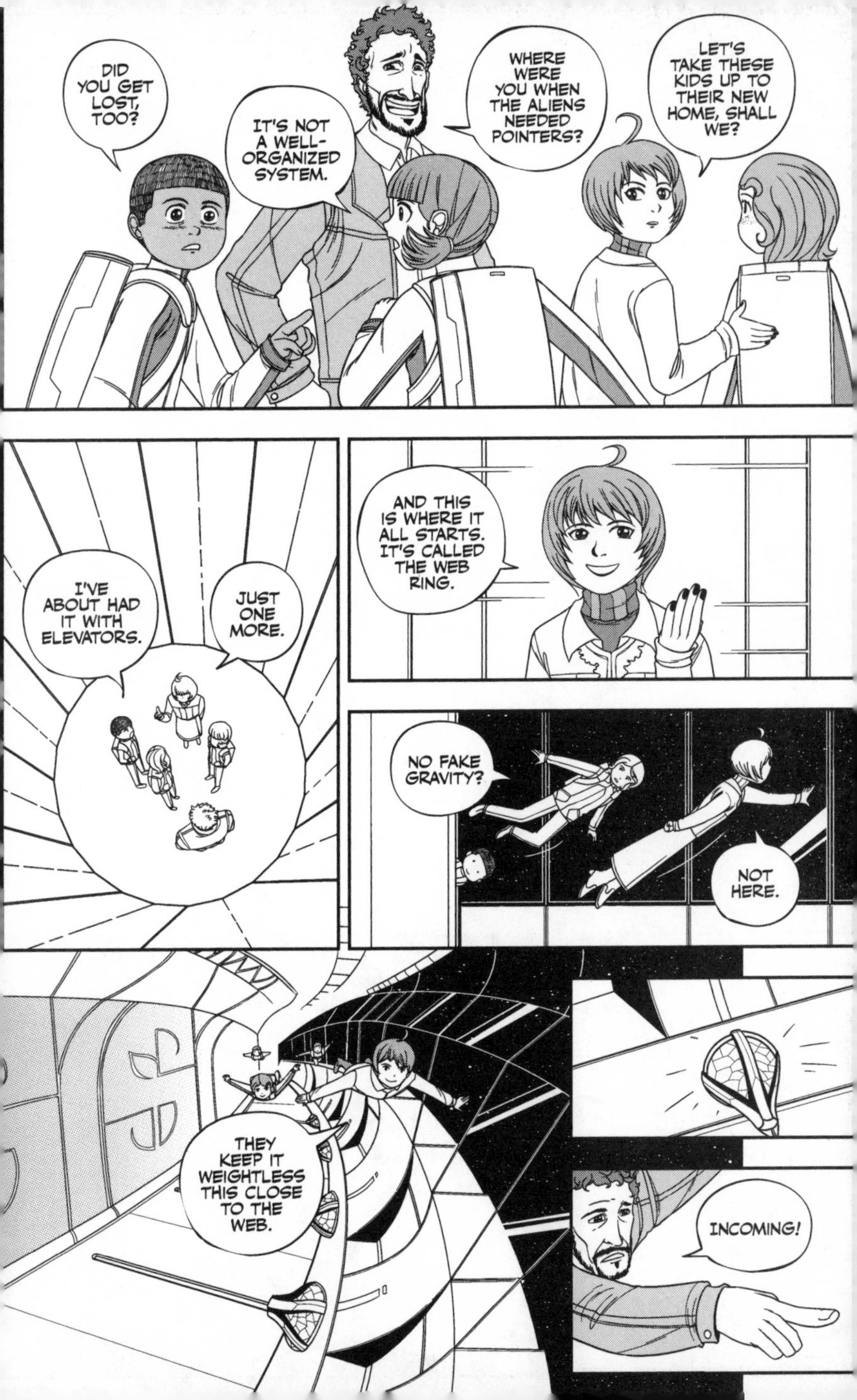
DID YOU GET LOST, TOO?
IT'S NOT A WELL-ORGANIZED SYSTEM.
WHERE WERE YOU WHEN THE ALIENS NEEDED POINTERS?
LET'S TAKE THESE KIDS UP TO THEIR NEW HOME, SHALL WE?
I'VE ABOUT HAD IT WITH ELEVATORS.
JUST ONE MORE.
AND THIS IS WHERE IT ALL STARTS. IT'S CALLED THE WEB RING.
NO FAKE GRAVITY?
NOT HERE.
THEY KEEP IT WEIGHTLESS THIS CLOSE TO THE WEB.
INCOMING!

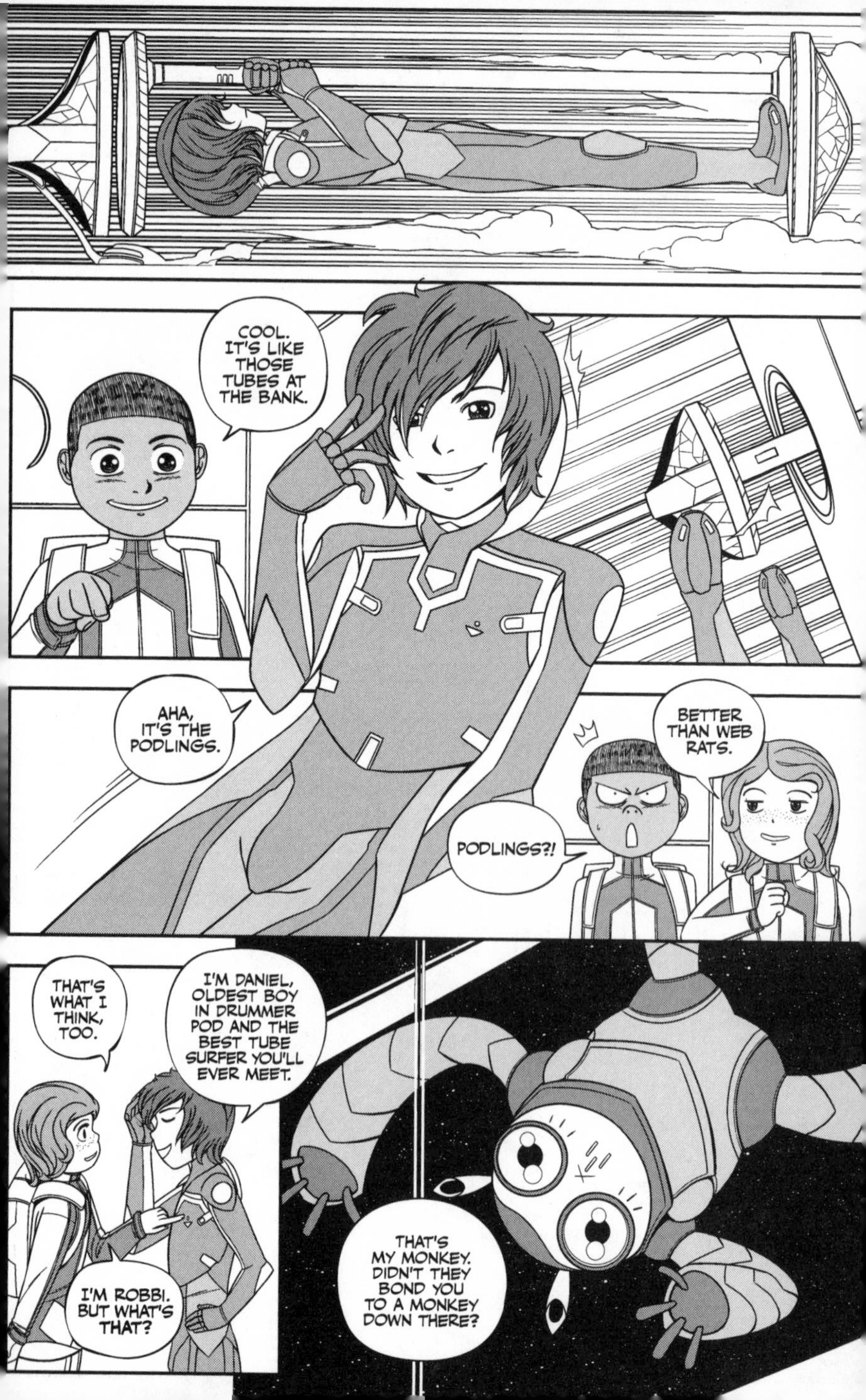
COOL. IT'S LIKE THOSE TUBES AT THE BANK.
AHA, IT'S THE PODLINGS.
BETTER THAN WEB RATS.
PODLINGS?!
THAT'S WHAT I THINK, TOO.
I'M DANIEL, OLDEST BOY IN DRUMMER POD AND THE BEST TUBE SURFER YOU'LL EVER MEET.
I'M ROBBI. BUT WHAT'S THAT?
THAT'S MY MONKEY. DIDN'T THEY BOND YOU TO A MONKEY DOWN THERE?

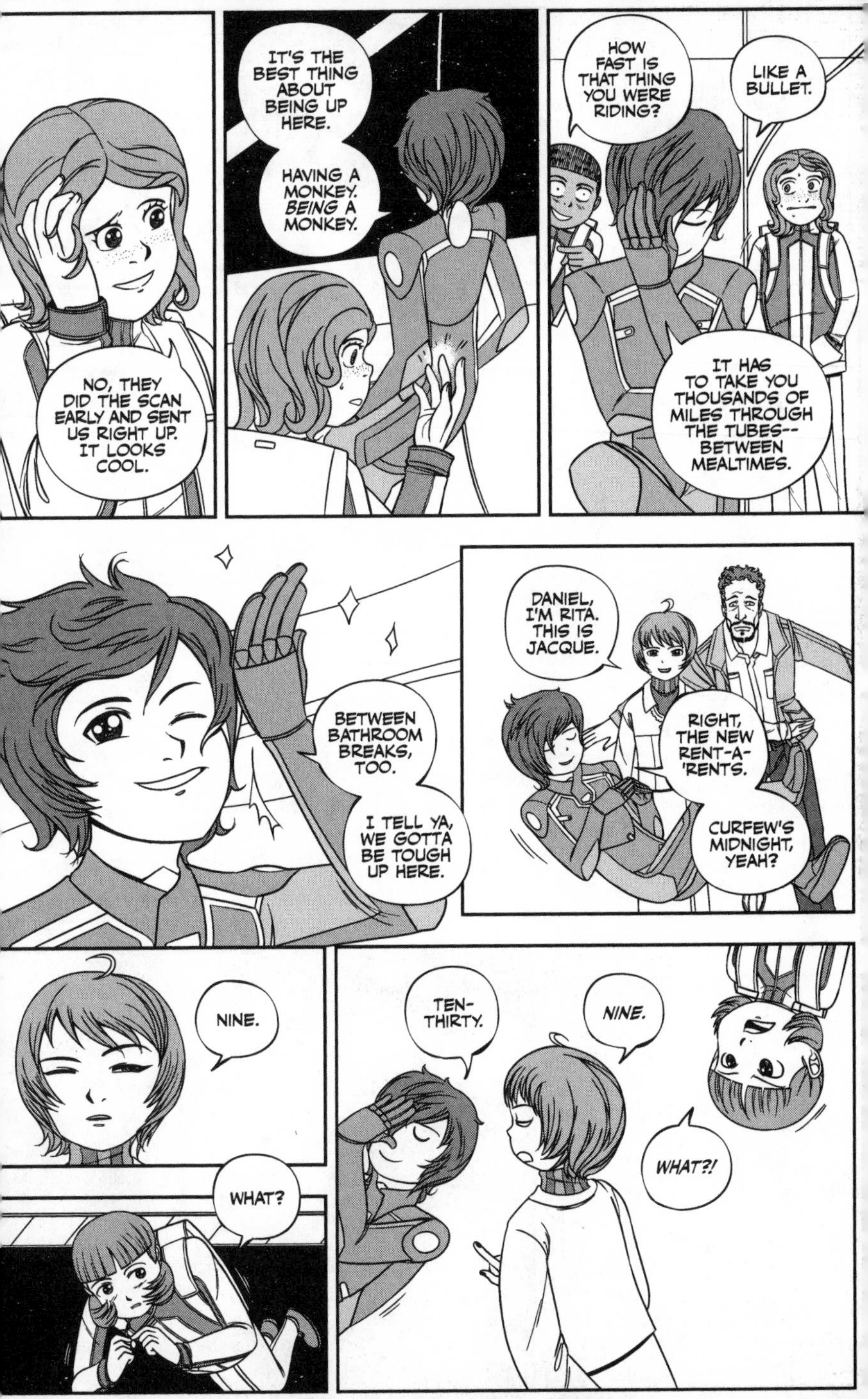

NO, THEY DID THE SCAN EARLY AND SENT US RIGHT UP. IT LOOKS COOL.
IT'S THE BEST THING ABOUT BEING UP HERE.
HAVING A MONKEY. *BEING* A MONKEY.
HOW FAST IS THAT THING YOU WERE RIDING?
LIKE A BULLET.
IT HAS TO TAKE YOU THOUSANDS OF MILES THROUGH THE TUBES--BETWEEN MEALTIMES.
BETWEEN BATHROOM BREAKS, TOO.
I TELL YA, WE GOTTA BE TOUGH UP HERE.
DANIEL, I'M RITA. THIS IS JACQUE.
RIGHT, THE NEW RENT-A-'RENTS.
CURFEW'S MIDNIGHT, YEAH?
NINE.
WHAT?
TEN-THIRTY.
NINE.
WHAT?!

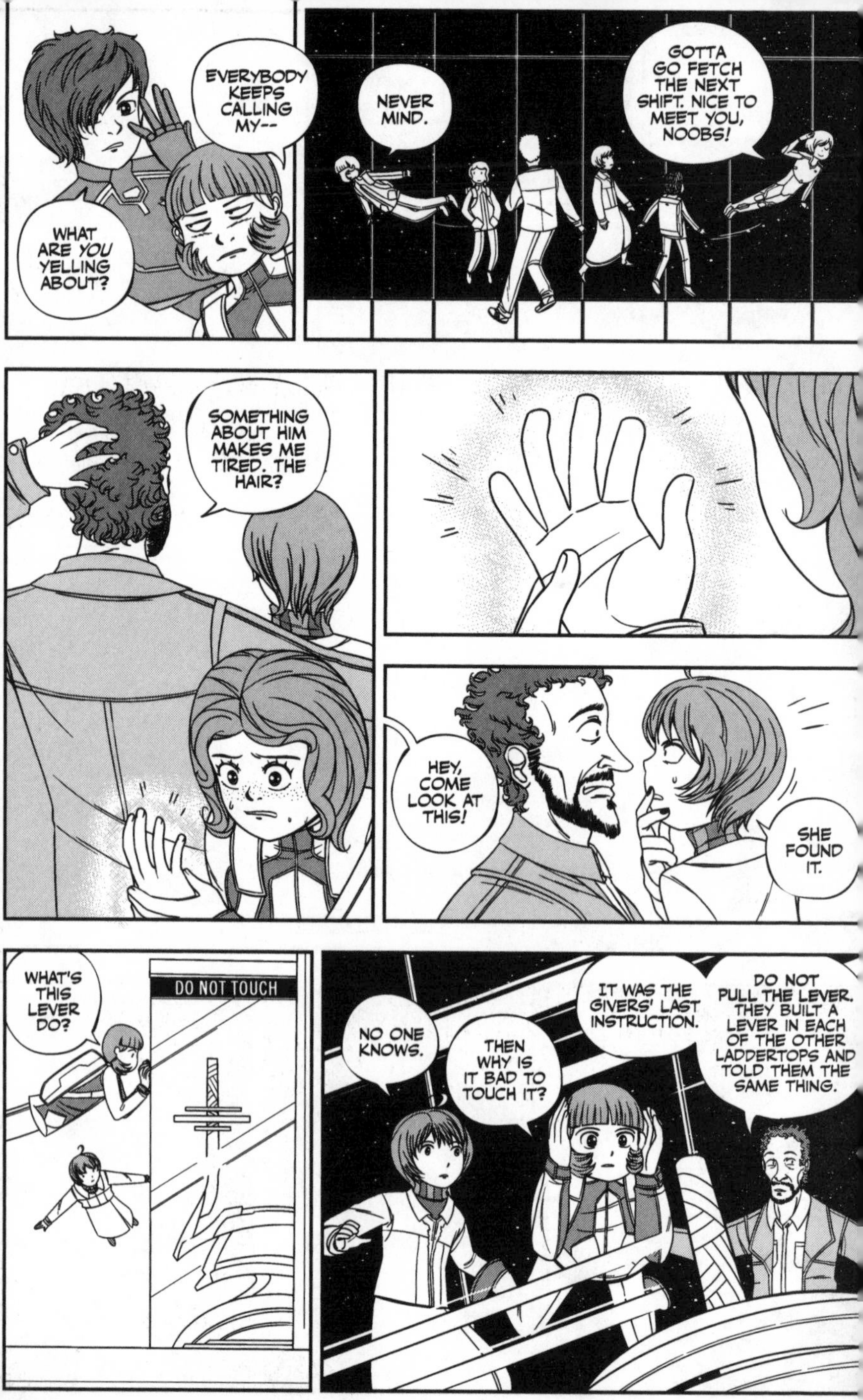
EVERYBODY KEEPS CALLING MY--
WHAT ARE *YOU* YELLING ABOUT?
NEVER MIND.
GOTTA GO FETCH THE NEXT SHIFT. NICE TO MEET YOU, NOOBS!
SOMETHING ABOUT HIM MAKES ME TIRED. THE HAIR?
HEY, COME LOOK AT THIS!
SHE FOUND IT.
WHAT'S THIS LEVER DO?
DO NOT TOUCH
NO ONE KNOWS.
THEN WHY IS IT BAD TO TOUCH IT?
IT WAS THE GIVERS' LAST INSTRUCTION.
DO NOT PULL THE LEVER. THEY BUILT A LEVER IN EACH OF THE OTHER LADDERTOPS AND TOLD THEM THE SAME THING.

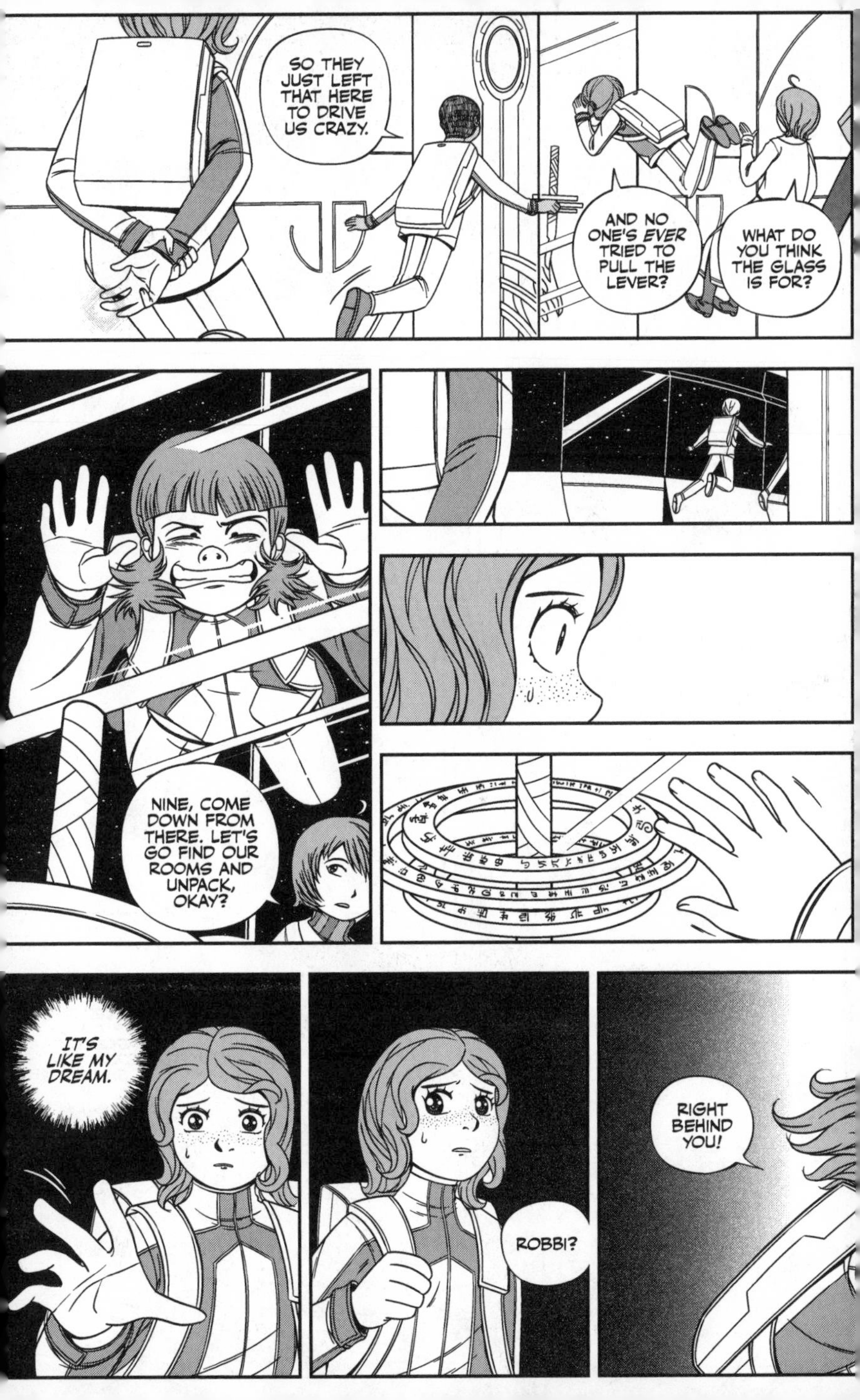
SO THEY JUST LEFT THAT HERE TO DRIVE US CRAZY.
AND NO ONE'S *EVER* TRIED TO PULL THE LEVER?
WHAT DO YOU THINK THE GLASS IS FOR?
NINE, COME DOWN FROM THERE. LET'S GO FIND OUR ROOMS AND UNPACK, OKAY?
IT'S LIKE MY DREAM.
ROBBI?
RIGHT BEHIND YOU!

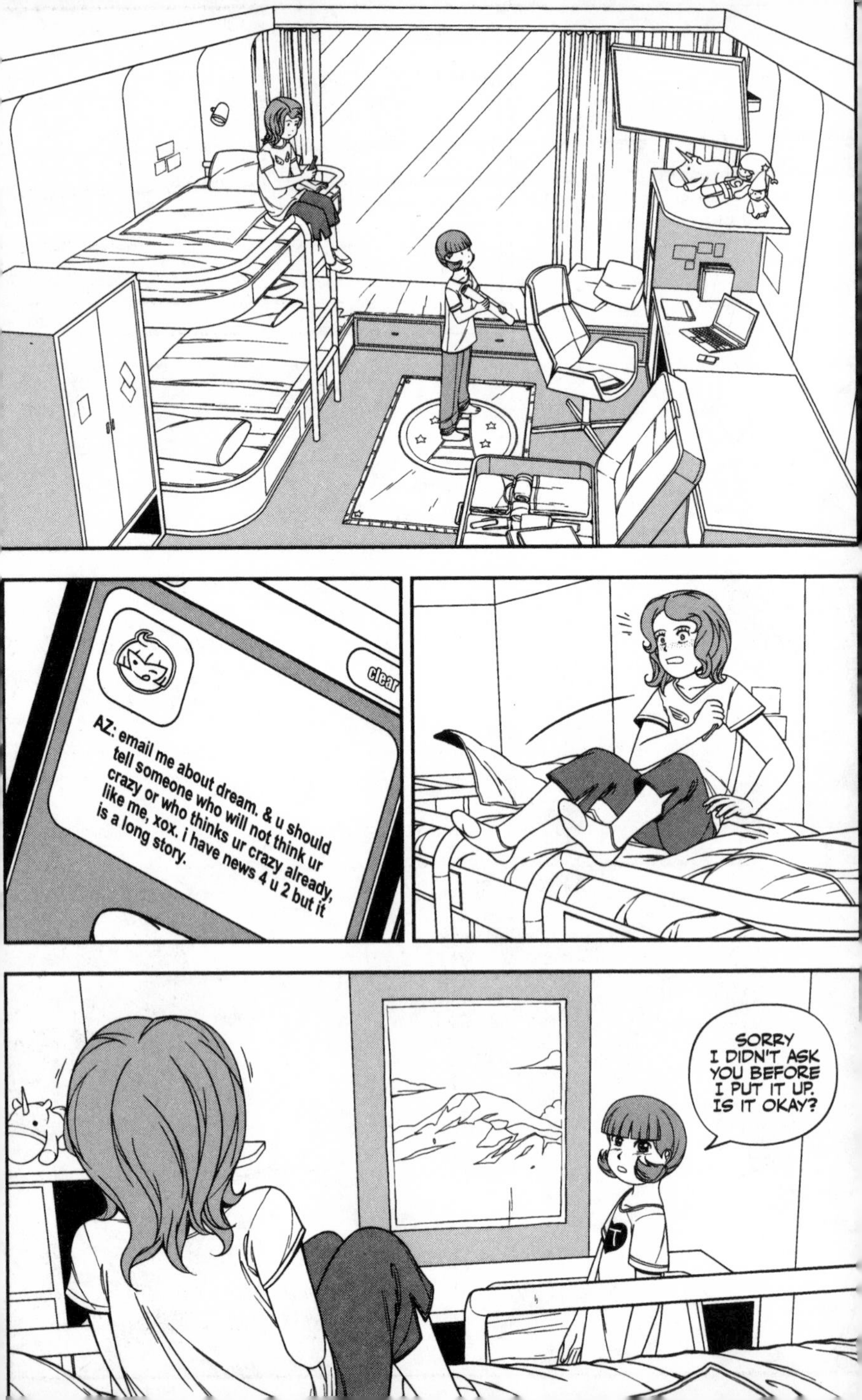
clear
AZ: email me about dream. & u should tell someone who will not think ur crazy or who thinks ur crazy already, like me, xox. i have news 4 u 2 but it is a long story.
SORRY I DIDN'T ASK YOU BEFORE I PUT IT UP. IS IT OKAY?

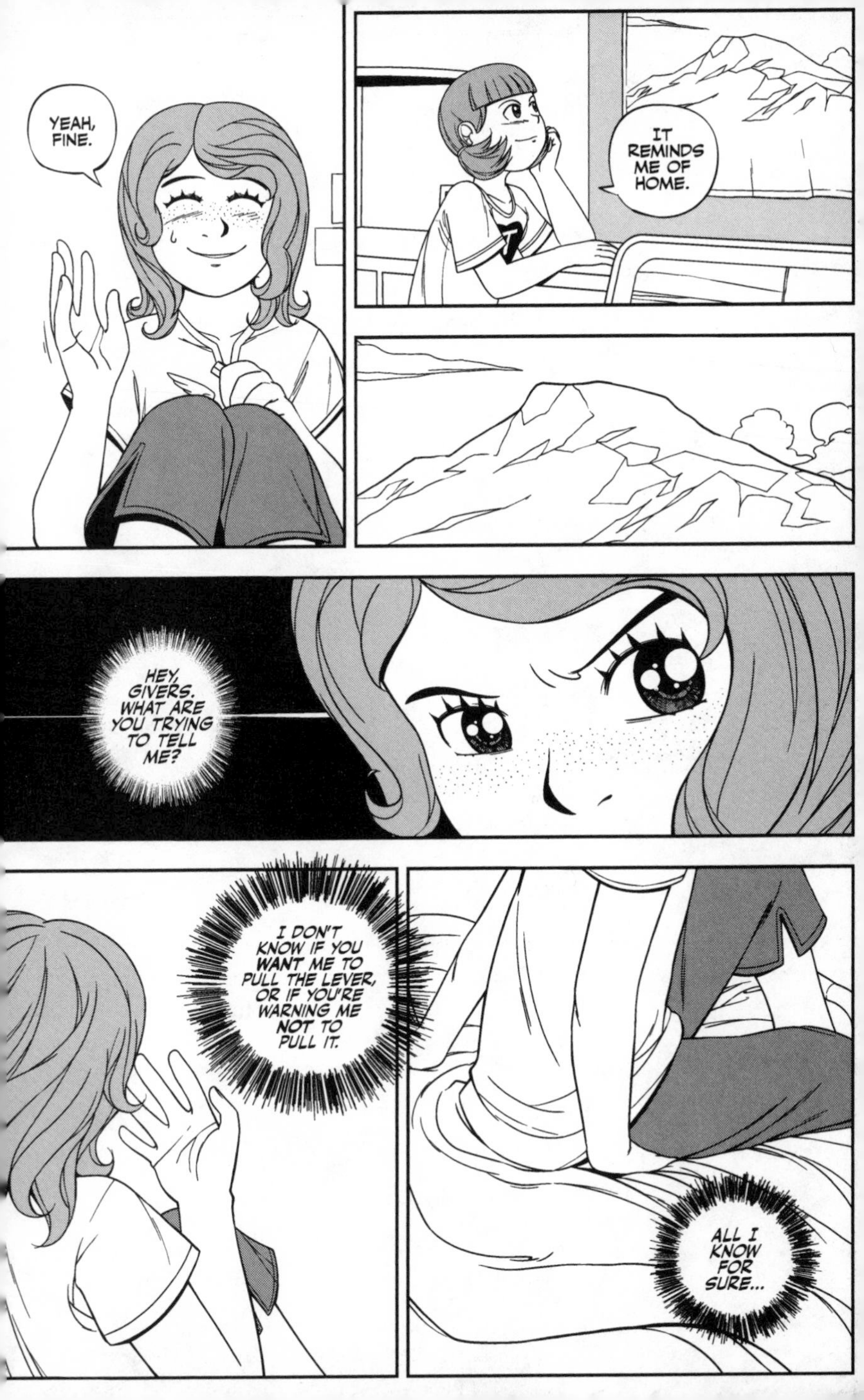
YEAH, FINE.
IT REMINDS ME OF HOME.
HEY, GIVERS. WHAT ARE YOU TRYING TO TELL ME?
I DON'T KNOW IF YOU WANT ME TO PULL THE LEVER, OR IF YOU'RE WARNING ME NOT TO PULL IT.
ALL I KNOW FOR SURE...

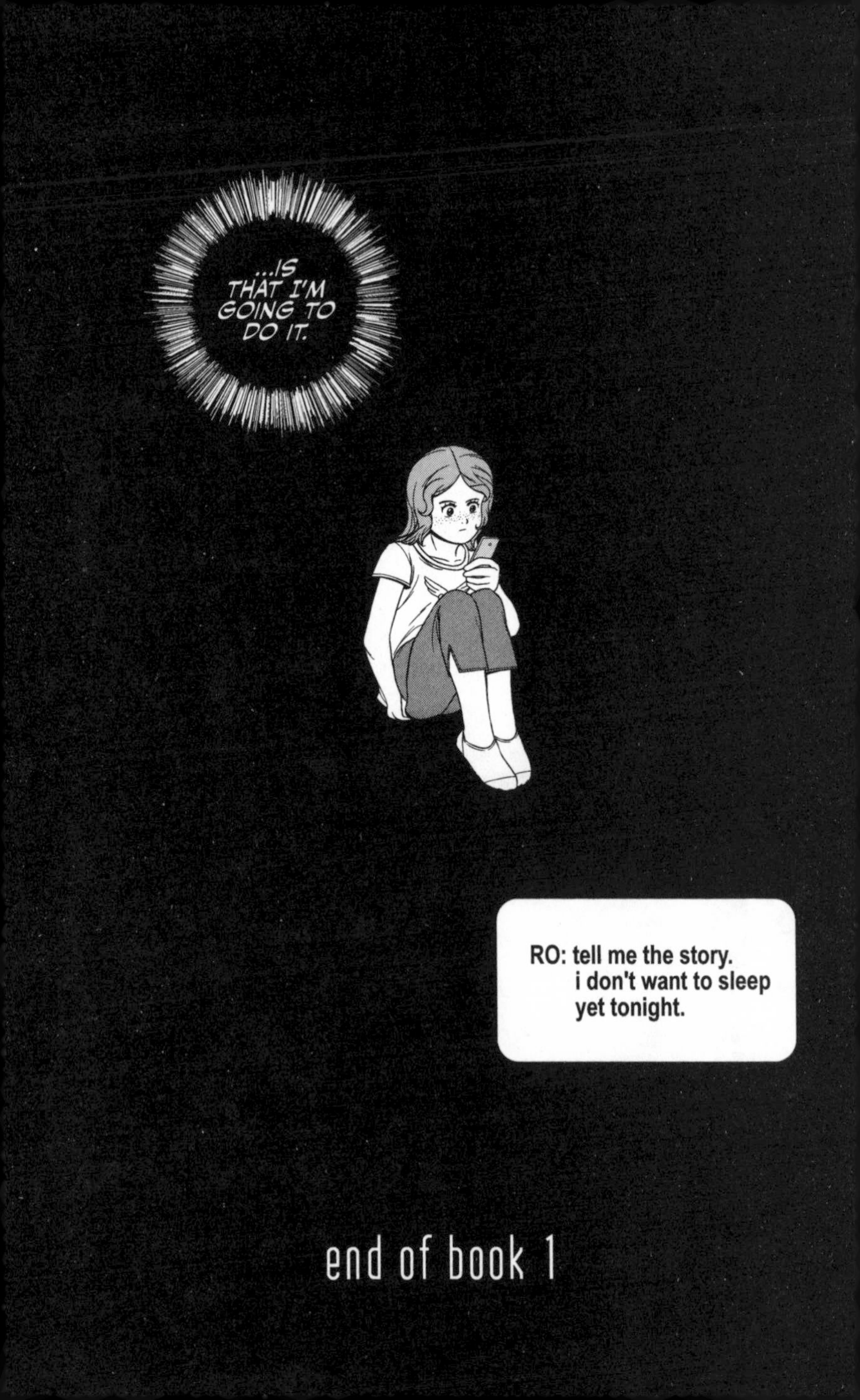
...IS THAT I'M GOING TO DO IT.
RO: tell me the story. i don't want to sleep yet tonight.
end of book 1

LADDERTOP
CHARACTER DESIGNS

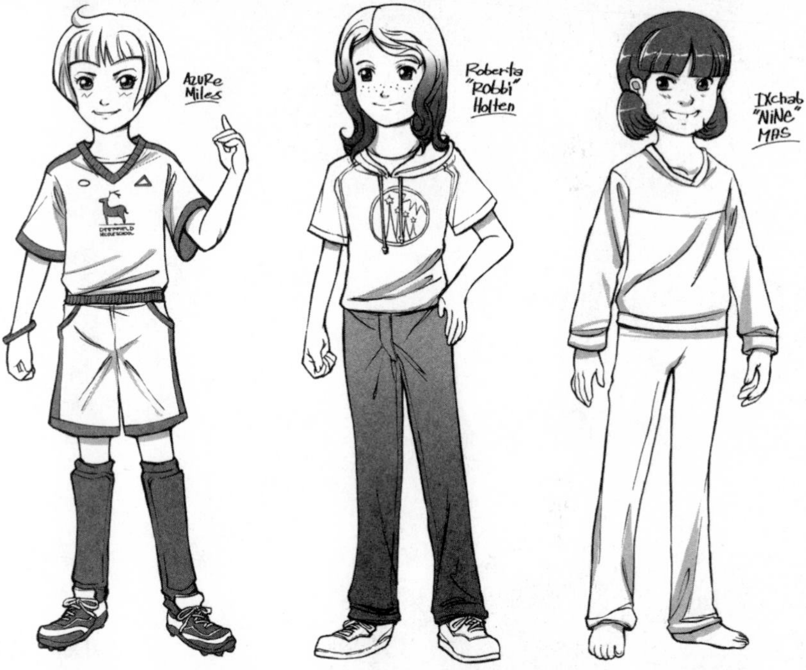
AzURe Miles
Roberta "Robbi" Holten
IXchab "NiNe" MAS

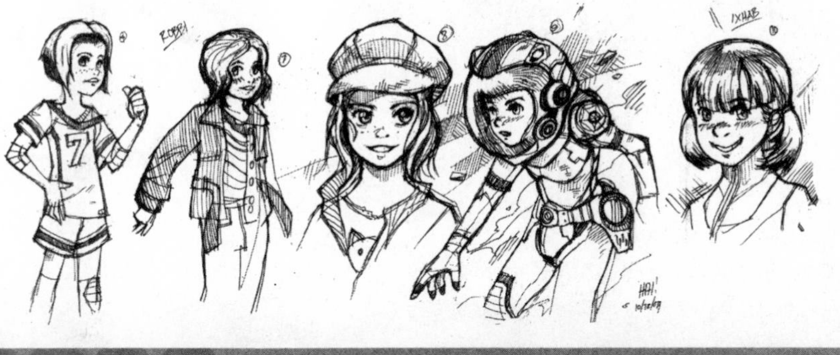
ROBBI
IXHAB
HA!

LADDERTOP

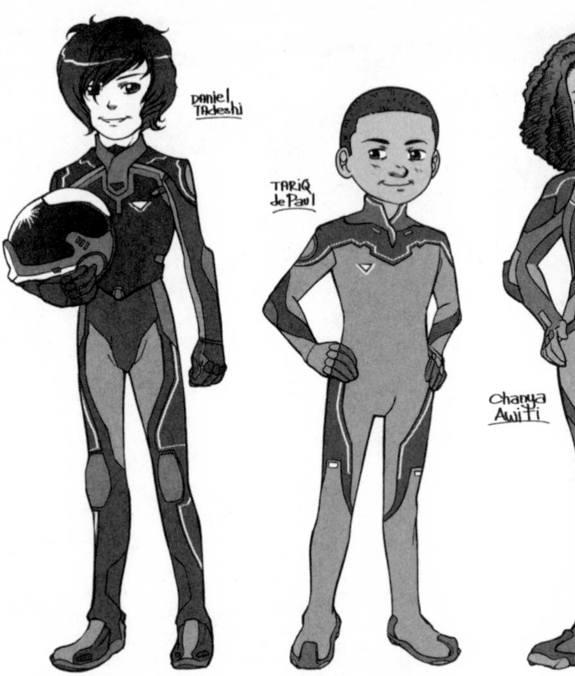

Daniel Tadeshi
TARIQ de Paul
Chanya Awiti

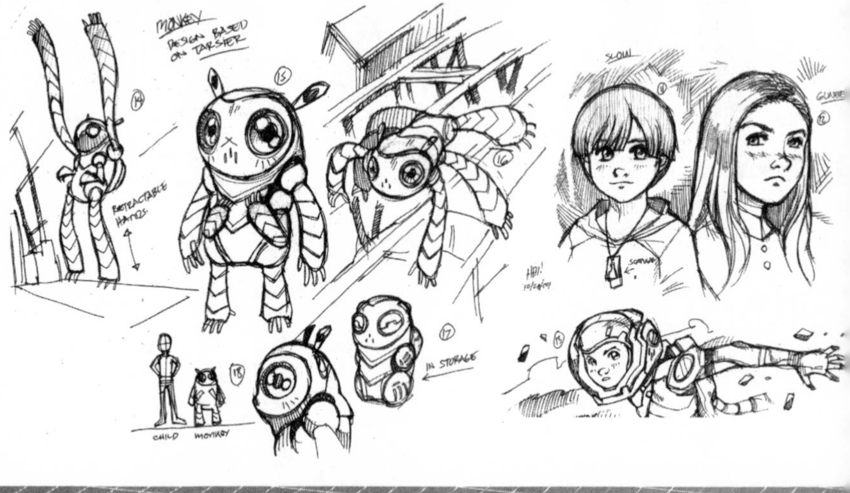

MONKEY
DESIGN BASED ON TARSIER
RETRACTABLE HANDS
STORAGE
CHILD
MONKEY
SLOW

CHARACTER DESIGNS

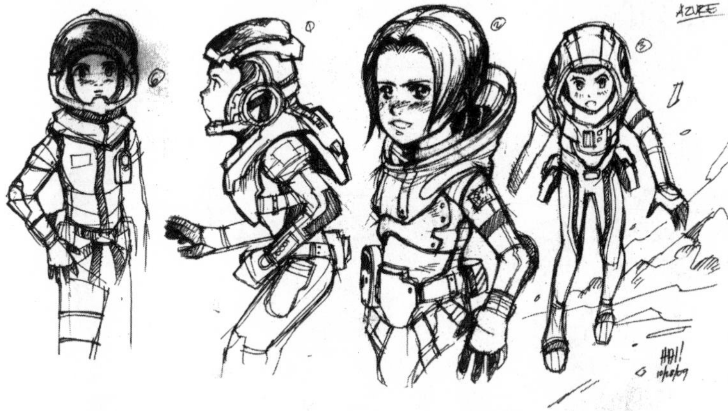
AZURE

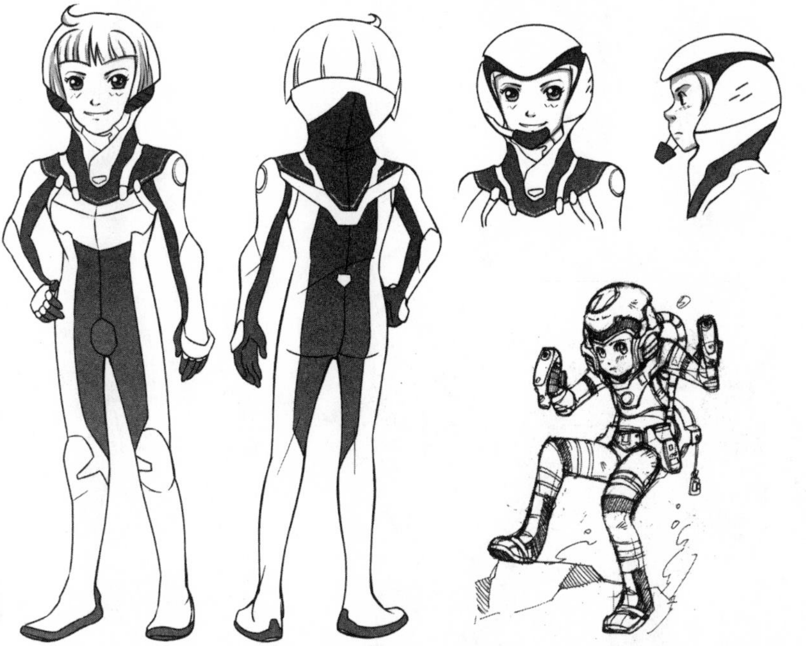

NULL-GRAVITY
TRAINING SUIT

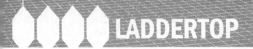

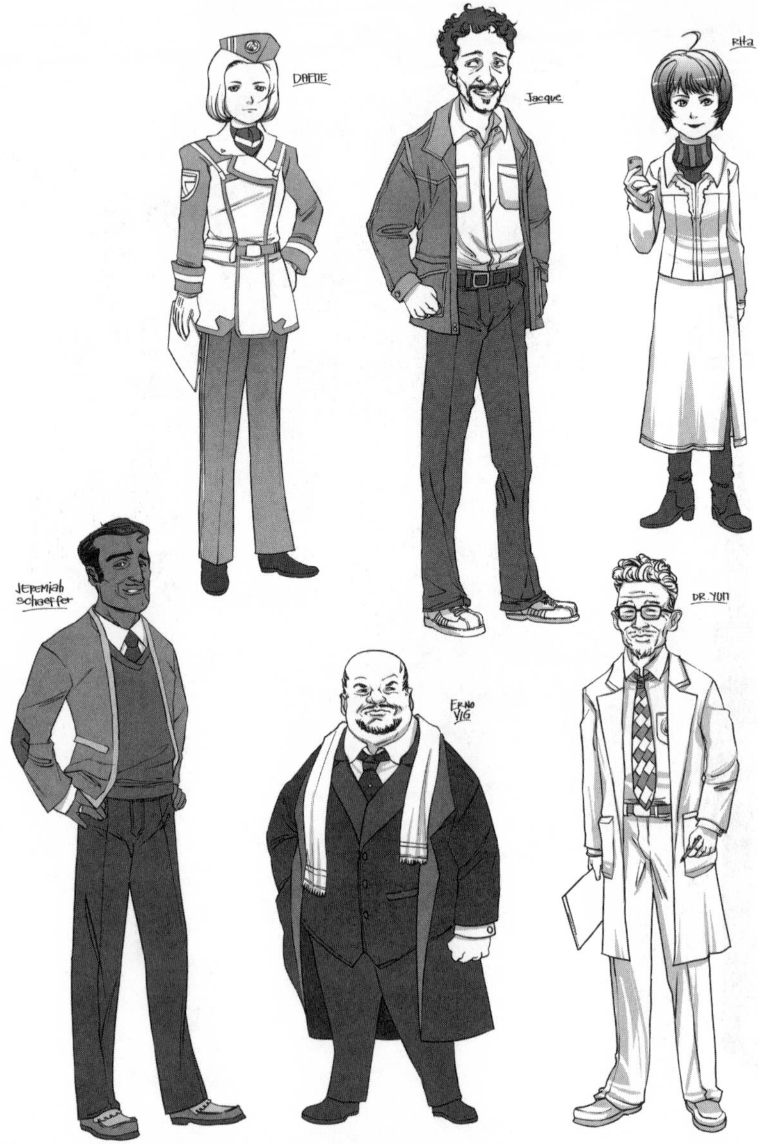
DAFNE
Jacque
Rita
Jeremiah Schaeffer
ERNO VIG
DR. YUN

CHARACTER DESIGNS

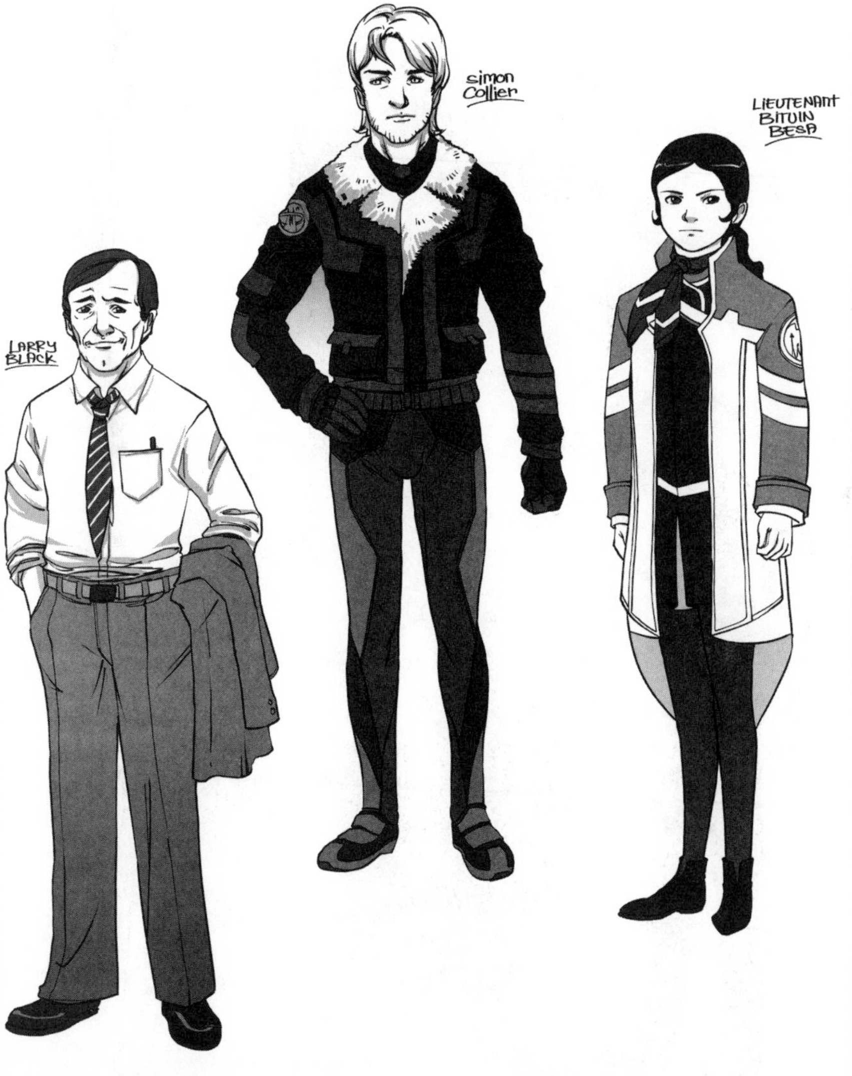
LARRY BLACK
simon Collier
LIEUTENANT BITUIN BESA

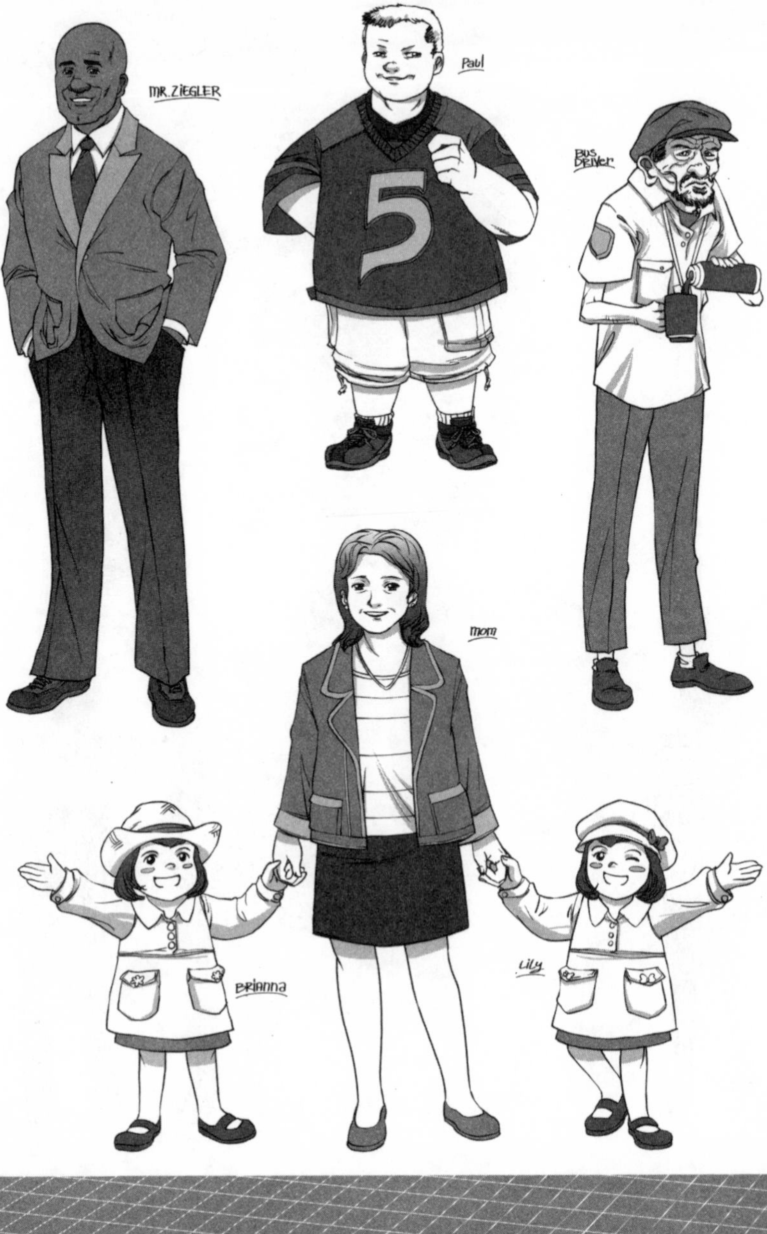
MR. ZIEGLER
Paul
Bus Driver
mom
Brianna
Lily

CHARACTER DESIGNS

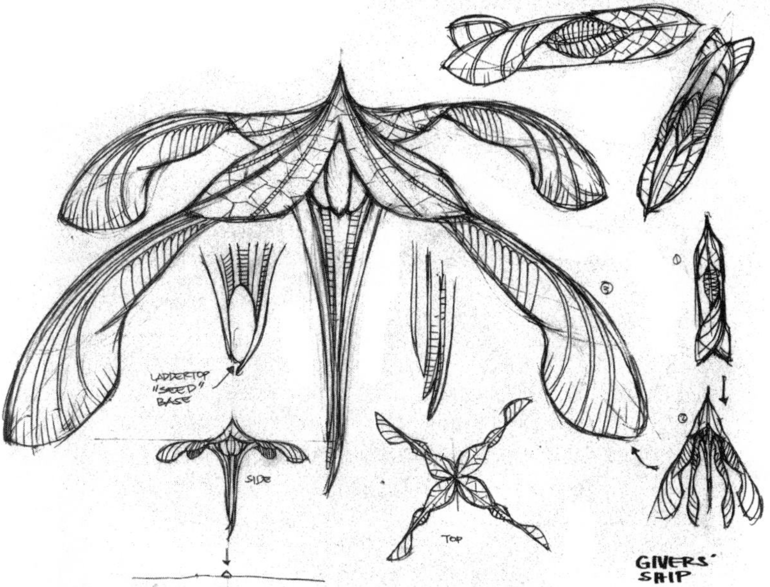
LADDERTOP "SEED" BASE
SIDE
TOP
GIVERS' SHIP

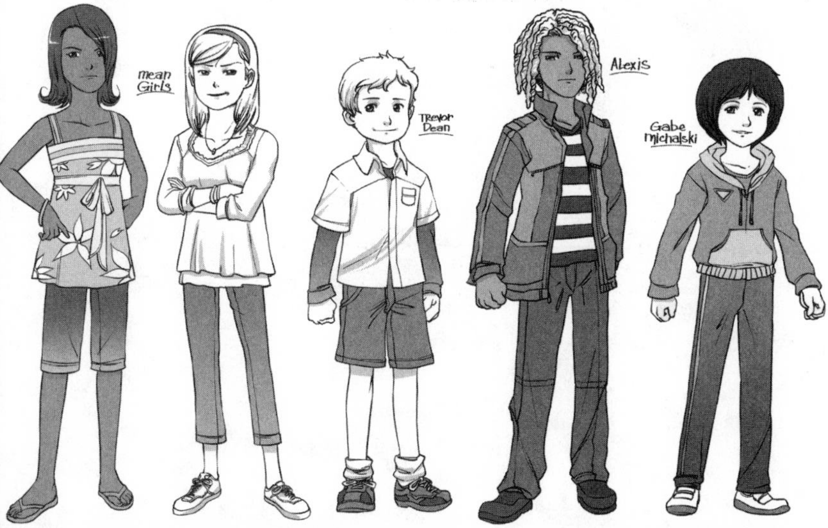
mean Girls
Trevor Dean
Alexis
Gabe Michalski

Orson Scott Card is best known for the novels *Ender's Game, The Lost Gate*, and *Pathfinder*, and, in the world of comics, for *Ultimate Iron Man* for Marvel. He lives in Greensboro, North Carolina.

Emily Janice Card is an award-winning reader of audiobooks, including *The Lost Summer of Louisa May Alcott, Special Topics in Calamity Physics*, and *Podkayne of Mars*. She also wrote, codirected, and acted in *Jane Austen's Fight Club*.

Zina Margaret Card is a junior in the high school drama program at Weaver Academy for the Performing and Visual Arts in Greensboro, North Carolina. A longtime fan of anime and manga, she recently played Katharina in *The Taming of the Shrew*.

Honoel A. Ibardolaza is an award-winning children's book writer and illustrator. He is also a manga and comic artist whose published works include *Blade for Barter*. You can find him at www.honoel.com.